This book comes with access to more content online.

Quiz yourself, test your progress,
and score high on test day!

Register your book or ebook at
www.dummies.com/go/getaccess

Select your product, and then follow the prompts
to validate your purchase.

You'll receive an email with your PIN and instructions.

PHR®/SPHR®
Exam

2nd Edition with Online Practice

by Sandra M. Reed, SPHR, SHRM-SCP

A Wiley Brand

PHR®/SPHR® Exam For Dummies®, 2nd Edition with Online Practice

Published by: **John Wiley & Sons, Inc.,** 111 River Street, Hoboken, NJ 07030-5774, www.wiley.com

Copyright © 2021 by John Wiley & Sons, Inc., Hoboken, New Jersey

Published simultaneously in Canada

For general information on our other products and services, please contact our Customer Care Department within the U.S. at 877-762-2974, outside the U.S. at 317-572-3993, or fax 317-572-4002. For technical support, please visit https://hub.wiley.com/community/support/dummies.

Wiley publishes in a variety of print and electronic formats and by print-on-demand. Some material included with standard print versions of this book may not be included in e-books or in print-on-demand. If this book refers to media such as a CD or DVD that is not included in the version you purchased, you may download this material at http://booksupport.wiley.com. For more information about Wiley products, visit www.wiley.com.

Library of Congress Control Number: 2020950196

ISBN 978-1-119-72489-6 (pbk); ISBN 978-1-119-72479-7 (ebk); ISBN 978-1-119-72490-2 (ebk)

Manufactured in the United States of America

SKY10023409_122220

Contents at a Glance

Table of Contents

Introduction

I wrote this book for all the HR professionals who are intent on leaving no stone unturned on their quest for the PHR or SPHR designation. It rounds out the edges of the preparation process, seeking to keep you on track and focused on the steps necessary to pass.

PHR/SPHR Exam For Dummies, 2nd Edition, also is a reminder that it's not about what you know at this stage in the process, but rather what you *don't* know that requires your full attention.

This book is for the tenacious and the curious and the self-deprecating, possibly because I find humility an attractive trait in individuals getting ready for a tough test. Those traits can keep your mind open and your eyes alert. Resolute curiosity can force you to grab a thread and follow it all the way to the end, which is the absolute best way to master and apply the information that you're about to discover while getting ready for these exams.

About This Book

The focus of *PHR/SPHR Exam For Dummies* is to orient you, the experienced HR professional, to the task at hand: getting ready to become professionally certified. With pass rates low and nerves high, this guidebook takes you on your preparation journey, serving as a resource to get you organized and introduce you to key elements of these tests. In no other preparation resource will you find

>> An advanced discussion of the exam content outlines and their importance

>> A review of how the knowledge and objectives work together

>> Information on how to use the internet to enhance your efforts

>> A study of the HR Certification Institute's (HRCI) website (www.hrci.org) and the exam content outline for content markers

Furthermore, adult learners tend to do better when they understand how information applies to them. In this case, taking a 50,000-foot view of key exam concepts and exam preparation activities allows you to take control of the exam prep process. As with anything worth doing, a haphazard, unstructured approach to preparation won't serve a positive outcome. Just as a true career isn't an accident, neither is successful certification — it takes both planning and strategic execution.

The primary purpose of your exam preparation activities is to successfully pass a fairly difficult test. For this reason, I include two sample tests in this book — one for the PHR and one for the SPHR. These exams are similar to the one that you'll see on test day — 175 questions directly related to the exam content outlines. Although I provide bubble sheets for easy use, also consider putting your answers on a blank piece of paper so you can use the tests again.

Foolish Assumptions

Assumptions are simply things that I think I already know about you that guided my decisions on what to include in this book. For the PHR and SPHR exams, they are as follows:

>> You're an experienced HR professional. Because exam eligibility is based on years of practical experience, even with a bit of education, I know that you know the basics of HR.

>> You're preparing for an exam, not looking for *HR in a jar*. This book is about what you need to do to prepare to take a test about HR. It doesn't teach you all you need to know about the field of human resources. In fact, the purpose of this book is to guide you to multiple resources for exam preparation.

>> You have a baseline knowledge of business and management principles. Corporate America, small businesses, and nonprofits all have shared HR and business needs. I assume that you're a working professional in one of these categories and understand business terms such as *strategy* and *organizational structure*.

>> You know how to conduct internet research. So much of what you need to pass the tests can be found online, and I encourage you throughout the book to do so.

Probably the most impressive assumption I make about you is that you're self-motivated, driven, and determined. Successful performers aren't generally satisfied with the status quo. If you're reaching out to take one of these tests, you're among those individuals who demand more out of themselves and by extension, your preparation resources. For this reason in this book, I recommend adding study time, admonish you to take an expanded view of a topic, and encourage you to create other dimensions to the content. You must find it and touch it and interpret it yourself to fully grasp the nuances of the exam content. This process requires that you take control of your study time and resources. Leaving it to a single author or only your past work experience isn't enough to get you through. I need you to tap into that drive and commit to doing what it takes to pass the first time around, or at least be a heck of a lot better for it after the process.

Icons Used in This Book

Consistent with the *For Dummies* series is the use of special icons. They serve as markers for information that may be of increased importance or interesting. I incorporate the following icons:

In general, I use this icon when you have a special opportunity to apply a behavior in its easiest form. In most cases, a tip can save you both time and energy, building upon the experience of those individuals who have gone before you.

I use this icon to reinforce an important principle. Pay attention to this information because it's important.

This icon directs you to some examples of the types of questions that appear on the PHR and SPHR exams. It also gives you examples of how the content may be represented in the workplace.

The information flagged by this icon may trip you up. The warning may be due to a topic's complexity, level of difficulty, or commonly reported mistakes.

Beyond This Book

In addition to the content of this book, you can view some related material online, including additional information about each exam. You can access a free Cheat Sheet at dummies.com. Just type "PHR/SPHR Exam For Dummies cheat sheet" in the search box.

An added feature to the online content is two additional exams to support your learning. Taking multiple practice exams is an absolute must as you get ready for several reasons:

>> The exam level of difficulty requires that you're familiar with question phrasing and multiple-choice setup. Keep in mind that these questions, also called *items,* can be highly situational. Taking practice exams can remove that element of surprise.

>> Answer distractors are common obstacles to a passing score. My online practice exams help condition your brain to recognize and eliminate the obvious wrong answers, increasing your chance of making a correct selection.

>> The online practice tests include a description of the right and wrong answers, which makes the practice exams extremely valuable, because they're much more than another bank of questions. Taking these exams also helps you master content.

The general recommendation is that you can't take too many practice assessments, and this book plus the online content is an excellent place to start. To gain access to additional tests and practice online, all you have to do is register. Just follow these simple steps:

1. Register your book or e-book at Dummies.com to get your PIN. Go to www.dummies.com/go/getaccess.

2. Select your product from the drop-down list on that page.

3. Follow the prompts to validate your product, and then check your email for a confirmation message that includes your PIN and instructions for logging in.

TIP

If you do not receive this email within two hours, please check your spam folder before contacting us through our Technical Support website at http://support.wiley.com or by phone at 877-762-2974.

Now you're ready to go! You can come back to the practice material as often as you want — simply log in with the username and password you created during your initial login. No need to enter the access code a second time.

Where to Go from Here

One of the reasons why preparing for this exam has been reported to be difficult is the sheer volume of reading that is required. This book can help a bit with all that reading. This book is modular in that you don't have to read it in order from cover to cover. Feel free to pick and choose the bits that you think will serve you best.

I wrote it so that you can pick any chapter and begin reading. To the ordered mind, doing so may be an unusual prospect, so go ahead and proceed in chapter order — the content will bear up to the pressure. For those of you who are only interested in certain exam elements, you have come to the right place. Feel free to bounce around or even begin at the end by starting with a practice exam to simply see how you fare. That may highlight for you a correct starting point for your unique preparation needs.

If you need some help in finding somewhere to begin, scan the table of contents or the index, find a few topics that interest you, and jump in.

Regardless of where you begin, the absolute *first* and most important step is to build a study plan. This book is full of useful tips and information to fill in the blanks of a plan, so maximize your investment by taking heed and writing down your plans. What gets measured gets done, so strengthen your odds by getting organized.

1

Getting Started with the PHR/SPHR Exam

Get a firm grasp of the structure for the PHR and SPHR so that you can begin to prepare a plan of attack to study for the exam.

Figure out the exam eligibility to ensure that you're qualified to take the right exam.

Know how to talk to your boss about taking the test and how you may persuade her to pay for the test.

Select proper resources so you maximize your study efforts and have access to what you need to know in preparing for a passing score.

Identify the different types of questions on the PHR and SPHR in order to be able to figure out the best way to answer them.

Familiarize yourself with the ins and outs of test day to make sure that you show up ready to go.

IN THIS CHAPTER

» Looking at the certification process

» Figuring out which test you need to take and signing up

» Seeing how the exam is structured and scored

» Getting ready to start

» Perusing core exam content

Chapter **1**

Introducing the PHR/SPHR Exam: Just the Basics, Please

Preparing to sit for either the Professional in Human Resources (PHR) or the Senior Professional in Human Resources (SPHR) exam means that you're investing in yourself through professional certification to differentiate your talent from the rest of the pack. It indicates a professional curiosity and commitment to excellence that characterizes the human resources (HR) profession. In fact, the PHR and the SPHR remain two of the most sought-after designations in the HR industry. This is demonstrated by a Dow Jones/Inc. Magazine study that found that 93 percent of Fortune 500 companies employ HRCI certification holders.

The reasons to become certified are many. Personally, you may be seeking validation of your knowledge and competencies. Professionally, you may desire more job responsibilities or pay increases. Regardless of your reasons, earning the designatory letters (PHR or SPHR) to place next to your name is the mark of a skilled and competent professional. This chapter serves as your launch pad to the rest of the book and your journey toward the title.

Summarizing the Certification Process

Sitting for the exam is but one step in your journey toward demonstrating professional excellence. There are several steps before (and recertifying after) that must be part of your planning process. The Human Resource Certification Institute (HRCI) defines the six steps that are required for successful certification:

1. **Meet the exam eligibility requirements.**

2. **Complete the application process.**

3. **Schedule your exam appointment at an approved testing center.**

4. **Prepare for the exam using the Exam Content Outline (ECO).**

5. **Follow the strict procedures on exam day.**

6. **Apply for recertification through continuing education and other means.**

I explore each of these steps throughout this book.

PHR or SPHR: Which Exam Is Right for You

One of the first decisions you'll have to make is which exam to take. The Human Resource Certification Institute (HRCI) offers eight accredited designations in the field of human resources. For purposes of this study guide, I discuss the institute's flagship (and most popular) accreditations: the Professional in Human Resources (PHR) and the Senior Professional in Human Resources (SPHR). Before selecting the proper exam, you must first determine your eligibility.

Exam eligibility

The PHR and the SPHR are both knowledge- and competency-based, and thus require you to complete a certain number of professional-level years of work before being eligible to sit for the exam. The PHR exam is recommended for individuals with a broad knowledge of the operational side of the HR house, and those with at least one to four years of related experience (dependent upon level of education completed). The SPHR exam is better suited for individuals with a background in strategic HR management, validated by four to seven years of professional level experience or education. HRCI defines *professional-level* experience as roles that include

>> The ability to use independent judgment and discretion in performing work duties.

>> A level of specialized knowledge in the HR field with some authority for decision-making.

>> In-depth work requirements, such as data gathering, analysis and interpretation.

>> Interaction with a broad range of individuals, including key personnel.

>> Individual accountability for results.

REMEMBER

You don't need a college degree in human resources to be eligible to take the PHR and SPHR exams.

HRCI's *Certification Handbook* identifies the full eligibility requirements for the PHR and SPHR exams. It's definitely worth reviewing while you're making your decision. Table 1-1 gives you a summary of that information.

TABLE 1-1 Figuring Out Which Exam Is Right

PHR	SPHR
A minimum of one year of experience in a professional-level HR position with a master's degree or higher	A minimum of four years of experience in a professional-level HR position with a master's degree or higher.
or	or
A minimum of two years of experience in a professional-level HR position with a bachelor's degree	A minimum of five years of experience in a professional-level HR position with a bachelor's degree
or	or
A minimum of four years of experience in a professional-level HR position with less than a bachelor's degree	A minimum of seven years of experience in a professional-level HR position with less than a bachelor's degree

The Cheat Sheet found at www.dummies.com is your go-to resource to help you pick the right test (Just type "PHR/SPHR Exam For Dummies cheat sheet" in the search box). It includes information related to all the exam eligibility requirements and assessing the amount of time you have available to study.

TIP

If neither of these exams seems right for you, don't forget about the six other certifications available from HRCI. For example, the Associate in Human Resources (aPHR) is a great choice for those just beginning their career in the human resource field. It is ideal for those with no previous HR experience, as it does not require professional-level experience to be eligible for the exam. Many students use the same preparation material for the PHR exam, and report great success — not to mention a significant knowledge boost and jump start for their next certification!

Comparing the two exams

Taking the right exam has an effect on more than simply making the preparation process less stressful. Choosing the appropriate test also can impact your future job performance and earnings potential. Think about applying for an upper-level HR job that requires exposure, experience, and problem-solving in business management and strategy that may be validated by the SPHR credential. Suppose that you squeak by the SPHR exam and are successfully certified. If you get the job based on an SPHR credential but don't have the depth and breadth of practical experience that goes along with it, more than likely you'll struggle in the role. Taking the right exam also allows you to engage in the proper recertification activities.

The professional certification process is an investment in your career, not a one-time shot at a credential. Starting with the PHR is perfectly reasonable (it's what I did). You can get the baseline under your belt and then, assuming you meet the eligibility requirements, chase after the SPHR in the following year or two. The knowledge gained by studying and recertifying has served many HR professionals well time and time again, opening doors that would have remained closed without the credentials.

HRCI defines the ideal candidate for each exam. Table 1-2 provides this insight to help you make the right choice.

Just because you can doesn't mean that you should. For example, just because you have 20 years of experience as a recruiter doesn't necessarily mean that you're ready to take the SPHR exam. For this reason, you should consider the *breadth* of your experience, not just your specialties, and plan accordingly.

TABLE 1-2   **Ideal Traits for PHR and SPHR Candidates**

PHR	SPHR
The candidate reports to another HR professional.	The candidate is responsible for the HR function at the company, either independently or with staff.
The candidate's job responsibilities impact the function of HR rather than the company as a whole.	The candidate manages the relationships necessary to achieve organizational outcomes, including with employees and within departments.
The candidate doesn't have progressive HR experience due to length of time in the industry.	The candidate understands both general business principles and industry-specific conventions (both HR and their company industries).

REMEMBER

A general rule: Use HRCI's years of experience qualifier and apply it to the top two areas of exam content, which looks something like this:

» **PHR:** For the PHR, about 60 percent of the exam content is in the areas of Employee & Labor Relations (39 percent) and Business Management (20 percent), Aim for the minimum years of experience requirements in *each* of these top areas. For example, if you have a master's degree, you should be fine if you have one year of applied experience in Employee & Labor Relations and 1 year of experience in Business Management (assuming you are otherwise eligible).

» **SPHR:** For the SPHR, more than half the exam content is built from the functional areas of Leadership and Strategy (40 percent) and Employee Relations & Engagement (20 percent). For someone with less than a bachelor's degree, this information translates to seven years of experience in *each* of these top functional areas.

These tips are for study purposes only — remember, everyone is different, and each exam has its own eligibility requirements. For the time-pressed professional, spend a larger percentage of your available study time in these top two functional areas.

WARNING

Don't quickly dismiss these percentages as overkill. Take a moment and look at the exam pass rates (69 percent PHR and 60 percent SPHR in 2019) or read the online forums of failed exam takers condemning HRCI for exam level difficulty. Consider just for a moment that *diluting the exam value* by making it easier is less effective than individuals simply *choosing the right exam* and *properly preparing* the first time. It's also worth noting that professional exams for Information Technicians and Paralegals share similar levels of difficulty. Would you hire one of these professionals if a novice could pass their certification exam with little prep or demonstrated experience? Of course not. If we as HR professionals are to be credible business partners our exams must be thorough and demonstrate excellence. Do the preparation work — you will be better for it.

Making your decision: Certification is a journey, not an event

Many individuals believe that if they meet the SPHR exam eligibility requirements, then they should start there. However, this assumption should be carefully considered for three reasons:

» If you take the SPHR and fail it the first time around, you'll have to pay a second exam fee to take it again (unless you buy insurance). If you're not sure, start with the PHR. You will benefit from gathering a baseline of knowledge and then can go round two with the SPHR on firm ground. Passing the PHR first and then taking the SPHR is a much better use of your exam fee dollars, and most importantly, it spreads your learning out over an extended period of time.

This impacts long-term retention for career application. At the end of the day, career progression and mastery really is the point of putting you through the process.

» Depending on the amount of time that you have available to study, reaching for the SPHR first may make for an unnecessarily stressful exam preparation process. Unless you have unlimited time to study and very few other obligations such as work and family, spreading your certification efforts over time is perfectly reasonable.

» Rome wasn't built in a day, and neither is your career. Both exams require recertification credits with a goal of lifelong learning. Instead of recertifying your PHR exam with webinars and classes, take the time to study and successfully pass the SPHR exam. Renewal, refreshment, and most importantly, *relevance* are the keys to a successful career in HR, and this path allows for all three.

Still undecided?

The best way to know where you stand is to invest in a couple of practice exams, which are designed to assess your level of knowledge before any studying or preparation has occurred. Don't worry if you don't pass the practice test; passing on your first or even second time isn't the goal. The purpose is to measure where you are at so you can anticipate what it will take to get you to a passing score and what subject materials you need to spend time studying.

If you're truly undecided, take both a PHR and an SPHR practice test and compare scores. This investment is worthwhile and may very well give you the answer that you're searching for. At the very least, you'll now be ready to create a study plan that targets your low scores.

If you are really worried, consider purchasing second chance insurance (SCI) when you submit your exam application. SCI is an optional, prepaid insurance policy that allow you to retake the same exam without any additional fees or having to reapply.

TIP

You can find a practice PHR test in Chapter 17 and an SPHR test in Chapter 19. (Chapter 18 provides the answer explanations for the practice PHR test, and the SPHR answer explanations are in Chapter 20.) You can also find PHR and SPHR practice tests online at www.dummies.com/go/getaccess. (See the Introduction for more info on the online practie tests.)

Applying for Your Exam

Now that you have made the tough decision on your exam-of-choice, it's time to complete the application process. It begins by creating an account at HRCI.org. This is important, as the account will be where all the details of your certification journey will be housed going forward — including where you log recertification credits after successful certification.

Completing your application online

The application process begins by inputting your certificant information. These are your personal details, but please note: The full name you enter here *must* match the name on your legal, unexpired, valid, government-issued identification documents, such as a driver's license or passport. Getting this step right is *critical* to avoid a hassle on exam day when you are required to present proof of ID before being allowed to test.

Logging your education and experience comes next. This step will be used to determine your eligibility to sit for your chosen exam and will be subject to audit and verification. Failure to accurately input this data could result in your application being rejected or nullified.

Remember to log experience that is related to human resources, even if you did not hold an HR title when performing the tasks. Think about it — how many "supervisors" do you know that are required to hire, discipline, and make decisions about pay? This is all credible, additional experience for purposes of determining whether you have the experiential chops to master the exam.

If you don't qualify based on number of years of experience or education, apply for the aPHR! It's perfect for managers with job functions other than HR and entry-level HR, and it doesn't have the same professional-level experience requirements as the PHR and SPHR.

From here, it's about the money! While the fees can change, as of 2020 the application fee for both exams was $100. The exam fees are

>> $395 USD for the PHR

>> $495 USD for the SPHR

A couple of times a year, HRCI offers discounts on the application fee (not the exam fee). Consider following them on social media such as Twitter (@HRCI_Official) and LinkedIn (HRCI in Alexandria, VA), where they advertise these specials. I also retweet their stuff regularly along with other nuggets of exam preparation resources. Find me on Twitter at @mat_schwartz.

Once your application has been submitted, you will receive a confirmation of receipt from HRCI within one business day. You will receive a separate email with your application status. You must wait until you receive your "authorization to test" email, which is the green light to go ahead and schedule your exam date.

Approved exam eligibility is valid for 120 calendar days. This means the exam must be scheduled and taken within those four months or the candidate will have to reapply — and pay the fees again!

Scheduling the exam online

As of 2020, HRCI partners with Pearson VUE to deliver the PHR and SPHR exam (more on this in Chapter 4). Go to pearsonvue.com/hrci to schedule your test-day appointment using the same legal name from your HRCI registration, the HRCI 9-digit eligibility ID found on your HRCI application summary, your phone number, the exam type, and finally, your preferred date, time, and location.

Any exam rescheduling must be done with Pearson VUE, and there is a nonrefundable rescheduling fee.

During the Covid-19 pandemic of 2020, HRCI received temporary approval to offer remote-proctored exams. It is unclear whether this practice will be continued. Prior to the pandemic, both the PHR and SPHR had to be taken at a proctored Pearson VUE physical location.

Knowing What to Expect on the Exams

Anticipation is often worse than the actual experience, which seems to hold particularly true for both the PHR and SPHR exam day. The chapters in Part 1 are all about sharing with you what to expect on the big day. The following sections give you a quick overview.

Looking at the exams' structure and types of questions

Both exams have questions that are written by certified HR professionals who are not necessarily academics. In fact, exam item writers go through a series of stem/option (answers) iterations in order to come to a "best answer" consensus by those actively practicing in the field of HR. This is actually what makes these exams fairly difficult, as each question may have what looks like to be multiple correct answers. HRCI correlates exam scores to the years of experience that are required for the tests, which is in part to justify the need for practical work experience for a successful test. Furthermore, as part of the accreditation process, the exam content is built from the exam bodies of knowledge (BOK). The exam's BOK are based on an analysis of the HR field as a whole.

Chapter 3 discusses the exam structure, including a review of the different types of test questions. Each question may be worded differently and include traditional multiple choice, multiple choice/ multiple response, fill in the blank, drag and drop and scenario-based questions. Each exam item may be phrased as a question, an open-ended statement, or a statement. For all question types, you will be asked to select the best answer. This is an attempt to measure your response based on a "real-world" situation. Some options are written as distractors, looking correct but not the best decision in the context of the scenario given.

HRCI's *Certification Handbook* notes that each question will focus on one of the following three areas:

>> **Knowledge/comprehension:** Recalling factual material, such as definitions

>> **Application/problem solving:** Applying familiar principles or generalizations to solve real-life problems

>> **Synthesis/evaluation:** Combining different elements and using critical thinking skills to solve a complex problem

To become familiar with these question types, practice exams (such as the ones included in this book) are highly recommended.

Grasping how the exams are scored

Many test takers are really only concerned with passing or failing, which is fine. Students must have a total scaled score of 500 to pass these exams.

However, the exams have two types of scores that affect what you need to pass:

>> **Raw:** The *raw score* is the actual number of items answered correctly on your test.

>> **Scaled:** The *scaled score* represents the difficulty level of the random exam you received.

There are thousands of PHR and SPHR test questions. You only have to answer 175 of them. You may receive 175 of the questions that are rated as difficult, whereas the person next to you may receive 175 of the fairly easy ones. That means that you'll be allowed some wiggle room while still needing to achieve the scaled score of 500 in order to pass. It's an exercise in fairness.

REMEMBER

Don't leave a question unanswered. Scoring is based on the number of correct answers, so leaving an item blank — even if it's an educated guess — eliminates the possibility of that item counting in your scaled score. Refer to Chapter 3 for some strategies about guessing on the PHR and SPHR exams.

Preparing to Tackle the Exam

Very few individuals take this test with no preparation. The degree to which you prepare is based on your unique work experience and education. Preparation tactics include the following (Chapter 2 discusses these factors in greater detail):

>> **Study plans:** A study plan is a tool that you design. It's a written plan of attack that addresses the things that make you unique — your specific strengths and weaknesses and the amount of time you have available to study — which means that you'll need to have a general idea of your exam date and assessment scores. I'm not a fan of absolute statements, but I make an exception here: Successful test takers *must* have a written plan of attack. Get organized and stay organized to ensure that you don't miss studying critical exam content.

>> **Assessment and practice exams:** You can't possibly know the extent of your strengths and weaknesses without taking an initial assessment test. Additionally, you may be as knowledgeable as any other successful candidate, but applying that knowledge takes preparation. Many individuals report suffering from severe test anxiety or have not taken a formal test in many years. Practice exams help with training your brain to think through how to apply your working knowledge while becoming familiar with a time-based, difficult exam.

>> **Study groups:** Another option for getting ready for the exam is to join a study group. You can join a group either through a college campus or independently. Chapter 2 discusses the pros and cons of this support option.

TIP

HRCI does not endorse one prep product over another, instead recommending that you use multiple preparation resources to study for the exam. They do, however, partner with preparation providers (some that offer money-back guarantees if you don't pass) to offer bundled pricing, and this is a cost-effective way to get started!

Tackling the 24 Hours before, during, and after the Exam

Regardless of how long you prepare for the exam, nothing is quite like the trio — the day before, the day of, and the day after the exam day.

>> **Before the test:** You'll need to make many decisions to prepare for the 24 hours before test day. For example, some individuals prefer to book a hotel room near the exam facility, which minimizes the possibility of heavy traffic and allows for a quiet evening before to review. I actually drove the route to the testing center the day before so that I could minimize my tendency to get lost while driving! Regardless of your decision, in the 24 hours before your test, turn off the cell phone, TV, and other distractions, and concentrate on a relaxed state of mind. Make sure that you get a good night's rest.

>> **On exam day:** Exam-day basics should focus on stamina. Sitting in a small room for a few hours while your brain is drained isn't an easy task. Distractors such as nerves, fatigue, and hunger are real threats to success. For this reason, having a plan of attack before you're faced with the conditions is helpful. Chapter 4 discusses more strategies on taking breaks and eating snacks to keep you focused.

>> **After the test:** I'm confident that you'll feel a sense of relief as you answer the last question. In some cases, you may have marked questions for review and will need to go back and finish them before you cross the finish line. You will be given the choice to take a quick survey while

the results are calculated. The good news is, you will know before you leave the desk if you pass or fail! If you fail the exam, a more detailed score report will be mailed to you so you can see how close you were and in what functional areas you didn't pass. Regardless of a pass or fail score, you have just spent several weeks immersing yourself in the world of HR — go home and celebrate! Chapter 5 gives you some ideas on how to begin to apply this new knowledge on your job.

At the end of the day, you are a unique individual with individual needs, and no one-size-fits-all solution exists to how well you manage before, during, and after the test. Some students swear by cramming the night before, whereas others say doing so confused them. Eating a large meal before the test was impossible for some, whereas others knew that low blood sugar during the exam would sink them. Others believe that only a successful exam is reason to be proud of themselves — which is just not true. The preparation process will make you stronger regardless of the outcome of your first attempt. Knowing your needs and extracting advice that meets those needs is the purpose of these discussions so that you can be at maximum mental performance level when it counts.

TIP

On exam day, you don't need to bring a calculator. Most math-related questions are written to be easily calculated. Don't worry, though. If you prefer a calculator, one is available on the desktop computer from which you take your exam.

Examining the Core Subject Areas on the Exam

Both exams have unique functional areas in terms of content, and you need to know what to do with this information in order for it to serve you. Similar to the test questions, you must be able to apply the knowledge from a workplace perspective to be successful. Each exam has five functional areas. These sections provide a brief overview of what you can expect about the functional areas of the PHR and SPHR exams. I include chapter references to continue the discovery.

REMEMBER

A note about Federal Employment Law: As seasoned practitioners, we all know that employment law changes from year to year. However, the exam content outlines are only updated every five to seven years or so. HRCI tells us that exam candidates are responsible for knowing the HR laws that are in place at the time of their exam. For this reason, regardless of the exam prep resource you use, you may need some additional research to ensure your knowledge of best legal practices is up-to-date. Final note: The exam includes questions related to federal laws and regulations, not state laws.

PHR

PHR test questions are designed for the operational practitioner of human resources. The exam goes beyond the foundations of an entry-level performer and bumps right up against the strategic skills required of their human resource bosses. While the functional area titles of the PHR and SPHR exams are similar, the content weight and focus are different.

Functional area 01 — Business Management

Second only to functional area 05 in exam content, Business Management makes up 20 percent of PHR exam questions. The focus is heavily weighted toward executing HR activities in alignment with the business, such as industry best practices, the company mission and vision, as well as taking care to avoid litigation related to employment law violations. Discover more about this important content in Chapter 7.

Functional area 02 — Talent Planning and Acquisition

At 16 percent, the Talent Planning and Acquisition area of the PHR should not give you (too much) trouble. Take care to study concepts such as federal labor law and its impact on hiring practices; creative candidate sourcing techniques; and the cycle of acquiring talent within the organization, from recruitment to negotiating employment offers. You can read more about this subject area in Chapter 8.

Functional area 03 — Learning and Development

Learning & Development (L & D) has evolved from a strict focus on training design and delivery. In today's world, it relates to a generalist's ability to advise managers and team members on professional growth, career plans and replacement planning efforts that support business strategies. At only 10 percent of the exam content, focus on how L & D supports the larger scope of the Business Management and Talent Planning and Acquisition functional areas. See what this might look like in Chapter 9.

Functional area 04 — Total Rewards

Implementing and managing total rewards programs provides 15 percent of the PHR exam content. It starts with the critical function of managing employee payroll, and rounds out with the ability to understand and administer effective employee benefit programs. Chapter 10 includes an overview of content related to this functional area.

Functional area 05 — Employee Relations and Engagement

HRCI saved the most comprehensive section of the PHR exam for last. This section deals with matters related to HR functions throughout the employee life cycle and collecting/interpreting data related to employee engagement levels at each stage. It makes up a whopping 39 percent of the total exam, so PHR hopefuls must pay particular attention. Federal requirements related to diversity, inclusion, health and safety, employee policies, discipline, and separations are all measured here in the functional area of Employee and Labor Relations. From previous versions of the PHR Exam Content Outline, you will find content related to employee performance management migrated to this section as well. Begin your studying with the content review found in Chapter 11.

SPHR

SPHR test questions are highly scenario-based and require the ability to integrate information from *all* functional areas in your analysis. This exam is designed for senior leaders who help shape business strategy and position their companies to successfully navigate the business landscape — inside the workplace and out.

Functional area 01 — Leadership and Strategy

Formerly called Business Management and Strategy, the Leadership and Strategy functional area of the SPHR exam makes up 40 percent of total exam content. It focuses on developing HR strategies that are in alignment with business strategy, and draws heavily from the domains of Business Management (such as business metrics and operations) and Organizational Development (such as managing change and behavior). Chapter 12 summarizes this, along with the other people-management elements present in this content area.

Functional area 02 — Talent Planning and Acquisition

The functional area of Talent Planning and Acquisition carries the same punch on both exams, coming in at 16 percent. For the SPHR, this content is derived from strategies designed to plan for, attract, and retain talent. Look for questions about workforce planning (such as expansion and downsizing) and cultural integration (such as onboarding and socialization). As with all content on the SPHR, pay special attention to measuring the results of these activities, which is discussed in more detail in Chapter 13.

Functional area 03 — Learning and Development

Learning and Development (L & D) is about more than just training workers. At 12 percent of the SPHR exam content, it is tied closely to organizational development and expands upon the idea that training and performance management can help organizations meet both current and future needs. For this reason (as in practice), L & D activities cascade out from Talent Planning and Acquisition functions. Among the exam objectives, expect to see HR behaviors such as evaluating training strategies and succession planning. You can read more about this subject area in Chapter 14.

Functional area 04 — Total Rewards

Similar to L & D, content in the Total Rewards function on the SPHR exam makes up about 12 percent. Labor costs are often the top expense for organizations, so oversight of this function — and the measurement of results — is critical for senior HR leaders. This includes heavy emphasis on the design of creative compensation strategies, such as incentives and executive pay, as well as analyzing the effectiveness of employee benefit plans. Check out Chapter 15 to get a good feel for what you need to know about this subject area for the SPHR exam.

Functional area 05 — Employee Relations and Engagement

Not just about union management anymore, this functional area has evolved to include the management of all relationships in the workplace. From an exam perspective, it makes up the second highest amount of content, 20 percent. This includes factors related to measuring and improving employee satisfaction, building diversity and inclusion initiatives, and of course, the original concepts of managing a union/management relationship. In 2018, the content from the former Risk Management functional area was migrated here as well. Head to Chapter 16 for more information about this subject area.

Remembering the Core Knowledge Requirements

One of the major changes of the 2018 exam content updates was the absorption of the core knowledge requirements within each functional area. Prior to 2018, it was a separate section that was not directly tied to specific exam areas. In 2018, HRCI moved this content into its relevant functional areas, further sorted by exam. This may be in part because the HRCI exams seek to measure competencies (skills, abilities, practices) as opposed to only book knowledge.

Found at the end of each section with the heading "Knowledge of:" you will find a numeric listing of the data required for successful application of the HR responsibilities being measured on each exam. The Knowledge and Responsibilities of the exam content outlines form the full framework for the PHR and SPHR exams — you must know them well. Chapter 2 provides a more in-depth perspective on this content.

Understanding That You Can't Be Taught the Exam

HRCI makes no secret that these exams can't be taught. Yet individuals who fail the exams gnash their teeth and wail loudly, wondering how they're supposed to prepare for an exam that has no precise preparation resource. Thinking such as this is unfair and takes an unrealistic perspective, for the following reasons:

>> **The exam is deeply experience based.** Writing an exam (or study guide) that gauges every exam taker's level of experience and breaks down the content into the right-size piece for every person's palette is impossible. Having the right number of years of experience doesn't guarantee that you'll pass. The quality, depth, and breadth of the experience get you an invitation to the certified members' lounge.

>> **The exam isn't about rote memorization and to suggest that it must become so is diluting the value for those professionals who are certified and the profession as a whole.** Dumbing it down into memorizable pieces mocks the profession because it doesn't translate into practice. Imagine binding HR professionals to textbook answers and one-size-fits-all strategies. C-suite executives would take one cross-eyed look at that approach and go rogue, exposing businesses to risk and devaluing an HR professional's role. Talk about why executives avoid HR! This approach damages HR's credibility and effectiveness.

>> **The homework, research, and creative studying methods make you a better HR practitioner.** You'll come out of the preparation trial-by-fire well-seasoned and tempered to be the business partner that your enterprise needs. Unless you hope to go back to party planning and payroll, jump on the bandwagon and dig deep. These exams aren't for the faint at heart.

>> **Just because you fail doesn't mean that you aren't good at your job.** You may not be a good test taker. The testing room may have been too hot. Perhaps you aced one area, but you need more rounding out in others. Toughen up and try again. As an HR professional, you need to be the model of resilience for those impacted by your talent, and inflating your ability or transferring blame serves no one. Having a do-over is okay. Review how far you came in terms of knowledge before you began preparing compared to test day. Honor your growth and how far you have come by believing in yourself and trying again. And guess what — you'll have earned the certification.

MY EXAM JOURNEY

Making the decision to become professionally certified certainly helps your career, but the decision is also highly personal. Fear of failure, fear of success, and worry about the exam level difficulty are a host of pitfalls that may keep you from being successful. I hope my own journey can help you in your journey.

I left the world of full-time HR the day my son was born and began teaching classes at night. I realized that to be credible, I needed to get my PHR certification. Back in the days of the pencil-and-paper test, I self-studied with a group, sat for the exam, and passed after waiting six weeks for the results.

Fast-forward several years. Now with two children, I found out that I was being laid off from my teaching position. I worried a bit at the time because I didn't have any sort of college degree, and I felt that I wouldn't be a competitive candidate in the market. I remembered that the process of getting certified the first time renewed my interest and taught me so much more about HR, so I decided to go the SPHR route while my final students were finishing their program. I self-studied again, this time with the internet and several preparation books. My exam date was right around Christmas, and I remember how nervous I was while listening to my audio recordings as I drove to the hotel in the city where my testing center was located. I crammed the night before and remember sitting on the bed surrounded by my books, papers, and flash cards. I felt guilty for being away from home and completely unprepared, despite my studying efforts over the last 12 weeks. I had my "ah-ha" moment right then and there, when suddenly the processes began to make sense. The common denominators declared themselves, and the information linking functional area to functional area took shape. I sat for the SPHR exam the next morning, finishing an hour early and passing on the first try. Now I just needed to do something with the credential.

Although I had a strong desire to stay home with my kids, I wanted and needed to put my newfound knowledge to use. So when I found that the Society for Human Resource Management (SHRM) accepted proposals for case studies and learning modules, I jumped on it, having three projects accepted and published. I began HR consulting as a sideline and soon started writing test-prep books about the exams.

The PHR and SPHR certifications allowed me to pursue my passion while still living the life that I loved with my children, who are now 19 and 15 years old. Certification has validated my talent and opened doors that would have firmly remained closed without it — it gave me options. Try not to worry about the pass rates and the time commitment. Accept that a career of passion and excellence is an important piece of the puzzle to finding fulfillment. Seize the tiger by the tail and go for it.

IN THIS CHAPTER

» Anticipating the content of the PHR and SPHR exams

» Benefitting from practice exams

» Putting together a study plan

» Seeing whether your employer will pay for certification

» Finding resources online

» Discovering core knowledge

Chapter **2**

Preparing for the Exam

All exams aren't created equal, nor are all exam takers the same. Hence, you must consider both the exam selection and your individual skill set when preparing for the PHR or the SPHR.

"Pass it ugly" is a phrase I use to remind overachievers that they don't need to ace this exam. All they have to do is pass it. Having a comprehensive study plan is critical when preparing for the exam because it ensures that you focus on the *right* things, not necessarily on *all* things.

Focusing on the right things begins by anticipating exam content, comparing the content to your individual assessment results, and accessing resources that are uniquely suited to your exam readiness.

This chapter discusses tips, tricks, and best practices that take into account your unique ability and resource availability and how you can get organized for maximum effect. As with all things HR, proper planning is the first activity leading to ultimate success.

Considering Exam Weights by Functional Area

Weighting the exam content allows the test builders to rank information in the order of importance and level of difficulty. Exam weights are expressed as percentages — the higher the percentage, the more important or difficult the information and the more likely it is that you will see it on your test.

For example, the functional area of Leadership and Strategy weighs in at approximately 40 percent of the content of the SPHR exam, making it a top priority for SPHR exam takers. PHR candidates should pay special attention to the category of Employee and Labor Relations, weighting in at 39 percent of that exam.

HRCI has this to say about exam weighting:

"The weighting indicates the percentage each Functional Area contributes to the exam total. If you were to add each Functional Area's weight, the total would equal 100 percent. This allows you to see how much each Functional Area contributes to the total exam."

From this we can infer that certain functional areas and questions will carry more weight in calculating your final score — and that you will probably see much more content related to the depth of these areas on your respective exam. Take a look at the calculations of Tables 2-1 and 2-2 to give you a glimpse at what this may look like.

TABLE 2-1   PHR Exam Weights

Functional Area	Exam Weight	Number of Questions
Business Management	20 percent	35
Talent Planning and Acquisition	16 percent	28
Learning and Development	10 percent	18
Total Rewards	15 percent	27
Employee and Labor Relations	39 percent	68

TABLE 2-2   SPHR Exam Weights

Functional Area	Exam Weight	Number of Questions
Leadership and Strategy	40 percent	70
Talent Planning and Acquisition	16 percent	28
Learning and Development	12 percent	21
Total Rewards	12 percent	21
Employee Relations and Engagement	20 percent	35

REMEMBER

The two exams may have similar content, but the exam questions will be different. For example, even though both exams may have questions related to recruiting, the PHR exam will deal with operational specificity, whereas the SPHR exam will be more focused on oversight and strategic implications. Here are two sample questions asking a very similar question with a different correct answer to illustrate this difference.

First the PHR question:

EXAMPLE

A position has just opened for a quality technician in the Research and Development department of the company you work for. The position is part time, requires some education, and could have a flexible schedule for the right talent. Which of the following recruiting sources would BEST result in qualified applicants?

(A) Staffing agencies

(B) College or trade school recruiting

(C) Online sources, such as recruiting sites and social media

(D) Daycares and elementary schools

Although all of the answers have potiential to result in a qualified individual, the correct answer is Choice (B). College or trade schools is a targeted resource and most likely to have candidates who are interested in part-time work while having some education/skill in the field. Choice (A) is a more expensive option than necessary at this stage of the recruit and for this type of hire. Choice (D) doesn't target the labor pool adequately. Choice (C) is a broader scope than may be necessary for this job opening.

Now the SPHR question:

EXAMPLE

ABC Manufacturing has launched a total quality management program in order to be eligible to service international clientele. As a result, the company will need to regularly add quality inspectors to its R & D department over the next three to five years, with newly trained employees being deployed to the national and global clients in need. The position will be part time, require some technical aptitude, and have nontraditional hours. Which of the following recruitment sources would BEST result in a steady flow of qualified candidates?

(A) Staffing agencies

(B) College or trade school recruiting

(C) Online sources, such as recruiting sites and social media

(D) Daycares and elementary schools

In this example, Choice (A) is best. A global staffing agency with locations near clients can help HR build the partnership necessary for a sustained effort. Choices (B) and (C) are quite useful for short-term recruiting needs but don't achieve the regional partnership necessary to achieve sustainable results. Choice (D) isn't targeted at all toward the position.

REMEMBER

Being armed with information about the exams, such as assessment results and question formatting, can feel a bit overwhelming. The exam content is already cumbersome and tricky, and tracking and managing information *about* the exams rather than what is *on* the exams may seem unnecessary. However, doing the legwork before you dive into the exam content is worth it. It can reduce anxiety and ensure that you have adequate time to prepare for both the exam content and the pitfalls to avoid. In this case, context matters.

Practicing for Results

Practice doesn't make perfect, it simply makes the material you study permanent. This means that the wrong kind of practice can have a negative effect on your test outcome. Simply studying content and expecting to apply it successfully in an exam setting isn't enough. Your goal should be to be an accomplished test taker by test day (the day of judgment).

REMEMBER

Use practice exams to focus on one of two things:

>> **Content review:** In content review, the goal is to get you to dive into the exam objectives to test your knowledge. Use the tests to study different concepts and reinforce what you know and don't know.

>> **Exam simulations:** These not only measure your knowledge, but they also simulate testing conditions. It may have been a while since you last sat for an exam, so you're likely unfamiliar with protocols and format. In order to simulate exam-day conditions, be sure to take practice tests that are at least 175 questions and that give you only three hours to complete them. When you take the test, be sure to watch the time so you properly pace yourself and get used to answering each question in just over a minute. Practice marking questions for review and

changing your answers to see if your first choice was correct. If yes, alter your technique to *not* change answers and see if that works better. Doing so can help you decide how to handle the unknown when you're faced with the real deal.

In order to benefit from practice exams, you need to take as many as possible. Doing so takes planning and a clear understanding of what you're trying to measure. (Refer to the section "Building a Study Plan Strategy" later in this chapter to help you create a plan.) The next two sections focus on how practice exams can help you and what you can do to get maximum results from them.

Reaping the benefits from practice exams

In order to get the most out of taking practice exams, you need to use your time wisely. You want to practice with as many as you can before you take the actual exam. These tips can help you maximize your results.

When you're practicing with content review (rather than simulation) in mind, consider the following:

>> **Take the practice tests open book.** Practice exams can serve many masters, one of which is to teach you exam content. The assessments in this book include a comprehensive answer review that explains both the correct and the incorrect answers. Taking the tests open book can align your studying efforts with the application to the test, the most effective way to master this material.

>> **Look for the answers online and see what reading material or videos are related to that question.** If you have time, studying the test questions this way creates a depth of knowledge that is transferable to the exam. The exams are designed to measure not only knowledge, but experience as well. Real-world examples of the concepts surface online, giving you an experience-based perspective for future recall. Take the concept of "emergency response, business continuity, and disaster recovery strategies" (knowledge requirements on both exams) as an example. When you type this phrase into your search engine, one of the top (non-ad) results will be ready.gov. Here you can find all sorts of relevant strategies and practices that candidates can use to understand the real-world application of this objective.

Many of the exam objectives start with phrases such as "design and manage . . ." or "implement and evaluate. . . ." Use your resources (starting with the Exam Content Outline first) to begin to understand what the question is asking you to answer.

TIP

When going online to study, stay away from lawyer websites or generic databases. Search for sites that end in *.org* or *.gov* to ensure that you're applying the right material. Credible journal sites are also a good place for free to low-cost information, giving you insight into trends and current practices in the field of HR. Popular ones include www.forbes.com and www.hbr.org *(Harvard Business Review)*. Check out www.dummies.com/extras/phrsphrexam for a list of ten apps that are good resources. One exception: I do subscribe to podcasts from labor attorneys. It helps me stay up-to-date on the complex issues surrounding legislation such as the interpretation of the 2019 FLSA Overtime rules. One of my favorites is New York attorney Michael Schmidt's "Employment Law Now" podcast.

>> **While taking a practice exam, check your answers as you go.** Doing so can ensure that you're learning the information correctly and not storing incorrect information. Focus on the content of the questions and the right answers (and why they're correct). Then take another test and trust your gut.

When you're focusing on exam simulation when taking practice exams, keep these tips in mind:

REMEMBER

>> **Practice using similar tools to those that will be available at the professional testing site.** For example, use an online calculator for the math questions. Use noise-cancelling headphones or ear buds to gauge your comfort level with the tools provided onsite. Most importantly, time yourself, allowing approximately one minute per question, to train your mind to the pace of the exam. These conditioning strategies will serve to minimize your anxiety and give you insights into your individual preferences.

The more practice exams you take, the more opportunities you have to simulate exam-day conditions and determine your personal preferences, all while learning content. These are worthy investments that should not be underestimated.

>> **Mimic the conditions of test day as closely as possible.** Doing so is just as important to exam preparation as learning the content, because it minimizes the likelihood of unpleasant surprises on test day. Set aside three hours with no distractions (no ringing phone, no needy pets, and no demanding co-workers). Your goal is to answer all 175 questions in three hours. For example, practice at the same time of day your exam is scheduled for. Be aware of other common distractions that happen under those conditions, such as hunger or fatigue. Know before exam day how you're going to handle these common distractors so that you don't inadvertently sabotage your success by being unprepared for the unexpected.

TIP

Determine whether you can sit for three hours without using the restroom. It may seem somewhat silly, but you want to make sure that you're comfortable with the exact conditions that you'll face at the testing center. Plan ahead at home during a practice test rather than on game day. If you can't sit that long without using the restroom, then you should account for a quick bathroom break in determining the amount of time that you'll have to answer each question.

Making the right selection

Several options for practice exams are available, and they range from online tests to the paper-and-pencil variety. I recommend the online solutions because you'll be taking the exam online. This book has both types of tests — written ones in the book and online versions (see the Introduction) — for you to practice.

Building a Study Plan Strategy

Having a study plan in place is a smart strategy for preparing for the PHR and SPHR exams. A study plan can direct your efforts and keep you focused on meeting your goal of passing so that you can achieve the three or four initials after your name. These exams aren't for the faint of heart, which is why an organized commitment is essential. A little planning goes a long way, and these sections describe the ins and outs of writing your plan.

Being organized keeps you focused

Taking the time to prepare your plan and get organized holds you accountable. You know what your expectations are and what you need to accomplish on a daily basis. (If your approach is less structured, you may be tempted to study when you can, which can create anxiety on test day and decrease your chances of success.)

You can use different tools to create your study plan, depending on your preference. Three options include

>> **Calendar:** A calendar allows you to create a bird's-eye view of your preparations. Working backward from your test date, block out a specific time each week in which you'll study. One strategy is to allocate at least two weeks per functional area. Another strategy is to allocate three weeks for the top three areas in content (see the preceding Tables 2-1 and 2-2).

>> **Digital Planners:** Several free or low-cost apps and online tools are available to help you keep track of your progress and build the discipline necessary for successful preparation. Find one that not only allows you to plan out your weekly activities, but also sends you digital reminders of your commitment.

>> **To-do checklist:** A to-do list is a great way to capture your study activities. You can create a simple checklist by functional area that includes a reminder to use the exam preparation resources that you have selected. Head to www.dummies.com/extras/phrsphrexam for a sample checklist that you can use to get you started. You can use it to give you ideas on how to create your own to-do list, or you can print it and use it verbatim, whichever works best for you. It directs you to specific studying activities, such as reading your selected exam preparation study guide and answering the chapter review questions where available. You'll find it is a helpful way to ensure that you're leaving no resource unexplored as you study the material.

TIP

Get creative as you approach the material. Rote memorization is not only boring, but it may not lead to long-term retention. A good checklist takes you beyond flash cards and reminds you to tap into multiple ways of learning for maximum effectiveness. Schedule time in your plan to build mind maps and affinity diagrams, crossword puzzles, and digital flash cards. Watch videos and consider opposing viewpoints so that you see a complex issue — such as union membership — from all perspectives. Don't forget to tap into your network! You are most likely connected to several subject-matter experts, so job shadow or interview them to really get that applied viewpoint.

Writing a study plan: The how-to

You may not have sat for an exam in a long period of time, so the prospect of writing a study plan may be daunting. The good news is that there isn't a single best practice in preparing for this exam. It's the collection of multiple efforts that will help you perform well and reach your goal. This section highlights some of the best ways to get your plan started to have maximum effect on your studying effort. Get started here and expand as you see fit.

TIP

To create your own study plan, follow these easy steps:

1. **Select your practice exam resources.**

   Align your preparation with HRCI's exam objectives. I recommend that you focus on resources that are content driven, such as a study guide or a website. These resources should include functional review questions, flash cards, quizzes, and other study activities that serve you. HRCI recommends that you select multiple resources to prepare for these tests.

   Many adults prefer to learn online, and there are options for self-paced studying. Several major universities offer self-paced courses, as do individual authors and businesses. In Part 3, I recommend a plethora of websites that can serve you in your study plan.

   HRCI also offers a *Guide to the Human Resource Body of Knowledge* (HRBoK), a comprehensive desktop reference guide that covers the fundamentals of human resource management and written by yours truly. This is a good starting point as you begin to assemble your study resources.

2. **Identify the areas that you'll study after taking the assessment exams based on the exam weights.**

   Take one or two assessments *prior* to beginning your studying efforts to get a baseline of your current readiness. Focus on the data in Tables 2-1 and 2.2 to know what content areas to study. If you scored low on your assessment in an area that carries a heavier content weight on your exam, you should build extra time into your study plan to assure preparedness come exam day.

3. **Decide how much time you'll study per week.**

   Because these exams have five areas to address, you should plan for at least two weeks per functional area, or ten weeks, depending on your assessment scores. Hence, focus on the content areas that you scored lower on and that have more questions on the exam.

   Include practice exams in your overall study calendar. Add at least another three practice exams for review, preferably one per section. Approximately two weeks prior to your exam date, take at least two more exam simulations. Remember that no single preparation resource has all the content of the PHR and SPHR exams; authors don't have special access to the exams, and out of the thousands of possible questions, your exam will be made of just 175. Immersing yourself in practice exams from multiple resources not only acclimates you to the question wording, but also exposes you to broader exam content, increasing your odds of seeing something familiar on the test.

TIP

Everyone has different preferences and needs as they prepare for this test, so there really is no wrong way to study. Do your best to incorporate studying into your everyday activities. For example, if you exercise on a regular basis, make an audio recording using your phone and play it back while on the treadmill. If you're a parent who reads to your infant at night, read aloud from your textbook instead of from the regular titles; your baby won't mind what you read as long as he hears your voice. Or, ask your tween to quiz you with a flash-card deck, showing her how hard you're willing to work to prepare for something you want.

Employing the Principles: Going Deeper

To fully immerse yourself in the preparation experience, you need to find and access multiple experts. Finding a complete study guide is critical, but not enough. The next couple of sections point you in the direction of other resources to create depth from which to draw on exam day.

HRCI's suggested authors

In addition to the Exam Content Outlines and the HRBoK, HRCI has identified must-reads by authors such as:

>> **Warren Bennis:** Bennis is a management theorist in the areas of leadership and behavior management. In general, he states that the traditional organization structure of top-down authority is less effective than democratic or collaborative leadership. Although he has authored several books, you should take a strong look at his work on Douglas McGregor, one of the fathers of humanistic behavior management in the field of industrial psychology. The principles of both of these authors are very likely to be in one form or another on the exams.

>> **Charles Handy:** Handy is best known for his work on organizational strategy, so SPHR candidates should accord special study time to studying his theories. In short, he discusses the need for businesses to function as a community, with rights and shared responsibilities.

>> **Geert Hofstede:** A well-respected social psychologist, Hofstede pioneered work in the field of organizational culture. He developed the idea of dimensions of culture, specifically that individuals are "group animals" responding to a moral code of conduct and values that must exist in an organizational community. Familiarize yourself with the concepts of power distance, individualism versus collectivism, masculinity versus femininity, long- versus short-term orientation, and indulgence versus restraint.

>> **Henry Mintzberg:** The author of several management books, Mintzberg talks quite a bit about balancing the power of economic structures, in which he includes organizations. For purposes of the exams, take a look at his model of ten managerial roles.

>> **Kenichi Ohmae:** Ohmae may be best known for his role in illuminating the Lean manufacturing principles in the West. Started by Toyota in Japan, Lean is a quality management program with the goal of stripping out waste and engaging in just-in-time production. His work, however, is quite broad and focuses on both operations and strategy, making him a necessary read for both PHR and SPHR exam takers.

>> **Michael Porter:** If you've taken any management strategy classes, you probably have heard of Porter's five forces. His work on environmental scanning reminds us that there are several external pressures that affect organizational success. This includes supplier power, buyer power, competitive rivalry, threat of substitution, and threat of new entry.

>> **C.K. Prahalad:** Prahalad makes for good company on this list of pioneers. Much of his work was focused on corporate strategy and the need for business to break through traditional competitive boundaries and invent new markets. A great example of this is his book titled *The Fortune at the Bottom of the Pyramid* (Wharton School Publishing), which discusses how organizations can compete and profit while eradicating poverty.

>> **Edgar Schein:** A prolific author, Schein's work in organizational culture, leadership, and management theory is quite broad. PHR candidates can benefit from his work on modern career pathing and leadership development. SPHR candidates should go deep in his works about organizational culture and its impact on outcomes.

>> **Peter Senge:** Organizational learning is the focus of Senge's work. He viewed organizations as one whole system with interrelated parts (departments) that are completely dependent upon organizational health. Called *systems thinking,* it's the fifth discipline of how organizations learn, integrating the other four that include personal mastery, mental models, shared vision, and team learning.

>> **Dave Ulrich's Scorecards:** You must spend time on business and HR scorecards, and Ulrich is the man to help you. As HR practitioners, it's your responsibility to develop measurements that help your company make data-driven decisions. His work talks about what must be measured and the tools you may use to do so.

Many of these subject-matter experts post on social media. Follow them and read their blogs and posts daily, a good practice for after the exam as well!

Online business sites

The exam BOK is updated every five or so years, and item writers use popular business research sources (along with field studies, peer-reviewed research, and a host of other techniques) to increase the relevance of the exam to the current business climate. Here are four credible sources that are a must-visit for supplemental exam materials:

>> **McKinsey & Company:** An international management consulting firm, this company doesn't just consult, it researches and shares findings online at www.mckinsey.com. Sign up for its tweets or emails and incorporate its articles in your daily mash of studying. Its topics are quite diverse and range from broader issues, such as global business, to more topical issues, like the impact of obesity on the workforce.

>> **The Boston Consulting Group (BCG):** The BCG publishes information through its website (www.bcg.com). It includes a host of business-related information, including global perspectives, CEO engagement, technology, and business transformations. You can view the group's information online or sign up for its magazine to strengthen your studying efforts.

>> **Deloitte:** Another global company, Deloitte is most relevant to the exams based on its surveys and business articles. Some of the topics covered at Deloitte University Press include CFO focus, business analytics, risk management, and performance. Check out www.deloitte.com.

>> **Re:Work:** It's probably no surprise that a company with a mission to organize the world's information has found a way to study the science of the workplace and publish it's findings. The content found at https://rework.withgoogle.com is well worth a day's study, specifically to watch their videos and read through the modern-day case studies and research findings.

>> **Inc.com:** In 2017, HRCI experts wrote content for a sponsored series titled "HRCI View." The series includes tons of relevant commentary on trends and issues in the human resource industry, and this can help reinforce that experiential perspective that is so necessary to a passing score. Find this series at www.inc.com/hrci.

Techniques

You may be wondering how you're going to find the time to go deep and study all the material on the PHR or SPHR exams. At this stage of your studying, I must emphasize how critical your daily commitment is to success. Reading all of these books and absorbing enough to apply to the exam is ideal, but probably not necessary. Instead, consider implementing the following study goals:

>> Commit to spending 10 or 20 minutes each day outside of your normal study time to research the authors from the previous section "HRCI's suggested authors" and their work.

>> Watch videos online where the authors give lectures, which may be the best way to immerse yourself in what *they* believed was important about their work.

>> Create a master document or flash cards of what you believe is most relevant, focusing on themes of leadership development, company culture, metrics, and strategy.

>> Look for common threads between these authors and articles, and extract what best applies to the exam objectives.

As with so many other facets of these tests, proper planning and development of meaningful study tools can ease your mind and get you ready for exam day.

MAKING OUTLINES WHEN YOU STUDY

The internet is the perfect place to download fact sheets from government websites on labor laws such as the Fair Labor Standards Act (FLSA), Americans with Disabilities Act, and Title VII of the Civil Rights Act of 1964. Use the knowledge requirements for each functional area to make sure that you're hitting the main points of each law as it applies in an employment context.

Be sure and do something other than just print the fact sheets or the entire body of law. Your mind may be saturated with written content at this point, and labor law is especially tough to chew through. Think about creating a mind map or Venn diagram, looking for relationships and common threads as these labor laws apply to the functional area of choice. For example, Title VII of the Civil Rights Act of 1964 applies to multiple functional areas, as shown in the following figure. There is no wrong way to do this, so modify these tools to best suit the information.

I like binders to keep all of this online material. You can print out your diagrams and make notes while you work, then store them in the proper section for later review. Doing so is especially helpful if you take an assessment test closer to exam day when you can narrow your studying efforts to sections in which you didn't perform well — your binder will be just the place to start. The more tech-savvy among us may prefer to use their smart devices to take photographs or screenshots of these resources so they can study them on-the-go.

REMEMBER

You're not studying for an MBA, so focus your time on the application of these principles to the exam objectives. Taking a broader view of this material may be interesting, but not purposeful to the one goal that you're focusing on — getting a passing score.

Finally, trust yourself and your talent. What seems overwhelming at first glance will eventually come together in an identifiable shape, and you'll see how these pieces fit together in your job as an HR professional. That awareness can help you apply the knowledge to the exam questions, so don't give up if at first it seems fragmented and unconnected. Build the foundation, and the "aha" moment will come.

Considering a Study Group: Yes or No?

A study group puts you in touch with other individuals like you and creates a level of accountability that may be the difference between a pass or fail score. According to HRCI there were more than 13,000 HR professionals who sat for the exams in 2019. This doesn't count those who applied but have not yet tested or those still in preparation mode. This means that there are plenty of individuals you may partner with to tackle the studying. The following sections identify the pros and cons to joining (or forming) a study group to help you decide if one is right for you.

Noting the benefits of a study group

When preparing to take the PHR or SPHR, you may want to join a study group, which has these advantages, the same ones Abraham Maslow wrote about in his "Hierarchy of Needs" (more in this coming up later in this chapter):

» **Belonging:** Adults are motivated when they belong to a group of peers with similar needs and desires. Aligning yourself with others in a study group creates a sense of camaraderie while reiterating the fact that you aren't, in fact, alone on this journey.

» **Self-esteem:** Most people want to contribute and believe that they have the knowledge and experience necessary to pass this exam. HR professionals have varying degrees of knowledge and experience that can only be shared in a study group. You'll bring knowledge to the table that others may not have, increasing your self-esteem and your confidence. For example, I have never worked in a union environment. Having someone in my study group who had gave me an in-depth look at how the exam content applied in the workplace, thereby increasing my understanding and exam application.

» **Self-actualization:** The top level of Maslow's hierarchy speaks to the need for individuals to realize their full potential. Sitting alone in a dark corner at a coffee shop trying to jam facts into your head doesn't inspire confidence or motivation to achieve your full potential — in this case, passing the exam. Coming together in a group motivates you to reach up and out with others beyond everyone's current capabilities and knowledge.

Note that adults' internal needs drive many of these benefits, yet you can obtain the solutions from external sources. Take yourself and this investment seriously enough to do whatever it takes to get you to a passing score.

SETTING GOALS

Similar to the other theories of motivation that you'll study during this process, goal-setting is one way to gain momentum toward success. It's not enough to simply say, "I will pass this test." Your goals must be much more specific and measurable if you're going to achieve them. Thus, "I will spend ten hours this week studying. I will read two chapters of the book and take all practice exams associated with those chapters" is a better goal than "I will study this week."

Writing down your goals is another visualization technique that increases your odds of a passing score. This process requires you to be thoughtful about what you want and what you plan to do to achieve it.

Finally, create a level of accountability by publicly declaring your intent. At our house, we review at Sunday night dinner what needs to get done in the upcoming week. It allows us to share what we plan to achieve while coordinating and marshalling the resources necessary to do so. Making it a family affair also makes it more personal, which is an excellent motivator.

Identifying the challenges of a study group

Challenges to participating in a study group are uniquely personal. A variety of issues may revolve around inconvenient meeting times or dates, incompatibility with other group members, or other special group needs that are difficult to accommodate. Other challenges may be a lack of the necessary diversity of knowledge to add value to your specific areas of weakness.

Keep in mind, however, the old adage: "The best way to learn something is to teach it." If you find yourself the strongest person in the group, take advantage by teaching a concept in which you have extensive knowledge/experience *or* one in which you need a crash course.

Selecting the right group or exam prep class

If you decide to join a study group (or an exam prep class), I recommend that you reach out to your local professional networking group to identify individuals who are seeking certification during the same time frame as you. Doing so can ensure that the timing is conducive to your study plan and that you have access to support when needed. When looking to find the right study group, ask yourself these questions:

>> How long does the group plan to study? How often do they intend to meet? Is it too long or too short for your needs?

>> Is the group instructor-led? What do you need? Are the other members or the facilitator experts or novices? Will the group add depth to your existing knowledge or teach you new things?

>> Do the other group members have work experience and application that you lack?

>> How much of the class is self-paced rather than face-to-face? Can they fit the activities around your schedule?

Finding the right study group takes effort. You may prefer to join an online forum where information is exchanged or join a group that meets face-to-face on a regular schedule to maximize accountability factors. Your goal in getting answers to these questions is to identify the deal breakers, not the excuses.

Keeping your group on task

If you decide to go with a group, note that the participants of the group you join can be the difference between productive and nonproductive time. For example, you may attend the first few sessions and realize that the participants have simply banded together out of fear or have have shifted responsibility of their success to a group leader. If this happens, practice those leadership skills and intervene. Establish the goals of the weekly meeting together and encourage others to actively participate in their own success. The last thing you want is to waste your precious study time on unrelated topics. Here are a few suggestions on keeping your study group on task:

>> **Assign PowerPoint quizzes.** Have each participant create a PowerPoint presentation in the early weeks. Post a full question on one slide followed by the answer on the next slide. Ask the question and then discuss together what the correct answer may be. Then show the answer. If your group has it right, move on. If wrong, all should search through the study material to find the right answer.

>> **Have individual members present a short lesson to the others.** Assign an area where a member is weak. There is plenty of evidence that teaching others aids in long-term retention of information. Thus, by assigning an area of weakness, you convert it to a strength.

>> **Agree to create 100 digital flash cards and share them with each other.** You can use a resource such as Quizlet (https://quizlet.com) or GoConqr (www.goconqr.com). This way you gain the efforts of all group members and make your own study time more efficient.

>> **Assign a video scavenger hunt in which members troll the internet for relevant videos in each functional area.** End your group meetings by watching a video segment as a group and discussing the video.

Make these sessions as productive as possible to ensure the most effective use of your time. Apply your natural leadership skills to drive the efforts, and you won't be disappointed by the amount of learning you all will gain as a result.

Asking Your Employer to Pay for Certification

Asking your employer to foot the bill for all or part of the certification is reasonable. HRCI's preparation bundles (that include exam fees) can run upward of $1000 so any support for this would be welcome to many. Success is all in the approach. Here are a few helpful tips:

>> **Collect information regarding the exact costs, including the application fee, the exam fee, the study material and the cost of a study group.** Consult your company handbook to see if your company offers a tuition reimbursement or professional development program. Be sure to research the value of certification and why you'll be a better employee.

>> **Research your current job description and the job description of the position that you eventually want.** How will certification add to your current job responsibilities? How will certification prepare you for the next step? Will certification allow you to mentor others down the same path? Having these answers prior to making a request will help you answer the *only* question your boss will have, which is "What's in it for us?"

>> **Schedule a face-to-face meeting with your boss to present the information, make the request, and convey your dedication to this journey.** If you try to make your request informally or by email, he may not take the time to give your request the proper consideration. Ask for a special meeting so you can present the information professionally, and be sure to focus on the increased benefits that your certification will have for the company, organization, or department.

>> **If full reimbursement is not an option, ask your manager if she is willing to pay for half or perhaps cover the exam fee.** A "no" answer may be a timing issue, especially if your manager has a training budget that has to be considered. Giving her plenty of time to plan for the request may lead to a successful outcome, even if you have to postpone your exam date to coincide with the budget.

Even if you walk away empty-handed, you have notified your manager that you're a committed professional, ready and willing to take on new challenges and create depth in your career.

Talk to your accountant about the option of writing the expense off as professional development education to maintain skills. The cost may be a tax deduction.

Using the Internet for Additional Resources

Finding resources that address both knowledge and practical application has never been easier than it is today with the availability of information online. This section identifies credible internet resources that you can use to go deeper in your studying efforts.

Functional Area 01

The focus of this area of the exam is on becoming strong business partners, so look for resources online that address business and management concepts (not necessarily HR specific). Consider the few below to get you started.

The Balanced Scorecard Institute

This website (www.balancedscorecard.org) is an excellent place to seek out additional information regarding strategic planning, intervention strategies, and most important for the SPHR candidate, tools of metrics. It includes videos, white papers, Q&As, and more to help you understand both the process and the tool. Click on the Resources tab to read articles, success stories, and frequently asked questions.

PHR candidates, there is something here for you as well! Understanding how different departments contribute to overall success will give you insights into how to practice HR with strategy in mind.

Society for Human Resource Management

The Society for Human Resource Management (SHRM) is a distinguished and highly credible resource for HR professionals. Go to www.shrm.org. Although membership is required for full access to the information relevant to today's practitioner, you can access many free resources.

Part of SHRM's academic initiatives is to further the education of the emerging HR worker. As such, the website offers free educational resources, which include case studies and learning modules available for download, written by subject-matter experts throughout the United States.

SHRM also partners with other reliable agencies such as ANSI to define industry standards. These publications are also available on SHRM's website.

The Free Management Library

The Free Management Library is a robust resource for all things business. As the title indicates, it's a library of information related to approximately 650 topics and contains more than 10,000 links to additional information and resources. For purposes of Business Management, you can access the library at http://managementhelp.org and search for the any relevant term (I recommend starting in the "Organizations" category). You are going to want to bookmark this one!

Federal Accounting Standards Advisory Board

Managing financial risks can be supported by employing the generally accepted accounting principles (GAAP) in the workplace. Found at www.fasab.gov, the advisory board has links to other websites and the complete standards of best practices. Use this website to help understand accepted ways to record financials and establish controls to reduce financial risks in reporting.

Functional Area 02

In this area, it is all about finding the talent to meet current and future demand. Search online for information related to sourcing talent and the many legal pitfalls to avoid when hiring and managing people. I have found that government resources are the best for this so I listed my go-tos below.

The United States Department of Labor

The Department of Labor (DOL) is the stronghold of all things labor law, administering and enforcing more than 150 employment standards. Visiting this website (www.dol.gov) gives you access to information related to the major labor laws that you need to understand for these tests, including the Fair Labor Standards Act (FLSA), Occupational Safety and Health Act (OSHA), Employee Retirement Income Security Act (ERISA), and the Consolidated Omnibus Budget Reconciliation Act (COBRA).

The DOL is sorted by sections, such as wage and hour laws and safety, along with unions and military protections. My recommendation is that you access this website *daily* and immerse yourself in the fact sheets. If you're less motivated by going online, print out the fact sheets all at once and review them in chunks or transfer the information to index cards for portable use.

The Equal Employment Opportunity Commission

The Equal Employment Opportunity Commission (EEOC) (www.eeoc.gov) exists to enforce Title VII of the Civil Rights Act of 1964 and all its amendments that prohibit discrimination in the workplace. It has been around for more than 50 years and has the authority to sue companies for illegal discrimination on behalf of workers. In its original form, the law prohibited employment discrimination on the basis of race, ethnicity, national origin, and gender.

The website is a gold mine of information, ranging from videos sharing the history of the agency and anti-discrimination laws to statistics and trends that justify the need for enforcement. I have used it for classroom research on real-world case studies into what is and isn't unlawful discrimination. Go to the publications page for fact sheets on discrimination related to religion, age, disability, and more. Cross-reference these fact sheets with how these protected classes were added to law. It may have been as amendments to Title VII or by executive order. This site creates depth in your knowledge and provides insight into the process that will serve you on the exams.

The Uniform Guidelines on Employee Selection Procedures

The Uniform Guidelines on Employee Selection Procedures (UGESP) is yet another acronym related to Talent Planning and Acquisition. It is the result of a need to have uniform guidelines recognized by agencies such as the DOL and the EEOC when considering the proper (translation: nondiscriminatory and job-related) use of tests and other hiring criteria during the selection process. At this site (www.uniformguidelines.com), you can find information related to the different types of validity, the concept of reliability, what employment actions the criteria apply to, and more.

O*Net

O*Net (www.onetonline.org) is possibly the best-kept secret of a free HR resource on the web. O*Net is short for Occupational Information Network and is a database sponsored in part by the DOL. This database houses hundreds of occupations and their job-related content from tasks, duties, and responsibilities to both the cognitive and physical skills and abilities that are necessary for successful completion of each job.

HR professionals use this site to build job descriptions, link to local salary survey information, and identify employment trends in specific job classifications. For exam preparation, focus on the content model, which describes the anatomy of an occupation. It's also helpful to jump into the numbers provided by the Bureau of Labor Statistics (BLS) to get a sense of the job climate by the numbers. All of this preparation should round out your reasoning and application of this information to a day in the life of an HR professional.

Functional Area 03

Once employees are hired and in place, it falls to HR teams to effectively manage the talent for both performance and retention. Much is available online related to best practices to build an engaged workforce.

The Association of Talent Development

The Association of Talent Development (ATD) (www.td.org) is still well known under its former name, the American Society of Training and Development (ASTD). As with so many HR organizations, there was a need for a more global focus, prompting the renaming.

Click on any ATD webcast description and check out how these training experts write learning objectives. Terms like "discover how" and "find out about" are excellent examples of how to accomplish the HRD task of writing training outcomes. Or just browse its most current content, such as the article titled *Workplace Equity through L & D* or *Digital Transformation Is Mission Critical*, both highly relevant to your exam objectives. Doing so will help you get a sense about what is most important in this exam domain.

One of the great things about HR is that if you don't enjoy all aspects of the job, you can choose to specialize. Many HR professionals decide that training and development is their cup of tea. ATD offers several *communities of practice* for support. These communities consist of subject-matter experts in multiple areas of relevance for these exams. For exam candidates, I recommend that you visit the communities of

>> **Learning and Development:** Although this section has a lot of great information regarding training interventions for performance management, one of my favorite aspects is the learning blog. Written by multiple experts, it allows for a rich, experience-based perspective of training and the real-world challenges faced in the design and delivery of effective programs.

>> **Career Development:** This community focuses the spotlight on taking control of careers and using coaching to underscore training. Free webcasts and descriptions of a trainer competency model illustrate the need for a broad skill set. Skills for trainers include change management, coaching, and the ability to manage learning programs. If you're a member, you can also explore the career navigator tool, which assesses your current self-described skill set and compares it to your dream job requirements and competencies.

>> **Learning Technology:** Training programs must be agile, and old-school methods of teaching in a brick-and-mortar classroom are no longer the obvious nor best solution. This community engages visitors with e-learning, innovation, mobile learning (m-learning), and social learning concepts, just to name a few.

In addition, SPHR candidates should go even deeper into communities made up of

>> **Management:** This area is devoted to helping managers respond to the moving targets that make up most of their days. Topics include tackling succession planning, implementing change, dealing with productivity issues, conflict management, and managing a multigenerational workforce.

- >> **Human Capital:** The description of this community is that of helping employers manage the employment life cycle. Although fairly broad in application, it makes sense in that the human capital — also called people, talent, and resources — must be effectively managed at all stages from recruiting to separation. Strolling through this digital community takes you to topics such as coaching, diversity, and executive coaching (another SPHR favorite).

- >> **Senior Leaders and Executives:** This section has some great blogs dedicated to developing both future leaders and current CEOs. Other attention-getting headlines in this community include selecting the right team members for projects and examining the different leadership styles of executives, such as transactional, transformational, and laissez-faire.

- >> **Global HRD:** One core knowledge requirement in this area suggests that SPHR candidates be able to apply information relating to international law and societal norms, so be sure and search for related data in this community. Other issues examined are how to communicate with global teams and how to handle unique management differences among countries.

Even though much of the content is available only to members, you can still access plenty of it for free, which makes this site a worthwhile stop on the prep journey. Options include scrolling through its blogs or signing up for its newsletters to stay connected to emerging content in this very important exam domain for both the PHR and SPHR.

Chief Learning Officer Magazine

I prefer to get this magazine mailed to me, because I already have a crowded email inbox that has me approaching information overload. Having a hard copy magazine delivered to the office or home sets the content apart from email, providing a psychological nudge that it's important for me to pick it up and look at it, rather than simply hit delete.

You may, however, prefer to visit www.clomedia.com. On this site, spend the bulk of your time on the research and results pages. You can download many of the documents for review. If you're taking the SPHR, search for work related to learning metrics, the learning organization, and organizational development. If you're taking the PHR, seek out information relating to training development and design and performance appraisals.

Talent Management

Similar to the *Chief Learning Officer Magazine*, Talent Management, a subscription service, offers a plethora of HRD information that goes both deep and wide. At www.talentmgt.com, you can find research and reports about how to manage high-potential employees, develop succession plans, and identify the emerging trends of the field. This site is your full-service resource for all things HRD. Use it to gain clarity on unfamiliar exam objectives or simply to freshen up your resources when you're feeling burnt out on others.

American Evaluation Association

At this site (www.eval.org), you can find a free e-library that you can access to download academic and peer-reviewed research related to the HRD function of these exams. The e-library features scientific research that both directs and supports the efforts of professional trainers and evaluators; it's well worth a regular visit as you study this section of the exam.

Functional Area 04

With a focus on total rewards, online resources should offer a robust view of ways to effectively and creatively reward employees to maximize retention. It is worth noting that wage and hour law violations continue to make up an extremely high percentage of litigation, so online resources should include ways to stay in compliance. Look for sites such as the ones listed below that address national and global issues, not those of individual states.

Department of Labor

Also noted earlier in the Talent Planning and Acquisition area, the United States Department of Labor (DOL) (www.dol.gov) is worth another review in the context of wages and hours. The DOL is the government agency charged with oversight of the pertinent information related to Total Rewards including

>> **Wage and hour laws:** Minimum wage, child labor, and overtime are the big three in terms of wage and hour compliance. As with many other labor laws, the FLSA was passed in response to the social climate of the time when employers were taking advantage of individuals desperate for work during the Depression. Similarly, Social Security and Medicare were also passed within this decade. The DOL is the place to find fact sheets and enforcement guidelines to supplement your preparation efforts.

>> **Health and benefits:** Although employer mandates continue to be defined, the days of voluntary health benefits for employees has been severely diluted in recent years by the passage of the Patient Protection and Affordable Care Act (PPACA), commonly known as Obamacare. The DOL website offers consumers information on what they need to know about ACA health benefits and compliance assistance for employers. The website also includes compliance information for COBRA, the Health Insurance Portability and Accountability Act (HIPAA), and the Genetic Information Nondiscrimination Act (GINA).

>> **Retirement:** Supplementary retirement continues to be a voluntary benefit offered by employers. However, it becomes heavily regulated after plans are in place. The DOL can offer employer information on how to comply with the ERISA and fact sheets about cash balance plans and traditional pension plans.

World at Work

Formerly known as the American Compensation Association, World at Work (www.worldatwork.org) is an excellent resource for all things in the world of compensation and benefits. You can find free information related to compensation strategies and how total reward practices impact an organization's competitiveness. Use this site as a resource to research pay concepts such as pay equity, distributive justice, and practices for variable pay plans.

World at Work also has membership opportunities. There are many options to specialize in the various practices of human resources. They also offer specialist certifications that are excellent options for the developing HR professional with a passion for compensation and benefits.

Internal Revenue Service

The IRS (www.irs.gov) is surprisingly an excellent resource for making decisions about compensation. In addition to existing laws, IRS opinion letters are worth a review as you study the area of Total Rewards. Use the site to find information about the following:

>> **Independent contractors (IC) versus employees:** An *independent contractor* is an individual doing work for your company who isn't an employee. Meanwhile, an *employee* is one for which the employer of record is responsible for taxes and benefits and is granted the protection of general labor law. Properly classifying individuals who do work for your organization has a tax impact, so getting it right is important to the IRS. Improper classification can cost companies a

lot of money in penalties and interest. The fundamental factor that distinguishes between an IC and an employee is *degree of control*. The greater the control over the work, the more likely the person is an employee. Factors include behavioral, financial, and the type of relationship.

>> **Updated forms:** The IRS publishes new W-4 forms for each calendar year. These forms must be completed upon hire so that proper payroll deductions can be made.

>> **Employee business expenses:** The IRS website has loads of information pertaining to actual business expenses and employee business expenses. Categories include business travel, mileage reimbursement rates, entertainment expenses, and corporate gifts.

Functional Area 05

For both the PHR and the SPHR exam, this last functional area carries a heavy weighting, marking it as critical content for success. To optimize the online resources, such as those that follow, plan extra study time and creative ways to learn the material.

The National Labor Relations Board

The NLRB (www.nlrb.gov) is the governing body of the union-organizing process. This site has excellent information and pertinent details of the three major acts (NLRA, LMRA, and LMRDA) affecting unions in the United States. You can also find fact sheets on key amendments and interpretations related to HR issues such as social media. However, you may find most valuable the graphs illustrating the election process as well as the process for filing an unfair labor practice charge.

Department of Homeland Security

The Department of Homeland Security (DHS) is an excellent source of information, both personally and professionally. You can find information on how to prepare businesses for emergencies, conduct a Business Impact Analysis (BIA) and generally stay informed on employer obligations to protect our teams. Access them at www.dhs.gov.

American Arbitration Association

Found at www.adr.org, the American Arbitration Association is a nonprofit organization tasked with governing the entire arbitration process, from filing to closure. The organization's website offers resources that educate individuals and companies on key concepts related to arbitration and mediation.

You can search for court rulings and common forms used throughout the process to help you visualize and relate the process to your own workplace. This information can add an experience dimension that's vital to both the PHR and SPHR exams.

AFL-CIO

One of the best repositories of information on both the history and relevant current issues affecting unions and workers is the AFL-CIO. The self-described "umbrella federation for America's unions," its website (www.aflcio.org) has videos and blogs full of information.

Although definitely a *biased* viewpoint, the website still can be helpful when viewing the unionizing issues from the other's perspective. Use this checklist to take your studying online to discover

>> What industries are covered by unions in the United States?

>> What are worker center partnerships?

>> When and how did unions rise in the United States?

>> How has globalization impacted union organizing and coverage of workers?

Occupational Safety and Health Administration

The OSHA website has always been an important resource used to describe an employers' responsibility to provide safe and healthy place of work. This includes protecting workers from disease. Many HR professionals found themselves accessing the OSH website for daily updates during the COVID-19 pandemic as the requirements seemed to change with each passing day. Remember — many states choose to enact their own health and safety laws. While this is important for daily practice, you must learn the national health and safety requirements for employers found at www.osha.gov.

Applying Core Knowledge

As you may be aware, a major change to the 2018 updates was the splitting of the PHR and SPHR exam content outlines. The benefit of this was a more appropriate measure of what each candidate should understand and be able to do at the different stages of their careers. A disadvantage is that there is some fundamental knowledge that serves as a benchmark to our practice that both PHR and SPHR candidates must know and be able to apply. I have chosen to address this in the book in three ways.

First, both PHR and SPHR candidates need to study the federal labor law appendix at the end of this book and through other resources. This knowledge will be useful for both exams and help individuals be better business partners.

Secondly, some exam concepts are highly operational, so I went deeper in the chapters for the PHR exam. However, SPHR teams may need that baseline of knowledge from which to apply their objectives strategically. In these cases, I simply note in the SPHR chapters where to go in the book when a refresher is needed.

Finally, the 2018 updates eliminated the Core Knowledge and Risk Management functional area from the exams, spreading the content throughout the remaining domains. These have been absorbed and distinguished in the appropriate chapters. However, there are several concepts that are inherently necessary to know about for both exams. These include

>> Diversity and inclusion

>> Human relations

>> Motivation

>> Health, safety, and security

>> Collective bargaining

These topics are covered next and should be included in BOTH PHR and SPHR candidate study plans.

Sharing the value of diversity and inclusiveness

A CNN Business report in 2020 written by Johnny C. Taylor of SHRM clearly articulated the excruciating fact that businesses are failing at their diversity and inclusiveness practices. It's not that they want to fail or don't recognize the value in succeeding. It may be that organizations are underestimating the magnitude of what this commitment entails. Successful implementation of these practices requires a significant investment of resources — financial and human.

Diversity is represented at two levels: surface and deep. When looking to build an organizational design intervention aimed at increasing diversity, some employers stop at surface level — those observable characteristics such as race or gender. While this is a good first step, focusing only on demographic diversity does not equate to fairness, nor does it harness the benefits that a diverse workforce brings. We must go deeper, and begin to understand the values, attitudes, and beliefs held by individuals and then find ways to include these elements into HR practices, such as hiring, as well as in day-to-day operations. For example, who is leading committees? How are problems solved? What voices are being heard? What behaviors get rewarded, and which ones are disciplined?

In order to ensure that diversity and inclusion efforts are tied to organizational results, the process of improving diversity and inclusion initiatives should be treated similar to strategic planning and systems development. Take a page from Uber's playbook as an example. After the bruising headline-making behavior of co-founder and former CEO Travis Kalanick (including his handling of sexual harassment at work) that resulted in his resignation, the new CEO knew he had an uphill road to redefining the culture and establishing trust. Instead of going on an executive retreat with senior leaders to write a new set of values, he conducted a poll of all stakeholders. The result? Twelve hundred employee submissions that were voted on more than 22,000 times resulted in a final set of eight values, one of which was simply: "We celebrate differences."

Of course, having a diversity component as part of the written values is good, but it's not enough to truly affect change or repair damage. Leadership teams must take steps to practice what they preach if they truly want to change their culture. This begins with a comparison of current state to desired state, and then the creation of an action plan to bridge the gap. The process will never fully be complete, as HR must lead the way in measuring program effectiveness and recommending real-time changes as needed.

DIVERSITY ON A NATIONAL SCALE

Did you know that in 2020, eight of the sitting Supreme Court justices held law degrees from either Yale or Harvard? While an impressive bunch who clearly were educated by the top scholars of our time, think about how the lack of diversity on the highest court in the land affects justice in America. How do you think laws would change or precedent would be set if our Justices were educated at more diverse schools, such as Temple University's Beasley School of Law in Philadelphia, or Washburn University School of Law in Kansas? What values might be better represented if the educational backgrounds of the Justices were more diverse?

Hiring a C-suite leader of diversity and inclusion is another common step employers are taking. Keep in mind, however, that if HR requires 20 years of experience of this candidate, they could be creating a *barrier to an effective hire* in two ways:

>> First, this role has not existed for that long.

>> Second, protected class groups that can offer the necessary perspective are historically underrepresented at senior levels in all industries.

HR can serve their teams well by clearly defining the desired outcome of the role and then recruiting for competencies that go beyond education or experience.

Human resources can also help improve outcomes (and manage risk) through the use of HR audits. This involves reviewing hiring data, compensation data, and demographics at all organizational levels and measuring for disparate impact (see the sidebar "Calculating disparate impact"). If lack of diversity or unlawful behavior comes to light, they must take steps to remedy the situation.

CALCULATING DISPARATE IMPACT

Metrics continue to be a valuable tool in the day-to-day operations of HR. To measure disparate impact, you must call upon the definitions from Uniform Guidelines on Employee Selection Procedures (UGESP):

"Disparate treatment occurs where members of a race, sex, or ethnic group have been denied the same employment, promotion, membership, or other employment opportunities as have been available to other employees or applicants."

The UGESP provides the formula for calculating when a disparate, or an adverse, impact has occurred:

"A selection rate for any race, sex, or ethnic group which is less than four-fifths (or 80 percent) of the rate for the group with the highest rate. . .."

This means that you can calculate the rate of terminations of protected class groups when compared to nonprotected class groups by using the four-fifths rule. Here is an example:

Christmas Trees Inc.'s busy season has ended, and as has been the case in past practices, it must lay off workers. Of its 500 employees, 100 employees older than 40 and 75 employees younger than 40 were selected for termination. Of the 500 total employees, 200 were older than 40, with the remaining 300 younger than 40. To calculate whether disparate impact occurred against older workers, do the following:

1. **Calculate the layoff selection rate for the workers older than 40:**

$$100 \div 200 = 50\%$$

2. **Calculate the layoff selection rate for workers who are younger than 40:**

$$75 \div 300 = 25\%$$

3. **Divide the selection rates to identify the impact ratio:**

$$25 \div 50 = 5\%$$

The impact ratio of 0.5 percent is less than 0.8 percent, so there is evidence that disparate impact occurred. Find more information on disparate impact (also referred to as *adverse impact*) at www.uniformguidelines.com.

Ultimately, being good stewards of the lives (and livelihoods) of the individuals who choose to work with us is a primary purpose of our industry. It begins by building healthy ways to manage all relationships at work — the hierarchical and the network. This happens by taking a good look at some of the more nontransactional aspects of HR.

Applying human relations

Human relations is many things, including a science. This means that there is a substantial body of research available on — wait for it — how to *be human* and *treat humans*. While it may seem counterintuitive, this data can be useful to outline some of the more important behaviors that affect relationships at work.

The key element of human relations hinges on how we can make employees feel like valued, contributing members of our organization, and not just numbers. This approach goes back to the 1920s, when researchers discovered that employees work for reasons beyond economics. Organizational behaviors that supported the other, more "human" needs will help build an engaged workforce. And as modern-day studies show, an engaged workforce leads to positive job attitudes, such as improved job satisfaction, greater worker engagement, and an increased organizational commitment.

A basic model for human relations includes three fundamentals that leaders should remember:

>> **Attitudes toward people:** Our employees share a set of common needs, including being respected and valued for their contributions.

>> **Amount and kind of participation:** We must consider the "whole" of employees as opposed to only their output. This includes giving them the context behind decision-making and allowing teams to be self-directed where appropriate.

>> **Expectations:** How information is shared is just as important as what kind of information is shared. These processes establish expectations and can satisfy basic needs for belonging and esteem. Modern-day application includes applying motivational techniques to discover how to change and drive adult behavior.

TIP

The three factors noted in the model of human relations is an excellent lens through which to measure a company's diversity and inclusive practices.

Using theories of motivation

There is so much data out there about how to motivate workers. When faced with an underperforming employee, many supervisors take up the cry, "We need to pay them more." With limited budgets and job worth factors, HR needs to model and communicate ways that supervisors can motivate their team members beyond the paycheck.

There are three categories of the theories of motivation: content, process, and reinforcement:

>> **Content theories** of motivation are founded on the idea that there are ways we can explain and predict employee behaviors. These theories include one of the more famous, Abraham Maslow's hierarchy of needs. Depicted as a pyramid, Maslow's theory indicates that until the lower needs are met, the higher needs will never be a motivating factor in an employee's behavioral choices. The order of needs, starting from the bottom, are physiological, safety, belonging, esteem, and eventually, self-actualization. Many years after Maslow, Frederick Herzberg published an expanded version called the *two-factor theory* that helped clarify what factors motivate (*intrinsic,* such as personal pride in performance), and what factors are dis-satisfiers (*extrinsic,* such as salary).

JOB CHARACTERISTICS MODEL

The way jobs are structured can serve as an extrinsic motivator for individuals. A 2012 study of federal workers validated the Job Characteristics Theory (JCT) built by Richard Hackman and Greg R. Oldham. JCT is a model of *how* the work is organized and the characteristics of the tasks that will have a direct influence on employee performance. The five characteristics are as follows:

- **Task identity:** Employees who know the whole as opposed to only the parts feel a sense of achievement when the task is complete.

- **Task significance:** The more important the task or body of work, the greater the impact it has on others and the more it contributes to a sense of purpose.

- **Skill variety:** The ability to use multiple skill sets in work contributes to a sense of fulfillment and reduces boredom.

- **Autonomy:** The extent to which an employee is allowed to use independent judgment affects her sense of control over her work life.

- **Feedback:** Feedback gives employees the information they need to be successful. Most employees crave both positive and constructive feedback.

The Association for Talent Development published an article about the 2012 study of federal workers. Check it out at http://www.td.org and search for the title *Job Characteristics Key to Motivating Federal Employees* to find out more.

>> **Process theories** are grounded by principles that seek to understand the employee needs that drive behavioral choices. These include J. Stacy Adams's *equity theory* (employees are motivated when their rewards are equal to their efforts) and Victor Vroom's *expectancy theory* (people believe they can do the work, they know they will be rewarded, and the rewards are worth the effort).

>> **Reinforcement theories** take free will out of the equation, benchmarked by the ideas that we are all conditioned through reward and punishment to act. The behavioral scientist BF Skinner wrote his *operant conditioning theory*, which noted that all human behaviors are learned through reinforcement — either positive or negative. If you have ever had trouble leaving a slot machine, you have experienced conditioning through rewards that occurred on a schedule of reinforcement.

All three theories are true to a certain extent! Regardless of which one you subscribe to or which one feels most natural, you can use the knowledge to begin to change behavior, a major focus of organizational risk management techniques.

Managing enterprise risk

You can understand the risks to the business or project through the following filters. It's helpful to get organized by understanding these big three areas of knowledge:

>> **Financial risks:** Financial risks include corporate espionage, sabotage, embezzlement, and other types of theft. Minimizing these risks may be best accomplished through the use of technology to limit access to sensitive information. HR can also develop policies and procedures such as procurement policies, credit card and expense policies, and ones that limit loss from these work efforts through checks and balances.

> » **Physical risks:** The employees' physical well-being used to be the largest focus of workplace safety efforts, so a lot of information is related to this HR activity. Target your studying on education and prevention efforts such as compliance with safety standards and common-sense work rules. Areas include hazard communication, workplace safety, emergency response, and violence prevention.
>
> » **Information risks:** The loss of critical information can be devastating to both the employer and employee. The exam objectives and knowledge components address information risks through the use of data security techniques, such as passwords and monitoring software.

EXAMPLE

The BEST way to protect confidential employee information is to

(A) Not collect it in the first place

(B) Store it digitally, with no paper trail

(C) Limit access to only those who need to refer to the data for business purposes

(D) Create a buddy system in which information is accessed only with witnesses present

The correct answer is (C). Whether confidential information is stored as paper files or digitally, HR must control access through passwords and keys. Choice (A) is unrealistic because labor laws require that employers collect and store information. Choice (B) doesn't address protecting the information, just the storage, so it's an incomplete answer. Choice (D) is unrealistic and unnecessary for the types of information collected and stored by HR.

Complying with safety standards in the workplace

The Occupational Safety and Health Act (OSHA) and administration are your go-to resources for workplace safety compliance. As with all of the functional areas, each begins with the need for HR professionals to ensure that activities are compliant with the law. The exam objectives take you on a nice little journey to tell you how to do so, as Figure 2-1 illustrates.

All you have to do is fill in the blanks of the requirements. Look at some examples of OSHA standards on how you can accomplish these tasks:

> » **Hazard assessment:** Although the exam objective calls them a *needs assessment,* OSHA gets a bit more specific. OSHA requires you to conduct a hazard assessment to determine, for example, what personal protective equipment is required for each job, and OSHA asks you to conduct a job hazard analysis to identify hazards before they cause injury. OSHA publishes the top ten most cited standards on its website, and it's a good idea to be familiar with these hazards and relevant compliance requirements for the exams. Ones that seem to make the top ten year after year include fall protection, hazard communication, scaffolding, respiratory protection, powered industrial trucks, lockout/tagout, ladders, electrical, wiring methods, machine guarding.
>
> » **Injury and illness prevention programs (IIPP):** OSHA identifies the common elements that should be present in all company IIPP. Although some states may have differing standards, all must meet or exceed federal requirements. Therefore, you can confidently assume the baselines will include management leadership, worker participation, hazard identification, hazard prevention and control, education and training, and program evaluation and improvement.

TIP

> Obtain a copy of your employer's IIPP and compare it to the common elements defined by OSHA. Doing so can give you an experience layer to apply to the exam requirement.

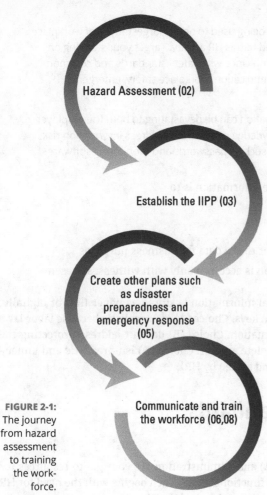

FIGURE 2-1:
The journey
from hazard
assessment
to training
the work-
force.

Hazard Assessment (02)

Establish the IIPP (03)

Create other plans such
as disaster
preparedness and
emergency response
(05)

Communicate and train
the workforce (06,08)

© John Wiley & Sons, Inc.

» **Disaster preparedness and emergency response:** Called emergency preparedness by OSHA, compliance efforts focus on both disaster response and recovery. In some standards, OSHA requires companies with more than ten employees to have these plans in writing. I provide a more detailed look at this HR activity in the next section.

» **Training of the workforce:** Most OSHA compliance efforts require some measure of communicating hazards to employees. Communicating hazards is most often accomplished through employee training. Accurate documentation of training efforts includes a description of the training content, the date(s) of training, who conducted the training, and signatures of the training participants.

» **General duty clause:** OSHA states that employers are required to provide their employees with a place of employment that "is free from recognizable hazards that are causing or likely to cause death or serious harm to employees." This is more commonly referred to as the *general duty clause*. The courts have interpreted OSHA's general duty clause to mean that an employer has a legal obligation to provide a workplace free of conditions or activities that either the employer or industry recognizes as hazardous and that cause, or are likely to cause, death or serious physical harm to employees when there is a feasible method to abate the hazard.

EXAMPLE

How should an employer communicate the contents of an IIPP?

(A) Give it to employees at the time of hire.

(B) Make it available on a company intranet.

(C) Conduct annual training on the various hazards addressed in the IIPP.

(D) All of the above

The correct answer is (D). There are several acceptable methods for communicating the contents of the employer's injury and illness prevention program (IIPP), and they include a need to present it at the time of hire, Choice (A); giving employees access if they have questions, as in Choice (B); and conducting compliance training for known hazards that are identified in the document, Choice (C).

Creating preparedness plans

The Federal Emergency Management Agency (www.fema.gov/) is an excellent resource for businesses. The agency's website has free checklists and disaster preparedness materials that you can use to brush up on your disaster preparedness knowledge for the exams. FEMA also has a five-step process for designing an effective workplace preparedness plan. This plan is an excellent way to approach the process and compare your organization's current plan.

According to the FEMA, these steps include the following:

1. Manage the program.

The first step establishes a committed leadership effort out of the gate, which means that HR may need to make the case to executive management that resource allocation will provide a return on investment should a disaster occur. Communicating customer and financial impacts and identifying mitigation efforts such as insurance coverage are both elements to gaining upper management buy-in at this stage.

2. Conduct the needs assessment and business impact analysis.

Upon getting the green light, the planning stage formally begins, which involves identifying potential hazards that could affect your business. A commonsense approach may be helpful. For example, earthquakes are likely in California, whereas hurricane preparedness is more likely in the Southern states. Large corporations in multiple locations must create custom programs suited to the unique natural threats in the communities of business.

3. Implement the plan.

As with all great plans, proper execution is arguably the most important step. It actually begins by writing the multitude of plans that are identified as necessary in the assessment process. Consider business continuity plans, information technology plans to recover data, and the crisis communication plan so that information flows as freely as possible in the middle of a crisis.

REMEMBER

An *ad hoc committee* is one that meets to address a specific need. Identifying participants for an ad hoc crisis management meeting may be a helpful prevention effort. Use job titles rather than employee names for a practical approach to maintenance, but be sure the participants are properly trained in their roles.

4. Test and conduct simulations and drills.

Employee training is a significant element of program effectiveness. Rather than holding classroom-based training, hands-on simulations and exercises are more likely to condition employees on how to respond in an emergency. Where possible, bring in outside experts to validate the company's point of view. These experts are also helpful in spotting program deficiencies before a crisis, enhancing the overall effect of a good response plan.

5. Update, maintain, and improve the program.

As an R & D technician once put it to me, his goal was to "break it, then build it better." This stress-the-system philosophy serves the program improvement step of disaster preparedness well. Running the tests and simulations on a regular basis should identify where the program is deficient. Calendaring this activity on an annual basis allows HR to update the plan based on business changes such as expansions, turnover of key personnel, and training of new hires.

Reducing the risk of workplace violence

Although the exam content appears to focus on having a plan to respond to workplace violence, OSHA also addresses the issue in its standards. Refer to www.osha.gov/SLTC/workplaceviolence for OSHA's specific definition of workplace violence. In addition, OSHA has conducted research to identify who is at greatest risk for workplace violence and concluded that positions that involve an exchange of money, working in isolated locations, and working with unstable individuals all have an increased risk for violence on the job.

As with most safety standards, the employer's response should be aimed at reducing the risk of harm to its employees. This effort begins by having a zero-tolerance policy for any intimidating or violent behavior in the workplace. OSHA also offers support in the development of a workplace violence prevention program, which aligns your work efforts with the exam objective. These programs include policy development, employee training, and administrative controls.

Another area of concern for employers includes the threat of terrorism. FEMA describes several different types of potential terrorism threats, including biological, cyber, chemical, and nuclear. Visit www.ready.gov/business, an excellent resource to find out more about employer responsibilities. This website is a public service campaign affiliated with FEMA. Ready.gov states that more than 40 percent of businesses affected by a natural or man-made disaster never reopen. From an HR perspective, you should anticipate questions on the exam that relate to preparing your company to respond as quickly and effectively as possible to avoid short-term or long-term business impact.

EXAMPLE

Disaster preparedness is most effective when built on a foundation of what?

(A) Leadership

(B) Regulatory compliance

(C) Business needs

(D) Understanding hazards

The correct answer is (A). A foundation of leadership commitment involves providing the resources necessary to prepare. Choices (B), (C), and (D) are all important, but unlikely without the commitment of the executive management team.

EXAMPLE

What type of data is generally included in a confidentiality agreement?

(A) Dates of employment

(B) Definition of property not to be disclosed

(C) An agreement to not solicit competitors upon employee separation

(D) The proper storage methods of confidential data

The correct answer is (B). A *confidentiality agreement* defines the types of property that must be kept private, including trade secrets and customer lists. Dates of employment, Choice (A), aren't included, but the term dates of the contract are identified. Choice (C) is an element of a nonsolicitation/noncompete agreement, and Choice (D) isn't a general item of a confidentiality agreement.

TIP

Note that social media issues in employment continue to emerge. Wise employers (and their HR counsel) must stay up-to-date on court interpretation of existing law pertaining to social media use in the workplace. Check out the blog at (www.socialmediaemploymentlawblog.com/) to stay up-to-date on all things social media.

Completing common reports and tools

As with all the other functional areas of human resources, risk management has a fair share of paperwork. These reports and tools are very useful in demonstrating compliance with safety laws, such as the safety audit and safety training matrix. Other reports assist employers in making decisions about risk, such as workers' compensation reports and data reports from their human resource information system. Read on for more information about these useful options.

SAFETY AUDITS

Safety audits differ from hazard assessments in that they're used to evaluate compliance with safety programs rather than identify hazards. Even though hazard identification may certainly be a byproduct, their primary focus is to evaluate whether the controls established in the safety planning process are firmly rooted in place. Depending on the need, a safety audit can be conducted by visual walkthroughs, data collection, drills, or stressing the system to see what works and what doesn't.

WORKERS' COMPENSATION REPORTS

Keeping track of workers' compensation claims should be a monthly activity. Doing so requires HR professionals to be familiar with the workers' compensation laws in their states. The compensation reports help track the accrued versus paid amounts on open claims and allow you to manage the accruals where possible by working with the administrator. Compensation reports are useful to trigger status checks on injured workers still off work. This gives you the opportunity to engage in one of the exam objectives by building return-to-work programs such as modified duty. By doing so, the employee returning to work in a limited capacity is paid through regular payroll rather than through the workers' compensation insurance, lowering the overall claim costs. Because workers' compensation insurance is experience rated, this strategy is an effective way to keep insurance costs down long term.

TIP

The OSH Academy has several free resources, including sample checklists. It is a great option for students and safety professionals. Check it out at www.oshatrain.org.

SAFETY TRAINING MATRIX

Depending on the industry from which you practice, safety training can be a mixed bag.

A *training matrix* is a spreadsheet that compiles all of the required safety training in one place. Figure 2-2 gives you an example of one such matrix that can be modified on several levels to account for the who, what, where, when, and how often aspects of safety training. It can also help employers demonstrate a commitment to compliance.

Another option is to utilize your human resource information system (HRIS) to track dates and send reminders to management that safety training is coming due. Managing it from the time of hire and through the tenure of the employees is a streamlined way to keep track and run reports.

2015 Smith Brothers, Inc.			Spring	Spring	Fall	Fall	Fall	2 Yr Expiration	Fall
Training Resource			Who	Who	Local Fire Department	Train the Trainer	Who	Consultant	Who
Employee#	Name		Accident Investigation/ Prevention Signs And Tags	IIPP plans- disaster, emergency	Fire Extinguisher	Forklift	(SDS) Hazcom Training & Fall Protection	Supervisor Harassment Training	Employee Harassment Training
1	Samantha Jones		–	–			–	–	–
2	Archie Martin		–						–
3	Emma Russell					–			
4	Stan Smith		–			–	–	–	
5	Ethan Taylor		–			–	–		

FIGURE 2-2: A sample safety training matrix.

© John Wiley & Sons, Inc.

Navigating labor union implications

Unions tend to target the baseline needs of employees — job security, better pay and benefits, and safer working conditions. In their early years, these elements were subject to employer discretion, which led to all sorts of horror stories for employees. Now that these bits are actually addressed via labor law (such as the FLSA, PPACA, and OSHA), unions have been in a continual decline. Regardless, the labor laws governing the employer and unions must be understood for the exams.

Understanding compliance

Some days, it feels like all you do in your job is try to figure out how to comply with labor law. Employee relations therefore includes the ability to navigate an especially complex web of regulations, particularly because it applies to the right of employees to form unions.

Passed in 1935 and enforced by the National Labor Relations Board (NLRB), the National Labor Relations Act (NLRA) gave workers the right to organize, including striking against employers who were treating them unfairly. This act sets restrictions on employers during the union-organizing process, attempting to ensure that workers may collect together unfettered to make a decision about whether to unionize or not. For purposes of this exam, you should understand the two types of lawful strikes protected by the NLRA:

>> **Economic strike:** An *economic strike* is when employees refuse to work because they want higher wages, shorter working hours, or better working conditions. Economic strikers can't be discharged, but the employer may replace them.

>> **Unfair labor practice (ULP) strike:** An *unfair labor practice strike* occurs when workers are protesting a prohibited employer behavior. Prohibited behavior includes the employer threatening or interfering with a worker's right to organize, or refusing to bargain in good faith. The employer may not discharge or permanently replace ULP strikers.

The NLRB also defines the phrase *protected concerted activity*, which applies to most American workers whether organized in a union or not. According to the NLRB, concerted activity ". . . is when two or more employees take action for their mutual aid or protection regarding terms and conditions of employment. A single employee may also engage in protected concerted activity if he or she is acting on the authority of other employees, bringing group complaints to the employer's attention, trying to induce group action, or seeking to prepare for group action."

A few examples of protected concerted activities are

>> Two or more employees addressing their employer about improving their pay

>> Two or more employees discussing work-related issues beyond pay, such as safety concerns, with each other

>> An employee speaking to an employer on behalf of one or more co-workers about improving workplace conditions

This describes the collective behaviors of workers that are protected as part of the union-organizing activities, and the protection exists for activity that occurs in the workplace, in the parking lot, outside of the workplace, and online, such as through social media.

In 1947, Congress felt compelled to respond to the growing imbalance of power that the unions had gained, so it passed the Labor-Management Relations Act (LMRA). This act focused on defining union unfair labor practices and gave examples of prohibited policies and strikes. These prohibited practices include

>> **Wildcat strikes:** When workers walk off the job without union authorization to strike, they're considered to have *gone wild,* hence the name *wildcat strike.* The LMRA prohibits these strikes.

>> **Secondary boycotts:** A *secondary boycott* occurs when employees refuse to work at their company because their company buys from another site that is on strike.

>> **Jurisdictional strikes:** Think of a jurisdictional strike as a territory dispute. These strikes occur when unions are engaged in a turf war over who should be able to represent a group of workers.

TIP

Visit the National Labor Relations Board's website to find out more about lawful and unlawful strikes at www.nlrb.gov/strikes.

The Labor-Management Reporting and Disclosure Act (LMRDA) was passed in 1959, and it created a bill of rights for union members. This bill of rights gave equal status to union members in terms of voicing opinions, and the bill restricted the dues increases to those that were passed by a majority vote of members. The LMRDA was necessary because there was evidence of corrupt union practices that didn't serve the interests of the union members.

REMEMBER

Context matters on these exams. Think about what was going on in 1935 when the NLRA was passed. The effects of the Great Depression were severe, and worker exploitation was the norm. Employees were looking for security and fair treatment. By the time the LMRA was passed in 1947, the unions had used strikes as threats to shut down businesses and were impacting commerce, so Congress responded with a bill to balance the equation. More than 20 years after unions had been officially recognized, the LMRDA was passed in response to reports of corruption among union leadership.

An interesting read on this time of labor organizing is *The Hoffa Wars: The Rise and Fall of Jimmy Hoffa* by Dan E. Moldea (Open Road Media). Hoffa helped fight for the right to organize as a young man, and as a union leader he engaged in the corrupt practices that led in some part to the protections necessary under the LMRDA. Understanding context should help you relate exam questions that are tied to reasoning.

Union organizing

Regardless of the overall decline of unions, the essence of union organizing has remained fairly constant. The process, along with the various types of unfair labor practices (ULP) that can occur at each stage, looks like this:

>> **The campaign:** A *union campaign* is similar to a political campaign in that the union and the employer are opponents with the winner decided by a majority vote. The union may contact employees at home or hold offsite meetings to woo employees over to its side, which is accomplished when at least 30 percent of the targeted workers sign authorization cards, authorizing a vote. Campaign strategies include signage, mailers, phone calls, town hall meetings, and propaganda — it's an intense time for all involved.

For the exams, note the various unfair labor practices that may occur. An employer may not interfere with, restrain, or coerce employees during a union campaign. Examples of prohibited behavior include promising employees benefits if they remain union free, polling employees to determine their support of the union, and photographing or videotaping employees engaged in protected activities.

>> **Representation election:** After 30 percent of the targeted workers have signed authorization cards, a representation election is scheduled. A *union ballot* (voting card for employees to cast their vote) is created showing the candidates (the union and the employer) petitioning to be the employee representative. The option that receives the most votes of the majority that voted (not number of employees) wins. For this reason, many employers subject to a representation election encourage *all* affected employees in the bargaining unit to vote.

ULPs that may occur during the representation election include an employer spying on voting activity, threatening employees who vote one way, or trying to bribe workers to vote in the employer's favor.

>> **Union certification:** The NLRB issues official certification after a successful election. The union is now authorized by the employees to make decisions on their behalf through the collective bargaining process.

>> **Collective bargaining:** Union employees are no longer at-will (see the common law doctrines later in this chapter for more on employment at-will); an employment contract governs them. The union and the employer negotiate the contract, which addresses typical issues such as wages, hours, pensions, seniority, working conditions, and cause for discipline or termination. HR supports this stage by providing the data necessary for contract costing, such as the cost of labor and benefits. The contract also stipulates the length of the contract, grievance procedures (such as arbitration or mediation), and any security provisions desired by the union. A union may file a ULP against the employer during the collective bargaining process if the employer fails to send someone in with the authority to bargain in good faith.

>> **Ratification:** After an agreement has been reached through collective bargaining, the union representatives take it back to the workers who vote whether to accept the terms. A union may be charged with a ULP if it lacks transparency in presenting the final contract to the union members or changes parts of the agreement after the membership has voted to ratify.

REMEMBER

A bargaining unit consists of only the employees eligible to be represented by a union. These employees must have shared interests, such as supervision, wages, benefits, physical location, and industry description.

The *community of interest* doctrine establishes the criteria that must be met in order to be considered a bargaining unit. It states that the proposed members of a bargaining unit have enough shared employment interests that an agent can effectively represent the group without conflict. Supervisors can't be part of a bargaining unit because they're considered part of the management team rather than part of the labor. For follow-up, study the NLRB's definition of a supervisor, which is especially important because there have been several attempts by employers to categorize groups of employees as supervisors (such as nurses) in order to impede their ability to organize.

After the agreement is in place, a union steward, who is both an employee of the company and a union official, is put into place to handle employee grievances. For larger issues, union members may strike against their employer by refusing to come to work.

EXAMPLE

In dispute resolution, what do conciliation, mediation, and arbitration all have in common?

(A) They are all binding legal decisions.

(B) They are all required by the UGESP.

(C) All three are conducted by third-party individuals.

(D) All three are required to be included in employment contracts.

The correct answer is (C). Conciliation, mediation, and arbitration are alternative dispute methods that use neutral third parties to attempt to resolve employee complaints. Conciliation and mediation decisions aren't legally binding, whereas arbitration decisions are, so Choice (A) is incorrect. None of the three options are mandated by the Uniform Guidelines on Employee Selection Procedures, nor must they be included as part of employment contracts, making Choices (B) and (D) false.

Common law doctrines

In addition to the labor code, Employee and Labor Relations deals with employees' rights granted by law, called statutory rights. Examples include the right to be free from harassment in the workplace and the right to privacy. Added to these laws must be a conversation about common law doctrines. A common law doctrine doesn't require an act of Congress to have the force of law; it's based on consistent court interpretations. Because of these court interpretations, HR professionals have to stay up-to-date on new lawsuits and court rulings every year, because the status of HR law changes with each ruling.

More than likely, the PHR and SPHR exams will ask you questions about the common law doctrine of employment at-will (EAW). *EAW* is the right for either party in employment to terminate the relationship at any time. Employers don't have to give a reason, and employees don't have to give notice. The challenges with true EAW come in the form of three exceptions:

>> **Public policy exception:** Employees may not be terminated for engaging in a protected activity. Examples include filing a workers' compensation claim or refusing to alter employee timecards to avoid overtime payments.

>> **Good faith and fair dealing:** The duty of *good faith and fair dealing* is simply the expectation that employers should act in a fair manner when making employment decisions. An employer can't fire an employee under the at-will doctrine to avoid paying a large sales commission or fire an older worker to avoid retirement obligations.

>> **Implied contract:** If an employee has longevity and good performance reviews, an *implied contract* may exist, which means that the at-will doctrine is no longer in effect, and the employee may only be terminated for cause. Implied contracts have been created by statements from supervisors to the effect of "as long as you do good work, you'll have a job here for life."

Formal employment contracts such as ones used for executive leaders and collective bargaining agreements are examples of explicit contracts that negate employment at-will.

A SPECIAL ISSUE FOR THE SPHR: UNION AVOIDANCE

Employers want to avoid union organizing when possible. While in some industries an organized work-force is business as usual, there are some steps SPHR leaders can do to reduce this relationship from developing at their place of work. They include

- **Aligning ELR activities with the company mission, vision, and values:** Writing polices and activating procedures in alignment with the corporate mission, vision and values (MVV) will help to ensure that employees are on the same page with management. Doing so communicates to an employee that she is part of a bigger picture and encourages a direct line of communication between management and employees. Supporting this link reduces the need for a third-party facilitator.

- **Training the supervisors to be a fair and accurate reflection of the MVV:** An old saying goes, "Employees don't leave companies; they leave bosses." Twisted up a bit, one could argue that employees don't invite a union in, but rather bad managers open the door. As a result, training supervisors, coaching leaders, and teaching management to model desired behavior is a frontline defense against union organizing.

- **Evaluating management and program effectiveness:** Soliciting employee feedback isn't enough. HR must take action. And taking action doesn't mean giving employees everything they ask for, but rather communicating to employees the information used to arrive at a decision.

- **Putting policies to good use:** No-solicitation and open-door policies are preventive in nature, but they must be applied judiciously to avoid charges of interference. If you're taking the SPHR, familiarize yourself with how and why policies can help avoid a positive outcome to a union election.

Remember that so much of HR is about relationships, and any efforts made toward fostering a positive culture will help improve employee job satisfaction. This supports union avoidance efforts in that happy employees generally do not seek out union representation.

Be sure to seek out additional information about utilizing third-party union busters as part of the resistance efforts should a campaign get going at your facility.

EXAMPLE

The common law doctrine of at-will employment can be defined as

- **(A)** refusing to hire an individual based on a protected class characteristic
- **(B)** holding the employer liable for the actions of its supervisors
- **(C)** providing an untrue employment reference
- **(D)** being able to terminate an employee at any time, for any reason, unless unlawful

The correct answer is (D). The common law doctrine of employment at-will states that the employer or employee may terminate the relationship at any time, for any reason, unless prohibited by law. Choice (A) refers to unlawful discrimination. Choice (B) is the common law doctrine known as *respondeat superior*, and Choice (C) is defamation of character or slander.

In addition to common law doctrines, there is another set of laws *not* passed by Congress that require employer compliance. They're called *executive orders*, signed off by the President of the United States. The exam-related executive orders mainly identify classes of protected groups.

Chapter 3

Identifying the Question Types and Strategizing to Answer Them

You may be aware that the questions on both the PHR and SPHR exams are tricky and that first-time test takers have low pass rates. Because you're reading this book, you are clearly taking your test preparation seriously and are doing everything you can to be successful.

With 175 questions and three hours to complete the exam, you have approximately one minute to answer each question. Some questions may take you longer to interpret, while others will be smooth sailing.

This chapter explains the types of questions that you'll encounter on the test and how to tackle them on test day.

Having a Plan to Answer the Questions

Preparing for the test and answering the questions can be similar to the way a golfer approaches a shot. "Approaching a shot" refers to how the golfer goes through a few phases of preparation before actually swinging the club. He selects the right club, stands back to view the landscape, tees up the ball, and squares up to the shot. This all happens before he ever makes contact with the ball. Addressing this exam requires the same mindset. You can follow this list to break down the tactical approach to the PHR and SPHR exam questions:

1. **Read the question thoroughly.**

Doing so helps you figure out what knowledge you must access to select the right and determine what part of your studying will best serve you.

2. **Look for clues in the question.**

These clues can precisely pinpoint what the question is asking such as action words (describe, interpret), centering the question around employer size, or from the view point of the employer as opposed to the employee.

3. **Select the best answer.**

Apply the answer to the question to ensure that it's correct and then make the selection on your monitor. If you're still unsure, mark that question for later review, but do not leave the answer blank.

Interpreting the Content While Conquering the Form

Many of your study resources may focus your attention on the exam content, which is good. What is missing, however, is the need for you to conquer the format of the exam because it can be challenging. Both the PHR and SPHR exams have thousands of questions in the test bank, of which 175 will be randomly assigned to your exam. The PHR and SPHR exams have weighted questions, with difficulty levels in three ranges — easy, medium, and hard — interspersed throughout the entire exam.

What you can't predict is the precise exam objectives from which you'll see questions. No clear map lays out how the exams present the problems. You may get the more difficult questions earlier and the easier ones later. Or the exam may get progressively more difficult. What will be consistent is the weight of exam content by functional area.

No matter, being prepared for the different types of questions can help you better navigate the exam so that you don't panic when you encounter questions that are more difficult. The following sections break down the questions and answer options on the exams so that you know what to expect.

REMEMBER

The great news about this type of variety in question stems is that you may find answers to other questions in the questions themselves, which is how marking for review can come in very handy.

Understanding how the questions are formed

The majority of the questions on both exams are multiple choice with four possible options. The *stems*, or premise of the question, are phrased in a few different ways, which I discuss here. These sections focus on the questions (so I don't focus on providing answer explanations).

Direct questions

These types of items ask a specific question, usually offering background information or a summary. Here is an example of a direct question.

EXAMPLE

What type of interview bias is the result of the interviewer applying a widely held but not necessarily true characteristic to an applicant, often based on a protected class characteristic?

(A) Similar to me

(B) Stereotype

(C) Discrimination

(D) Horn effect

The correct answer is (B).

HRCI recently introduced "alternative item types", a fancy way to identify direct questions that are not traditional multiple choice. New to 2018, you will see drag and drop and multiple response types of questions on the PHR and SPHR.

Incomplete statements

Traditionally recognized as a fill-in-the-blank style, these types of questions ask you to finish a thought or statement. The following example illustrates this type of question.

EXAMPLE

A stereotype is an example of interview_____?

(A) bias

(B) discrimination

(C) judgment

(D) error

The correct answer is (A).

Scenario questions

Scenario questions are phrased to mirror typical HR situations. They're designed to measure how well you're able to apply your knowledge to a work simulation. Especially on the SPHR exam, you may be given one scenario in which two or three questions follow. You should be able to apply facts from multiple functional areas. When you encounter these questions, be prepared to first take a broad view and then strip it down to what the question is really asking.

EXAMPLE

Kendall is a recruiter interviewing several candidates for an accounting clerk position. He rates Iris, an Asian female candidate, very highly qualified, mainly because he has heard that Asian people are highly intelligent and good at math. This is an example of what kind of interviewer bias?

(A) Unlawful discrimination

(B) Bias

(C) Stereotype

(D) The halo effect

The correct answer is (C).

EXAMPLE

Which of the following are stages in the business life cycle (select all that apply):

(A) Start-up

(B) Infancy

(C) Decline

(D) Maturity

The correct answers are (A), (C), and (D).

The matching/drag and drops are questions that show two lists — one in Column A and one in Column B. The question asks you to drag an item from Column A to its matching description in Column B.

EXAMPLE

Match the following HR activity to the reason for the process:

A. Onboarding	To help a new employee assimilate to the new work environment.
B. Workforce Planning	To respond to external factors affecting how work gets done
C. Orientation	To anticipate the future hiring needs of an organization.
D. Restructuring	To meet specific compliance requirements at the time of hire

The correct answers are as follows:

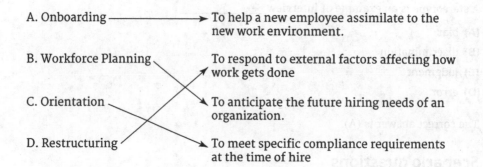

A. Onboarding ⟶ To help a new employee assimilate to the new work environment.

B. Workforce Planning ⟶ To respond to external factors affecting how work gets done

C. Orientation ⟶ To anticipate the future hiring needs of an organization.

D. Restructuring ⟶ To meet specific compliance requirements at the time of hire

Spotting the target: The correct answer

One of my favorite strategies to recommend for selecting the right answer is to anticipate it before you even read the answer choices. This strategy requires knowledge about the core subjects and the ability to predict what the answer choices may be. This strategy isn't a guessing technique. It's a technique designed to focus your thinking on what the question is asking so that you recognize the most likely answer when you read the options.

Each question is likely to look like there are multiple "right" answers. When faced with this, always defer to the application in the workplace. Think about the impact of an answer from the employee's perspective, and then from the employer's perspective. Consider the answers from a federal versus a state perspective and remind yourself that these exams are based on federal law. Re-read the question and make sure that you understand what it's asking before making your answer choice. For example, a question asking you to *implement* a plan may have answer options related to design, execute, and measure. All answers are vital to the planning process, but only one is directly related to implementation (execute), which would be the correct answer.

TIP

To use this strategy, stick to these steps:

1. **Read the questions twice.**

2. **Before looking at the available answers, identify the correct answer in your mind.**

3. **After you're confident that you know the answer, scan the options for the most similar choice to your conclusion.**

   When you allow yourself to find the answer naturally, you're less likely to be swayed by the distractors.

REMEMBER

The best way to determine whether this strategy works for you is to take a practice exam where you can try it. Measure your comfort level and confidence, not just the final score. Refer to Chapter 2 for more information about the importance of taking practice exams.

In addition to predicting the correct answer, other effective strategies can help you narrow your choices. They include the following:

» **Eliminate the obvious.** Writing wrong answers is more difficult than you may think for the exam preparers. Look for slight variations in wording or partially correct answers. Search for clues such as synonyms or phrases in the answer that mirror that of the question. Find the *distractors* (extraneous information included as an answer or in the question stem that isn't relevant; refer to the next section for more help on how to locate distractors) that include correct information, but don't actually answer the question. If you know these techniques ahead of time, you can practice spotting them on exam simulations. Make it a challenge when you take practice exams.

» **Apply your knowledge.** An incorrect answer choice may answer part of the question but not all of it. Incorrect choices serve to confuse you, because you know part of the answer choice is correct, so you think that perhaps it may be right. Think about how you would accomplish the activity on the job. Ask yourself important questions: What information would you need and what actions would you take? What resources would be necessary, and most importantly, what would be the desired outcome? From this process, you should be able to spot the answer option that best reflects the answers to your workforce application.

With this example question, I illustrate this strategy at work. Go ahead and use this strategy and then read the answer explanation to see how you did.

EXAMPLE

Where would be the best place to find information about local labor market trends?

(A) Your city's chamber of commerce

(B) The state's workforce development agency

(C) The Department of Labor

(D) The Bureau of Labor Statistics

The correct answer is (B). Although all choices may offer you variations of labor market trends, applying the preceding techniques can help you arrive at the best answer. Rereading the question can help you identify a key word — *local*. You can eliminate Choices (C) and (D) because they're national resources. Both (A) and (B) address the locality issue, so apply your working knowledge of this practice. An experienced HR professional knows that chambers of commerce don't actively collect labor market data and serve more in the capacity of employer lobbyists. Therefore, Choice (B) is the best answer.

REMEMBER

Half of your brain is focused on the structure of the question and interpreting the stem, whereas the other half is engaged in applying your knowledge to find the answer. Both of these functions are important to arriving at the correct conclusion. Compartmentalizing these activities during practice trains your brain to acknowledge each half during the test, minimizing anxiety because you're prepared for successful analysis.

Navigating the answer distractors

In addition to the two good answer choices, an exam question usually also has distractors. The difference between a distractor and a clearly wrong answer is that the distractors are plausible.

Distractors can show up in a couple of different places:

» **In the question stem:** This extraneous information isn't relevant to the correct answer.

» **In one of the four answer choices:** Some distractors are answers based on common misconceptions. Others aren't relevant to the question (such as a state requirement rather than a federal one). Some distractors are true statements that don't answer the actual question. Worse yet are the distractors that are close to the actual correct answer, but with a slight variation that renders it second best.

Practicing this approach may take a bit of time at first. The clock eventually will matter for these practice exams, but during your earlier practice sessions, your focus should be on training your brain to think critically through each exam item.

Here is an example of a question with distractors.

Which of the following is an HR implication of the *Griggs vs. Duke Power Company* Supreme Court case?

(A) Punitive damages for sexual harassment may now be tied to organizational size.

(B) Tests used for employment selection should be job related.

(C) Employment discrimination now includes categories of age, gender, and military status.

(D) Labor unions must now keep records of financial dealings in accordance with both state and federal laws.

The correct answer is (B). All statements sound true, but the court case deals with employment selection tests. To answer this question, you need to know the basics of the court case. If you knew that *Griggs vs. Duke Power* is considered the benchmark case that established the need for employment tests to be job related, you could eliminate Choice (A) because the case isn't related to claims of sexual harassment, Choice (C) because the case didn't address protected categories, and Choice (D) because the case didn't involve labor unions.

Recognizing Special Circumstances

Just relying on your experience and education alone isn't enough when answering questions on the exams. The exam body of knowledge (BOK) is built upon industry best practices that are examined each year through the use of subject-matter experts, peer-reviewed journals, and the use of certified HR professionals to write the exam items. The following sections point you in the right direction when it comes to mastering the nuances that exist on both exams.

Test takers are only tested on subject matter included in the exam content outline. Study these exam objectives to find clues to HR best practices. Refer to each chapter for the specific objectives, or find them online at www.hrci.org.

Maneuvering through the "best" pitfall

Both the PHR and SPHR exams rely heavily on the concept of the *best* answer. It means that in a group of experts, all would agree that the answer is the best answer to a given premise. The exams use these types of questions to measure how well you're able to apply your work experience to an exam item.

To tackle these types of questions, keep in mind that you're looking for the answer that serves the exam objectives and the industry as a whole. It may not be the choice that is true all the time, and it certainly won't be an absolute statement with terms such as *never* or *always*. Here are a few strategies to help you get to the correct answer:

» **Find the most ethical answer.** Ethics is a huge consideration of the profession and often must serve as the final element in your decision-making. Let it serve you with these types of questions.

» **Select the choice that best serves the employee.** Erring on the side of the employee is rarely the wrong thing to do at work and often is the best choice for managing risk. This strategy reduces your risk of selecting the wrong answer. Be sure when employing this strategy that the question doesn't specify an advantage for the employer.

» **Look for similarities and differences in the answer options.** If two answers seem to be correct, compare them against each other to identify the difference and similarity, and then reread the question. Apply both answers while considering the difference/similarity and choose what makes most sense.

» **Picture the response scrutinized in court.** You're the expert at work, and you have the responsibility to give solid advice. Look for the answer that would hold up best if you had to publish your response or defend an employment action in court.

» **Select the choice that is an industry best practice.** For this strategy to work, you must have mastered the exam BOK. Although you may answer differently for your own employer, these questions are measuring what best reflects the HR industry best practices.

The practice exams will help familiarize you with these types of questions, so invest in as many credible resources as your budget allows. Refer to Chapter 2 for more information about taking practice exams.

Here is an example of a *best* question. Use these strategies and review the answer explanation to see how you did.

EXAMPLE

The BEST reason to conduct a labor market analysis is to increase an organization's

(A) knowledge of local trends

(B) assessment of workforce skill sets

(C) identification of workforce requirements

(D) brand awareness

The correct answer is (A). In many *best* questions, all the answers appear to be appropriate, so it's up to you to apply critical-thinking skills to the choices. In Choice (B), a labor market analysis collects trends that impact the workforce skill sets, but it's only one component of the information gathered. Brand awareness, Choice (D), could certainly be a byproduct of trolling the market for information, but it isn't a directly related goal of the effort. Choice (C) is an internal activity, not an external effort.

Working with extremes — always, never, most, least

Answer choices that contain absolutes such as *never, none, all,* or *always* are virtually never correct. Absolutes must apply to all circumstances, and HR professionals know that very few things in day-to-day activities are universal. For this reason, eliminating these answers as incorrect is a safe bet.

A bit more difficult to navigate are the *most* and *least* questions. These types of questions tell you right away that all four answers apply in some fashion, and your job is to apply independent judgment and work experience to rate them in order of importance or likelihood of occurrence.

REMEMBER

To solve these *most* and *least* problems, keep these points in mind:

>> Think about what you would do if the situation were presented to you on the job.

>> Consider the facts that you would gather or what resources you would employ.

>> Address the legal issues that may or may not be associated with the question presented.

Consider the following example of a *most/least* problem.

EXAMPLE

OSHA discovered at your place of work that noise levels exceed the maximum levels allowed. Which of the following choices is LEAST likely to result in hazard abatement?

(A) Introduce a policy requiring employees to wear ear protection.

(B) Reinstate the manufacturing guards that control the volume of the machinery.

(C) Call out an expert to measure and confirm the original decibel findings.

(D) Discipline the employees for failing to wear their earmuffs.

The correct answer is (D). Disciplining employees for failing to wear ear protection won't solve the root cause, which is the goal of hazard abatement efforts. A policy (Choice [A]) won't result in compliance, although it certainly launches the process. Calling in the experts (Choice [C]) is a better answer, because it seeks to find the root cause of the issue. Choice (B) is a critical component to compliance, because the machine guards for noise protection had been bypassed.

Dealing with the unknown

You'll inevitably run into a question (or a few) where you simply won't know the answer. Don't be surprised when you encounter one. Stay calm and don't panic. Here are some strategies to deal with the unknown:

>> **Trust your first instinct.** Try not to overthink the question. If you really don't know the answer, trust your first instinct and move on, marking it for review if time permits.

>> **Make an educated guess.** Making a guess is better than leaving an answer blank. You had to qualify by experience and education to take the exam, and you have dedicated the time in advance to prepare, so you can make a pretty good guess at what may be correct.

REMEMBER

Guessing is actually an extremely important test-taking strategy. You start with a score of zero and build up points for every correct answer. If you leave an answer blank, you guarantee that you'll get zero points for the question. Guessing incorrectly doesn't hurt you; you simply won't get the points for the question. Leaving it blank altogether is a mistake.

>> **Skip it and go back.** Marking questions for review is a good way to address the unknown. Other questions may actually help you answer the headache questions. You may, however, want to at least take an educated guess, just in case you run out of review time at the end of the exam.

CHANGING YOUR ANSWER

TIP

Some test takers choose to stick with their first answer, whereas others use the review process to make changes. The only way to know which approach works for you is to try them both. Remember that you probably haven't sat for an exam in a while, so what used to work for you may no longer be effective.

Take a practice exam in which you don't go back and change your answers and compare it to a practice exam where you allow yourself to make adjustments. Or, you can take a single exam and practice changing some answers but not others. During the exam, write down the question numbers of those answers that you changed and the questions for which you wanted to change the answer but didn't. Measure which technique worked best for you. Try this approach a couple of times to make sure that you're confident in your approach on test day. Refer to Chapter 2 for more advice on how you can prepare for the exam.

Chapter **4**

Surviving Test Day

Taking the PHR or SPHR exam can be downright nerve-wracking. Those nerves can make you stop eating, eat too much, or lose sleep leading up to test day. They can show up in physical ways like shallow breathing, rashes, stomachaches, or headaches. Yet nerves also have the power to motivate you, sharpening your focus and strengthening your resolve. What you do in the week immediately preceding test day and on the day of the test can help you harness the positive energy to apply toward exam success.

Read Chapter 2 and take my advice to give yourself plenty of time to study, review, and take exam simulations. Regardless of your preparation activities, however, test anxiety is a very real phenomenon that you should consider in your preparation. Knowing what to expect can help reduce the anxiety, eliminate distractors, and allow you to focus on what you came to do. This chapter examines what you can do to ease your nerves and perform well the days before and on test day.

Leading Up: The Days before the Test

During the Coronavirus pandemic of 2020, HRCI got special permission to offer the exams remotely through Pearson VUE. It is as yet unclear if this practice will continue. Regardless, it is the smart option to think about what you can do prior to the big day.

Planning ahead allows you to make arrangements to tour the testing facility or get a good deal on a hotel room if you want to stay over the night before. Making decisions about cramming and packing your bag for the testing hours alleviates possible missteps or worse, forgetting the government-approved ID that gets you in the door. These are just examples of what the following section examines. I also offer tips, tricks, and strategies for you to incorporate into your preparation activities.

Similarly, if taking the exam remotely, you'll need to think about where you can take the exam without interruption and in compliance with the guidelines for a remotely proctored test (camera access, talking out loud, and so on).

Avoid alcoholic beverages the night before the exam. They can lead to dehydration, causing you to overload on water the day of your test. Too many bathroom breaks in the three-hour time frame will be a waste of your allotted time.

Cramming: Yes or no?

Some popular theorists say that cramming for your exam or putting off studying until the last moment — the week or the night before the test — is useless. Short-term memory gains are often at the expense of lost information elsewhere, which is especially true if your late-night studying breaches your normal sleep patterns, because a well-rested exam taker is more successful than one who just pulled an all-nighter.

Allow me to propose a compromise. Although a panicky study session the night before isn't the best way to spend your evening hours, a well-planned, systematic review of difficult-to-understand concepts may be just the sedate activity that is a natural extension of your regular study patterns.

Keep notes during your weekly study sessions of topics that you've struggled with or that you need to understand more clearly. Then during the week before your exam, engage in one or more of these activities:

>> **Watch videos.** Most of your studying has probably been of the reading sort, fighting your way through the language of academia and a hodgepodge of MBA terms like *paradigms* and *deltas*. In the week before your exam, engage in watching videos produced by credible experts, such as authors or professional associations, regarding the muddier concepts. You can find many of these types of videos on free websites such as www.youtube.com. Both SHRM and HRCI have their own YouTube channels that I recommend you subscribe to.

>> **Stick to your review schedule.** Accelerating the amount of time you spend reviewing is fine; however, be aware of your limits. The week before the exam isn't the time to learn new concepts. Focus then on reviewing the familiar or go deeper in the more difficult. Chapter 2 helps you put together your study plan.

>> **Write exam questions or create a presentation.** Doing so is harder than you think. The best way to learn something is to teach it, so writing exam questions or preparing a PowerPoint presentation as though you're getting ready to train on a difficult topic forces you to look at the material in an objective way. Strip the concept down to its core, seeking out information to teach rather than to learn. Doing so gives you greater control and less fear over the concept that has eluded retention in your information-overloaded mind.

You alone need to decide whether a modified cramming schedule works for you. Abandoning all preparation activity the night before may be unrealistic for some individuals, yet quite a relief for others. Don't judge yourself after you have made a decision either way; just trust your instincts and do what feels right for you.

Eyeing the lay of the land: The testing facilities

HRCI has contracted with Pearson VUE to administer the exams. The company has hundreds of computer-based facilities around the United States (and internationally). After you have been approved to sit for the exam (see Chapter 1), you'll be directed to the Pearson VUE's website to schedule your exam. At this time, you'll be able to select the facility where you'll test and take note of the address and phone number.

Familiarizing yourself with the testing environment

When taking the test, you'll be in a room filled with workstations and computer monitors. Pearson VUE administers many different exams, not just the PHR and SPHR. As a result, test takers have different appointment times. This means that on test day, you may have people coming in and going out of the testing room. Your goal is to stay focused and not worry about other test takers who are working more quickly than you. They may have started before you or have a shorter test, so be aware of this fact and ignore the movement as best as you can.

Plan to arrive at least 30 minutes prior to your scheduled start time. When checking in, you'll need to present proper identification (refer to the later section, for specifics). When you check in, Pearson VUE also takes your photo and a biometric scan of either your fingerprint or palm.

In accordance with HRCI's policies, no personal items will be allowed in the testing room. This includes food/drinks, equipment, bags, notes, phones, pagers, watches, and wallets. You may bring in a sweater or blazer, but you'll need to show that the pockets are empty. All testing rooms are recorded.

Items such as face masks, glasses, bandages, and hearing aids (without remote controls) are allowed in the testing room, but the test administrator will ask to visually inspect them prior to the start of your exam.

Everyone receives a ten-minute tutorial on how to use the program before the start of the exam and a survey at the end of the exam while the results are calculated. The three-hour time window does not include the time it takes to complete these items. All examinees will receive an erasable note board to take into the exam room with them, and the computer has a calculator available online for any math problems.

TIP

Pearson VUE has the ability to set up alternative testing accommodations such as a separate testing room, special breaks, and extra testing time to accommodate individuals with a disability. Don't hesitate to ask for these accommodations when scheduling your exam. You may have to provide proof of disability, so if you need accommodation, it is best to request it beforehand rather than hope it will be available on exam day.

The Time Is Here: Exam Day

The day of the exam has finally arrived. All your effort and preparedness is literally about to be put to the test. But your preparations aren't finished yet. A few important pieces of advice that I cover in these sections can increase your chances of success over the next few hours.

TIP

Regardless of how you feel when you wake up, be sure and eat a decent meal. Focus on proteins such as eggs, cheese, or nuts to fill you up and fuel your brain. Avoid sugary foods, such as donuts or candy bars, and energy drinks that may result in an energy crash halfway through the exam. Keep in mind that carb-heavy foods may make you feel heavy and sleepy, affecting your performance. Resist the urge to avoid food altogether, because you'll need the fuel it provides for the mental marathon that you're about to begin.

On the day of the exam, stop studying. Give yourself a pep talk and visualize yourself succeeding. Refer to the later section, "Remembering the ABCs of Exam Day" for more information.

Pearson VUE is meticulous for security to ensure the integrity of the exams isn't breached and that you are who you say you are on exam day. Make sure that you arrive at least 30 minutes prior to your scheduled time to allow for security procedures. You must present an unexpired, government-issued ID when registering, when entering the test room, and when returning from a break. Acceptable IDs include a valid

>> Drivers license or state ID card

>> Military identification card

>> Passport

>> National identification card

Make sure the identification you use matches the name on your application exactly, including the use of middle initials or hyphenated names. The two items shouldn't have any discrepancies. Furthermore, your primary ID must have your photo and signature. If you present an ID without either, you'll need a backup form of ID that has the missing element. Keep in mind that the backup ID must match your name on the application exactly as well. You won't be permitted to test if they don't match.

HRCI's *Certification Handbook* gives several examples of acceptable/nonacceptable name variances. Table 4-1 gives a few such examples; however, it is best to ask if you are uncertain.

TABLE 4-1 **Acceptable versus Unacceptable Name Variance**

Name on HRCI Application	Name on Government-Issued ID	Acceptable?
Chi Xing-Lu	Sandy X. Lu	No
Chi Xing-Lu	Chi X Lu	Yes
Sandra M. Reed	Sandra Michelle Reed	Yes

Finally, Pearson VUE will ask you to write a digital signature for comparison on the identification you bring to the exam room.

TIP

If you aren't sure what forms of ID will be accepted at your test center or just want to double-check, don't wait until exam day. Call your testing facility or contact HRCI toll free at 866-898-4724 to verify that your ID will be accepted. You want to avoid (or take steps to correct) any potential issues before the morning of test day.

Remembering the ABCs of Exam Day

A few common factors can contribute to success on test day, no matter your education or experience. Here are three important tips that can help you get in the right frame of mind.

Attitude: Believe that you can succeed

To prove my point, conduct a web search on the term "the power of positive thinking" and you may be surprised at the amount of material that is available on the impact of how a person's attitude affects successful outcomes. From peer-reviewed research to bestselling books, you can find a ton of information about the impact of the positive perception of your life, knowledge, skills, and abilities.

REMEMBER

Test day is not the first time you should practice having a positive mindset! Your attitude toward your study time, the materials that you use, and the choices that you make can substantially influence how prepared you feel going into exam day. Negative self-talk is harmful, so focus on positive psychology, even when you consider that you might fail on the first try. Certification is truly about the journey. You're guaranteed to come out more informed and competent in your job, making this exercise well worth every second of preparation, regardless of a pass or fail score.

Breathing: It matters more than you may think

Regulating your breathing is important to clearing your mind and sharpening your focus. "In through your nose, out through your mouth" may feel silly, but your body needs regulated oxygen to perform optimally. In fact, taking too many shallow breaths can actually increase anxiety and even cause you to hyperventilate.

When you're in your deepest point of sleep, your breathing is even, causing your heart rate to steady and your body to remain calm. Focusing on your breathing while you're awake can manifest those same benefits. Become conscious of your breathing while you're taking exam simulations or during your preparation activities so that you train your body to shift automatically into this calm state when you encounter the material. Conscious regulation of your breathing sends messages to your brain, impacting clarity and eliminating fuzzy thinking.

Knowing how to breathe better has many benefits to overall health. For purposes of exam preparation, proper breathing calms the fight-or-flight instinct that everyone has when faced with high stress or perceived dangerous situations. Symptoms that you're anxious include a rapid heartbeat, sweaty palms, and temperature changes such as flushing or feeling cold. Proper breathing requires that you take in air through your nose and then push it out from your stomach through your mouth. Here are a few training tips to help you master this technique:

>> Put one hand on your stomach and the other hand on your chest. When you breathe in, your stomach should rise more than your chest, which means the air is being drawn all the way to the base of your lungs.

>> Exhale slowly through your mouth. As a general rule, your exhale should be twice as long as the inhale.

>> Repeat four or five times until you feel the calming results of a slower heartbeat or normalized temperature.

Meditation is another technique that may help you enter a calmer state, which is especially useful if you suffer from test-taking or performance anxiety. Although many methods are available, look for one that addresses the basics of concentration or focuses your mind on one thought at a time. Concentrating on a simple word or phrase clears the mind of negative talk and other distractions that elevate your nerves. Effective meditation relies on breathing. Combine the two techniques by finding a calming word or phrase that you can repeat in your mind during the previous breathing exercise. Favorites may be "I am calm," "I am relaxed," "I am peaceful," or "I am thankful." If you're more serious about tackling meditation in your study plan, check out the latest edition of *Meditation For Dummies* by Stephan Bodian (Wiley).

Confidence: Expect success

True confidence requires that you're *honest* about your capabilities and effort up to test day. Believe in yourself, knowing that you've prepared for the test and done what you need to succeed. However, if you go into your exam day expecting to fail, you may not be as motivated to perform because in your mind, the outcome is already set.

Getting to a true confident state requires that you ask yourself these questions long before exam day:

>> **Are you taking the right test?** Too often, exam takers reach for the SPHR before they're truly ready. Make sure to pay attention to your assessment scores and be willing to change exams if they aren't up to par. (Refer to Chapter 2 for more information about assessment tests.) It's better to pay the fee to change the test than to sit for an exam that you aren't ready for and fail.

>> **Are you respecting your study time?** Be honest. You alone know your true level of effort. Are you being too hard on yourself and minimizing your efforts, or are you being too generous, according effort where it really doesn't belong? The good news is that you don't have to share this answer with anyone — it's just between you and your psyche, so don't be afraid to explore at will. If you know you aren't doing as much as you should to prepare, don't let it derail you. What matters is that you focus on the task at hand and get back at it!

>> **What stereotypes or negative self-talk has crossed your mind?** Negative self-talk erodes confidence. During the test thinking things like "I can't do this" or "I knew this test was going to be too hard for me" keeps you from doing best. Focusing on what you *don't* know comes at the expense of your ability to focus on what you *do* know. Getting control of those thoughts before they change your behavior is key. If, during the test, you begin to think negative thoughts, stifle them by taking a deep breath and changing the statement to a psychologically positive alternative. For example, "I should have studied harder" can be converted to "I am going to apply what I know." Or "I'm not good at taking tests" can be changed to "I'm putting myself out there and am going to get this done."

A note of encouragement: I have had so many students who come to me worried that they are not equal to the task because they don't have a formal degree. As a person who didn't finish her degrees until well into her 40s, I understand this sense of inferiority all too well! But let me share this good news: Being an excellent HR professional doesn't require a formal college degree, nor is it dominated by one race or gender. Human resources is relevant in all industries and important in all the major countries where the work of business is getting done. You'll be successfully certified based solely on your talent, preparation, and performance, and taking this step in your career signals your dedication. Be proud of yourself.

After the Test: What to Expect

Congratulations. You clicked the finish button and completed a strenuous experience. However, before you can leave, you have a few small tasks to do — most importantly receiving your score. These sections explain what you need to do after you finish.

Completing the survey

Before you find out how you performed, you'll be asked to complete a short survey conducted by HRCI. The survey asks a few general questions, such as how you prepared for the exam. Don't worry though, because the answers aren't scored. HRCI uses this information to help make recommendations to other students on the studying habits of successful exam takers, so be as honest and thoughtful as possible.

Getting your results

After the timer wheel stops spinning, your preliminary results report will tell you if you passed or failed. The screen will show "congratulations, you passed" or "did not pass." You'll receive a printout of the result while your official results will be sent via email or mail. You need a scaled score of at least 500 to pass either the PHR or SPHR exam.

If you passed

The official results that you'll receive via email or mail shows a snapshot of how you did in each of the functional areas for use in future development activities. These reports won't show your overall score because HRCI doesn't want the score reports being misused. For example, if I scored 510 points and another candidate scored 520 points, those additional points don't necessarily mean she is a better HR candidate than me.

You should wait to use the initials after your name or communicate your exam results until you receive the formal score report from HRCI within four to six weeks of your test date. At that point, you can search the directory of certified professionals for your name at www.hrci.org.

Successful candidates will receive an email from HRCI congratulating them on the accomplishment and telling them how to create a digital badge for their social media accounts, emails, and résumé. This is more than just bragging rights — a digital badge serves as verification that you are indeed a newly minted member of the professionally certified.

You may also request a paper certificate through HRCI's online store.

TIP

Proudly displaying your new credentials in a signature line is an exciting way to communicate this professional achievement. The correct way to do so is to use the proper acronym with no punctuation and to display the credentials in the order received. For example, "Kinsey Millhone, SPHR" is correct. "Kinsey Millhone, S.P.H.R" is incorrect.

If you didn't pass

Your official score report will compare your individual result with the score you needed to pass. You'll also see your overall performance, so that you know what areas need to be improved upon prior to retaking the test. Your score will be in a range of 100–499; the closer to that scaled score of 500 this number is, the closer you were to passing!

The report will also break down your performance by functional area so that you can see where you underperformed. Use this as the starting point for retaking the exam.

In order to retake the exam, you must wait 90 days (regardless of whether you purchased second-chance insurance). There is no waiting period if an unsuccessful candidate wants to change the exam type (such as from the failed SPHR to the PHR or aPHR).

2
Managing the Basics: Pre-Test Fundamentals

IN THIS PART . . .

Track the latest trends in human resources.

Explore how HR professionals are required to be business partners, not just support staff, serving as both the employer and employee advocate while companies navigate change.

Review the huge list of HRCI terms that you need to study.

Chapter **5**

Career Day: Life of a Certified HR Professional

The history of what are currently known as the PHR and SPHR exams is really quite interesting. Under its earlier name, the Society for Human Resources (SHRM) commissioned a task force based on a study of industrial relations in the 1960s. The focus was on whether or not the field of human resources was a true profession, similar to that of a lawyer, doctor, or accountant. This study and other studies identified characteristics that must exist in order for a body of work to be defined as a profession. Because these other industries weren't a perfect fit for the practice of HR, the discussion evolved until it was decided that the HR profession must

» **Be a full-time responsibility:** In human resources, the tasks, duties, and responsibilities are performed on a full-time basis in many functional areas. Examples include training, compensation, and safety.

» **Have a body of knowledge (BOK) from which schools could teach:** The HR body of knowledge forms the basis for the PHR and SPHR exams, and there is a process for updating and certifying the BOK approximately every five years.

» **Have a professional association, along with competency and knowledge certifications:** The Society for Human Resource Management (SHRM) is perhaps the most well-known HR association. In 1976, the Human Resource Certification Institute (HRCI) began offering the HR exams known today as the PHR and SPHR. Several other related professional associations have been linked to the business of HR, including World at Work (total rewards) and the Association for Talent Development (training and organizational development). Both of these associations have certifications for HR professionals.

» **Be governed by a code of ethics:** Although SHRM and other groups have codes of ethics, the exam-relevant code of ethics is published by HRCI. It includes standards for professional responsibility, professional development, ethical leadership, fairness and integrity, conflict of interest management, as well as how you should use that information.

Since the 1960s, a pattern has emerged. Agencies have changed names, exams have changed names, and content has developed and evolved; it has certainly been a work in progress. The same can be said of your career. An HR professional must continue to evolve to keep pace with this ever-changing profession. Although your choice to pursue certification is a strategic career move, it also serves a larger goal that brings everyone to the same table. The preparation process teaches all one language and helps everyone apply best practices to their workplaces while mentoring a new generation of talent. Your effort demonstrates a commitment to professional excellence and fits perfectly within the spirit that guides the evolution of our industry.

This chapter explores a day in the life of a certified HR professional that takes into account current trends for which you must prepare, the emerging role and responsibilities of your position of trust within the company that you serve, and how to best apply your knowledge on the job.

Tracking Trends in Human Resources

Like any business function, HR has lots of data that can be tracked and measured. In fact, much of HR's history runs parallel to the evolution of business as a whole. For this reason, it's not enough to only seek education in HR. You must commit to being a business resource for the industry in which you practice. Although HR can support industries from mining to medical administration, these industries have completely different needs from an organizational perspective. So, bouncing from industry to industry on your HR career path isn't wise; find your enterprise and begin to specialize.

Trends in human resources allow you to keep pace both with your profession and best business practices. These exams update every five or so years for that very reason. HRCI recognizes that how well people do their jobs changes based on several factors, including the role of education in the field, technology advances, global consumer markets, and the ebb and flow of the supply and demand of talent. I discuss these factors in more detail in the following sections.

Understanding educational trends

These exams support a baseline of knowledge that you must have in order to be successful. In fact, the process of preparing for these exams may make you feel like you're in graduate school. In addition, these exams require recertification, which means those individuals certified must engage in development activities that support the variety of exam objectives based on best practices. The great news is that getting and staying educated has truly never been easier in the HR field.

Emerging trends in HR education must begin with a discussion of the virtual playing field. The traditional classroom is no longer the only place to go to learn, and options are available for every budget. If you have some money to invest, consider an online master's degree in HR from universities such as Cornell or Penn State. These programs are often a *hybrid* — a blend of online, virtual learning, and a few weeks of the year spent on campus.

HRCI is well-ahead of the need for nontraditional training and certification options to help practitioners stay up-to-date and relevant in the field. In 2018 they introduced micro-certifications via their upSkill initiative. Specialized certifications that are available include

>> California HR

>> HR in Social Media

>> Confidentiality and Technology

» Risk Management

» Workforce Analytics

This is a very cost-effective way to continue your education and stay relevant.

WARNING

When you're researching educational opportunities for your HR career or studying for either the PHR or SPHR exam, make sure the sources that you're using for your informal or formal online HR education are reputable. Just because something is on the internet doesn't make it true. Look for clues such as websites ending in *.org*, *.gov*, or *.edu*. Don't rely on websites that are written by the general public or driven by opinions. Stay away from online groups that have political agendas or other bits that may render them biased advisors.

Clarifying the role of HR

The role of HR has continued to evolve alongside the needs of the employers that they support. The stereotype of party planners has been replaced with a vision of business partners, participating in strategic planning and supporting the core competencies. You can easily view the role of an HR professional through the lens of a PEST analysis — the political, economic, social, and technological changes in the industry:

» **Political:** The most obvious way that the political climate impacts how the role of an HR professional has changed is the abundance of labor law. Changes to healthcare and immigration reform are highly visible examples of why you must stay up-to-date every year. These exams test you not only on labor law, but also on the role of HR in lobbying efforts to effect change.

» **Economic:** Like many other industries, HR hunkers down to weather out tough economies. HR is different from other jobs, however, in that HR professionals also help organizations create solutions when things get tight. Recent examples include managing work furloughs, controlling benefits costs, and retaining key people. Demonstrating the value of HR through leadership and excellence will likely pop up on the exams.

» **Social:** Several social indicators that have impacted how the HR role has evolved are likely to be on the exams. They include the need for employees to find balance in their work and family lives, the management of a multigenerational workforce, and the global landscape from which many companies now compete.

» **Technological:** The need for cellphone policies and the popularity of learning management systems (LMS) are just two examples of the broad impact technology has had on how HR does business. Other examples include the use of technology for employee self-service, virtual interviewing, and the need to manage and protect employee and customer confidential information.

REMEMBER

Social media is an exam-relevant example of how a PEST analysis can help you go deeper into content. For example,

The *political* climate is being shaken up by the National Labor Relations Board, claiming that employees' right to post complaints online about their working conditions or pay is a protected activity.

The *economic* climate has driven an increase in the use of social media to find both jobs and workers.

Socially, the employer brand is often communicated via social media websites through videos and employee testimonials.

Although *technology* has improved efficiencies, many of today's workers report surfing personal social media sites while on the job, which certainly has an impact on productivity.

Another useful acronym to describe the environment in which we practice our craft is VUCA (you are also likely to see this on the exams). A VUCA environment is characterized by

>> **Volatility:** Business environments can be highly volatile, a term often used to describe the ups and downs of the stock market. So it is with HR, and therefore, HR professionals need to be flexible and nimble, able to respond to frequent and rapid change.

>> **Uncertainty:** Many of the decisions HR has to make come down to choosing the option that "sucks the least." The role of HR professionals is to advise management and team members on difficult situations in which the outcome is less than certain. It requires an exercise in neutrality in order to avoid any unintended consequences of HR's actions.

>> **Complexity:** As the adjective describes, the situations in which HR is called upon to act on a daily basis can be quite complex, with multiple stakeholders and implications. Many of the issues are connected, making necessary the ability to anticipate the effect of one decision on other factors, often referred to as "the domino effect."

>> **Ambiguity:** Humans are complex, emotional creatures with varying needs, motivators, and personalities. Working within systems designed to manage the talent is by nature ambiguous, requiring HR professionals to be good listeners and creative problem-solvers. There is rarely a one-size-fits-all solution for the demands made on HR personnel's time.

REMEMBER

The term *business partner* (BP) is a good way to understand what companies need from their HR people. A good BP understands the business, not just his job. A BP comprehends the finances, seeking ways to respond to threats while maintaining a competitive advantage in the relevant market. Because HR doesn't generate direct revenue, the department must find other ways to demonstrate value by continuing to evolve right alongside the business that is supported.

Use the PEST and VUCA acronyms to interpret a muddy exam objective as part of your studying efforts. Suggestions include HR needs such as substance abuse, union organizing, and hiring veterans.

Using the Statistics

Understanding who is currently certified and what is most valuable to employers will help you set the course for a successful career in HR. Even if you fail the PHR or the SPHR exam on your first attempt, the information you have gained while studying has already made you a more valuable business partner and hirable candidate. Don't give up! You're already living this day in the life of HR, so reaching higher is simply an extension of what you already know. The stats in these sections show you that you're in great company.

Identifying who is certified and why this information is important

HRCI offers a wide range of exams, certifying more than 500,000 professionals over the last 40 years in 125 countries. The HRCI exams have evolved along with the profession, adding tests in HR disciplines that are broad in scope, yet address the global diversity that the industry represents. The HRCI reports some important numbers in 2020 to give you some perspective:

>> **PHR:** 73,170 certified professionals.

>> **SPHR:** 49,300 certified professionals.

>> Of those certified, 38 percent serve in specialist roles, whereas 33 percent are managers.

>> More than 13,000 individuals tested in 2019.

>> Similar to other professional exams in degree of difficulty, both the PHR and SPHR exams have pass rates that run from 60 to 70 percent on average.

This information is useful for you to determine how competitive your market is for human resource jobs and validates that passing this exam will help set you apart from the rest.

Leveraging the impact of certification on salary

The choice to become certified is often quite personal. Although directly related to your professional development, it's a personal achievement that distinguishes you in your industrial community. The feeling of pride and accomplishment that successful certification brings is legitimate — you worked hard! The impact of certification reaches beyond just the documentation of your talent, though. In 2018, Payscale reported the percent of increase in pay associated with professional HR certifications as 31.6 percent. They also found that this increases exponentially over the lifetime of a career.

This same report found that holding a professional certification in HR increases the odds of promotion, sometimes by as much as 24.8 percent.

This information is quite important for you when it comes time to leverage your new credentials to impact your salary and career trajectory, because it demonstrates the *value* of your certification. It can also help you measure the ROI of your preparation costs.

REMEMBER

Communicating your success is the first step on the path to leveraging your success. In fact, if you're anything like the thousands of other exam takers, more than likely everyone at work knew you were preparing for this exam — reading prep books at lunch, searching online for unfamiliar terms, and sharing new information as you discovered it. In short, you geeked out on all things HR for a period of time, which is excellent news. It gives you the opportunity to triumphantly enter the workplace the day after the exam and announce that your effort paid off. Here are some tips on how to get a raise post-certification:

>> **Do more prep work.** Ask your boss before the exam what your options will be for career growth after you're successfully certified. Establishing the expectations early on aligns your boss with your goals and allows her to gain any approvals before the big day. You may still need to be groomed for that next promotion, but at least you'll know what to expect.

>> **Ask directly.** Take yourself seriously. You'll just have passed a difficult exam, and that effort should be recognized. Depending on the culture of your work environment, that recognition may come in different forms.

>> **Establish a plan.** Receiving increased pay, a title change, or a promotion is *not* unreasonable for the newly certified HR professional, but it may take some time. If you've already done the legwork pre-test, then you know that the plan is to increase your pay. If the company you work for isn't able to financially reward your professional success, perhaps the company can offer other ways for you to benefit, such as gaining a senior title. A title is nothing to scoff at, because it demonstrates professional growth on your résumé.

REMEMBER

You chose to go down the road of certification for a reason, and it certainly wasn't the path of least resistance. You must have your own career plan to help you decide whether you should stay with your current company or look elsewhere for opportunities. Where possible, job changes should serve your résumé, not just your pocketbook.

Applying Your Knowledge on the Job

At the end of the day, whether you're able to get a pay increase or not, your role at work is going to change. It's not just because you now have initials next to your name. The preparation process taught you new things, and as the consummate professional that you are, you'll begin to seek change in your workgroup.

These changes will apply in two areas:

TIP

» **In your department:** Depending on the size of your HR department, you may suddenly become a go-to person for input and advice. If so, consider mentoring a co-worker and coaching him down the certification path. Make it a goal for everyone in the department to become certified so that you're all speaking the same HR language. In another scenario, you may be an HR department of one. If so, I'm sure that you'll have identified areas for increased efficiencies within your workspace all throughout the exam prep process. Proper planning and staying organized will keep you from becoming overwhelmed.

» Focus on one or two projects at a time, like auditing Form I-9s or researching employee benefit plans (sooner than the month before open enrollment). Create a master annual HR calendar to schedule special projects.

» **Companywide:** Seeking change companywide can be more of an uphill battle. Begin by making sure management understands what your new certification means. Tell the decision-makers what you studied and how you feel it can benefit the company. This conversation isn't one-way, either. Make sure that you're listening to the executives, managers, and supervisors to avoid being labeled an academic. Some of the concepts you have learned during your studying aren't a one-size-fits-all solution. Common ground is where the meaningful change occurs.

Focusing on staying relevant: Continuing your education

The expectation of the newly certified HR professional is that you continue to engage in professional development activities; therefore, both the PHR and SPHR certifications are valid for three years. That means that you must recertify your credentials in one of two ways: Retake the exam or earn credits. Not surprisingly, many choose to earn the 60 recertification credits over the three-year active window rather than sit for the exam again.

Recertification credits aren't difficult to obtain, but you need to be on the lookout for opportunities. Approved activities may fall into any of the following categories:

» **Continuing education:** Part of the HRCI code of ethics is that HR professionals commit to professional development. Taking classes, attending seminars, and participating in webinars are all activities that can go toward recertifying your credential.

>> **Instruction:** Teaching an HR class or a topic on which you're an expert is a great way to reinforce your learning while mentoring others. Perhaps you can guest speak at your local university or present at an HR networking luncheon.

>> **On-the-job training (OJT):** The classic OJT works for recertification credits. These credits typically need to be for tasks or responsibilities that are new to your role.

>> **Research/publications:** With the abundance of online publishing, blogs, and e-newsletters, plenty of opportunities are out there for you to write on an HR topic that may be trendy or of interest to other professionals. Conducting field, boots-on-the-ground research and sharing your findings is another creative and job-related way to get recertified.

>> **Leadership:** Leading teams or projects are not only bonus worthy, but they also will earn you recertification credits with proper documentation.

>> **Professional membership:** Log any professional memberships you have such as SHRM or ATD for additional credits.

There is also no need to look only for approved programs. After you're certified, you'll be able to go into your HRCI profile and log work activities or educational activities to submit along with your recertification application. Just know that all activities must be HR related. HRCI notes that if you can answer "yes" to any of the following questions, the activity most likely qualifies for recertification credits:

>> Can I connect the activity to one of the responsibility or knowledge statements found in the HRCI Exam Content Outline for my certification?

>> Will the activity add to my knowledge of the HR profession?

>> Does the activity focus on my professional development rather than my personal development? (For example, topics such as *How to Reduce Stress*, *Developing Your Network for Success,* and *Personal Dynamics* do not qualify.)

Demonstrating knowledge: Positively impacting your employer

Business as usual isn't always the best policy, but wanting to change too much too fast can actually damage your credibility. Think carefully about what is book smart compared to changes that your employer or teammates can reasonably be expected to tolerate. There will come a time, however, when you really must speak up and advocate for a change. How you do so will be the difference between being viewed as a hero or the office pariah. Ways to constructively offer feedback to your team or company include

>> **Seek to understand.** Asking the right questions about why a process is in place can help you understand the desired outcome.

>> **Know the facts.** After you understand what the company needs from a person or process, you can begin to gather data. Strive to *be the expert* when it comes to the numbers and statistics to ensure that your idea is the best course of action. You must not only know your job, but also the industry and business functions that you support. Do things such as work the production line, answer the phones, ship the widgets, work the night shift; in short, live the impact your suggestions may have on your people or processes.

>> **Be flexible.** After you comprehend the outcome and have all the facts, you may have to abandon your attempt because it may not be the right option. You may also work with the management team on a *buffet solution,* where you take a little bit from here and a little bit from there and mash it all together. A commitment to a collaborative, flexible effort will help you gain trust.

>> **Time it right.** Timing has two issues that you must consider:

- **How you present your ideas:** Trying to gain permission in the hallway while your boss is walking into a meeting isn't the time to articulate your thoughts. You're bound to short-change your ideas. Be prepared to argue a *business case* before approaching management with a change proposal.

- **When you present your ideas:** Many businesses have seasons, so proper planning can help you and your management team work around these peak times of year. For example, the best time to introduce new point-of-service software in retail is not November or December.

>> **Speak the language of business.** HR people often have to be chameleons, blending into all organizational environments and departments. Know the priorities of the groups that you serve, and speak to those needs before anything else. If the VP of HR needs business metrics, be sure to include a system to deliver them.

>> **Study change management techniques.** *Change management* (the process of systematically coordinating and managing change in the workplace) is a well-researched topic. Become the change management guru at your organization, bringing others along with you. Most people fear change, and fear is a powerful deterrent to any behavior, no matter how well designed. Teaching your company to embrace the new can help them compete — a win for all who work there.

Know that your long-term impact may take time to materialize. It may even take a change of leadership or business strategy to launch your ideas. Having a consistent, flexible approach can help you gain trust and create a successful business partnership.

Constructively criticizing: What to do when you disagree

Constructive conflict is the fuel that drives the corporate engine. If everyone always agrees when a new topic is introduced, you should question whether you have an engaged management team or workforce. The good news is that docile compliance isn't a typical state of work; opportunities abound for lively disagreements about people, products and services, or work procedures. Not only will you need to help facilitate these conversations, but you also will often be the instigator of the conflict. For this reason, in any disagreement, you should first understand your role. Determine whether you're there to facilitate the dialogue in a neutral fashion or to provide constructive feedback about why you disagree.

Here I discuss a few important topics to guide you through this process of communication, which includes the ability to *facilitate* dialogue rather than *teach* a topic and provide constructive feedback and guidance where necessary.

Grasping the role of facilitation

Facilitation is the art of suspending your own opinions and beliefs while delicately extracting tiny little bombs of information from others without detonation. It requires the ability to ask questions, reframe comments where necessary, and keep participants focused on the business at hand. Start by identifying the common goals and shared rewards, and then work backward to identify what must be done to get there. In facilitation, you aren't the expert.

Providing constructive feedback

Constructive feedback is similar to facilitation, except that you're now a participant in the arena. Although the focus must still be on business needs, you're now actively trying to modify behavior. The foundation of this feedback must be courtesy, dignity, and respect. Most individuals aren't devising diabolical plans of disruption at work in the morning while brushing their teeth. They have a reason for behaving the way they behave, and they deserve the courtesy of understanding their motivation and reasoning before being expected to jump on the bandwagon of change. Consider using humor where appropriate, asking for their opinions on how to make something better, or talking of your own mistakes and what you learned from them.

REMEMBER

Keep in mind that providing constructive feedback isn't punitive. Find a way to show the individual why his work life will be better if he takes your feedback and applies it to his job. Then be sure to follow up to see how it's working for him. This approach to coaching becomes a flexible win-win for both parties.

Chapter **6**

Examining HRCI's Glossary of Terms

I n addition to the multiple resources already discussed prior to this chapter, it is important to know about — and how to use — HRCI's Glossary of Terms. Tools can quickly become overwhelming if you don't know how to use them correctly, and this chapter focuses on how to be most efficient with a large amount of data.

As the name implies, the glossary is an index of common HR-related terms along with their definitions. These terms may be used to help individuals prepare for the exams; however, the glossary is not an all-inclusive dictionary of words related to the practice of human resources. This is a blessing and a curse. It is a blessing because learning these terms can provide context, and a preparer can begin to understand the nuances of the language that drives our day-to-day work activities. However, because the terms are not written specifically as an exam preparation product, there is no distinction between what a PHR candidate versus an SPHR candidate should know. Regardless, it is worth including the glossary as part of a comprehensive study plan.

Deciding How to Study

"How do you eat an elephant? One bite at a time." As the saying illustrates, the best way to use this document is to chunk it out. The glossary is presented alphabetically and includes a short descriptor of the term followed by the full definition. The process of sorting and ordering is in and of itself learning, so account for enough time in your study plan to make the effort valuable.

If you view this study tool through the lens of the adult learning styles, you can begin to see all the possibilities:

>> **Visual learners:** Take the time to color code the terms based on functional area. Consider green for terms related to compensation, pink for terms related to employee relations, and so on. You could also create a table with the exam functional areas as headings, and migrate each term to its proper location.

>> **Tactile learners:** Type up a set of flash cards using an online resource. Make sure the app you use is mobile friendly so you can use this whenever and wherever you find some downtime.

>> **Auditory learners:** Record yourself reading the terms and their definitions aloud. My suggestion is to do this in microbursts and listen to them when you find yourself idle or waiting, such as while driving or standing in line at the grocery store.

Of course, there is nothing wrong with a good old-fashioned set of index cards. The practice of writing them out by hand is a tactile way to become more familiar with the terms.

TIP

The study website goconqr.com has users (like me) with these terms already built into flash cards. Find me there at "Sandra Reed. Teacher" and you should be able to access the tools I have already begun. While I am an advocate for doing the work yourself as part of the learning process, this is a great shortcut if you need to save time!

The Terms

absenteeism: not coming to work because of illness or personal problems; many companies calculate the rate of absenteeism of their employees, which is the average number of days they do not come to work

accountability: an obligation to accept responsibility for one's actions

accrual: an accounting method that recognizes a company's financial performance by recording income and expenses at the time a transaction occurs, rather than when a payment is received or an invoice is paid

acquiring organization: the business or organization that is buying another business

acquisition: a process in which one organization buys another organization

active listening: a communication method that a listener uses to interpret and evaluate information from a speaker

ad hoc: a solution to a specific problem that is not planned, or cannot be used in other situations

ADA: a U.S. law that prevents an organization or person from discriminating against an employee because of physical or mental disabilities

ADDIE model: a process for designing training programs that has five steps: analysis, design, development, implementation, and evaluation

ADR: a method for resolving a disagreement without going through formal legal procedures

advocacy: supporting an idea or cause, influencing outcomes

affirmative action: an activity designed to correct previous inequality that may have existed for certain groups or classes of people

align: to place in a line or arrange in a similar way

alliance: a partnership between organizations that helps both sides

allowance: money for a specific purpose

Angoff method: a way to set the standard score for passing a test

antitrust: regulations that promote fair competition among businesses

appeal: to challenge an official decision (for example, in court)

appraisals: assessments of the value or performance of something (example: job appraisals)

apprentice: a person learning a trade or skill from a qualified person for a specific length of time

arbitration: the process of coming to an agreement about something without using a judge or court

assessment center: a system of tests and interviews that evaluate employee performance and help companies select the right people for job positions

assignee: a person who is on (or will go on) an international work assignment

assignment: a job, usually in a new location

assimilation: the process of becoming a member of a team, organization, or culture

asynchronous learning: a teaching method where the students and teachers are online at different times

ATS: computer software that helps an organization recruit employees

attrition: the number of employees that leave the organization for any of the following reasons: resignation, termination, end of agreement, retirement, sickness, or death

authority: someone with extensive knowledge of a specific subject; a person in a superior position

background check: gathering data to determine the accuracy of a candidate's experience and records during employment screening (for example, verifying personal data, checking credentials, determining any criminal activity)

balanced scorecard: a method or tool that organizations use to measure the success of their strategies by looking at both financial and nonfinancial areas

balance-sheet approach: a way to set the salary and living allowances for employees on international assignments

BARS — Behaviorally Anchored Rating Scales: a type of performance rating scale designed to combine both qualitative and quantitative data to the employee appraisal process. BARS compare an individual's performance against specific examples of behavior that are attached to numerical ratings.

base salary: compensation that does not include benefits, bonuses, or commissions

behavioral interview: interview process to predict future performance based upon how the candidate acted in past work situations

benchmarks: a basis for judging or measuring something else

beneficiary: a person who is eligible to gain benefits under a will, insurance policy, retirement plan, or other contract

benefits: compensation that the employee receives in addition to a base salary (for example, health insurance, company housing, company meals, clothing allowance, pension, gym membership, and so on)

best practices: the methods, processes, or activities that have proven to produce outstanding results for organizations

biodata: a shortened term for "biographical data": information about a person's education, background, and work history

blackout period: a brief period in which employees cannot access or change things about their retirement or investment plans

blended learning: a learning method that combines face-to-face teaching with online learning

brain drain: when smart and talented people leave their own country for better opportunities

brainstorming: a method in which individuals or groups spontaneously find solutions to a problem

breakdown (analysis): analyzing and classifying, such as an analysis of revenue sources or a report on attrition numbers

breakdown (failure): a collapse, such as a communication or equipment failure

briefings: discussions which provide detailed information

brownfield operations: reuse of land previously used for industry or manufacturing

business continuity plan: a plan which identifies threats and risks facing a company in order to protect its employees and assets, allowing for better preparation to continue its operations during a disaster or emergency

business unit: a specific area of an organization, such as marketing, accounting, or production

buy-in: acquiring backing or sponsorship from a person or group

career development: an employee's progress through each stage in his or her career

career ladder promotion: job advancement through a series of defined positions, from lower level to higher level

career management: preparing, implementing, and monitoring the career path of employees, with a focus on the goals and needs of the organization

career planning: taking steps to improve professional skills and create new opportunities

cascading goals: goals that an organization sets at a high level, which flow down as goals for departments and then become goals for specific people

cause-and-effect diagram: a visual tool to organize factors that contribute to certain outcomes; also called a "fishbone" diagram

Caux Principles: a set of ethical principles developed for global organizations by the Caux Round Table, a group of global business leaders from around the world

center of excellence: a team or division that uses best practices within a specific area to achieve business goals

central tendency: a measure of the middle of a statistical distribution of data

certification: confirmation of specific achievements or characteristics given by an authority, usually by issuing a certificate or diploma after a test

chain of command: the sequence of power in an organization, from the top to the next levels of authority

change agent: a person or department that deliberately causes change within an organization

civil law: regulations set by countries or legislative groups about the rights of people (different from common laws, which are set by judges)

clause: a part of a document, agreement, proposal, or contract that gives more detail

cloud computing: using a network of remote servers hosted on the internet to access, manage, and process data, rather than using a local server

coaching: a method of developing specific skills in which a coach gives information and objective feedback to a person or group

code of conduct: a written description of the principles, behaviors, and responsibilities that an organization expects of its employees

codetermination: an organizational structure in which employees share responsibility for the operation of a company

cognitive ability: thinking skills and mental abilities

commercial diplomacy: negotiations between countries about policies on international trade or investment

common law: laws established by court decisions and legal precedence (different from civil laws, which are regulations set by nations or legislative groups)

commuter assignment: an international job that requires an employee to live in one country and work in another country, and to travel regularly between them (for example, an expatriate who lives in Bahrain and works in Saudi Arabia)

compa-ratio: a number comparing a person's salary to other salaries for the same job; the comparison ratio is calculated by taking a person's salary and comparing it to the midpoint of other salaries (if a person earns $45,000 per year in a job where the salary midpoint is $50,000 per year, the compa-ratio is $45,000/$50,000 = 90%)

compensation: everything that an employee receives for working, including pay and non-monetary benefits

competencies: the skills, behaviors, and knowledge that are needed to succeed in a specific job

competency model: a list of the behaviors, skills, and knowledge needed to do well in a specific job

competency-based pay: pay based on the skills and knowledge that make an employee valuable to an organization

competency-based questions: questions designed to determine the candidate's ability to handle the job and handle specific situations

complaint procedure (see also **grievance procedure**): the steps that employees must follow when they want to express their concerns about work-related issues to their employer

compliance: following established laws, guidelines, or rules

comply: to obey requests, laws, or guidelines

conflict resolution: method of negotiating agreements or solving problems

consolidation: combining separate companies, functional areas, or product lines; in finance, combining the assets, equity, liabilities, and operating accounts of a company with those of its subsidiaries

contingent worker: a person who is hired part time to work under a contract or for a fixed period of time

contract manufacturing: a production method in which one company hires another company to manufacture parts or goods under its label and according to its specifications

core competency: the skills or knowledge that an organization or employee needs to do its work

core values: the basis upon which the employees of an organization make decisions, plan strategies, and interact with others

corporate citizenship: a practice in which organizations take steps to improve their employees' lives and the communities in which they operate

corporate culture: the values, language, rules, procedures, expectations, and processes that affect how employees of an organization think, act, and view the world

corporate social responsibility: a business philosophy in which an organization helps to improve social and environmental problems

co-sourcing: a business practice in which the employees of a company work with an outside organization to perform a service

cost per hire: the amount of money needed to recruit a new employee, which includes advertising, recruiting fees, referral fees, travel expenses, and relocation costs

cost-benefit analysis: a financial review of various options to determine if the benefits are greater than the costs

cost-of-living adjustment: an increase or decrease in pay based upon changes in economic conditions in a geographic location or country

cost-sharing: method of saving money by dividing the costs of a program, project, or business operation

credentials: proof of a person's earned authority, status, or rights, usually in writing (for example, a university diploma, or proof of passing a professional exam)

criterion: a test, standard, or rule on which something is judged or measured

Critical Incident Appraisal: a method of performance appraisal which involves identifying and describing specific events (or incidents) where the employee succeeds or is in need of improvement

cross-border: taking place across the geographic boundaries of two or more countries (for example, cross-border trade)

cross-border employee: an employee who works across geographic boundaries, such as an international business traveler or a short- or long-term international assignee

cross-cultural: involving two or more cultures (such as national, regional, or professional cultures)

cross-cultural training: programs that provide information to help a person live and work successfully in a different culture (for example, teaching about cultural values, beliefs and practices, communication styles, business protocols, and daily living resources)

cross-training: teaching employees the skills and responsibilities of other positions in the company to increase their effectiveness and to provide greater staffing flexibility in the organization

cultural coaching: giving support and suggestions to help employees achieve greater success with different cultures

cultural intelligence: a person's ability to function in multicultural situations and to interact appropriately with people from different backgrounds

cultural novelty: the difference between a person's native culture and a new culture, and the degree of difficulty in adjusting to the new culture

culture: the values and beliefs that shape a specific group of people (for example, organizational culture, national culture, generational culture, and professional culture)

culture shock: the disorientation a person feels when experiencing an unfamiliar way of life due to immigration or a visit to a new country

danger premium: extra pay that employees receive for working in dangerous jobs or places (for example, environments that are hazardous or politically unstable)

dashboard: a means of simplifying complex data to provide users with a performance summary on a single page or screen

days to fill: the average number of days it takes to hire someone for open job positions

dedicated HR: a human resources position that works only on HR responsibilities within an organization

deductive reasoning: a method of reasoning that forms a conclusion from general information; the opposite of inductive reasoning, where a conclusion is formed from particular facts

deferred compensation plan: a pension program which allows an employee to contribute a portion of income over time to be paid as a lump sum at retirement when the employee's income tax rate will be lower

defined benefit plan: a retirement plan that tells participants exactly how much money they will receive on a specific later date (usually the day they retire). Also known as **defined contribution plan** or **defined retirement plan.**

Delphi technique: a method of forecasting where a group of experts provide individual opinions which are later shared in order to reach a more objective decision

demographics: statistics about groups of people that give information such as age, gender, income, and ethnic background

designated: something intended for a specific person or purpose

development: something that has happened, or the act of making or improving something

didactic: intending to teach or demonstrate

differential: change in value of one item compared to another (for example, a "cost-of-living differential" is the difference between the price of goods bought in the home country compared to the price of similar goods in the host country)

disability: a physical or mental condition that limits, but does not prevent, the performance of certain tasks (for example, a person who is blind or deaf)

dispute resolution: resolving conflict between people or groups (for example, lawsuits, arbitration, and mediation)

distance learning: a method of education that uses TV, audio or video tapes, computers, and the internet instead of traditional classroom teaching, where students are physically present with their teacher

distributed training: a method of training that allows instructors, students, and content to be located in different places. This type of training can be used together with a traditional classroom or it can be used to create virtual classrooms.

diversity: a combination of various people working together, often with differences in culture, race, generation, gender, or religion

divestiture: property which an organization sells or gives to another organization (for example, a company sells a business unit)

document retention: managing employee data and records as required by the organization or rule or law

domestic organization: an organization that does business and is based in the country where it is established, unlike a multinational organization, which does business in more than one country

downsizing: a decrease in a company's workforce to create efficiency and profitability

downward communication: information that is conveyed by upper management to lower-level employees in the organization

drive: to push or move forward a plan or project

due diligence: the gathering and analysis of important information related to a business acquisition or merger, such as assets and liabilities, contracts, and benefit plans

due process: in the U.S., how a government enforces laws to protect its citizens (for example, guaranteeing a person a fair trial)

EAP (employee assistance program): services and counseling that employees receive to help them solve problems that could affect their work productivity (for example, counseling for drug or alcohol problems or family issues)

economic valuation: giving monetary value to environmental factors (for example, the quality of air and water, which are not normally part of a financial valuation)

EEO: a U.S. law that guarantees equal treatment and respect for all employees

e-learning: a method of education where students attend classes on a computer or on the internet

eligible: to be qualified to participate in a program or apply for a job

employee benefits: payments or allowances that organizations give to their employees (for example, medical insurance, social security taxes, pension contributions, education reimbursement, and car or clothing allowances)

employee engagement: a measurement of employees' involvement, satisfaction, happiness, and loyalty with their employment (how hard they work and how long they stay with their organization)

employee handbook: a manual that contains information about an organization's policies, procedures, and benefits

employee relations: interaction between employees and an organization (for example, communications, conflict resolution, compliance with legal regulations, career development, and performance measurement)

employee retention: an organization's techniques to keep its employees

employee self-service: a trend in human resources management that allows employees to handle many job-related tasks (such as updates to their personnel data) using technology

employee turnover: the percentage of a company's employees that must be replaced at any time

Employee Value Proposition: the balance of benefits and rewards an employee receives in return for their performance on the job. In addition to compensation, intangible rewards may include development opportunities, challenging and meaningful work, or an attractive organizational culture.

employer branding: the image an organization presents to its employees, stakeholders, and customers

employer of choice: an organization that people want to work for because it attracts, motivates, and keeps good employees

employer-paid benefits: benefits that an organization gives its employees in addition to salary (for example, medical insurance, payments to retirement funds, allowances for cars or clothing)

employment at-will: an employment agreement in which an employee can quit, or can be fired, at any time and for any reason

employment branding: process of turning an organization into an "employer of choice"

empowerment: the ability for employees to manage their work, share information, and make decisions without close supervision

environmental responsibility: the management of products and processes that show concern for health, safety, and the environment

environmental scanning: acquiring and using information about the internal and external business environments that influence an organization's strategy (for example, determining how to respond to a talent shortage)

equity compensation: noncash payment reflecting an ownership interest in a company (for example, stock options and restricted stock)

equity partnership: an agreement for a person or organization to own part of a company by providing start-up funds to the business

ergonomic: designed to be comfortable and avoid injuries (for example, an ergonomic chair or keyboard)

ERP (Enterprise Resource Planning): computer software that combines information from all areas of an organization (such as finance, human resources, operations, and materials), and also manages contact with people outside the organization (such as customers, suppliers, and stakeholders)

ESOP (Employee Stock Ownership Plan): a tax-qualified benefit plan with defined contributions that allows employees to own shares in a company

essential functions: an employee's main responsibilities or tasks to succeed in a job

ethnocentric staffing orientation: filling important positions in an international organization by choosing new hires from the country where the organization has its headquarters

ethnocentrism: the belief that one's own culture is the center of everything and other cultures are less effective or less important

ethnorelativism: the ability to recognize different values and behaviors as cultural and not universal

exempt-level experience: a U.S. term which describes employees who work however many hours are necessary to perform the tasks of their position. They do not receive overtime pay, unlike hourly workers.

exit interview: an interview that HR has with an employee to get feedback about the job the employee held, the work environment, and the organization

expatriate: an employee who has been transferred from their country of citizenship ("home country") to live and work in another country ("host country")

expatriate assignment: a position in one country which is filled by a person from another country who moves there to live and work

external forces: things that occur outside of an organization that might affect its financial health, employees, products, services, or customers (for example, political, economic, or environmental challenges)

extraterritorial laws: laws from one country that apply to that country's citizens when they travel or live in countries where they might be exempt from some local laws. Similar exceptions can apply to companies operating abroad.

extraterritoriality: being exempt from the laws of the foreign country in which one is living (for example, foreign diplomats)

extrinsic rewards: work or actions where the motivating factors are material and are measured through monetary benefits, grades, prizes, and praise

face-to-face: interacting while in the presence of another person, as opposed to on the telephone, a webinar, or email

feasibility study: research and analysis to determine if a project will succeed

federal regulations: in the U.S., laws that apply in every state (as opposed to laws unique to every state)

fiduciary responsibility: a legal duty to act solely in the interest of another person without benefit, profit, or conflict of interest unless expressly permitted to do so by the other person

financial viability: the ability of an organization to achieve financial goals, growth, and stability, while also paying expenses and debt

flextime: a work schedule that allows changes in the beginning and end of the workday without reducing the number of hours worked per week

forced distribution: a performance measurement system which ranks employees against each other and according to predetermined categories such as excellent, good, or poor

forecasting: analyzing the probability of future outcomes to help lessen uncertainty

foreign compulsion exception: when a law of an organization's home country does not apply because it is in conflict with laws of the country where the organization is doing business

foreign direct investment: an overseas investment in structures, equipment, or property controlled by a foreign corporation

foreign service premiums: extra pay that an employee receives for accepting an international work assignment

foreign subsidiary: a company that is more than 50 percent owned or controlled by a parent organization in another country

formalization: the degree to which processes and procedures define job functions and organizational structure

forum shopping: the practice of trying to get a trial held in a location that is most likely to produce a favorable result (also known as **jurisdiction shopping**)

franchising: selling a license for the use of a trademark, product, or service in order to do business a certain way and receiving ongoing payment for the license

fringe benefits: payments that the employee receives, other than or in addition to a salary, such as health insurance

front-back structure: an organization that has two parts: one part that focuses on the customers and the market (the "front"), and one part that develops products and services (the "back")

full-time equivalent (FTE): a percentage comparing the number of hours that an organization's part-time employees work to the number of hours that full-time employees work

functional area: a department in which people have similar specialties or skills (for example, the accounting or IT department in an organization)

functional HR: the human resources role within an organization that focuses on strategy, recruitment, management, and the direction of the people in the organization

functional structure: a department or division where people have similar specialties or skills (for example, the accounting or IT department in an organization)

gap analysis: an analysis process which helps an organization compare its actual performance with its potential performance

generalization: a perception based on observations (for example, "Americans are usually friendly"); different from a stereotype (for example, "All Americans are friendly")

geocentric staffing orientation: the practice of choosing the best employees for a job, regardless of their nationality or where the job is located

geographic structure: an organizational model in which divisions, functions, or departments are organized by location in a specific country or region

global ethics policy: an outline of how a company expects employees to behave around the world, often intended to prevent bribery and corruption

global integration: working to promote an effective combination of different people, products, services, and systems throughout the world

global mindset: a perspective that helps people understand and function successfully in a range of cultures, markets, and organizations

global mobility: the transfer of employees from one part of the world to another

global organization: an organization that views the whole world as one market and does not divide it into separate markets by country

global staffing: the process of identifying the number and type of employees an organization needs worldwide, and searching for the best candidates

Global Sullivan Principles: a voluntary set of rules to help an organization advance human rights and equality

global talent acquisition: actions an organization takes to make sure it has employees with the right skills to accomplish its worldwide goals

global team: a group of employees who are working on the same project but who are located in different countries or come from different cultures

globalization: changes in society and the world as a result of economic trade and cultural exchange

glocalization: characteristic of a company that "thinks globally, but acts locally"; when a company has a strong presence both in its own country and around the world

going rate approach: a method for determining the salary of an employee on an international assignment; the salary is based on pay rates in the employee's home country

governance: system of rules and processes an organization creates in order to comply with local and international laws, accounting rules, ethical norms, and environmental and social codes of conduct

graphic rating scale: a method of giving employees a numerical rating for having certain traits (for example, being reliable or honest)

greenfield operation: start up of a new business plant or operation, usually in a new location

grievance: a cause of distress that can lead to an official complaint (for example, difficult work conditions)

grievance procedure (see also **complaint procedure**): the steps that employees must follow when they want to express their concerns about work-related issues to their employer

grossed-up income: a practice in which a company increases an expatriate's base pay in order to cover the additional taxes the expatriate owes because of extra benefits and overseas allowances

group consensus: a decision process in which a group of people agree to a decision or come to the same conclusion

halo effect: the transfer of the positive qualities of a person or thing to related people or things

hard skills: teachable skills that can be quantified such as typing, writing, reading, calculating math, or using a specific computer program

hardship premium: extra payment or benefits that an expatriate receives on assignment in a country where the living and working conditions are challenging

hardships: situations in a country that cause political or economic uncertainty that make it challenging for expatriates to live and work. Often, expatriates receive extra "hardship pay."

head count: the number of employees an organization has on its payroll

head hunter: an informal name for an employment recruiter, sometimes referred to as an executive search firm

head hunting: the practice of recruiting employees from one company to work at another company

healthcare benefits: company sponsored medical plans which help employees pay for the cost of doctor visits, hospitalization, surgery, and so on

hidden costs: expenses such as maintenance, supplies, training, upgrades, and other costs in addition to the purchase price

high-context culture: a culture that communicates indirectly, through the context of a situation more than through words, and that builds relationships slowly (for example, Japan)

high-performance work culture: an organizational culture where employees at all levels are inspired to do their best, thereby consistently producing outstanding results

high-potential or "hi-po": employees who have the capacity to grow into higher levels of leadership in the organization

HIPAA: Health Insurance Portability and Accountability Act (HIPAA) protects American workers in assuring the continuation of health insurance coverage and protects their medical privacy

histogram: a bar graph that shows the upper and lower limits in a set of data

home-country compensation: expatriate salary that stays the same while the employee is on assignment (for example, if an employee is relocated from Tokyo to London, he or she continues to receive the Tokyo salary along with expatriate benefits)

homogeneous: description of a group whose members are all the same or similar (for example, people from the same background and heritage); opposite of heterogeneous

host-country nationals: employees or other people who are citizens of the country where a person is working on an expatriate assignment (also known as **local nationals**)

hostile environment harassment: a situation in which an employee's co-workers create an uncomfortable work environment, often through inappropriate sexual behavior or discrimination

HR: function within an organization that focuses on implementing organizational strategy, as well as recruitment, management, and providing direction for the people who work in the organization

HR audit: an evaluation of the strengths, weaknesses, and development needs of human resources required for organizational performance

HR business partner: a role in which human resources works closely with an organization to develop strategies and achieve business results

HR partner: a manager or department that has a relationship with HR in order to provide services to the organization

HRD: the part of human resource management that deals with training employees and giving them the skills they need to do their jobs both now and in the future

HRIS: technology that supports human resources functions

human capital: employees' knowledge, talents, and skills that add to the value of the organization

human capital management (HCM): the practices and processes for managing employees who are considered to be an asset to the organization

human capital strategy: methods and tools for recruiting, managing, and keeping important employees

hybrid structure: an organizational model that combines different operational, functional, product, and geographic structures

ILO: a department of the United Nations that deals with human and labor rights

ILO conventions: international standards for employers and employees that become international law when a certain number of governments have adopted them

in-basket exercise: a test used to hire or promote employees to management positions. The test measures the candidate's ability to prioritize and respond to daily tasks.

incentive: a monetary or nonmonetary reward to motivate an employee (for example, a bonus or extra time off)

indemnity: compensation paid for injuries, damages, or unfulfilled obligations

independent contractors: workers who contract to do specific work for other people or organizations and are not considered employees

indirect compensation: nonmonetary rewards or benefits for employees such as annual leave, health insurance, company car, or mobile phone

individualism: cultural belief that the individual is the most important part of society; one of Hofstede's cultural dimensions, opposite of collectivism

inducement: a benefit that management offers to employees as motivation for producing specific results

industrial relations: the relationship between the management of an industrial enterprise and its employees, as guided by specific laws and regulations

ineligible: not suitable to participate in a program or apply for a job

informants: people who provide business, social, or cultural data to others

initiatives: actions related to new ideas or to starting new plans

inpatriate: a foreign employee who is on a work assignment in the country where an organization's headquarters are located

insourcing: assigning a job to an internal department instead of to an outside organization; opposite of outsourcing

instant awards: rewards for employees that are provided immediately after the desired behavior is produced

integrate: to combine or bring together different parts

intellectual property: an original invention or something created by the mind, which is usually protected by patents, trademarks, or copyrights

intercultural: involving or representing different cultures (for example, intercultural communication, intercultural competency, or intercultural marriage)

internal equity: making sure that employees with jobs of similar value to the organization receive equal compensation

internal forces: key people and influences inside an organization that shape its future (the opposite of external forces, such as the economy and competitors)

internal rate of return: a calculation of the average return each year during the life of an investment

internal recruitment: seeking current employees within the organization to apply for upcoming job openings

international assignee: a person who moves to a new country to work on an international assignment

international organization: a company that has operations and services in different parts of the world

interpersonal skills: effective social qualities for communicating and building good relationships with different people

interpretation: an explanation of the meaning of something; translating spoken language

interpreter: someone who translates spoken language by speaking or signing

intranet: a restricted computer network which only allows authorized people to access the site (for example, a company intranet that only allows its employees access to its data)

intrinsic reward: non-material motivation which comes from personal satisfaction (for example, job status, job satisfaction, or human interest)

investments: money and capital which are spent in order to make more money (examples: stocks, bonds, real estate)

job analysis: a study of the major tasks and responsibilities of jobs to determine their importance and relation to other jobs in a company

job bidding: a process whereby applicants compete with each other for a position

job classification: an arrangement of different types of employment or grades within an organization according to skills, experience, or training

job competencies: the skills and behaviors that will help an employee succeed in a specific job

job description: written document describing an employee's work activities

job enlargement: increasing the scope of a job by extending duties and responsibilities, generally without changing pay or status

job enrichment: a way to motivate employees by giving them greater responsibilities and more variety in their work

job evaluation: the process of measuring how much a job is worth (for example, in order to set the salary and other benefits)

job family: groups of occupations based upon the type of work performed, skills, education, training, and credentials

job grade: a means of determining different job levels and pay scales based upon the required knowledge, skills, and abilities

job hazard analysis: an assessment of potential causes and consequences of risks in a particular organization or its environment

job matching: the use of objective skill assessment data combined with common sense to determine the best fit for an employee to a specific job

job opening: a position that has not been filled in an organization

job posting: a notice for a vacant position that an organization publicizes internally or externally

job preview: a strategy for introducing job candidates to the realities of the position, both good and bad, prior to making a hiring decision

job ranking: a job evaluation method that compares jobs to each other based on their importance to the organization

job requisition: a procedure used when a company wants to hire a new employee to fill a position

job rotation: a way to develop employees by giving them different jobs to perform

job shadowing: learning a new job by watching another employee work

job sharing: an employment option where two or more employees share the responsibilities of one full-time position

job specification: a description of employee qualifications required to perform a specific job

job-content-based job evaluation: a way of estimating how much a person should be paid based on what they do

joint venture: when two or more organizations work together and share risks and rewards (also called "JV")

jurisdiction: the right and power to interpret and apply the law, often within a certain geographical region

key talent: employees that perform extremely good work and are highly valued by the organization

kidnap and ransom insurance: policies that reimburse employees' losses due to kidnapping or extortion in high-risk areas of the world

knowledge management: the process of gathering, documenting, and sharing important information to improve the performance of employees and the organization

KPI: a measure an organization uses to see its progress and show what it needs to improve

labor union: a group of employees with the same job who join together to ask their employers for things such as better wages, benefits, or working conditions

lag the market: a compensation strategy that is lower than the average pay rate

lagging indicators: signs that confirm the economy has already changed (for example, the unemployment rate)

laissez-faire: an economic theory that is strongly against any government interference in business affairs

lateral move: when an employee decides to change positions in the organization without a difference in the level of responsibilities and compensation

layoff: temporary suspension or termination of an employee or groups of employees because of business reasons

lead the market: a compensation strategy that is higher than the average pay rate

leadership: the ability to influence other people or groups to achieve a goal

leadership development: investment in programs to help current leaders become more effective and to build future leaders

leadership pipeline: the people in a company who will be developed to move into higher levels of leadership over time

leading indicators: signs that show the economy will change before it does (for example, a rise or fall in interest rates)

learning curve: the time it takes for a person to acquire new information and skills and to perform successfully

learning effectiveness model: measuring the impact of employee training and development programs on business goals

learning management system (LMS): computer software that administers, tracks, and reports on employee development opportunities such as classroom and online events, e-learning programs, and training content

learning organization: an organization that encourages employee development, innovation, and continuous learning in order to remain competitive in the business environment

learning pace: the time it takes for a person to understand and retain information

learning portal: internet site where employees can use educational resources

learning style: the way people process new information and learn most effectively. For example, some people learn best visually, through lectures, or by reading; others learn best by action or doing.

lease: an agreement for a person or organization to rent a property (leasee) from its owner (leasor) for a specific period of time and amount of money

leave of absence (LOA): a period of time that an employee is given to be on leave, away from work; it can be either paid or unpaid and either short- or long-term in duration

leniency error: rating employees higher than their actual performance deserves

leverage: the act of applying a small investment to bring a high level of return

liaison: a communication link between people or groups

licensing: a written contract in which the owner of a trademark or intellectual property gives rights to a licensee to use, produce, or sell a product or service

line management: work groups that conduct the major business of an organization, such as manufacturing or sales

loan: money or goods that a person or organization lends temporarily, usually charging interest

localization compensation strategy: salary for an international assignee that is the same as the salary that a local employee receives for a similar job

long-term assignment: a job in a different culture that lasts longer than six months, usually three to five years

low-context culture: a culture that communicates directly, using words more than situations, and that builds relationships quickly (for example, the United States)

lump-sum compensation: an extra amount of money paid one time rather than on a regular basis. For example, an expatriate may receive a lump-sum payment to cover the extra costs of the assignment related to housing, taxes, dependent education, and transportation.

management contract: an arrangement in which a person or company operates a project or business in return for a fee

mandatory benefits: laws which outline benefits to provide economic security for employees and their dependents

manpower: the total number of individuals who make up the workforce of an organization

market index: the total value of stocks or other investments and showing the current worth against a base value from a specific date

market salary survey: review of median pay for specific positions in the same labor market

market-based job evaluation: an evaluation that compares the salaries for particular jobs offered on the external job market

marketplace: a physical or virtual place in which business operates (for example, the global marketplace, or the online marketplace)

masculinity: term used in cultural studies to represent work-oriented societies; one of Hofstede's Cultural Dimensions; the opposite of femininity

Maslow's hierarchy: a method of ranking human needs in a pyramid, with basic physical needs (such as obtaining food and shelter) at the bottom, and psychological needs (such as creative expression) at the top

mastery: great ability and knowledge of some subject or activity

matrix structure: a system of managing staff where employees have more than one reporting relationship. For example, they could report to a direct supervisor as well as a team leader.

mean: an average determined by adding up a group of numbers, and then dividing that total by the number of numbers. For example, here's how to calculate the mean of "10, 20, 30, 40, 50": First, add the numbers (10 + 20 + 30 + 40 + 50 = 150); then count the numbers (5); and then divide the total by the number of numbers (150/5 = 30).

median: the middle number in a series. For example, in the series "13, 13, 13, 13, 14, 14, 16, 18, 21", the median is 14, with four numbers to the left and four numbers to the right.

mediation: an attempt to help other people or groups come to an agreement

mentee: a less experienced employee who is being supported or guided by a more experienced employee

mentoring: when an experienced person shares knowledge with someone who has less experience

merger: two or more organizations that come together through a purchase, acquisition, or sharing of resources. Usually the new organization saves money by eliminating duplicate jobs.

merger & acquisition (M&A): the process of legally combining two organizations. They may join together and unite their assets (merger), or one may purchase the other (acquisition).

merit increase: an increase in wages for meeting or exceeding the performance goals of a job

metrics: a set of measurements that quantify results: for example, performance measures, return on investment (ROI), or turnover rates

minimum wage: the lowest hourly, daily or monthly salary that employers must legally pay to employees or workers

mission statement: a short description of the main purpose of an organization, which does not change (unlike strategy and business practices, which can change frequently)

mobility: an HR term that refers to employees and their families who move from one location to another

mobility premium: extra salary paid to expatriates to encourage them to move to a new country (also known as **overseas premium**)

mode: the value that occurs most often in a series of number. In the following series of numbers, 8 is the mode: 6, 5, 8, 3, 7, 8, 9, 8, 4.

module: one section of a training program which is presented alone or as part of a series of other units

moonlighting: to have a second job in addition to full-time employment

moral absolutes: the idea that there is a clear definition of what is right and wrong

motivation: reasons or influences that lead to specific desired behavior such as commitment to a job or continuing efforts to achieve a goal

multicultural: employees of diverse cultures and backgrounds who are part of an organization's workforce

multinational organization: a company that has its headquarters in one country and has offices and operations in other countries; also known as a multinational corporation (MNC)

multinational pooling: combining different employee benefit programs in a multinational organization to save money and control risks

needs analysis: assessing the present situation to determine the steps necessary to reach a desired future goal

nepotism: a practice where people of influence appoint their relatives or friends to positions in a business, even though they may be less qualified than other candidates

network: a group of people who connect with one another; a computer system that allows people to access shared resources and data

NGO: any nonprofit, voluntary, and independent organization that is not connected with any government, and that usually works to improve social or environmental conditions

non-compete agreement: a legal document which prevents an employee from starting a competing business or disclosing trade secrets for a specific period of time

norms: a standard model or pattern which is considered typical

offshoring: transferring service or manufacturing operations to a foreign country where there is a supply of skilled, less costly labor

onboarding: the process of helping new employees learn the organization's policies, procedures, and culture in addition to their job responsibilities

one-on-one: person-to-person communication, such as a conversation between two employees

on-the-job experience: the skills and knowledge a person learns from day-to-day work experience

on-the-job training: acquiring knowledge, practical skills, and competencies while engaged in daily work

open sourcing: made available for others to use or modify

organization chart: a graphic representation of how authority and responsibility is distributed within a company; includes all work processes of the company

organizational development: planned process that uses the principles of behavioral science to improve the way an organization functions

organizational structure: the way that employees and processes are grouped into departments or functions in an organization, along with a description of reporting relationships

outplacement: services that help an employee find a new job (for example, writing résumés, networking skills, and counseling)

outsourcing: transferring certain business functions outside of the organization so that the organization can focus on core activities (examples of outsourced functions include data processing, telemarketing, and manufacturing)

outstanding: money that a person or organization has borrowed but not yet paid back

overhead: direct costs associated with operating a business, such as rent, salaries, benefits, equipment, technology, and so on

overtime: extra time worked beyond the normal hours of employment or the payment for extra time worked

ownership interest: owning part of a company or business

parent-country nationals: people who live and work abroad but are citizens of the country where an organization's headquarters is located

pareto chart: a vertical bar graph in which values are plotted in decreasing order of frequency, from left to right; often used in quality control

parochialism: a view of the world that does not consider other ways of living and working

passing score: the number of correct answers required to pass a test

pay for performance: a payment strategy where management links an employee's pay to desired results, behaviors, or goals

peers: people who are similar to one another in age, background, profession, or status

per diem: the amount of money a person receives for working for one day, or the amount an organization allows an employee to spend on expenses each day (for example, meals and hotels on a business trip)

performance appraisals: a method of measuring how effective employees are

performance management: the process of setting goals, measuring progress, and rewarding or correcting performance for employees

performance management system: the process of helping people perform to the best of their abilities, which begins by defining a job, and ends when an employee leaves the organization

performance review: a documented discussion about an employee's development and performance that involves managers, HR, and the employee

performance standards: the behaviors and results that management expects employees to achieve on the job

performance-based pay: pay linked to how well the employee meets expectations; better performance results in more pay

permanent assignment: an employee's regular or usual job or position in a company

perquisites (perks): special nonmonetary privileges (such as a car or club membership) that come with senior job positions; also called executive perks or fringe benefits

PEST analysis: political, economical, socio-political and technological (PEST) data that is gathered and reviewed by organizations for planning purposes. Other versions of this acronym add the terms *environmental* and *legal,* making the acronym PESTLE.

phantom stock arrangement: a technique in which a company gives its employees the benefits that come with owning stock, including "dividends," but does not actually give them stock in the company

piece rate: a wage system in which the employee is paid for each unit of production at a fixed rate

placement: finding suitable jobs for applicants

planned absence: missing work after asking permission in advance, such as for vacation or a medical appointment

plateaued careers: inability of employees to advance further in the company due to mediocre performance or lack of opportunities

policy: a method to help guide and make decisions

political unrest: unrest, agitation, or turmoil about a government's actions or beliefs

polycentric staffing orientation: recruiting host-country nationals to manage subsidiaries in their own country, and recruiting parent-country nationals to fill management positions at headquarters

power distance: a term Geert Hofstede uses in his cultural theory to describe hierarchical relationships between people in a culture. For example, high power distance means there are strong hierarchical relationships. Low power distance means greater equality and accessibility among the population.

predictive validity: the extent to which a score on a scale or test predicts future behavior

premiums: payments employees receive for meeting goals by a certain time; also, payments for insurance

prescreen: to examine or interview before further selection processes occur in order to determine the best potential candidates

prevailing wage: the hourly wage, usual benefits, and overtime that most workers receive in a certain location

primacy errors: incorrect conclusions where the first impression of someone or something continues despite contradictory evidence

process-flow analysis: a diagram used to assess business processes; sometimes called "process mapping"

proctor: a person who monitors another person or activity (for example, someone who supervises an exam)

product structure: a method of organizing a company in which the departments are grouped by product

progress review: formal or informal evaluation of an employee's progress toward goals and recommendations for improvements and development

progressive discipline: a series of corrective actions aimed at an employee to resolve a problem or improve performance

project management: a methodical approach to planning and guiding project processes from start to finish

promotion: advancement of an employee's rank, usually with greater responsibility and more money

proprietary: rights of property ownership relating to key information, materials, or methods developed by an organization

psychological contract: an unwritten agreement of the mutual beliefs, perceptions, and informal obligations between an employer and an employee, which influence how they interact

purchase: buy or acquire something through payment or barter

quantification: giving a number to a measurement of something

raise: an increase in salary that an employee receives, often for good performance

range: the amount covered, or the amount of difference (for example, a "salary range" is the difference between the lowest and highest amount paid for a particular job)

range penetration: an employee's pay compared to the total pay range for the same job function

ranked performance: rating employees from best to worst against each other according to a standard measurement system

ransom: a demand for money or other goods in exchange for releasing a person or property

reasonable accommodation: changing the process of applying for a job or the work environment for a qualified person with a disability

recency errors: incorrect conclusions due to recent actions that are weighed more heavily than overall performance

record retention schedule: a listing of key documents and the length of time that each is required by law to be stored or disposed of by the organization

recruitment: process of attracting, screening, and hiring qualified people for a job

red flag: an indicator of a problem, or something that calls for attention

redeployment: a change in an employee's location or task, often to reduce layoffs or to make the best use of employees

reduce turnover: to retain employees and lower the number of vacancies in a company

reduction in force (RIF): loss of employment positions due to lack of funding or change in work requirements

redundancies: elimination or reduction of jobs because of downsizing or outsourcing

re-entry shock: the transition challenges that a person experiences when returning to his or her home country after living in another culture

reference check: contact with a job applicant's past employers, or other references, to verify the applicant's job history, performance, and educational qualifications

referral program: recruitment method that rewards employees for recommending candidates

regiocentric staffing orientation: focus on recruitment and hiring of employees within a particular region with opportunities for inter-regional transfers

reimbursements: payments made for money already spent (for example, a company pays an employee for the cost of travel or supplies after the employee has spent his or her own money)

reliability: having the same results after many tests

relocation: transferring employees to another location for work

relocation services: help given to relocating employees (for example, pre-departure orientation, home-finding, tax and legal advice, and in-country assistance)

remuneration: money paid for work, including wages, commissions, bonuses, overtime pay, and pay for holidays, vacations, and sickness

remuneration surveys: surveys that gather information on what other companies pay employees and what kind of benefits they provide

repatriate: to return home from an international work assignment

repatriation: the return of an employee to the home country after living in another country (for example, an expatriate going home from an international assignment)

replacement planning: using past performance to identify employees who can fill future vacancies (unlike succession planning, which focuses on future potential)

reprimand: fair warning given to an employee who violates an organization's rules and may result in dismissal

responsibility: a task that is part of an employee's job description

restricted stock: stock with rules about when it can be sold (restricted stock is usually issued as part of a salary package, and has a time limit on when it can be fully transferred)

retention: methods of motivating employees to stay with the organization and making sure employees are satisfied and rewarded

return on investment (ROI): performance measure used to evaluate the financial outcome of an investment

reverse culture shock: the often-unanticipated disorientation resulting from "re-entry" back into one's home culture after an expatriate assignment

risk management: the process of analyzing potential threats and deciding how to prevent them

role behavior: how a person acts as appropriate to a particular job function or position

role play: to perform an action or attitude in a simulation in order to understand a different viewpoint

rule of law: all citizens are subject to the laws of their country, no individual is above the law, and everyone must obey it

sabbatical leave: a benefit provided by some organizations that allows eligible employees paid time off during a specific time period for study, rest, or travel

salary midpoint: the amount of money between the highest and lowest amount paid for a particular job

salary range: the lowest and highest wages paid to employees who work in the same or similar jobs

Sarbanes-Oxley Act: a broad range of legal regulations that strengthen corporate accounting controls in the United States

scaled score: a conversion of a raw score to a common scale that can be used for comparison

scatter diagram: a graph with a vertical and horizontal axis with dots at each data point; also called a "scatter plot" or "dot chart"

scored questions: the total number of right and wrong questions on an exam (for example, pre-test questions do not count)

screening tool: an instrument used in employee selection to help assess job suitability (for example, in-basket exercises, psychometric tests, and cultural adaptability inventories)

selection: method for choosing the best candidate for a job

self-assessment: evaluation of one's own performance, abilities, and developmental needs

separation rate: the ratio of the number of employees who leave their jobs to the total number of employees in the organization

service level agreement (SLA): a legal document that describes the specific work that a service provider will deliver to the organization for an agreed amount of money

severance: an additional payment (other than salary) given to an employee when employment termination occurs

sexual harassment: unwelcome verbal, visual, or physical conduct of a sexual nature that is offensive or inappropriate

shared services: an operational approach where each country or unit uses administrative services from a central source rather than repeating these services in different locations (examples of services include finance, purchasing, inventory, payroll, hiring, and information technology)

Sharia: the code of law from the Koran that regulates both civil and criminal justice as well as individual behaviors and morals

short-term: occurring over a brief time (for example, a short-term loan or a short-term assignment)

short-term assignment: a work assignment outside the home country that is usually less than six months long

sick leave: a specified number of days for paid time off due to illness, which is a required employment benefit in many countries

situational interview: a method of assessing a job candidate's skills by asking them how they would respond to specific work-related issues and problems

six sigma: a strategy to improve current business processes by continuously reviewing and revising them

skills inventory: a listing of the capabilities, experience, and goals of current employees as a tool for meeting the organization's human resource goals and objectives

S.M.A.R.T. goal setting: applying Specific, Measurable, Achievable, Relevant, and Time-based goals to help a company achieve business success

social media: technology that lets people communicate over the internet to share information and resources (for examples, Twitter, Facebook, LinkedIn, and podcasts)

social network: a group of people who interact because they have a common interest. The group communicates either in-person or using technology (for example, Facebook or Twitter).

social responsibility: an organization's voluntary obligation toward the good of the environment in which it operates

sourcing: identifying candidates who are qualified to do a job by using proactive recruiting techniques

span of control: the number of employees who report to one manager in an organization. The more people that a manager supervises, the wider the span of control.

split payroll: a method of paying expatriates that gives part of their salary in the currency of the home country and part of their salary in the currency of the host country

staff units: work groups that support the major business of an organization with activities such as accounting, customer service, maintenance, and personnel

staffing: the act of selecting, hiring, and training people for specific jobs, as well as reducing the workforce when needed

staffing system: the processes and technology used to create human resource efficiencies for employee management

stakeholder: a person, group, or organization that has a direct or indirect interest in the organization (for example, owners, investors, employees, suppliers, unions, or the community)

start-up: a company or business that recently began operating and is in an early phase of development

statutory benefit: employee benefits mandated by federal or local laws, such as social insurance and unemployment insurance

stay interview: a retention strategy that helps organizations understand why their employees remain with the organization and how they can motivate them to continue their employment

stereotype: an oversimplified opinion, image, or attitude that people from a particular group are all the same

stock option: a benefit which gives employees the right to buy or sell stock in their company at a certain price for a specific period of time

strategic alliance: an arrangement between two organizations to pursue common goals and share resources. Unlike a joint venture, the organizations do not form a new legal entity.

strategic partnership: a mutually beneficial relationship based upon the common goals of people or organizations

strategic planning: the process of defining a company's direction for the future in four stages: analysis, development, implementation, and evaluation

strategy: a plan of action that starts with examining the current state of an organization and then deciding how to achieve the best state for the organization's future

stretch objectives: setting personal or business targets that require extra effort to achieve

structured interview: interview approach whereby each interviewer asks a candidate exactly the same questions in exactly the same order

subsidiary: a company whose voting stock is more than 50 percent owned by another company. The company with the majority interest is called the "parent company."

substance abuse: use of habit-forming drugs or substances which impair behavior

succession planning: identifying and developing high-potential employees for the organization's future success

supervisor: someone who oversees employees in a department or business unit to assign tasks and make sure work is completed

supply chain management (SCM): process of planning, implementing, and controlling operations, which begins with acquiring raw materials and continues to customer delivery and support

sustainability: the capacity to stay, hold, or maintain something, such as a concept, economy, geography, environment, and so on

SWOT analysis: a strategic planning technique used to assess the internal and external environment in which a company operates, its strengths and weaknesses (internal), and opportunities and threats (external)

synchronous learning: type of e-learning in which participants interact without a time delay, which requires them to attend at specific times

talent management: the process of recruiting, integrating, and developing new workers, developing and keeping current workers, and attracting skilled workers

talent pool: a group of available skilled workers, or database of résumés, that a company can use to recruit in a particular location

targeted selection: an assessment of job-related behavior from the candidate's previous employment to predict future performance

tax bill: a document which lists the tax money owed to a government or legal body

tax equalization: a policy that makes sure that expatriates' combined home and host taxes are no more than they would have been paid if they had remained in their home country. The expatriate's company pays for any additional taxes (also known as **tax protection**).

telecommuting: a flexible work arrangement which allows part- or full-time employees to work at home via a computer

tenure: holding a permanent job or position without the need for periodic contract renewals

territorial rule: a rule that employees must follow the tax laws of the country where they are working

testing vendor: an organization that provides locations for people to take exams on certain dates

third-country national (TCN): an expatriate who works for a foreign company that is located in the host country (for example, a French person working in China for a German company)

third party: a person or group in addition to those who are directly involved, such as a company that supplies outsourced services to an organization

time-to-fill: the average number of days that a certain job position remains open

total compensation: an employee's complete pay package, including cash, benefits, and services

total quality management (TQM): a method for improving the organization by continuously changing its practices, structures, and systems

total rewards: financial and nonfinancial benefits that the employee sees as valuable

totalization agreement: an agreement between countries that says an expatriate only needs to pay social taxes to the country in which he or she is working

trainee: a person who is learning and practicing the necessary skills for a particular job

training method: a way of communicating skills and knowledge (for example, classroom training, distance learning, online training, and on-the-job-training)

transfer of learning: the continuous exchange of information, knowledge, and skills from one context to another

translation: changing a message from one language to another while keeping the meaning

transnational corporation (TNC): an organization whose operations, production, or service processes take place in more than one country and are interconnected

trend analysis: gathering information from the past to identify patterns which will help predict future outcomes

tuition reimbursement: a benefit whereby the employer provides full or partial payment for educational courses completed by employees

turnkey operation: business that includes everything needed to start operating in a certain location

uncertainty avoidance: one of Geert Hofstede's cultural dimensions which describes the degree to which cultures accept ambiguity and risk. For example, in cultures with high uncertainty avoidance, people prefer clear, formal rules. In cultures with low uncertainty avoidance, people are comfortable with flexible rules.

up-front: paid in advance, or invested as beginning capital

user interface: software that allows a human and a computer to share information

validate: to formalize an agreement; in testing, to confirm the accuracy

validity: the extent to which something is accurate (for example, the extent to which an exam actually measures what it claims to measure)

value added: products or services that are worth more because they have been improved or had something added to them

value chain: model of how businesses receive raw materials, add value to the raw materials, and sell finished products to customers

value proposition: the unique benefits, costs, and value that a business delivers to its customers

values: the lasting beliefs of members of a culture about what is good or desirable and what is not

variable pay plan: profit-sharing, incentives, bonuses, or commissions that align compensation with performance

vendor/supplier: a person or company that sells services and/or products, such as a recruiting firm, financial consultant, or relocation company

vicarious liability: a legal doctrine that makes a person liable for the negligence or crimes of another person

virtual team: a group of people who work in different times, locations, or organizations, who communicate using technology

vision statement: a written statement which clarifies what the organization wants to be in the future

voluntary benefits: extra benefits or discounted services offered to employees with little extra cost to the employer (for example, additional life insurance, gym memberships, and concierge services)

wage band: The lowest and highest wages paid to employees who work in the same or similar jobs

webinar: an interactive seminar on the internet (usually a live presentation)

weighting pattern: term used in statistics to show the frequency of different choices

well-being: a positive lifestyle which includes good health, enjoyable recreation and leisure time, and social belonging

wellness program: services to improve and maintain the health of employees

work unit: a business function that produces one product or focuses on a single area

workers' compensation claim: a document that an employee files asking for wage replacement for missed work and medical benefits due to injuries suffered on the job

workforce: the people working for a single company, industry, or a geographic region

workforce analytics: metrics used to determine the effectiveness of HR functions, such as turnover rates, organizational culture, and succession planning

workforce planning: identifying and analyzing what an organization needs to achieve its goals, in terms of the size, type, and quality of its employees

workforce rotation: the regular movement of employees from one function, time, or place to another, as needed

work-life balance: the ability to effectively manage time at work with the time spent on leisure or with family members

work-life balance programs: services to support the well-being of employees and to help them balance their jobs, families, and personal lives

workplace: a place, such as an office or factory, where people work

works councils: organizations that function like trade unions and represent the rights of workers. Works councils are most common in Europe and the United Kingdom.

zero-based budgeting: a budgeting process that requires that every budget item is approved instead of only budget changes being approved. No reference is made to previous budget expenditures.

3

The Ins and Outs
of the PHR Exam

IN THIS PART . . .

Review HRCI's exam functional areas and exam knowledge objectives, which are the most credible sources of what may be on your exam.

Discover ways to use the internet to expand your resources and knowledge so you can go beyond a textbook (and this book) for success.

Become knowledgeable about common HR reports and tools that are used in day-to-day operations. These exams are experienced based, so get ready by learning how to interpret and apply these fundamental reports and formulas.

Focus on exam-specific topics that are likely to show up on your test based on the exam objectives, knowledge components, and reports of other exam takers.

Practice your test-taking skills on a few example questions while studying critical HR topics.

Familiarize yourself with the language and acronyms of both business management and human resources so you can successfully interpret the exam questions.

Chapter 7

The Key to Success: PHR 01 Business Management

The business management functional area of the PHR exam is weighted at 20 percent. This means you can expect to see a fair number of questions related to this content area, along with a greater emphasis on getting the questions correct on exam day. HRCI defines this functional area as follows:

"Using information about the organization and business environment to reinforce expectations, influence decision-making and avoid risk."

This chapter helps you prepare for the PHR questions so that when you encounter them on the exams, you are ready!

Eyeing the Exam Objectives

Prior to the 2018 updates, this section was headed "Business Management and Strategy." It would appear that during HRCI's practice analysis study — which included gathering feedback from the active practitioners of HR — there was a consensus that PHR candidates need to understand *business* as opposed to *strategy*. These changes are reflected in the updated exam responsibilities and knowledge.

Responsibilities

Here is the list of Business Management responsibilities from HRCI that you will be tested on:

01 Interpret and apply information related to general business environment and industry best practices.

02 Reinforce the organization's core values and ethical and behavioral expectations through modeling, communication, and coaching.

03 Understand the role of cross-functional stakeholders in the organization and establish relationships to influence decision-making.

04 Recommend and implement best practices to mitigate risk (for example: lawsuits, internal/external threats).

05 Determine the significance of data for recommending organizational strategies (for example: attrition rates, diversity in hiring, time to hire, time-to-fill, ROI, success of training).

Knowledge

In addition to the major responsibilities listed above, there are also specific knowledge components that HRCI asks you to prepare for. In the functional area of Business Management this includes the following:

01 Vision, mission, values, and structure of the organization

02 Legislative and regulatory knowledge and procedures

03 Corporate governance procedures and compliance

04 Employee communications

05 Ethical and professional standards

06 Business elements of an organization (for example: other functions and departments, products, competition, customers, technology, demographics, culture, processes, safety, and security)

07 Existing HRIS, reporting tools, and other systems for effective data reporting and analysis

08 Change management theory, methods, and application

09 Risk management

10 Qualitative and quantitative methods and tools for analytics

11 Dealing with situations that are uncertain, unclear, or chaotic

Focusing on What You Need to Know about Business Management

Business Management is the functional area of the exam that focuses specifically on the need for human resources to be strategic business partners. It requires a thorough understanding of the relationships between human resources and the stakeholders. These stakeholders may include

>> Executive management

>> Employees and their families

>> Suppliers and vendors

>> Investors

>> Community

For purposes of Business Management, the stakeholders are anyone within or outside of the organization that has an interest in the future of the company. Meeting the needs of these stakeholders requires first a thorough understanding of the environment under which businesses perform.

The playing field

Business gets done at multiple levels, including local, regional, state, national, and global. Several forces influence an organization's ability to compete, and a useful way to remember them for the PHR is the acronym PESTLE:

>> **Political:** The political environment is perhaps the most significant driver of how rapidly the practice of human resources changes. Depending on the platform of the party in charge (Democrat or Republican in the United State's two-party system), HR will be tasked with interpreting intent and establishing priorities for the business.

>> **Economic:** The labor force is considered a pillar of economic health. This is most often communicated using the monthly unemployment numbers. A high unemployment rate at a local, state, or national level means that there are many people out of work. A low unemployment rate means the supply of qualified people is low. This, of course, drives business recruiting and compensation strategies.

>> **Social:** The 1960s are a classic example of how the social environment can drive workplace initiatives. The national feeling at the time was built on premises of freedom — not only freedom to act but also freedom from negative acts such as discrimination against women. The labor laws of the time period give a strong indication of how social changes can shape workplace behaviors. We are living in another time of active social changes, and the workplace landscape will have to evolve in response.

>> **Technological:** If it is true that technological capabilities double every two or so years, it is no surprise that the forces of technology serve as business disruptors. Not only can technology increase capacity, but it also creates pitfalls to avoid (such as privacy and denial of concerted activity).

>> **Legal:** An upcoming section on labor law describes the environment in which businesses must act. But it is not only the laws that apply to people management that influence organizational behaviors. There is also a need to understand the various regulations governing independent industries, such as the financial or food sectors of the United States.

>> **Environmental:** Closely tied to social forces, a renewed interest in environmental responsibility exists today. This means that employers must take heed of the impact of their operations on the environment, and take steps to minimize damage and improve sustainability.

If only we had a crystal ball, we could predict what changes the preceding PESTLE forces may have in store for us. We can, however, use our critical-thinking skills to at least anticipate what may be in the pipeline. Consider the impact of the COVID-19 pandemic of 2019 and 2020. We can anticipate an emergence of new Occupational Safety and Health regulations related to the flu season, such as requiring physical distancing at work or auditing disinfecting practices. Also from the headlines of 2020 came the horror of George Floyd's death, prompting protests. From this we may anticipate the need for a renewed allocation of our resources toward our diversity and inclusiveness practices. The debate over immigration reform rages on in politics, from which we may agree that we should look at our own workforces and make changes where appropriate. These are just a few examples. Can you think of other changes that may be coming based on any one of the preceding forces?

REMEMBER

PESTLE is often shortened to PEST; it is simply an abbreviated version of the tool. The letters have the same meaning in both versions.

Human resources is not only a function of business but also a champion of business, which requires professionals to have a solid understanding of basic business principles and a working knowledge of other departments within the company. Not only are you tasked with managing your own department, but you're also responsible for helping other department managers do the same. Think about what you know about finance or ponder the productivity standards of your workforce. As this chapter discusses, you must have enough working knowledge of these other business functions to add value and support your company's outcomes. These outcomes are a major part of the development of a business strategy, so we look at this next.

Working with other business functions

For purposes of the exam, knowing information related to the operational functions of business is important. These functions include a general understanding of finance, accounting, production, sales and marketing, customer service, purchasing, and information technology (IT).

Finance and accounting

Some people commonly misperceive accounting and finance as one and the same. Unfortunate for the amount of studying that you have to do, that's simply not true. The *finance* function of business management deals with making data-driven decisions using financial information and formulating strategies. It may also include establishing banking relationships to meet both current and future needs. The *accounting* function is more operational in nature, dealing primarily with accounts receivable and accounts payable. HR supports the accounting function through the development of key metrics, including budgets to execute workforce planning or human capital management plans.

Production

Production deals with producing the widgets from which a company generates revenue. It can be either products or services. Production is often considered the most important function of business because it remains firmly rooted at the heart of the company's core competency.

Because production (or services) is often a core competency, the PHR exam requires working knowledge of how HR can support productivity and the ancillary needs, such as quality, performance management, employee relations, and risk management.

Sales and marketing

Similar to finance and accounting, sales and marketing are separate yet related business functions. *Marketing* deals with issues such as determining what products or services to introduce to the market, branding the products and the company, and providing the collateral necessary to get the message into the marketplace. In turn, the *sales* department is responsible to sell the items that production is producing and marketing is offering. Symbiotic, as it were — it's all related.

Sales and marketing are conduits to profit. Therefore, expect to see questions related to the recruiting and selection of qualified professionals, commission-based pay structures, plus ongoing performance management of the behavior of these employees to positively impact growth.

Customer service

Customer service serves multiple roles within an organization, but viewing it is easiest from the perspectives of pre- and post-sale. Customers may have many questions before making a decision to buy, ranging from product details to purchase policies or warranties. After a sale, a customer may have an issue with a damaged product or the need to return a purchase. For this reason, HR best supports the customer service department through the hiring of talent, training on the skills necessary to problem-solve, and ensuring the ability to answer questions successfully regarding the products and services.

Purchasing

Purchasing is tied closely to the inventory management system that is in place within the organization. It's primarily a support function of production, solving issues related to incoming raw materials and the ancillary components necessary to build a product or operate a business. The PHR exam more than likely asks questions related to operational issues about conducting inventory or hiring purchasing agents.

Information technology (IT)

The impact of technology in the workplace is far reaching. In human resources, the use of Human Resource Information Systems (HRIS) helps to tie together the various elements present in the life cycle of the employee, as Figure 7-1 shows.

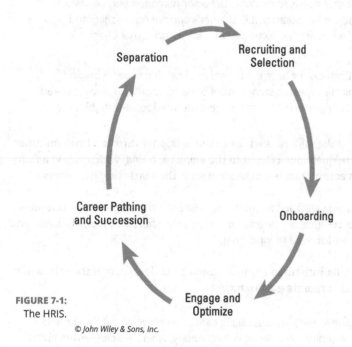

FIGURE 7-1:
The HRIS.

© *John Wiley & Sons, Inc.*

An HRIS system serves as a résumé database for recruiting, a compliance repository for training materials, and documentation of compensation and benefits as the employee matures within the company.

IT is also important in that it's the frontline of defense in the protection of customer and employee information.

Finally, IT provides the infrastructure necessary for the execution of most business operations.

On the PHR, prepare for content related to confidentiality issues and the electronic storage of records. You're also likely to be asked questions related to workforce planning, because technology can replace part of the existing workforce due to streamlined processes, or questions about the need to staff a new department with technical, noncore skill sets of talent.

Establishing internal and external relationships

Relationships are how business gets done, simply because people are at the core of work, and how people work together affects outcomes. *Internal relationships* exist between departments and co-workers as well as between supervisors and employees. Several exam components deal with these relationships, including the following:

>> **Managing change:** Change is an inevitable part of the day-to-day activities of an HR professional, and it occurs throughout all HR functions. Although driven by strategy, PHR candidates are tasked with implementing the changes throughout the business operations. When studying change management, you can easily identify solutions by looking at the functional areas of HR. For example, paying more for higher-level skill sets is a consideration of total rewards. Another example is shoring up your knowledge about union avoidance strategies when introducing change to a skeptical workforce, a function of employee relations.

>> **Motivating workers:** Among the core knowledge requirements of both exams is the need to motivate people to do the work that needs to be done. Behavior management has several theories that are grounded in scientific research. B.F. Skinner's *operant conditioning* and Abraham Maslow's *hierarchy of needs* are two examples of such theories that Chapter 2 covers in greater detail.

>> **Management development:** Both exams have the objective of helping supervisors and managers model and communicate expected standards of behavior. Some supervisors need help, and it's up to HR to identify opportunities for management development in this area.

External relationships reflect other stakeholders, such as customers, investors, and communities. On the exam, you should anticipate questions related to the *employer brand*, which is just a fancy name for the company reputation communicated in tandem with the marketing department.

Managing these relationships is often classified as the need to be both the employer and employee advocate. This HR task serves to remove obstacles, communicate shared responsibilities, and move the proverbial ball of business forward toward goals.

Managing external relationships falls into three organizational behaviors: corporate citizenship, corporate social responsibility, and corporate governance.

>> **Corporate citizenship,** according to HRCI, means taking care of employees and the communities where they live. This may be applied by offering volunteer pay, where employees are given a number of hours each month to work in their communities.

>> **Corporate social responsibility** is defined by HRCI as helping to improve social and environmental problems, such as building internet infrastructures in parts of the country where access is limited.

>> **Corporate governance** has a legal tinge to it. It refers to how an organization acts on its responsibilities to stakeholders. Laws beyond what we understand as labor laws exist to direct corporate governance behaviors that are related to antitrust, monopolies, and whistleblowing.

HRCI's Code of Ethical and Professional Responsibility

Ethics at work are behaviors that are considered moral or right. While organizations must comply with the law, laws don't exist for every single circumstance that may come up. It is up to an organization and its employees to act in accordance with who they want to be as business leaders.

The starting point for organizational ethical behavior is often found in their statement of values. Values define what the company holds dear as a business and what they are unwilling to compromise in the course of day-to-day operations.

REMEMBER

A values statement is often paired with an organization's mission (why they exist) and vision (where they want to be). Be prepared for questions on all three!

A code of ethics helps to communicate the expected standards of behavior and is accompanied by the employee handbook. Take, for example, the ethical requirements of a successful PHR credential holder (future you!). In order for a body of work to be considered a "profession," the industry must have a code of ethics.

Following is what the HRCI (www.hrci.org) has to say about the ethical and professional responsibilities of its certified professionals:

1. Professional Responsibility

As an HRCI certificant, you are responsible for adding value to the organizations you serve and contributing to the ethical success of those organizations. You accept professional responsibility for your individual decisions and actions. You are also an advocate for the HR profession by engaging in activities that enhance its credibility and value.

You will:

Adhere to the highest standards of ethical and professional behavior.

Measure the effectiveness of HR in contributing to or achieving organizational goals.

Comply with the law.

Work consistently within the values of the profession.

Strive to achieve the highest levels of service, performance, and social responsibility.

Advocate for the appropriate use and appreciation of human beings as employees.

Advocate openly and within the established forums for debate in order to influence decision-making and results.

2. Professional Development

As an HRCI certificant you must strive to meet the highest standards of competence and commit to strengthen your competencies on a continuous basis. You will:

Commit to continuous learning, skills development, and application of new knowledge related to both human resource management and the organizations you serve.

Contribute to the body of knowledge, the evolution of the profession, and the growth of individuals through teaching, research, and dissemination of knowledge.

3. Ethical Leadership

As an HRCI certificant you are expected to exhibit individual leadership as a role model for maintaining the highest standards of ethical conduct. You will:

Be ethical and act ethically in every professional interaction.

Question pending individual and group actions when necessary to ensure that decisions are ethical and are implemented in an ethical manner.

Seek expert guidance if ever in doubt about the ethical propriety of a situation.

Through teaching and mentoring, champion the development of others as ethical leaders in the profession and in organizations.

4. Fairness and Justice

As an HRCI certificant you are ethically responsible for promoting and fostering fairness and justice for all employees and their organizations. You will:

Respect the uniqueness and intrinsic worth of every individual.

Treat people with dignity, respect, and compassion to foster a trusting work environment free of harassment, intimidation, and unlawful discrimination.

Ensure that everyone has the opportunity to develop their skills and new competencies.

Assure an environment of inclusiveness and a commitment to diversity in the organizations you serve.

Develop, administer, and advocate policies and procedures that foster fair, consistent, and equitable treatment for all.

Regardless of personal interests, support decisions made by your organizations that are both ethical and legal.

Act in a responsible manner and practice sound management in the country or countries in which the organizations you serve operate.

5. Conflicts of Interest

As an HRCI certificant you must maintain a high level of trust with our stakeholders. You must protect the interests of those stakeholders as well as your professional integrity and should not engage in activities that create actual, apparent, or potential conflicts of interest. You will:

Adhere to and advocate the use of published policies on conflicts of interest within your organization.

Refrain from using your position for personal, material, or financial gain or the appearance of such.

Refrain from giving or seeking preferential treatment in the human resources processes.

Prioritize your obligations to identify conflicts of interest or the appearance thereof. When conflicts arise; you will disclose them to relevant stakeholders.

6. Use of Information

As an HRCI certificant you must consider and protect the rights of individuals, especially in the acquisition and dissemination of information while ensuring truthful communications and facilitating informed decision-making. You will:

Acquire and disseminate information through ethical and responsible means.

Ensure only appropriate information is used in decisions affecting the employment relationship.

Investigate the accuracy and source of information before allowing it to be used in employment-related decisions.

Maintain current and accurate HR information.

Safeguard restricted or confidential information.

Take appropriate steps to ensure the accuracy and completeness of all communicated information about HR policies and practices.

Take appropriate steps to ensure the accuracy and completeness of all communicated information used in HR-related training.

As you can see, being a professional practitioner of human resources is a huge responsibility. The exam objectives for the PHR further note that not only must we be familiar with the ethical standards of our business, our industry, and our profession, we must also communicate and model these standards in our daily practice.

TIP

Take the time to find the code of ethics within your organization. In what ways are you modeling these expectations? If one does not exist, what message might that be sending to your stakeholders? Take a deeper look and find the code of ethics for the industry you are in (academia, medical, farming, manufacturing, and so on). What are the similarities and differences between your organization and the industry in which you operate?

Risk Management

As noted previously, ethical leadership must take into account what is legal. As an HR practitioner of any length of time, you are probably aware of the labor law land mines that must be navigated on a regular basis. There is a misperception, however, in that a company's policies and behaviors can *prevent* a lawsuit. The truth is, any employee can file a claim with an enforcement agency at any time, whether the complaint is true or not, and the employer will have to respond. This slight shift in thinking hopefully will motivate you to focus your risk management efforts on legal practices, yes, but also to layer in defense mechanisms to prevent unlawful behaviors, and to defend a practice when (not if) you are called upon to do so.

A model to consider exists in establishing an affirmative defense against a sexual harassment claim. It may serve as a useful guide to understanding how to build best practices in general risk management practices:

> » **Have a written policy.** There is no single legal requirement that an employer have a written handbook. There are, however, several labor laws that require employers to have a written policy to demonstrate compliance. For this reason, a best practice is to have a single, collective document (the handbook) that can help comply with those requirements. While an employee handbook is ostensibly about communicating employee rights and responsibilities, it has morphed more into a legal document that establishes good faith intent to comply. Thus, having all policies reviewed by the labor attorney who may be called upon to defend said policies is a very, very good idea.

>> **Train employees.** Compliance training continues to be the area where many employers spend most of their training dollars. Training requirements exist for safety and health and harassment, just to name a couple. Various labor laws also manage how often training should occur, such as at the time of hire, annually, or every two or so years. HR must not only be familiar with federal requirements (exam focus), but the requirements of the states in which they operate (day-to-day focus).

>> **Investigate promptly.** Any time an employee makes a complaint, HR must take it seriously and embark on a neutral, fact-finding mission. In some cases, it is best to have an external resource conduct the investigation, but HR more often than not will be expected to handle the bulk of the detective work.

>> **Prohibit retaliation.** Claims of retaliation for exercising employee rights continue to cost employers millions of dollars — whether true or false. HR must champion this at all levels of the organization, from peer retaliation to the most egregious, retaliation by a person of authority, such as a supervisor.

Applying U.S. labor law

The purpose of labor law is to govern the relationship between the employer and the employee and protecting the employee from harmful or unfair employer actions. Labor laws exist in all the functional areas of HR.

Both the PHR and SPHR exams are unique in their question writing. Hoping for questions with answers that require simple regurgitation of facts isn't a good strategy. Your ability to *apply* the relevant labor laws to exam questions should be the focus of your exam preparation, not rote memorization of dates and numbers. Here is an example using the Americans with Disabilities Act (ADA).

The Americans with Disabilities Act applies to employers with 15 or more employees, prohibiting unlawful discrimination against qualified individuals with a disability. An individual with a disability is someone who has a physical or mental impairment that substantially limits a major life activity (such as walking, breathing, hearing, or seeing), who has a record of such impairment (such as successful treatment), or who is perceived to have such impairment (such as a facial disfigurement).

A qualified individual is one who has the knowledge, skills, and ability to perform the tasks, duties, and responsibilities of the job with or without reasonable accommodation.

Employers may claim undue hardship for failing to accommodate an otherwise qualified individual, but only on a case-by-case basis when considering the employer's size, financial resource availability, and the business structure in general.

Using this knowledge, answer the following question:

EXAMPLE

CPR Real Estate Investments has more than 300 independent real estate agents across the entire state of Kentucky who work on a commission-only basis. Administrative and management support is housed out of the corporate offices in Frankfort with three brand managers, three regional exempt-level managers, and five administrative support workers. One of the administrative support workers was recently diagnosed with fibromyalgia and needs every Friday and Monday off to seek treatment and recuperate until her follow-up appointment in four months. CPR refused to accommodate her because it is too small to absorb the new schedule. The worker quit and then filed a claim of unlawful discrimination under the ADA. Which of the following statements regarding this situation is true?

(A) CPR violated the employee's rights under the ADA.

(B) CPR did not violate her rights under the ADA.

(C) CPR violated her rights under the Family Medical Leave Act.

(D) CPR was correct in claiming undue hardship because nobody else could cover the responsibility.

The correct answer is (B). CPR didn't violate the employee's rights under the ADA for several reasons, making Choice (A) incorrect. The Family Medical Leave Act doesn't apply here because the employer doesn't have more than 50 full-time-equivalent employees, making Choice (C) incorrect. Choice (D) is more difficult because it's possible it's correct, but you don't have enough information to know whether it's correct.

Arriving at this answer requires knowledge of the ADA on several levels, including

>> **The number of employees:** CPR employs 300+ independent agents, meaning they're not employees. The ADA's threshold of 15 employees wasn't met by the 11 corporate workers.

>> **The definition of a qualified individual:** The employee was a qualified individual with an actual disability. *Qualified* means the individual can, with or without reasonable accommodation, perform the essential duties of the job. Depending on the severity and individual symptoms (such as the degree of limitations), this employee may be considered a qualified individual with a disability.

>> **The concept of undue hardship:** *Undue hardship* doesn't apply because she wasn't covered by the ADA. If she had been, the argument could be made that the employer didn't engage in an interactive process to find alternatives.

>> **Awareness of other labor laws:** Choice (C) was meant to distract you from the ADA issue. If you have knowledge of the FMLA, you would know that job protection is granted for up to 12 weeks for a serious health condition. However, the FMLA applies to employers with more than 50 full-time employees, so Choice (C) is incorrect.

As you can see in the example, your study activities for the multitude of labor laws may begin with the detailed facts, but they must end with application, application, application.

Tackling executive orders

The President of the United States (POTUS) signs an *executive order* (EO), and it carries the full weight of law. An executive order isn't passed by an act of Congress; POTUS bypasses Congress. Executive orders only apply to federal employees and federal contractors although they can have side effects on American citizens. For the exams, you should know eight or so EOs, and they include

>> **11246:** Passed in 1965, it prohibits unlawful discrimination based on race, creed, color, or national origin, requiring affirmative steps be taken in employment activities by federal contractors.

>> **11375:** Passed in 1967, it bans discrimination on the basis of sex for federal workers and for federal contractors.

>> **11478:** Prohibits discrimination in employment on the basis of race, color, religion, sex, national origin, handicap, and age for federal employees. Also mandates affirmative action to reach EEO goals.

>> **12138:** Created the National Women's Business Enterprise policy in 1979.

>> **13087:** Expanded protected class status to sexual orientation in 1998.

>> **13152:** Included status as a parent to the list of protected characteristics in 2000, referencing the care of dependents who can't care for themselves.

>> **13279:** Offered some relief to 11,246 faith-based organizations in 2002.

>> **13672:** Amends prior executive orders, preventing discrimination on gender identity (federal employees) and both gender identity and sexual orientation (for hiring by federal contractors).

>> **13932:** Authorized under President Trump in 2020, this EO seeks to reduce the emphasis of degree-based requirements for hiring federal workers.

Familiarizing yourself with the EOs is an act of context, not memorization, based on the fact that you can infer the answer by the leading numbers. They're numbered chronologically, so the orders that begin with the number 11 were passed prior to those that begin with 12 or 13. If you know, then, that the first relevant EO was passed in the 1960s, you can infer that it had something to do with civil rights. Align your studying methods of the EOs with these numbers, and your recall will be more meaningful than it would be through rote memorization.

EXAMPLE

If the President of the United States wanted to ban sensitivity training for federal workers without Congress's approval, which of the following tools would he use?

(A) A bill

(B) An executive order

(C) An amendment

(D) A joint resolution

The correct answer is (B). An executive order is a rule signed by the President of the United States that carriers the weight of law. It differs from a bill (Choice [A]) or a joint resolution (Choice [D]) in that a bill and a joint resolution must proceed through Congress in order to become a law. An amendment (Choice ([C]) is a Congressional change to existing law.

Managing Data

The output of data from the human resource department is significant. Much of the output is related to managing people, such as personnel files, payroll data, performance feedback . . . pick a functional area of HR and there is data associated with it. Having said that, the PHR exam is specific with what a practitioner should understand for the exams. It includes analyzing data for use in making strategic recommendations.

One example is that of turnover rates. Also called *attrition*, this rate is used to measure how many individuals left an organization due to voluntary quits, terminations, retirement, and layoffs. Calculating turnover at organizational and departmental levels can help senior leaders forecast the need for current and future talent. A simple calculation, it is expressed as a percentage by dividing the total number of separations by the total number of employees and then multiplying it by 100. As a general rule, any number above 15 percent should be cause for a strategic response. For this reason, many employers calculate turnover on a monthly basis, which allows for real-time response. In some industries a 15 percent turnover rate would be considered a gift (one report found that hourly retail workers had a turnover rate of 65 percent!). It is up to you to know the specifics of your industry and the goals of your employer.

Many stats that are used to analyze data at the PHR level are generated at the time of hire. Taking a look at recruiting success such as the time it takes from positon request to hire can help pin-point strategies to improve the recruiting process. Other metrics are driven by a desire to comply with labor law and initiate policies related to a positive culture. This may be measured by taking a look at how diverse your workforce population is. It requires demographic data collection at the point of hire and should be voluntary and anonymous.

TIP

Go online and check out the EEO-1 reporting requirements for employers. Even if you work for a small employer, it will inform you of the different types of demographic data that may be collected at the time of hire. A good starting point is www.eeoc.gov/employers/eeo-reports-surveys.

Return-on-investment calculations serve HR at all functional levels. For example, what is the return on investment of training outcomes? As you can see in Chapter 9, success of training should be included at the time of design.

Chapter **8**

Finding Resources: PHR 02 Talent Planning and Acquisition

The Talent Planning and Acquisition area of the PHR exam experienced some major shuffling in the 2018 updates. While the exam content outline still included workforce planning, it became more oriented toward the beginning of the employee life cycle. The exam weighting for this content area actually shrank (it used to make up the most content of the PHR exam at 24 percent) to only 16 percent. This is no cause for resting on your laurels, however. The PHR exam can still throw at you a question about the multitude of labor laws related to HR practice, so a robust review of the Federal Labor Law Appendix is in order. This chapter focuses specifically on what is most necessary to achieve a passing grade in this functional area, as evidenced by HRCI's summary:

"Identifying, attracting, and employing talent while following all federal laws related to the hiring process"

Noting What's Important about Talent Planning and Acquisition

Similar to the SPHR exam, this content area is made up of only three responsibilities. You may want to think of this content as talent's "origin" story — where do we source our people resources from, and how do we help them become productive members of our work society?

Responsibilities

HRCI defines the main responsibilities for exam preparation and practical application as follows:

01 Understand federal laws and organizational policies to adhere to legal and ethical requirements in hiring (for example: Title VII, nepotism, disparate impact, FLSA, independent contractors)

02 Develop and implement sourcing methods and techniques (for example: employee referrals, diversity groups, social media)

03 Execute the talent acquisition life cycle (for example: interviews, extending offers, background checks, negotiation)

Knowledge

In addition to the practical responsibilities of Talent Planning and Acquisition, this functional area includes knowledge components of the following:

12 Applicable federal laws and regulations related to talent planning and acquisition activities

13 Planning concepts and terms (for example: succession planning, forecasting)

14 Current market situation and talent pool availability

15 Staffing alternatives (for example: outsourcing, temporary employment)

16 Interviewing and selection techniques, concepts, and terms

17 Applicant tracking systems and/or methods

18 Impact of total rewards on recruitment and retention

19 Candidate/employee testing processes and procedures

20 Verbal and written offers/contract techniques

21 New-hire employee orientation processes and procedures

22 Internal workforce assessments (for example: skills testing, workforce demographics, analysis)

23 Transition techniques for corporate restructuring, mergers and acquisitions, due diligence process, offshoring, and divestitures

24 Metrics to assess past and future staffing effectiveness (for example: cost per hire, selection ratios, adverse impact)

Recognizing What Subjects to Study

In analyzing the HR function of Talent Planning and Acquisition, understanding the term *human resources* is important. Similar to the heavy use of acronyms in the industry, this term and its uses can be an obstacle to learning if not understood.

One way the term "human resources" is used is to reference the *human talent* or *human capital* — in short, the people doing the work. From brawn to brains, individual contributors to executives, these people are the resources toward which all our human resource efforts are applied.

The term "human resources" is also used to describe the framework for the domain of HR as follows:

- » **Profession:** The *profession* is that of a human resources professional — those individuals who are educated, certified, and professionally positioned to execute the best practices of the field.

- » **Field:** The *field* refers to the industry of human resources where vendors, suppliers, networks, associations, and experts exist to evolve the profession through research, education, and publication.

- » **Department:** The *department* is the functional area of an organization that takes the knowledge, skills, and abilities of the professional and applies them to the best practices of the industry toward the work of business.

The Talent Planning and Acquisition function of the exam places heavy emphasis on HR's ability to find the people resources necessary to achieve organizational strategies and goals.

Looking at the Life Cycle of the Employee

The function description published by HRCI in the HR Body of Knowledge focuses on the life cycle of the employee, beginning with recruitment and ending with organizational exits.

A lot of workforce planning efforts exist within each cycle, so understanding the activities from this perspective is important. Talent planning efforts begin with the strategic plan, where decisions about hiring needs are often made based on new business growth, including mergers and acquisitions or new product offerings. Decisions regarding layoffs or divestitures may also be identified during the planning process. The planning process is tied to strategic goals of one to three years. At minimum, a strong strategic plan will have benchmarks that determine whether hiring or firing is financially the right decision and what data should be collected and measured. While the strategic plan sits firmly within the domain of senior HR leaders, PHR candidates are most likely called upon to implement the actions. A good place to start is with labor law compliance. Take a look at Table 8-1 for a few examples of the impact of labor laws at the hiring stage.

TABLE 8-1 Time-of-Hire Application of Labor Law

Labor Law	Impact at Time of Hire
Americans with Disabilities Act	Prohibits the use of medical exams to qualify an applicant for employment
Uniform Guidelines on Employee Selection Procedures; Title VII of the Civil Rights Act of 1964	Requires all pre-employment tests be job related and nondiscriminatory in both intent and effect
Immigration Reform and Control Act	Requires that employers hire only those authorized to work in the United States and completion of Form I-9 within 72 hours of employment

While labor law is an important consideration in all areas of the life cycle, we begin the next section by reviewing the first opportunity a new hire has to engage with the company — the recruiting process.

Creating a Recruiting Process

The process of recruiting launches the employee life cycle. Figure 8-1 shows the steps in the recruiting process from the perspective of the exam objectives. Note that the recruiting process is separate from the selection process. Recruiting focuses on identifying and marketing open positions and sourcing methods such as employee referrals, diversity groups, and social media. The selection process is reflected in exam responsibility 03 and includes interviews, employment offers, background checks, and negotiating offers.

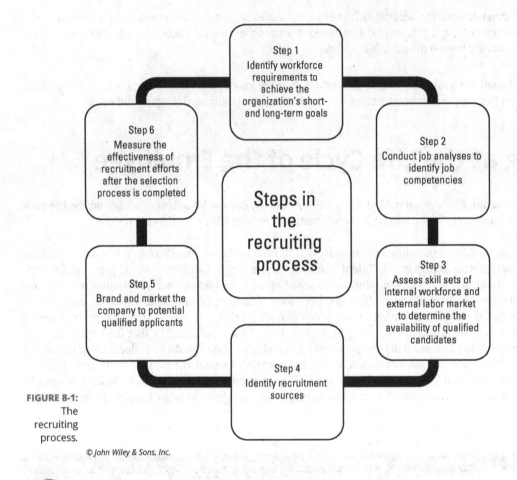

Steps in the recruiting process

Step 1
Identify workforce requirements to achieve the organization's short- and long-term goals

Step 2
Conduct job analyses to identify job competencies

Step 3
Assess skill sets of internal workforce and external labor market to determine the availability of qualified candidates

Step 4
Identify recruitment sources

Step 5
Brand and market the company to potential qualified applicants

Step 6
Measure the effectiveness of recruitment efforts after the selection process is completed

FIGURE 8-1:
The recruiting process.

© John Wiley & Sons, Inc.

REMEMBER

One important step in the recruitment process is the development of the employer brand. The *employer brand* is the company's reputation as an employer that the candidate experiences, which may include several facets related to effective communication such as:

>> **Application process:** So much of the recruiting process is now done online. Sources include social media sites such as LinkedIn, job boards such as Indeed, and the company's website, giving the applicants a glimpse into how the employer does business.

>> **Responsiveness:** After an application has been submitted, an individual will expect to hear back. Do applicants receive an automated email thanking them for their application? Is a nonselection letter sent if they aren't qualified? Too often, applicants submit their résumé into what feels like an inky void, never to be heard from again, which affects the employer's reputation.

>> **Availability of information:** Communicating the employer brand requires access to information about the company. Many employers have their own social media pages and utilize videos for maximum effect on why a candidate should come and work there. Applicants can read about the employer's mission, vision, and values, or find out about the benefits the company offers. They can see how many positions are open and view the locations and requirements of the jobs.

>> **Employee referrals:** A large percentage of consumers shop online. Next to price, product reviews rank high in searches. This concept applies to employers as well. People want to work for companies that they can trust or that they know something about. Employee testimonials are quite effective at communicating the employer brand. Employee referrals can be done in person at job fairs, via a company résumé, or by online videos.

These communication factors are dependent upon a well-organized HR department, and the exam varies in terms of what it asks about collecting, analyzing, and optimizing hiring data. Consider the functionality of an applicant tracking system (ATS) that operates as a one-stop shop for recruiters, with capacity to update job descriptions and job postings, run searches in the résumé database, and track applicants through the entire hiring process.

EXAMPLE

Building Blocks is a technology start-up that has to continuously recruit for specialist roles in the highly competitive city of Salt Lake in Utah. The company's major challenge was lack of name recognition, making it highly dependent on third-party vendors for placement solutions. As the new HR director, which of the following strategies should you recommend first?

(A) Contact the staffing agencies and negotiate better pricing on their fees.

(B) Start a company social media page and pay for exposure.

(C) Research HRIS solutions to better organize applicants.

(D) Develop an employer-brand campaign starting with videos of current employee testimonials.

The correct answer is (D). The lack of name recognition is this company's biggest challenge, and an employer-brand campaign utilizing videos and employee reviews is the best place to start. Neither Choice (A) nor Choice (D) addresses the name recognition challenge, and Choice (B) should be part of the larger brand campaign.

Operationally, this activity matches candidate knowledge, skills, and abilities (characteristics of people) with job tasks, duties, and responsibilities (characteristics of jobs) to predict person-to-job fit. Strategically, this process does three things: communicates company culture, accurately predicts future success on the job, and expands the ability of HR to successfully predict person-to-organization fit.

Selecting the Right Employees

Imagine a world where you have hundreds of résumés to review and they all have the skills for which you're seeking. The applicants are properly educated, have a strong work history, volunteer in their communities, and are reasonable about the starting salary. And then you wake up. The simple fact is that many employers are competing in two markets: the unemployed and the currently employed. Without the proper filters, recruiters will be forced into a review of hundreds (or thousands) of résumés of individuals who may or may not be qualified to do the job.

Using pre-employment tests

The Uniform Guidelines on Employee Selection Procedures (UGESP) state that *any* employment requirement is a test, and therefore, subject to two factors:

» **Reliability:** *Reliability* means that the test consistently delivers similar results of a candidate when measured over a period of time.

» **Validity:** *Validity* is a process of ensuring that the test measures what you say it measures.

EXAMINING GRIGGS VS. DUKE POWER

Griggs vs. Duke Power is a landmark Supreme Court decision made in 1971 that shaped the use of pre-employment tests. Its outcome: Even seemingly neutral employment requirements must be job related and not result in adverse impact against a protected class group. *Adverse impact* occurs when there is a significantly different rate of selection of protected class groups. Selection is not just about who is hired; it includes selection for promotion or participation in training programs as well.

Note that Duke Power had a history of discriminatory practices prior to the passage of the Civil Rights Act of 1964 by segregating black workers in one of its many departments, the labor department, and hiring only white people for the better jobs in other departments at significantly higher pay rates. Post 1964, Duke Power implemented a high-school diploma requirement for all positions available in the labor department. The high-school diploma became a condition of employment or to be eligible for transfer to other positions. The company claimed that it would enhance the overall quality of the company employees.

Furthermore, understand that the diploma and baseline skills testing became a requirement after Title VII was passed, effectively precluding African-American workers to transfer to better jobs. Thirteen employees filed suit under Title VII of the Civil Rights Act of 1964, stating that this requirement resulted in discriminatory practices against African Americans, because they have a substantially lower rate of graduation from high school than whites.

These charges were upheld, with final commentary focused not on the requirement itself, but the impact. The diploma requirement in and of itself was a neutral hiring tool; however, the tool resulted in disparate impact or substantial underrepresentation of a protected class group, rendering the outcome discriminatory.

You should understand five important principles for the exams that are the result of this landmark case:

● A test or other selection practice must be job related, and the burden of proof is on the employer to demonstrate that it didn't discriminate against an individual.

● An employer's intent not to discriminate is irrelevant. Having an otherwise neutral employment requirement that results in discrimination — regardless of intent — is unlawful.

● If a practice is "fair in form but discriminatory in operation," the court won't uphold it.

● Business necessity is the defense for any existing program that has adverse impact. Business necessity typically can be shown for safety sensitive positions or for religious positions that require a certain faith of their employees.

● Title VII doesn't forbid testing. However, the test must be job related or valid, in that performance on the test must be related to performance on the job.

You can find an audio version of the oral arguments in this case online at the NAACP's Legal Defense and Educational Fund (www.naacpldf.org/case-issue/griggs-v-duke-power-co).

For example, say an applicant takes a personality assessment as part of the selection process and scores very high in teamwork. This would be a reliable measure if at a future date, the employee retakes the test and scores very similarly to round one. This test would be valid if the individual were hired and found to be a collaborative worker. If the test results are inconsistent or don't accurately measure the behavior of the person on the job, the results and the test itself would be found to be unreliable and invalid.

The Uniform Guidelines specifically address the different types of validities. Here is a list of the types of validity studies you should be familiar with for the exams:

» **Face validity:** *Face validity* simply addresses whether the test appears to be measuring what it's supposed to be measuring. Thus, a driving test for the position of bus driver would be high on face validity. A math test for a bus driver would be low.

» **Criterion validity (concurrent versus predictive):** *Criterion validity* refers to whether the employment test predicts job performance either now *(concurrent validity)* or in the future *(predictive validity)*. In general, the *pure ability* of a test to predict performance now and in the future is criterion validity.

» **Content validity:** *Content validity* is often the most important for defending a lawsuit. If an employment test measures the same content as on the job, then it's high on content validity. For example, if you create an employment test using the job description for the content of the questions, you're likely to result in a test that is high on content validity.

In addition to being reliable and valid, employment tests must be job related (as demonstrated by content validity) and avoid unlawful discrimination based on protected class status. (Refer to the nearby sidebar for a court case that relates to pre-employment tests.)

Conducting interviews

Perhaps the most common hiring tool, the interview, is an opportunity for the organization to assess an applicant's person-to-job and person-to-organization fit. This is done by using various styles of questions in an attempt to predict future success in the role. These questions are a form of pre-employment test, and thus are subject to the requirements of the UGESP.

While some organizations pride themselves on creative interview questions (if you were an animal, what kind of animal would you be?), it is an HR best practice to encourage the use of one of the following question styles:

» **Behavioral:** Focused on past behavior. "How did you handle an angry customer in your last job?"

» **Nondirective:** Developed from an answer to a previous question. "How did you handle an angry customer in your last job?" After the candidate answers, you dive a little deeper such as "Why did you choose that approach?" or "What was the outcome of that approach?"

» **Situational:** Focused on future behavior. "How would you handle a customer that called in to complain about a company driver?"

Remember that regardless of the type of question asked, questions should reflect the requirements of the job for which the interviewee is applying.

Rarely does HR make the final hiring decision, which means that HR must train supervisors and others who are responsible for interviewing on the different forms of bias that can be present when making a hiring decision. These include the halo effect (ascribing positive meaning to a single attribute), the horn effect (placing emphasis on a negative aspect of behavior), similar-to-me bias (being more positive about interviewees who are like the rater), and failing to distinguish between candidates by rating them all as "middle of the road."

Once a hiring decision has been made, HR is challenged to extend an employment offer and negotiate salary.

TIP

Using Legos and asking candidates to build something and asking off-beat interview questions such as "What would a work Utopia look like in your world?" are actually gaining in popularity despite the associated risks. When employers are intent on using creative interviews, work with your teams to understand what competencies these tools are attempting to predict, and then document the data to demonstrate content validity. Good HR business partners communicate the risk and take steps to reduce it — they should not simply say "no."

Employment offers

While administrative on the surface, extending an offer of employment entails avoiding several land mines. This includes avoiding the development of a contract — explicit or implied — when using written offers. It also includes avoiding negating the concept of employment at-will, which means that either the employer or the new hire may exit the organization at any time and for any reason without notice to the other party.

Once a verbal or written offer of employment is extended, there is a high likelihood that a candidate may begin to negotiate salary. An HR best practice is to have already completed the wage survey so they understand the minimum and maximum range for the position. Beyond wages, you may be able to persuade an applicant in your favor by communicating the company benefits packages, paid-time-off offerings, and other nontangible benefits of joining your team.

For the more difficult-to-fill roles or more senior leadership roles, the availability and details of a Total Rewards package will take on significance and is discussed in more detail in Chapter 10.

The use of background checks

There are several ways an employer may access the background of applicant. These include checking the references on an application to verify the information, requesting transcripts to verify education, and taking copies of any professional certifications. For more extensive checks, most HR departments outsource the task to an agency that can access criminal convictions (never arrest records), motor vehicle history, and/or credit history. Any background investigation must begin with written authorization from the applicant and must be related to the job.

Once an applicant has accepted a job offer, the real work of integrating that person into the business begins.

A WORD ABOUT NEPOTISM

Nepotism is described as the practice of allowing family members to work at the same organization. Some companies outlaw it altogether. But in a tight labor market, this practice may be an effective way to staff for jobs. For this reason, HR best practices with regard to controlling the negative effects of nepotism — such as favoritism — are to have a policy that prohibits family members from working in the same department, supervising one another, or being placed in positions where collusion or conflict of interests could occur.

Comparing Orientation to Onboarding

Orientation and *onboarding* are terms that are often used interchangeably because some employers practice both as though they're one activity. However, they really are separate employee experiences. The simplest way to distinguish between the two is to note that orientation is an *event*, whereas onboarding is a *process*. For example, filling out post-hire paperwork is often done at orientation and only needs to be completed once. Mastering the tasks, duties, and responsibilities of the job occurs over time and is often part of the onboarding process. Table 8-2 describes more of the differences.

TABLE 8-2 **The Difference between Orientation and Onboarding**

Orientation	Onboarding
Is one to three days	Is 30 to 90 days or longer depending on the position (consider expatriation activities, for example)
Doesn't provide a fluid mechanism for employee feedback	Ends with a 30-, 60-, or 90-day, two-way review
Focuses on compliance training	Focuses on skills identification and development needs
Includes filling out proper hiring forms, such as Form I-9 and W-4	Embeds employee in company culture through development plans and objectives

Orientation is reflected on the exams through the administration of post-offer, pre-hire activities such as completing Form I-9, which verifies a new employee's identity and eligibility to work in the United States, and drug testing. The PHR exam also asks questions about the onboarding process, including how to develop the processes, implement the systems, and evaluate their effectiveness. Keep in mind that the affected employees include new hires, rehires, transfers, and potentially, the newly promoted.

Recognizing Common Reports and Tools

The talent planning function of human resources is an area with a lot of documentation requirements. From reporting new hires to analyzing the effectiveness of hiring sources, the need for formal documents and processes is evident all throughout this functional area. Some of the most common reports and tools that are likely to be examined on the tests are explained in these sections.

EEO-1 reporting

The EEO-1 report is a mandatory compliance survey for employers who meet the threshold requirements. It's a collection of employment statistics categorized on the Standard Form 100 by race/ethnicity, gender, and job category. The Equal Employment Opportunity Commission (EEOC) and the Office of Federal Contract Compliance use these findings to support enforcement and civil rights activities and to analyze employment trends across industries.

Make sure that you're familiar with completing this form in preparation for the exam, even if you aren't currently required to use it on the job.

Form I-9

Form I-9 is a document that verifies two things:

>> An employee's identity

>> An employee's eligibility to work in the United States

Required as part of the Immigration Reform and Control Act of 1996, this document must be completed within 72 hours of the new employee's first day of work for wages. This can be done electronically using E-Verify, or on paper.

For guidance on how to complete this one-page form, you can refer to the 96-page Handbook for Employers (M-274), published by the United States Citizen and Immigration Services (USCIS). It's a great addition to your study materials. Download a copy now at www.uscis.gov and search the "resources" section to download a copy. Assess your knowledge by finding answers to the following questions

>> May I accept a copy of documentation?

>> Do you need to fill out this form for independent contractors?

>> How can I correct a mistake made on Form I-9?

Fines for failing to complete this form properly range from $230 to $2,392 per error. Your bigger concern now, however, is to ensure you are prepared to answer questions about this process — including e-verify — for the exams.

TIP

Conduct a spot check of your files. Start by making sure that the most recent hires were given the most up-to-date version of Form I-9 published by USCIS.

Recruiting analysis

A *recruiting analysis* is a very simple document that you can create to track the effectiveness of various recruiting resources. This data is tracked by job and is helpful for future openings to know where qualified candidates are sourced from, the amount of time it takes to make the hire, and the overall cost to recruit. This information can then be translated into department budgets for anticipated openings, shrinking the amount of money and time spent on nonproductive recruiting sources in the future.

REMEMBER

You can measure the effectiveness of your recruiting efforts in these ways:

>> **Metrics:** *Metrics* refers to the number of candidates per source, number of hires per source, and ratio of résumés to interview. Define for your organization what is useful to measure, and apply a formula for data collection, review, and application.

>> **Feedback:** Interviewing new hires to get their opinions and feedback on the recruiting process is helpful to ensure the desired message is being sent during the process.

>> **Quality of hire:** Turnover ratios and performance measures are just two of the many ways that you can measure to ensure that the hires you're making are a good fit for the organization. Consider that you may hire ten employees from one source, but if they all turn over in the first six months, the recruiting source isn't effective.

>> **Validation of measures:** Looking for patterns of effective hires and determining which recruitment methods are more able to differentiate better from worse candidates is a worthy effort. Doing so helps narrow your focus and find qualified candidates for your employer the first time around in future hiring efforts.

Chapter 9

Sharpening Your Tools: PHR 03 Learning and Development

Just as the domain of Business Management focuses on the function of the business units and processes, Learning and Development (L&D) is all about the people and the culture and climate in which we ask them to perform. Doing so requires that we are positioned to execute this content area by:

> "Contributing to the organization's learning and development activities by implementing and evaluating programs, providing internal consultation, and providing data."

At only 10 percent of PHR exam content, we sharpen our focus on only what's most important.

Identifying What's Essential About Learning and Development

Effective HR technicians are adept at helping to manage both the business and the talent. This requires the ability to take a consultative approach in both plans and actions.

Responsibilities

HRCI focuses the L&D responsibilities around 3 key areas:

01 Provide consultation to managers and employees on professional growth and development opportunities.

02 Implement and evaluate career development and training programs (for example: career pathing, management training, mentorship).

03 Contribute to succession planning discussions with management by providing relevant data.

Knowledge

As with all exam content, each area has additional knowledge components to account for in your study plan. For L&D, you need an understanding of the following:

25 Applicable federal laws and regulations related to learning and development activities

26 Learning and development theories and applications

27 Training program facilitation, techniques, and delivery

28 Adult learning processes

29 Instructional design principles and processes (for example: needs analysis, process flow mapping)

30 Techniques to assess training program effectiveness, including use of applicable metrics

31 Organizational development (OD) methods, motivation methods, and problem-solving techniques

32 Task/process analysis

33 Coaching and mentoring techniques

34 Employee retention concepts and applications

35 Techniques to encourage creativity and innovation

Examining What You Need to Know for the Exam Regarding Learning and Development

The exam objectives explore L&D as an evolution of the people to improve their *effectiveness* in their current roles (ability to do the work well) while also being developed to meet future needs. Strong planning skills can help achieve this.

For example, an organization needs a strategic plan to guide it over a period of one to three years, just as an employee needs a career path that points her in the direction that you need (and she wants) to go. A *gap analysis* may be used to identify the differences between where a company is and where it wants to be, a tool that may also be used for disparity in employee performance.

Although the objectives address training specifically, the content also demands that you understand employee development beyond simple training, such as through training and development. The following sections describe these processes in more detail.

REMEMBER

PHR materials have changed the term definitions of *training* and *development* over time, and there are many different definitions in existence. Basically, *training* is teaching workers skills that they need now for the job, and *development* includes identifying and building the competencies needed for the future.

The design of training

"He needs training" is a common refrain of frustrated supervisors everywhere, and yet, training as a solution isn't always the right answer. The exam objectives tell you that a needs assessment is the first thing that you need to do to determine whether training is the appropriate intervention. A *training needs assessment* (TNA) is a tool used to identify the goals of training. A TNA can be used on a macro level to view the company from 50,000 feet during the strategic planning process. For example, if the company is introducing a new product or installing new software, the training need is fairly obvious. On a smaller scale, the training needs are generally viewed from three perspectives:

>> **Compliance:** So many labor laws, so little time. Training is often the second step to demonstrating compliance with various labor laws, bowing only to establishing a policy. Areas where training is required by law include harassment prevention and safety.

>> **Technical:** How to perform the work is another reason for training. Although most companies seek to hire individuals with at least some level of skill or experience, all jobs have a learning curve that must be nurtured through training efforts.

>> **Retention:** Many employers simply attempt to hire employees with the necessary skills required for the job. When this is impossible (or impractical), they may find that training current workers with the specific skills needed for new jobs is more effective. Training costs may prove to be much lower than recruitment costs. Also, employees may be less likely to leave an organization that is willing to offer more job security through training.

True organizational development activities take into account the powerful soft skill, helping employees develop in areas of communication, interpersonal skills, building trust, leadership, change management, and more. So many companies unfortunately are forced to allocate their training dollars and time to compliance and technical training, leaving the softer side of work woefully unexplored.

Regardless of the type of training, the exams ask you to apply your knowledge to a broad range of training applications, which include

>> **Instructional design:** Defining the objectives of the training must be the focus of any solid *instructional design* (a process to identify the systems, methods, and strategies of training). Exam prep materials often use a helpful acronym called ADDIE:

- **A**nalyze the need.
- **D**esign the training objectives.
- **D**evelop the training material.
- **I**mplement the training by teaching.
- **E**valuate the outcomes.

>> **Training delivery:** How the training is delivered is actually an important consideration. When training is selected as an intervention, a company must make many decisions. One decision is to identify whether the training should be formal, such as conducted by an outside expert, or informal, such as self-paced. You need to be familiar with training terms, such as *vestibule* (near-the-job training), *computer-based* training (online, CDs, software), and *contract learning* (self-identified competency learning at one's own pace).

>> **eLearning:** *eLearning* is the formal name for any training that students attend online or at a computer. Terms you should know for the exam include asynchronous and synchronous. *Asynchronous* training occurs when students and teachers are online at different times, whereas *synchronous* training is when participants are required to be online at the same time.

>> **mLearning:** A relatively new term, *mLearning* refers to mobile learning, or the ability of elearners to access training material on mobile devices. For training developers, mLearning requires decisions to be made about how the information will be delivered and upon what devices in order to modify content as necessary. For example, web-based learning that relies on mouse-click selections won't work on tablets that are touch screen. HR professionals need to become familiar with authoring tools that support this mode of training delivery.

>> **Measurement of training effectiveness:** The goal of most training activities is to transfer learning to the job, which requires that you're able to measure the effectiveness of a training program through the use of established metrics.

EXAMPLE

Nancy Jones created a measure of satisfaction with the training program using a 1 to 5 scale, with 1 being not at all satisfied and 5 being completely satisfied. This would be an example of what type of scaling:

(A) Nominal

(B) Ordinal

(C) Interval

(D) Ratio

The correct answer is (C). Choice (D) is incorrect because a 4 isn't twice as good as a 2. Choice (A) is incorrect because the measures aren't categories. The answer isn't ordinal, Choice (B), because this measure doesn't order the responses from higher to lower.

EXAMINING ADULT LEARNING STYLES

All trainers should take into account the learning styles of their employees. Many of them haven't been in a formal classroom in years, and yet HR professionals often hustle them into a conference room for the latest PowerPoint presentation without regard to how well they will absorb the material. Effective trainers know that people learn with their senses, and some senses are more dominant than others. Imagine for example, that a child enters a playground with his mother. A *visual learner* will watch how the other kids are playing and then mirror their behavior. An *auditory learner* may ask his mother what he should do, seeking verbal direction. A *tactile* or *kinesthetic learner* is likely to jump right in, grabbing a ball or digging his hands in the sand.

Now, imagine that this same child is all grown up and is required to learn a new software program. The visual learner will be most comfortable using a reference chart or reading the training manual. The auditory learner would benefit from watching a video on the key program features, listening to the trainer's voice. And the tactile learner just wants to get started, tap, tap, tapping away on the keyboard or clicking his way through the demo.

According to adult learning theory, adults are different than children in their process and approach to learning in the following ways:

• Adults have the need to know why they're learning something.

• Adults have a need to be self-directed.

• Adults bring more work-related experience into the learning situation.

• Adults enter into a learning experience with a problem-centered approach to learning.

• Adults are motivated to learn by both extrinsic and intrinsic motivators.

Developing employees

Many factors affect the need for agility in the workforce and innovative ways of doing business. Many organizations have not had the luxury of planning beyond a year or two as the rapid pace of change continues to demand a response — often outside the strategic plan! Consider globalization, technology, social activism, four generations in a single workplace — these all require that HR lead their teams to develop the skills necessary to adapt and go beyond current requirements. This is the crux of development activities. Some HR tools to use include:

>> **Assessing employee performance:** Classifying an employee as good or bad isn't sufficient for an organization to successfully compete. HR professionals must be able to help their organizations drill down into the core of what knowledge, skills, or abilities are necessary for benchmarked performance. The gap between the core and the talent may then be addressed, focusing resources on the root causes rather than the symptoms of employee performance.

>> **Creating career paths:** The term *career paths* was actually added to this objective in 2012. The field research and other studies used to update the exam content indicated that this aspect was important to the daily life of an HR professional. *Career path* is simply a plan of development for employees that addresses both strengths and weaknesses that must be addressed to prepare employees for their next step. Figure 9-1 illustrates the concept of *forced distribution,* where supervisors are asked to *distribute* their employees on a curve based on current status. This practice *forces* them to think through who their top performers are that should be developed for promotion, those who are to remain at status quo, and those who are underperforming. Note that the stars represent individual employees and that they can be at varying degrees of your career-pathing efforts. You should also know for the exams the different types of career paths. Employees may choose

- **Traditional:** Promoting up the ladder within their chosen field

- **Expert:** Focusing on being the best in their industry

- **Spiral:** Developing new skills over time, or combining new skills with old skills to create a new career

- **Transitory:** Developing skills by constantly moving into new positions or companies

>> **Managing high-potential employees:** *High-potential employees* (hi-po) are those employees who, if not properly managed, will take their talent and go. These individuals tend to not only have the skills and abilities to do the work that they're assigned, but they also have a high degree of internal motivation and drive. Often they have a career plan in mind and will exert the necessary effort and time commitment to learn new things or take advantage of opportunities. Allowing these employees to wilt on the vine is something that HR professionals must help their employers avoid through development plans, mentoring, and new skill development.

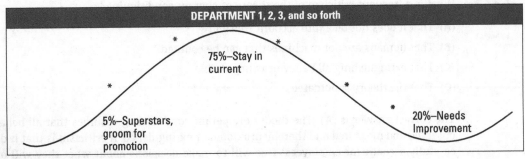

FIGURE 9-1: Forced distribution.

© John Wiley & Sons, Inc.

EXAMPLE

A supervisor has grouped her employees into three performance categories: develop for promotion, stay in current position, and needs improvement. Which strategy should she apply to the group of workers classified as needs improvement?

(A) Direct and assess

(B) Sustain and support

(C) Discipline and exit

(D) Retain and transfer

The correct answer is (A). In this strategy, the supervisor would provide clear direction to the employees needing improvement while assessing them for retention. Choice (B) isn't correct because sustaining poorly performing workers doesn't solve the issues. Choice (C) may not be the best strategy for all the employees, especially those who just need a bit of coaching to perform better. Choice (D) isn't a good strategy, because transferring poor performers into another department doesn't address the performance deficiencies.

REMEMBER

Picture in your mind a slot machine player in Las Vegas, Nevada. She inserts a few quarters, pushes a button or pulls a lever, and suddenly music is playing and lights are flashing. Every once in a while, she receives a payout — a reward for continued play. The lights, sounds, and reward all encourage her to continue putting money in the machine. B.F. Skinner used gambling as an example to describe his theory of *operant conditioning,* in which a specific action has a reward, conditioning people to expect certain outcomes.

Apply the theory of operant conditioning to your employees. They have — through individual and organizational behavior — been conditioned to act a certain way based on the rewards. The rewards may be *tangible,* such as pay or benefits, or *intangible,* such as supervisor praise or co-worker esteem. Harnessing these rewards and using them to encourage productivity is at the core of the successful management of employee behavior. You need to understand this theory and other theories of motivation in order to execute the responsibilities of this domain.

Don't forget about the vast number of videos online. A favorite of mine is one of Skinner that describes how he taught pigeons to read. It's well worth a few minutes of your time. Pick up on keywords such as *conditioning,* schedules of *reinforcement,* and *reward,* and think about how this theory ties into employee behavior management. Other important concepts of Skinner's theory are

>> **Positive reinforcement:** Behaviors that are followed by a reward tend to be repeated.

>> **Negative reinforcement:** Behaviors that are followed by undesirable consequences tend to disappear.

>> **Extinction:** The elimination of behaviors through failure to reward.

EXAMPLE

What is a frequent criticism of the theory of operant conditioning?

(A) That it does not take into account free will

(B) That humans are not machines that can be counted

(C) That extinguishing all behavior is impossible

(D) That the theory is outdated

The correct answer is (A). The theory of operant conditioning assumes that all behavior can be observed and measured and thereby promoted or extinguished. A criticism is that it doesn't successfully account for employees' free will to make decisions about what they will or won't do, regardless of reward or punishment. Choices (B), (C), and (D) are subjective views that require an opinion to be correct.

With regard to L&D specifics, training and employee motivation programs aren't just about training and managing behavior. It's the management of a larger network of programs and procedures that must be identified, developed, implemented, and evaluated. It includes the need for train-the-trainer programs to ensure proper facilitation or teaching of the class.

Making the most of data management

Several useful reports, tools, and processes support the function of L&D. They range from specific documents such as the replacement charts to the more detailed process of applying the ADDIE model to the process of training. Keep reading for more detail on how these tools apply to your exam.

Succession and replacement plans

Using data from career pathing is an excellent way to find out the needs, wants, and intent of team members. Finding out that Jaqueline wants to move into an HR department from accounting can be useful when developing not only her career path, but also an organization's succession and replacement charts.

HRCI defines these tools as follows:

>> **Succession planning:** *Succession planning* is determining and preparing for future talent needs. It includes identifying and developing high-potential employees for the organization's future success.

>> **Replacement planning:** Identifying employees to fill future vacancies is a function of *replacement planning.* It entails using past performance to identify employees who can fill future vacancies (unlike succession planning, which focuses on future potential).

Training needs assessment

A *training needs assessment* (TNA) is an analysis tool used prior to the design or delivery of training. It answers questions about whether there is a need for training. Strategic training needs assessment focuses on whether the employee knowledge, skills, and abilities (KSA) and performance support desired business outcomes. These objectives must be very clearly defined.

Table 9-1 shows you an example using a problem-solving technique regarding the whys. In this example, a company needs to improve customer satisfaction ratings for consumers who call in with a problem with a product.

Training design

After the training participants and the business outcomes have been identified, training design can begin, including what core competencies need to be improved and who should facilitate the training. In the example from Table 9-1, you can continue asking why until you drill down to the root, in which training may not be the only identifiable solution. When designing training, consider three primary considerations:

>> **Determining learner readiness:** Knowing the levels of readiness of learning participants is an important consideration when designing training. *Learner readiness* helps to design training that meets the specific needs of the workgroup being trained. For example, if you have an entry-level workforce, the training may need to be designed to teach baseline knowledge that then sets the employee up to learn more detailed principles. Another factor may be language barriers in the workplace. Employees whose first language isn't English may struggle to keep up, so you may need to conduct the training in another language or work with the employees to teach them basic English terms that will be used in the training.

TABLE 9-1 Remembering Why When Determining Training Needs

Why Question	Answer	Note
Why does the company need to improve these ratings?	The company received poor reviews online about its customer service.	If you stop asking why here, the training may be designed around communication or problem-solving, and you still don't have enough information to make a diagnosis.
Why did the company receive poor reviews?	The customer service representatives didn't have enough technical knowledge about the products to answer the consumers' questions.	If you stop asking why here, you may only address part of the problem.
Why were there issues related to certain products?	The issues were with new products that went to market before everyone was trained, and the product went out with faulty wiring.	So then, who needs to be trained? The correct answer is both the customer service reps in technical knowledge and the production workers in quality.

>> **Understanding different learning styles:** All adults have different learning styles, and the basics are auditory, visual, and tactile. Quality training is designed to incorporate strategies for all learning styles, such as the use of charts and graphs for visual learners, lecture and discussion for auditory learners, and hands-on exercise for the tactile learners in the training group. Refer to the earlier sidebar that discusses adult learning styles for more information on this important exam consideration.

>> **Designing training for transfer:** The third consideration is to prepare the content for transfer onto the job. The goals of training are to modify behavior and outcomes, so establishing learning objectives and supplying tools for transfer should be of utmost priority. Cross-reference the upcoming section "Training evaluation" to discover more about the modification of behavior and results as a goal of training.

Training development

After the training needs have been identified and the design of training addressed, choose and create (or purchase) the appropriate training tools. For purposes of the exam, copyright issues may come up, so it's important for trainers to use tools only for the purpose intended. It may be a violation of copyright laws if you don't.

Training implementation

The implementation of training is all about the action — how it will be delivered, when it will be scheduled, and who to invite as the participants. Method matters at this stage, and a few training delivery options you should be aware of for the exams include

>> **On-the-job training:** This training occurs when the employee is working. It may be through *job shadowing* (when an employee observes another employee doing the work) or doing the work while a trainer watches him, correcting the trainee as mistakes occur.

>> **Role-playing:** *Role-playing* is useful when there are relational duties as part of a job. Role-playing asks participants to act out a scenario, with the facilitator and other participants evaluating and discussing their responses. It can be uncomfortable for some to work in front

of a group or be critiqued by others, so the use of role-playing should be limited to employees who will gain maximum benefit, such as sales reps or customer service agents.

>> **Computer-based training (CBT):** CBT has continued to grow in popularity. CBT occurs online or is delivered via software. It's most beneficial for training that can be quantifiably measured through the use of review questions or scores. An extension of CBT is online training that may occur at the same time as the instructor is online (*synchronous*) or when the instructor and student are online at different times (*asynchronous*).

Training evaluation

Training isn't successful simply because you held the event, regardless of how fun or relevant the content was. Successful training occurs when participants are able to apply the knowledge or skill gained to their work environment, thus achieving the desired state — thus, the *E* in Addie standing for *evaluation*.

In the 1950s, Donald Kirkpatrick developed a method of evaluating training that includes four levels: reaction, learning, behavior, and results. Figure 9-2 shows these levels along with common tools used to successfully evaluate the training. Measuring training is highly dependent upon the identification of training objectives prior to design or delivery. Without these objectives, evaluating whether or not the training hit the targets is difficult.

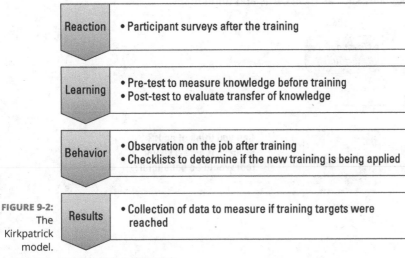

FIGURE 9-2: The Kirkpatrick model.

Courtesy of Kirkpatrick Partners

TIP

Several books and papers support the Kirkpatrick model at www.kirkpatrickpartners.com. These resources can help you go deeper into the concepts of training evaluation for the exam. At minimum, go online and review the site's thoughts on how this model has evolved and remains relevant in today's workplace.

EXAMPLE

Mary Jones managed Acme's Customer Service training program, in which Mary reviewed the proper way to greet customers. After all the employees went through the program, she asked the trainees' managers to measure how many times the employee greeted a new customer with a smile and welcome as they walked into the door. This form of measurement is at what level of Kirkpatrick's levels of training evaluation?

(A) Reaction

(B) Learning

(C) Behavior

(D) Results

The correct answer is (C). Kirkpatrick's evaluation of training at the behavior level measures the impact of training on the employees' work actions. In this case, the manager was measuring how the employees' conduct changed in direct relationship to what the employees had learned in class. An employee's reaction to training is measured by what he thought of the class, so Choice (A) is incorrect. Learning is measured by evaluating what knowledge was transferred, not behavior, so Choice (B) is incorrect. Results in this example would be evaluated by determining whether the training efforts made a difference to customers or how many of the employees were able to successfully apply the new behaviors, so Choice (D) isn't the best choice.

TIP

Get creative with your own learning style! Create a mind map such as the one found in Figure 9-3 using a resource such as www.goconqr.com. Join my group (Sandra Reed) and access resources from other exam candidates such as flash cards and mind maps.

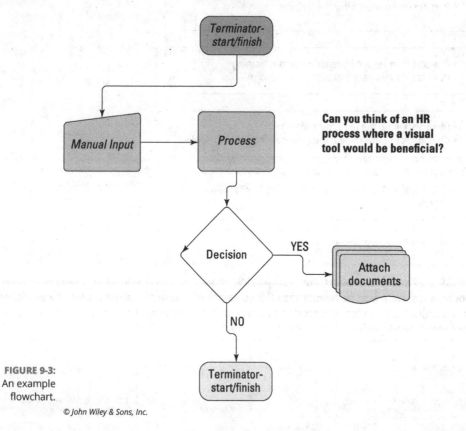

FIGURE 9-3:
An example
flowchart.

© John Wiley & Sons, Inc.

STUDYING FOR COMPREHENSION IN SIX HOURS

Print out the exam content area for the L&D function of the PHR. Look at your study schedule and allocate at least six hours as such:

- **Hours 1 and 2:** Search the internet for documents related to *each* exam objective and save or print the information. Sort this stuff by the exam objective, not by the documents' headings or titles. You must decide how the information applies to the test. This is transferring *knowledge*.

- **Hours 3 and 4:** Read through the documents from the first two hours, looking for common threads, themes, trends, or patterns in this field. Use highlighters or sticky notes to relate concepts and draw conclusions on where the functional area is heading. Draw conclusions about what information makes each exam objective related to the other, creating a web of connectivity. This activity teaches you *critical thinking*.

- **Hours 5 and 6:** Try and put each exam objective into a work context. Ask yourself questions about how the exam objective and related content would translate into your workplace. What are the obstacles? If already in place, how is it working? What measurements could you design to communicate effectiveness? This process supports your efforts toward applying *experience* to this domain.

You now literally have much of the information required to tackle this exam subject. Spread this exercise over a period of a week, and the knowledge, critical thinking, and experience perspectives will create depth to your learning. See if you can apply Kirkpatrick's four levels of training evaluation to this effort. What was your *reaction* to the exercise? Did it result in *learning*? How did it change your studying *behavior*? Were your *results* better on the assessment in L&D post training?

Chapter 10

Paying Your Dues: PHR 04 Total Rewards

The impact of Total Rewards in business is comprehensive. Compensation has existed since the days of the Romans when soldiers were paid in salt (where the term "salary" derives from) and in modern days is still one of the primary reasons individuals seek employment. Total Rewards have been packaged since early days as well, when apprentices were sponsored by experts who took on the responsibility of the worker's pay, training, safety, food, and housing. In addition to base pay, employee benefits can add a burden of 30 percent or more to the cost of having workers. The regulatory environment spends a lot of time in these areas, with many of the top reasons employers get sued being related to wage and hour violations. This chapter gives you an overview of these issues and more as it relates to the 15 percent of PHR exam content you will see on exam day.

Identifying the Exam Objectives for Total Rewards

The exam objectives related to Total Rewards are deceptively simple: compensation, benefits, and compliance with labor laws. Don't let this simplicity fool you however. Understanding Total Rewards for the exam will require in-depth, practical experience.

Responsibilities

The following list identifies the practical experience you will need to draw from in order to successfully pass the PHR:

01 Manage compensation-related information and support payroll issue resolution.

02 Implement and promote awareness of noncash rewards (for example: paid volunteer time, tuition assistance, workplace amenities, and employee recognition programs).

03 Implement benefit programs (for example: health plan, retirement plan, employee assistance plan, other insurance).

04 Administer federally compliant compensation and benefit programs.

Knowledge

In addition to the practical responsibilities listed above, a baseline of information will be required to accurately answer the questions on the PHR. Make sure and plan study time to review these topics:

36 Applicable federal laws and regulations related to total rewards

37 Compensation policies, processes, and analysis

38 Budgeting, payroll, and accounting practices related to compensation and benefits

39 Job analysis and evaluation concepts and methods

40 Job pricing and pay structures

41 Noncash compensation

42 Methods to align and benchmark compensation and benefits

43 Benefits programs' policies, processes, and analysis

Tackling the Key Points about Total Rewards

Total Rewards in the context of the PHR is bound by the framework of rewarding workers. This is done primarily through compensation and benefits programs. It begins by building the system from which employees are rewarded.

Structuring pay systems

Most employer plans will include a combination of direct and indirect forms of compensation.

Direct and indirect forms of compensation include cash and noncash components. Direct compensation includes hourly wages and salaries and variable pay such as commissions, bonuses or incentives. Indirect forms of compensation include noncash components such as health insurance and retirement plans. They may also include additional time off, such as volunteer leave, and tuition reimbursement programs. Nonmonetary compensation is generally found through perks, such as a car allowance, and paid training and recognition rewards. A total package is necessary in order to attract, retain, and reward team members.

Compensation philosophy

At a strategic level, an organization must make a decision about whether its comp systems will be based on *entitlement* or *performance.* An entitlement philosophy shows up in pay systems that give annual pay increases, such as those tied to cost of living. In a performance-oriented culture, compensation is tied to individual or team performance differences, also called "merit."

Building a pay system that meets the needs of either philosophy — or in some cases, a hybrid approach — is dependent on identifying the requirements of the job, done through job analysis and priced using job evaluation.

Job evaluation

A *job evaluation* seeks to value the findings of *job analysis* (the process of identifying the tasks, duties, and responsibilities of each job within the company) in an effort to make decisions about pay. The job evaluation process looks at the common factors among all jobs within the company and the market values for the positions. This data is then used to set pay rates. Common methods for evaluating jobs are

>> **Point:** The *point* method of job evaluation assigns a value to the *compensable factors* of a group of jobs (a job element that is common among a group of similar workers).

>> **Classification:** The *classification* method uses the job descriptions (written documents from the job analysis process that identify the tasks, duties, and responsibilities of each job) to group similar jobs into grades of pay. From this, minimum and maximum pay levels are set.

>> **Factor comparison:** More difficult than the other methods for job evaluation, the factor-comparison method assigns points to the job tasks, duties, and responsibilities as well as ranks jobs from highest to lowest according to their worth.

>> **Ranking:** The easiest of all evaluation methods, jobs are placed in order of importance.

EXAMPLE

What is one of the major disadvantages of using the ranking method to conduct a job evaluation?

(A) The data collected cannot be legally validated.

(B) The information collected is highly subjective.

(C) The entire job is considered, rather than the individual elements.

(D) Employees with similar jobs may perform them in different ways.

The correct answer is (C). The ranking method of job evaluation uses the whole job rather than the individual tasks, duties, and responsibilities. Validation studies refer to pre-employment tests, so Choice (A) is incorrect. The job data used for the job evaluation method isn't subjective because it refers to the output from a job analysis or job description, so Choice (B) is incorrect. Understanding how the work gets done so that it can be properly designed and compensated is important, so Choice (D) isn't a disadvantage.

Conducting wage surveys

Wage surveys, a tool used to collect data about average pay practices of the relevant market, are an important consideration when designing compensation plans for the following two main reasons:

>> **Labor as a percentage of overhead:** Paying too much for talent impacts the ability of a company to compete in the market. Increased overhead drives the cost of building the widgets or offering services. With inflated overhead, companies are forced to pass bloat to the consumer or compromise other important business outcomes such as quality. A subset to this concept is the decision to *lead* the market in pay rates, which ties directly into organizational strategy. A company that chooses a *differentiation strategy* (designing new or substantially different products from the competition) for its products or services may need to pay more for talent, but the expectation is that its products will be of superior quality, allowing the company to charge more to the consumer.

A strategy of *cost leadership* (in which being the lowest price in the market is the goal) is going to require compensation rates that lag or only match market pay in order to keep consumer prices down. Leading the market in pay rates increases overhead and therefore increases the cost of goods sold. Nevertheless, a company must conduct external wage surveys to align its pay practices with strategy.

» **The ability to compete for talent:** Regardless of organizational strategy, companies need to be able to compete for and retain talent in order to stay in business. Similar to executive compensation, supply and demand drives these decisions. Conducting regular wage surveys allows for greater agility in pay practices, giving businesses the opportunity to get ahead of issues before they become challenges that must be dealt with. In short, it's the difference between *managing* a pay practice and *handling* a pay issue.

Market surveys come with special issues of their own. *Benchmarking* jobs (the practice of comparing jobs to similar work in the industry) is the focus of conducting a pay survey, which can lead to charges of *collusion* (discussing pay practices with competitors) or *wage fixing* (artificially holding down wages or benefits). Any time competitors get together to exchange information, they must be careful not to artificially hold down wages for a group of workers. For that reason, many industries participate in wage surveys conducted by third parties with privacy firewalls.

REMEMBER

As a PHR candidate, you need to be skilled at managing outsourced vendors, so utilizing and managing a third-party vendor to conduct wage surveys may be an area for increased review.

Several large technology companies (competitors) agreed to not poach talent from each other in order to avoid wage inflation in their industry. Affected employees sued and won based on a violation of which act?

EXAMPLE

(A) Sherman Antitrust Act

(B) Fair Labor Standards Act

(C) Employee Retirement Income Security Act

(D) The Portal-to-Portal Act

The correct answer is (A). Several major technology companies were accused of agreeing to not poach employees from each other in order to avoid paying higher wages. Affected employees sued, accusing these companies of colluding to fix wages, a practice prohibited under the Sherman Antitrust Act. Choice (B), the Fair Labor Standards Act, established rules for minimum wages, overtime, and child labor. Choice (C), the Employee Retirement Income Security Act, regulates retirement plans, and Choice (D), the Portal-to-Portal Act, amended the Fair Labor Standards Act to define compensable time under the act.

Pay structures

After the job analysis and market wage surveys are complete, a company can begin to design *pay structures* (the framework that organizes how employees' pay is calculated). Considerations for the exam include understanding concepts related to exempt versus nonexempt workers (the employers' obligation to overtime and rest breaks), creating pay *grades* or *bands* (grouping similar jobs together and setting minimum and maximum pay levels), and evaluating existing pay rates to ensure equity. The result of these efforts may identify employees who are out of range for their positions. These employees are known as either

» **Green-circled employees:** Green is the color of money, and in the case of green-circled employees, their pay falls short of the established range. Exam candidates should understand strategies to address this deficiency, including a one-time increase or gradual increases until the employees' pay rate matches the pay grade.

>> **Red-circled employees:** Red means stop, as in, stop paying these employees above the range set for their position. HR can address employee pay rates that are above the grade by freezing wage increases or looking for opportunities to increase employee job responsibilities to account for the increased pay.

Pay compression

Pay compression occurs when the gap between *incumbents* (those currently doing the job) and new hires becomes small. This can happen for a variety of reasons, all generally related to the employer's lack of systems-based decision-making when it comes to company pay practices.

Pay adjustments

After a pay structure is in place, a system to account for pay adjustments must be established. Common pay adjustments include legal processing of *wage garnishments* (court ordered withholdings from employee pay to settle a financial obligation) and pay *increases* (giving an employee a raise or compensating for new job tasks through pay bumps).

Processing payroll

The processing of weekly or bi-weekly payroll can be nerve-wracking for the inexperienced. Fraught with opportunities for errors, it is also heavily regulated, and mistakes are costly, specifically because most employees are fully reliant upon their paychecks being correct. It is not just about cash in the bank account; it's about what that money allows them to do — feed their families, make the house payment, save for emergencies, and so on. An error in payroll creates not only a practical challenge, but also an emotional one as well. Getting this practice right should be of upmost priority for the HR technician.

Payroll is tied to many regulatory compliance needs. For example, processing a court-ordered garnishment of wages and turning over those funds to the proper counties is one area of concern. Recordkeeping and accuracy of pay stubs is another area of consideration. Tax-related issues are front and center when calculating net income and employer-owed payroll taxes, so HR departments often partner with accounting to ensure accuracy.

REMEMBER

Payroll and medical files both have a high level of confidentiality associated with their administration, so take steps to discover how to protect this delicate information.

Selecting and Communicating Employee Benefits

There is a long list of options when it comes to selecting benefits. These options include health and wellness offerings, retirement plans and contributions, employee assistance programs (EAPs), workers' compensation, Medicare, protected leave, and Social Security. Benefits may be voluntary or mandated by law, such as the leave rights defined under the Family Medical Leave Act. Some benefits are voluntary (such as retirement plans), but once an employer chooses to offer them, they are regulated. For these reasons, we spend a bit of time in this section focusing on a few of the laws you are likely to see questions about on the exam.

Understand that the components of labor law change on a very regular basis, sometimes every year! While you must stay up-to-date on the changes to labor laws at a state and national level for practical use, HRCI disclaims on the PHR exam content outline: "IF LAWS CHANGE: We realize that employment laws change constantly. Candidates are responsible for knowing the HR laws and regulations that are in effect at the time of their exam. This exam content outline took effect in 2018."

Violations of wage and hour laws are one of the most common complaints to the Department of Labor and other state agencies charged with enforcement. Because the PHR exam is focused on national law, we begin there.

Fair Labor Standards Act (FLSA)

The FLSA is the seminal law on managing employee rights and employer wage and hour responsibilities. It fundamentally does three things:

>> It requires employers to pay a premium rate for any hours worked over 40 in a week for nonexempt (hourly) workers, called *overtime*.

>> It creates the minimum wage that employers must pay to their workers.

>> It establishes controls regarding the employment of minors.

In addition, expansion of the requirements of the FLSA over the years include offering additional break time to nursing mothers, guidance on the salaries of tipped workers, and defining compensable time, the function of the Portal-to Portal Act.

The Portal-to-Portal Act is an amendment to the FLSA that clarifies what is compensable time (travel time, time spent putting on PPE, and so forth) and is well worth a robust study effort. Check out the summary from Cornell Law on the Portal-to-Portal Act at www.law.cornell.edu/cfr/text/29/790.5.

Studying the FLSA is a perfect time to point out how *context* can really enhance your learning. Think about what was happening socially and politically back in 1938 when the FLSA was passed. It was the middle of the Great Depression, and thousands were out of work. Those who were fortunate enough to have work had to work for any number of hours and for any amount of pay from their employer (overtime and minimum wage). Some families were desperate enough to send their children off to work (employment of minors). Knowing this can help you understand that President Roosevelt got the FLSA passed to address the issues of the day.

Do some research when studying the federal labor law appendix at the end of this book to discover the social and political context of the years in which the laws were enacted.

Employee Retirement Income and Security Act (ERISA)

The government doesn't require retirement plans to be offered to employees (yet). But when an employer chooses to administer a voluntary plan, ERISA (1974) is there to guide the process. Many employers choose to outsource the administration of retirement plans, which is about as complex as possible. That does not release them of liability, however, so a basic understanding of how to comply with this law is important. This includes providing members with retirement plan descriptions, establishing a fiduciary obligation for human resources (a higher level of legal responsibility to act in an ethical manner), and granting the employee the right to sue for malfeasance.

Of significance is not only the number of amendments that have since been tacked on to ERISA, but also how important they have become in shaping human resources. The two most noteworthy include the following:

>> **COBRA:** The Consolidated Omnibus Budget Reconciliation Act gives employees the option to continue healthcare coverage when a qualifying event — such as termination — occurs.

>> **HIPAA:** The Health Insurance Portability and Accountability Act expanded employee privacy rights related to medical information.

As you can see, HR practitioners must not only be familiar with the original text and requirements of the labor laws, but also the expansion of coverage through the use of amendments.

The Older Workers Benefit Protection Act (OWBPA)

The OWBPA is an amendment to the Age Discrimination in Employment Act (ADEA) of 1967. The ADEA was written with the intent to classify individuals over the age of 40 as protected class groups and thus entitled to nondiscriminatory employment decisions such as hiring, compensation, selection for training, and promotion.

It soon became clear that the law needed to be clarified and enhanced in three specific areas, and thus the OWBPA was passed to protect older workers in these situations:

>> When signing severance agreements that exchange payment for their right to sue for employment practice violations, older workers must have a written agreement in which they are advised and given time (21 days) to sign and/or to have an attorney review the proposed agreement.

>> When making decisions about downsizing the workforce, older workers cannot be targeted for separations and then subsequently replaced to manage salary levels.

>> When offering benefits, the employer is prohibited from considering the employee's age. Generally, employers must offer equal benefits to all workers, regardless of age.

REMEMBER

The concept of "employment-related decisions" is present in the application of all labor laws. These include decisions related to hiring, promotion, selection for training, compensation, eligibility for benefits, job assignment, locations, schedules, offering overtime, and so on. Basically, any decision related to the management of employees must be job related and nondiscriminatory in both intent and effect.

Social Security & Medicare

Another law that was passed during the Great Depression was Social Security & Medicare (SSI), a form of social insurance in which the government supplies financial assistance to eligible people. Medicare amended the Social Security Act in the 1960s, providing medical insurance for those who qualified. Both SSI and Medicare are taxes paid by both the employer and employee, calculated on a percentage of wages and deducted from each paycheck until the maximum amount is met.

Workers' compensation

Workers' compensation is required by federal law; however, individual states administer it. It offers medical care, wage replacement, rehabilitation, and survivor payments to employees injured on the job. Workers' compensation is a form of mandatory insurance that is entirely employer funded. Employees are also protected from retaliation for exercising their rights under this and other mandatory benefits.

Family Medical Leave Act (FMLA)

The FMLA provides job-protected leave to employees with a serious health condition. It applies to employers with 50 or more employees. Eligible employees are entitled to 12 weeks of unpaid leave for the birth of a child, for their own serious health condition, or for the serious health condition of a spouse, child, or parent. If an employee is the caregiver of an injured member of the military, the employee is entitled to 26 weeks of unpaid leave within a 12-month period to provide care. Eligible employees are those who have worked for a covered employer for more than 12 months and at least 1,250 hours.

Related to the FMLA, in response to the COVID-19 pandemic of 2019 and 2020, Congress passed two emergency laws affecting the employment of workers:

>> **The Families First Coronavirus Response Act and the Emergency Paid Leave Act:** This act expanded eligible leave time for those who are sick with COVID-19 or need to care for a family member who is sick, and addressed workers affected by school closures. It is set to expire in December of 2020.

>> **The Emergency Paid Leave Act:** This act established that employees affected by COVID-19 are entitled to an additional two weeks of paid sick leave. This is the only type of leave that is paid under the FMLA.

HR should regularly check the Department of Labor for updates to these emergency laws to ensure they are complying with the recordkeeping requirements, rates of pay, eligibility, and more (www. dol.gov/agencies/whd/pandemic/ffcra-questions#12).

While the COVID-specific amendments to the FLSA have expiration dates, understanding the context is important. An HR pro can predict, for example, that flus and other common illnesses may now be included under OSHA's general duty clause. The general duty clause states that "Each employer shall furnish to each of his employees work and a place of employment which are free from recognized hazards that are causing or are likely to cause death or serious physical harm to his employees." For this reason, employers should take steps every year to minimize employee exposure to the flu as part of their regular safety and health program.

These legal measures taken by Congress may also indicate that terminating employees for absences related to illness may be more difficult in the future. It also suggests that similar to programs required by Maine and New Jersey, employers may eventually be required to offer earned sick leave as part of their mandatory benefit offerings.

Patient Protection & Affordable Care Act

The Patient Protection & Affordable Care Act (PPACA) is the outcome of the government's attempt at healthcare reform that requires affected employers to offer employees health insurance. It requires that employers with 50 or more employees provide affordable health insurance options to their full-time-equivalent (FTE) workforce or be subject to a penalty.

COMMUNICATING THE BENEFIT OF EMPLOYEE BENEFITS

With the exception of ERISA, the benefits described here are mandatory. After they have been implemented, your employer has the option to offer several different types of voluntary benefits such as sick time, vacation leave, tuition reimbursement, or flexible scheduling. After your employer has decided which benefits to offer, HR must communicate to employees why they should take advantage of these benefits. With a diverse workgroup, these conversations can feel discombobulated. For example, baby boomers may be highly interested in the retirement match, but younger professionals may be more interested in tuition reimbursement. Employees with young families and those who are part-time college students may appreciate flexible scheduling.

Ultimately, conducting employee surveys to identify which benefits they prefer is a helpful way to offer and potentially pay for benefits that will increase employee satisfaction. This is one example of the types of reporting tools HR can use to become better business partners.

Taking Advantage of Common Reports and Tools

Streamlined reporting supports an employer's efforts toward compensation and benefits communication. Often, the practice of collecting the data can be quite revealing, and it can help employers make decisions about what benefits to offer in the future. The following sections are a few of the more common data collection and communication tools used in administering Total Rewards.

Hidden paychecks

Also called *total rewards statements, hidden paychecks* allow employers to communicate the true value of an employee's pay. A hidden paycheck summarizes individual employee base pay, incentives, and benefits. For example, say an employee's base pay is $50,000 per year; however, the employer contributions to health insurance and retirement plans add an additional $16,000, making the total value of the employment $66,000. This information is important for the employee to have, especially if she is considering leaving for what appears to be a better paying job. Total rewards statements are often given at the end of the calendar year, and many HRIS or payroll processing systems generate them automatically.

Benefits surveys

With increasing benefits costs outpacing inflation, the decision to offer benefits has a direct link to the profit and loss statement. Conducting an employee-needs survey to ask employees which benefits they would prefer helps employers offer options that are fully utilized. Surveys can be used to identify both the financial and nonfinancial desires of the workforce. Popular survey questions relate to additional health insurance, coverage for same-sex partners, family-friendly benefits like flexible schedules, the need for tuition reimbursement, and employee wellness incentives for weight loss or smoking cessation.

Exempt checklists

The FLSA allows employers to exempt certain workers from the payment of overtime wages if certain criteria are met. In some cases, a whole class of workers are exempt, such as outside salespersons. Other positions may require a more in-depth look at whether they're truly qualified for this exemption. Factors to consider include

» **Salary level:** As of January 2020, the FLSA mandates that all employees paid less than $35,568 per year ($684 per week) be nonexempt and eligible for overtime.

» **Job duties:** Meeting the salaried basis test isn't enough. To be correctly classified as exempt from overtime law, the employee must also meet the job duties requirement. Described by the FLSA as "high-level," the law further breaks down the exemption categories into the following:

- **Executive:** Defined by who is in charge. Even if a supervisor is a working supervisor, if she is the one who is in charge and truly has influence over personnel matters, she may qualify for exemption.

- **Professional:** Creative professionals and those jobs that are highly intellectual requiring an advanced degree, such as lawyers or architects, aren't entitled to overtime pay.

- **Administrative:** Administrative professionals support the work of business and are considered staff workers (as opposed to line workers who produce the goods or services). HR and finance are two examples of qualified administrative professionals. General clerical workers aren't.

EXAMPLE

FLSA standards specify that a job is exempt from overtime payments when

(A) the employees are paid on a commission basis

(B) the work is done by a tipped employee

(C) the work is conducted by an independent contractor

(D) the minimum pay rate equals at least $684 per week

The correct answer is (D). In order for any position to be classified as exempt under the Fair Labor Standards Act (FLSA), the pay rate must equal at least $684 (salary basis) per week. Choice (A) is incorrect because commissioned employees must be paid a minimum of one-and-one-half times the minimum wage for each hour worked. Choice (B) isn't a factor in determining whether an employee is exempt or nonexempt, so it's incorrect. An independent contractor isn't an employee, and therefore, isn't subject to labor laws, so Choice (C) isn't true.

REMEMBER

To meet the job duties requirement for exempt workers, you can't rely on job titles. The employee's tasks, duties, and responsibilities (TDR) and the knowledge, skill, and abilities (KSA) required to perform the work determine whether the employee is exempt.

Chapter **11**

Connecting the Dots: PHR 05 Employee and Labor Relations

The title of this HR function is telling. Employee and Labor Relations (ELR) is all about relationships. The first relationship is between the supervisor and his direct reports. The next relationship is between the employer and a union. The third relationship is between the union and its members. There are also relationships between co-workers. Finally, there is the relationship between the employees and the organization. And of course, all employment relationships have rights and responsibilities of both parties, making risk management necessary for success. The application of ELR principles is always toward one of these relationships that exist in the workplace. This chapter examines some of the specifics in more detail.

Navigating Employee & Labor Relations

One of the fundamental HR directives from the Employee and Labor Relations exam objectives is illustrated by the phrase "functional effectiveness." This refers to HR's ability to balance the many competing demands of stakeholders in a way that "results in results." Perhaps easier said than done, it is obviously important as these responsibilities make up the greatest amount of the weighted content you will see on exam day at 39 percent — or 59 of the 150 scored questions.

REMEMBER

Your exam will have 175 questions, but only 150 will be scored. Twenty-five are questions that are being validated by exam writers, and thus, your answers to these questions don't count toward your score. You won't know which questions are unscored.

Get your first sense of the framework for this HR function from HRCI's description of Employee and Labor Relations: "Manage, monitor, and/or promote legally compliant programs and policies that impact the employee experience throughout the employee life cycle."

Responsibilities

With so much of the PHR covering this content, it is no surprise that the responsibilities of ELR are comprehensive. Be prepared to face questions related to these topics:

01 Analyze functional effectiveness at each stage of the employee life cycle (for example: hiring, onboarding, development, retention, exit process, alumni program) and identify alternate approaches as needed.

02 Collect, analyze, summarize, and communicate employee engagement data.

03 Understand organizational culture, theories, and practices; identify opportunities and make recommendations.

04 Understand and apply knowledge of programs, federal laws, and regulations to promote outreach, diversity, and inclusion (for example: affirmative action, employee resource groups, community outreach, corporate responsibility).

05 Implement and support workplace programs relative to health, safety, security, and privacy following federal laws and regulations (for example: OSHA, workers' compensation, emergency response, workplace violence, substance abuse, legal postings).

06 Promote organizational policies and procedures (for example: employee handbook, SOPs, time and attendance, expenses).

07 Manage complaints or concerns involving employment practices, behavior, or working conditions, and escalate by providing information to appropriate stakeholders.

08 Promote techniques and tools for facilitating positive employee and labor relations with knowledge of applicable federal laws affecting union and non-union workplaces (for example: dispute/conflict resolution, anti-discrimination policies, sexual harassment).

09 Support and consult with management in performance management process (for example: employee reviews, promotions, recognition programs).

10 Support performance activities (for example: coaching, performance improvement plans, involuntary separations) and employment activities (for example: job eliminations, reductions in force) by managing corresponding legal risks.

Knowledge

In addition to the practical components listed above, there are additional knowledge requirements from which you will need to draw. These include the following:

44 General employee relations activities and analysis (for example, conducting investigations, researching grievances, working conditions, reports, and so on)

45 Applicable federal laws and procedures affecting employment, labor relations, safety, and security

46 Human relations, culture and values concepts, and applications to employees and organizations

47 Review and analysis process for assessing employee attitudes, opinions, and satisfaction

Focusing on What the Exam Covers in ELR

The majority of the content covered in this area relates to the environments in which we perform our human resource work. This includes the industries we are in, the markets where we compete, (global, national, regional, state, county, and of course, online) the talent we rely on, and the law. Understanding the business and market environments begins with the content you study in functional area 01, Business Management. Defining the parameters of the jobs and thus the supply of talent is the focus of functional area 02, Talent Planning and Acquisition. This continues through 03 and 04 as managing teams through Learning and Development and Total Rewards is a significant part of how HR contributes. What is left, then, is a conversation about the organizational culture and climate and the psychological and physical conditions in which HR asks its team members to perform.

REMEMBER

Several areas of content overlap remain between the PHR and SPHR, particularly in the area of Functional Area 05. These include

>> Human relations

>> Motivation

>> Diversity and inclusion

>> Health, safety, and security

>> Collective bargaining

For this reason, make sure to complete a thorough review of Chapter 2 where these topics are discussed in great detail.

Defining company culture and climate

The term *culture* is used in a few different ways throughout the exam objectives. It includes the diversity perspective of a group of people with a shared national origin that has a collective belief system, customs, and sometimes language that distinguishes it. These factors are protected class conditions; therefore, employers are not allowed to use them to make employment-related decisions.

The exam content also focuses on the conditions that define organizational culture. These conditions include values, customs, rituals, language, and artifacts, as well as the unspoken rules of engagement communicated through supervisor and employee behaviors. All these conditions can be useful in understanding the ELR components in these ways:

>> **Values:** A company that lives its values is setting a powerful standard for the day-to-day operations and behaviors of its employees. Core *values* are guidelines for how a company will behave toward its employees, customers, and other stakeholders. Values serve organizational culture by creating a shared commitment to a set of beliefs.

>> **Customs and rituals:** A *custom* is a traditional way of doing things, usually based on a family, religious, or collective belief. A *ritual* is a regular practice designed for a specific outcome.

>> **Language:** *Language* refers to the systems of communication in place at work. Tone, attitudes, body language, and even the unspoken behaviors communicated by executive decisions set the standard for company culture.

>> **Employer and employee behaviors:** How people act toward each other is an important indicator of the level of trust that exists within the walls of a business. Employers that do what they say they're going to do go a long way toward establishing a culture of goodwill. In addition, how employees behave toward each other sets the tone for a team environment working toward a common goal.

An added dimension to organizational culture is the intellectual achievements of a company. Everyone wants to be on a winning team — there is just something important about shared wins, which means how a company celebrates its successes matters. Note that every company has a culture (whether it knows it or not). HR's job is to help the company define and reinforce the factors that build a positive organizational culture.

EXAMPLE

A positive organizational culture may be influenced by which employee relations program?

(A) Health and wellness

(B) Diversity

(C) Union avoidance

(D) All of the above

The correct answer is (B). Diversity programs positively impact organizational culture by creating a more inclusive environment. Health and wellness programs are focused on the health, safety, and security of the workforce, so Choice (A) is incorrect. Companies create union-avoidance strategies primarily to avoid the unionization of the workforce, (although a positive organizational culture may be part of those strategies), so Choice (C) is incorrect.

After the culture is established, HR must take steps to monitor the climate and assess the effectiveness of ELR programs. These temperature checks appear throughout the exam and represent the stages of the employee life cycle. Based on the objectives, you should understand the use of the following:

>> **Focus groups:** Employee *focus groups* are a form of research used to gather feedback from workers on different employment issues. They send the message to employees that their feedback is valued and serve the organizational culture by improving employee *engagement* (the degree to which employees feel linked to company success). You should be aware that a focus group is considered a softer, more human way to gather information about employee needs because the results are communicated in words rather than numbers.

>> **Employee surveys:** Companies use *employee surveys* to both ask the employees what they need and measure the effectiveness of ELR programs, so devote some of your attention to the fundamentals of employee surveys. These fundamentals include the need to clearly identify the objective of the survey and communicate that objective when asking employees for their input. Management commitment to the findings should also be evaluated, because it's demotivating to ask employees for their feedback and then fail to act.

>> **Staff meetings:** A staff meeting is a tool used to both gather employee feedback on important issues and help employees feel involved. Staff meetings are broader than focus groups in that these meetings are regularly scheduled and serve to communicate information rather than specifically to ask for feedback.

>> **Exit interviews:** Exit interviews are another fairly specific form of gathering employee feedback. An *exit interview* is narrowly focused on asking separating workers why they're leaving the company. This data is then used to improve retention rates of the remaining employees.

While these tools are capable of collecting general data, the PHR exam asks you to apply an engagement filter based on the employee life cycle. It begins with the selection and onboarding process.

Early engagement techniques

While much of Chapter 8 is focused on engaging with applicants and new hires through employer branding and acculturation efforts, there is an opportunity to apply these fundamentals through the lens of ELR. Specifically, the beginning of the employee life cycle can predict retention — short- or long-term. For this reason, HR must find ways to communicate the company culture early and often.

Scroll through social media and you can see these efforts in play. Highly competitive companies send swag bags to new hires that include company merchandise or flowers to the home to say "welcome aboard." Other companies assign buddies for the first week to introduce team members and help them get the lay of the land. Onboarding sessions include training that goes beyond compliance to begin to communicate the norms and expectations. The key here is to unleash the creative talents of your HR team to help new hires feel welcome.

This is also an opportunity to optimize technology. For example, Cisco developed a check-in ritual that requires managers to assess how their team members are doing on different engagement factors such as finding opportunities to use their strengths and having critical conversations with their boss. Other questions, such as "What did you love or loathe about your job this week?", give employees space to communicate their weekly experiences and leaders the opportunity to respond, coach, or simply listen. Cisco's example demonstrates that, if built properly, the systems designed to engage new hires can be the building block for activities when it comes time to manage performance.

Building engagement through performance management

The performance management process is usually understood as the appraisal process, but a robust system affects so many positive employee outcomes! HR must take steps to provide feedback as part of a whole system, not just the performance review.

Providing performance feedback

The dreaded performance appraisal. Supervisors don't want to write them, and employees look forward to them only if they think that they're getting a raise. Supervisor and employee reports of dissatisfaction with the performance appraisal process continue to abound, and the dissatisfaction often is related to many things such as the following:

>> **Lack of clearly defined measurables:** Chapter 8 mentions that the effort that must go toward defining the tasks, duties, and responsibilities of the job must be matched with the knowledge, skills, and abilities necessary to perform. If this activity hasn't been successfully completed, having a meaningful feedback system in place for employees is nearly impossible.

>> **Rater errors:** Similar to the bias interviewers must avoid, performance rater errors dilute the effectiveness of the review process.

- The *recency effect* — where raters allow recent events to drive the feedback without looking at performance for the whole rating period — is especially prevalent, generally because most supervisors are crunched for time and often haven't properly documented employee performance for the entire year or quarter, thus being held hostage by their own memory.

- Another problem can be the *error of central tendency*, in which all employees are rated as average — no highs, no lows. Central tendency is the middle child of "all my employees are amazing" and "everybody needs to improve" — two other rater issues that HR must be on the lookout for when managing the process.

- Another error is the *primacy effect*, when raters allow first events to drive ratings. For example, when interviewing ten people in a row, there is often the tendency for raters to remember the first person that they interviewed more clearly than others.

- The *halo effect* refers to assuming that there are many positive things about a person based on one positive thing, such as the assumption that a person with excellent attendance must also be productive.

- Similarly, the *horn effect* refers to assuming many negative things about a person because there is an area in need of improvement.

TIP

The rater errors apply not only to the rating of employee performance, but also to interview bias that occurs during the hiring process. Study these errors from both perspectives for the exam.

>> **Perceptions of fairness:** Equity is a shared issue through all the functional areas of HR. From discriminatory hiring practices to disparity in compensation decisions, *fairness* is a concept in which you must become well-versed. Performance appraisals — especially when tied to pay increases — are quite the large target for claims of supervisor favoritism. HR can combat claims of favoritism by helping the raters understand the job criteria, by creating objective measurement criteria, and by training management on the expectations and purpose of the review process.

Employees may experience two types of inequities. They are important to mention for the exams because they apply to the perceptions employees have about any employment-related decision. They are as follows:

- **Procedural justice:** Employees consider an outcome acceptable if they believe the procedure used to make the decision is fair. For example, differences in pay are acceptable if the employees perceive the process to arrive at the disparity is both clear and reasonable, or a performance rating is fair if the right criteria were used to arrive at the final rating.

- **Distributive justice:** *Distributive justice* refers to the perception of fairness in the distribution of outcomes. If employees feel like their performance review was fair in comparison with how their peers did, their satisfaction with the outcome is likely to be perceived as acceptable. In compensation, distributive justice refers to the perception that the employees got the proper reward when compared to their effort.

Although the performance appraisal is probably the most recognized way of providing employee feedback, the exam doesn't stop there. Studiers should be prepared to review informal feedback as well, which includes daily, on-the-job comments; gaining feedback from employees through 360-degree reviews; and employee suggestion systems.

EXAMPLE

Which of the following sources would be consulted in a 360-degree review of an accounting clerk?

(A) The production manager

(B) The accounting manager

(C) A vendor

(D) All of the above

The correct answer is (D). In a 360-degree review, performance ratings are gathered from many different sources to evaluate the performance of an employee. The goal of this type of review is to measure how well the employee is supporting the stakeholders.

Performance appraisals

If ever there were a need to break the mold in HR and start over, the performance appraisal form would be the place to start. Kick up the dust at your company by starting the dialogue about what makes its performance appraisal forms irrelevant or meaningless. Be open to rewriting the document, but only do so after you have received feedback from your supervisors and employees about what they really want to know about how well or how poorly they're doing.

The actual performance appraisal tool should reflect what the company deems the most important of employee behavior, which may include quantifiable information, such as attendance and productivity, and the more subjective elements such as teamwork and attitude. The performance appraisal document should be both simple for the supervisor to complete and thorough enough to provide meaningful feedback to the employee.

REMEMBER

The performance appraisal is an excellent time to provide constructive feedback that is designed to help the employee be successful in the job and at the company. It is *not* the time to discipline an employee for performance deficiencies. That part of the employee life cycle requires a system of its own.

Applying discipline and conducting separations

When employee relations efforts such as providing performance feedback, coaching, and motivation techniques fail, many employers turn to discipline, up to and leading to termination. The ELR exam content refers to these concepts in a couple of ways:

>> As the end of the employee life cycle, such as through the design of an exit process that includes required paperwork to comply with labor law as well as getting feedback from the team member about why they are leaving. This is true for all types of separations, from the involuntary termination to the employee who quits, is laid off, or included in a reduction-in-force (RIF).

>> To use tools such as the performance improvement plan (PIP), an internal investigation to make recommendations and determine future actions.

HR must be skilled at handling difficult conversations and versed in neutral language. In separation meetings, they must take care to manage risk, while also understanding that the person being terminated is likely to have an emotional reaction requiring compassion and care.

Culture matters just as much at this stage of the employee life cycle as it does at the beginning. Particularly for team members who are leaving due to an RIF or job restructure, HR can offer support through résumé reviews, providing letters of recommendation, processing severance payments, and in some cases, hosting job fairs to help exiting members find new work.

EXAMPLE

In a termination meeting, managers should be counseled to

(A) be honest and direct

(B) keep the meeting as short as possible

(C) avoid conflict

(D) have another employee present.

The correct answer is (A). *Termination meetings* can be uncomfortable for both parties involved. It's best for a manager to be as honest and direct as possible without being condescending or combative. Keeping the meeting as brief as possible isn't a priority, so Choice (B) is incorrect. Avoiding conflict, Choice (C), may not be possible because employees aren't generally happy to be terminated, so a better choice would be for the supervisor to understand how to handle the conflict rather than avoid it. Choice (D) is a bit trickier because it's a good idea to have another person present; however, the witness should be a member of management, not an employee.

Using Policies and Procedures to Communicate

The words *policy* and *police* share origins, in that they refer to governing a population. In the workplace, policies are designed to communicate employer expectations and to comply with the various laws requiring that employees be notified of certain rights and responsibilities.

Employee handbooks and policy reviews

An *employee handbook* (written employment guide that documents employee rights and responsibilities) is the tool used by employers to document and communicate employment policies.

One example is in the area of sexual harassment prevention. In order for a company to be able to provide an affirmative defense against a charge of sexual harassment, the company first must have a policy in place that prohibits unlawful harassment. The harassment prevention policy would be used to train workers on appropriate conduct in the workplace, and the policy would reside in the handbook for future reference.

From the exam perspective, HRCI's ELR exam objective 06 states that you must understand how to:

> "Promote organizational policies and procedures (for example employee handbooks, SOPs, time and attendance, expenses")."

This means that you should be prepared to answer questions about how to create and monitor both policies and *procedures* for implementing said policies. Continuing with our sexual harassment example, the company would have a written policy that prohibits harassment in the workplace. HR would need to follow up by writing and communicating the procedure employees should use to report harassing behavior, such as "talk directly to your supervisor, to Human Resources, or to any other member of the management team" or "use the harassment hotline number to anonymously report."

Common reports and tools

In the area of ELR, the best advice is to remember that if it isn't documented, it never happened. Most human resource forms and documents are used to establish a paper trail of activity, ensuring that procedures are followed and both parties' interests are protected. These documents and forms are essential in ELR.

Standard forms

The list is really quite long of the various types of forms that make up the administrative debris that is part of HR. Some of the more common ones include

>> **Incident reports:** Employee incidents can be of any kind, running the spectrum from an injury or accident to a near-miss to an instance of a quality defect. Being able to accurately track this data allows for a focus on prevention. You can then use it to communicate expected standards of behavior to employees using real-time information.

>> **Disciplinary action:** If compensation and incentives are the carrot in employee motivation, then discipline is the stick in the realm of employee relations. Supervisors who notice negative behavior talk to the employee about what she needs to do to correct it and then document the conversation, which makes them much better positioned to make a longer-term decision about separation. It's fairer to the employee as well. Underperforming workers should be given the opportunity to correct their behavior before being placed on the path of discipline. When necessary, these initial conversations are used to justify more formal disciplinary action, up to and including termination.

>> **Request for time off:** Employees are generally granted time off through policies, and a way to track usage is necessary. The employee can give the request form to the supervisor in advance or, more common now, put in for the request through the HRIS or timekeeping system.

>> **Grievance or complaint:** Good employee relations management is paved as a two-way street. Supervisors should have a way to document performance, and employees should have a way to log complaints. From a claim of harassment to dissatisfaction with an employment decision, these objections are documented on a grievance form, which officially begins the grievance procedure.

Good forms aren't multipage documents. They're a quick checklist that reflects the core need of business to document occurrences and track efforts.

Employee suggestion systems

A form of *upward communication* (the direction of information moving up from the employees to management), employee suggestion systems are useful ways for employees to share their thoughts on specific issues with the management team.

One example of the use of suggestion systems is in quality management programs. Employee opinions on the elimination of waste or improved efficiencies is solicited, and a committee meets to evaluate the merit. This information can then be tied to incentives, which pay employees for implemented ideas, or gift cards to recognize employees who gave their opinion.

Encouraging employee suggestions is a worthwhile employee relations effort because employees are the experts in their jobs and are best positioned to provide impactful feedback. Asking for employees' opinions is an indication that the company and management desires to hear what employees have to say.

Agendas

An *agenda* isn't just a good business practice for meeting efficiency. Agendas are also necessary for corporations to communicate and record board of directors' activity. Corporations are required to have a board of directors, and boards must have meetings. An agenda announces to the stakeholders what will be covered, and the agenda becomes a part of the meeting record. The meeting frequency varies state by state, but standard protocol for meetings usually holds.

For example, a quorum must exist for the meeting to be held, and certain bylaws require the publishing of the meeting agenda in advance. Most meetings must have a record of the activity, so minutes are kept to accurately reflect the meeting outcomes and general follow-up.

Beyond the corporate governance efforts, the ELR exam objectives describe a need for employee involvement strategies through employee management committees, self-directed work teams, focus groups, and staff meetings. You should be familiar with not only how agendas can keep a meeting flowing smoothly and on topic, but also how an agenda serves as a record of what was discussed should a dispute arise in the future. For example, the National Labor Relations Act (NLRA) doesn't allow employers to dominate a labor organization. A labor organization may be said to exist if an employee committee is used to address policies or practices and the committee represents the opinions of other employees. If the employer directs the efforts or bargains with this group, an unlawful practice likely has occurred. In this example, an agenda can help defend or support this claim.

You must take a good, strong look at Chapter 2. It provides additional material that you must be able to apply on the PHR exam for successful certification.

REMEMBER

4

Digging into the SPHR Exam

Chapter 12

Building the Frame: SPHR 01 Leadership and Strategy

Leadership and Strategy is the functional area of the SPHR exam that focuses specifically on aligning business strategy with HR systems. It requires a thorough understanding of not only HR, but the unique conditions and risks under which the organizations must perform. Making up 40 percent of the exam content, questions related to this function are weighted higher than any other portion of the SPHR exam. You can also expect to see more questions related to these specific exam objectives, so it's important that you plan to use multiple resources to fully understand the concepts we touch on here.

HRCI defines this functional area as follows:

> "Leading the HR function by developing HR strategy, contributing to organizational strategy, influencing people management practices, and monitoring risk."

This chapter takes a look at some of the more important influencers of senior leader performance within companies and, of course, on the exam.

Leadership & Strategy Exam Objectives

It may be useful to put this exam domain in context using HRCI's changes to the exam bodies of knowledge. Prior to the 2018 exam updates, the PHR and SPHR exams shared content, with some exam objectives marked "SPHR only." We can infer by what remained intact after the updates that which is most important for senior leaders to understand and apply. Critical keywords to grasp as you study this section include "strategy," "alignment," and "metrics." The title change of the exam content also tells us that being strategic business partners is not just about aligning strategy to operations. It is about *leading* others through the changes often demanded as the result of organizational design and development initiatives.

Responsibilities

The work of strategic HR business partners is complex. This complexity is reflected in the exam responsibilities for the SPHR:

01 Develop and execute HR plans that are aligned to the organization's strategic plan (for example: HR strategic plans, budgets, business plans, service delivery plans, HRIS, technology).

02 Evaluate the applicability of federal laws and regulations to organizational strategy (for example: policies, programs, practices, business expansion/reduction).

03 Analyze and assess organizational practices that impact operations and people management to decide on the best available risk management strategy (for example: avoidance, mitigation, acceptance).

04 Interpret and use business metrics to assess and drive achievement of strategic goals and objectives (for example: key performance indicators, financial statements, budgets).

05 Design and evaluate HR data indicators to inform strategic actions within the organization (for example: turnover rates, cost per hire, retention rates).

06 Evaluate credibility and relevance of external information to make decisions and recommendations (for example: salary data, management trends, published surveys and studies, legal/regulatory analysis).

07 Contribute to the development of the organizational strategy and planning (for example: vision, mission, values, ethical conduct).

08 Develop and manage workplace practices that are aligned with the organization's statements of vision, values, and ethics to shape and reinforce organizational culture.

09 Design and manage effective change strategies to align organizational performance with the organization's strategic goals.

10 Establish and manage effective relationships with key stakeholders to influence organizational behavior and outcomes.

Knowledge

In addition to the responsibilities above, SPHR candidates must have fundamental knowledge about these topics:

01 Vision, mission, and values of an organization and applicable legal and regulatory requirements

02 Strategic planning process

03 Management functions, including planning, organizing, directing, and controlling

04 Corporate governance procedures and compliance

05 Business elements of an organization (for example: products, competition, customers, technology, demographics, culture, processes, safety, and security)

06 Third-party or vendor selection, contract negotiation, and management, including development of requests for proposals (RFPs)

07 Project management (for example: goals, timetables, deliverables, and procedures)

08 Technology to support HR activities

09 Budgeting, accounting, and financial concepts (for example: evaluating financial statements, budgets, accounting terms, and cost management)

10 Techniques and methods for organizational design (for example: outsourcing, shared services, organizational structures)

11 Methods of gathering data for strategic planning purposes (for example: Strengths, Weaknesses, Opportunities, and Threats [SWOT], and Political, Economic, Social, and Technological [PEST])

12 Qualitative and quantitative methods and tools used for analysis, interpretation, and decision-making purposes

13 Change management processes and techniques

14 Techniques for forecasting, planning, and predicting the impact of HR activities and programs across functional areas

15 Risk management

16 How to deal with situations that are uncertain, unclear, or chaotic

Directing Leadership and Strategy Initiatives

There is an old joke out there about the famous dancing partners Fred Astaire and Ginger Rogers. It notes that Ginger Rogers could do everything Fred Astaire did, but backwards and wearing high heels! This is suggestive of the environment under which human resource professionals must perform. Not only must they be creative problem solvers who are flexible enough to support business objectives, but they must also understand all aspects of the operations, build and maintain relationships with internal and external stakeholders, understand principles of organizational and individual behaviors, be neutral advisors to senior leaders, and manage risk — all while ensuring the "human" stays fully present in human resources. These (sometimes competing) demands can quickly become out-of-balance, as evidenced by the article titled "Why We Hate HR" (Fast Company, 2005) that came out many years ago. At its worst, teams stop coming to HR or relegate it to a single function, such as payroll or discipline. At best, HR is able to help teams navigate an environment that is VUCA — Volatile, Uncertain, Complex and Ambiguous — all the time. Having a plan is one way HR can create the framework of expectations; thus, the exam content in this domain is highly focused on the strategic planning process.

The Essence of Strategy

"The essence of strategy is choosing what not to do." —Michael E. Porter, Harvard Business School Professor and business strategist.

Strategy is another term for action plan or map. Think of a strategy in terms of military action:

>> The mission is established.

>> The environment is scanned for obstacles or threats.

>> A plan and timeline are developed to achieve the goal and deal with the obstacles.

>> The financial, equipment, and people resources are mustered.

>> Training is completed.

>> The tactical action steps begin.

>> All efforts are measured for success or failure.

A *strategic plan* is a high-level approach to business that includes the tactical steps necessary to succeed. The following sections break down some of the most important concepts for the SPHR.

Becoming a strategic partner

In no other functional area does the strategic planning process have more significance than in Functional Area 01 of the SPHR. The outcomes of this process are distributed throughout all HR functions with direct impact on other departments.

The strategic planning process is a series of events that result in a master plan. This plan is designed to achieve the corporate mission, goals, or strategic initiatives (sometimes referred to as interventions). Leaders collect data from multiple resources from inside and outside the organization to help write the plan. From there, tactical goals and actions are created.

During the planning process, threats and obstacles come to light, and it becomes necessary for the planners to create additional strategies, called *interventions*, to address these problems. These interventions address all the functional areas of HR. Options include restructuring jobs (Workforce Planning), developing training programs (Learning and Development), designing effective compensation plans (Total Rewards), and conducting risk assessments (Risk Management). Throughout these interventions, you're responsible for helping corporate leaders, managers, and employees work through the multiple changes that occur.

While mostly long-term oriented, circumstances can occur that require a more immediate response. One example of this is the COVID-19 pandemic of 2019–2020.

When COVID-19 hit, many employers were required to shutter their doors, putting more than 39 million Americans out of work. The Paycheck Protection Program (PPP) enacted by Congress that reimbursed employers for continuing to employ individuals during the first phase of the pandemic created additional strategic needs. They included making sure the funds were properly spent to avoid loan repayment and utilizing the funds to deploy the remaining talent to achieve the most urgent of business objectives without a complete sacrifice of the long-term plan.

COVID-19 created many other strategic considerations. Managing the exposure so that employees did not get sick was a key element to risk management, health, and safety. Preparing employees for remote work kept many HR professionals working late into the night, writing new policies, consulting with labor experts, and working with IT professionals to secure the data being generated from multiple at-home locations. Additionally, businesses with global operations had to respond on a larger scale from the perspective of containment, reopening where possible and dealing with supply chain interruptions. As businesses reopened, HR was faced with many opportunities to hire qualified talent and the pain of calling back to work employees who — due to additional unemployment funds and fear of the virus — were in some cases reluctant to report back to work when needed.

COVID-19 is a textbook example of the VUCA environment that opened this section, and illustrates how a plan is just that — a plan. HR must be nimble enough to react in the moment, reworking plans and objectives to meet the needs of their team members with an eye on the short-term demands and long-term recovery.

Interpreting strategic planning objectives

Several of the exam objectives address the strategic planning process. For example, Leadership and Strategy exam objective 01 gives clear direction for you when deciding what to study:

"Develop and execute HR plans that are aligned to the organization's strategic plan (for example, HR strategic plans, budgets, business plans, service delivery plans, HRIS, technology)."

In this exam objective, you must be familiar with the many types of plans that cascade down from the master version — both short- and long-term. This includes a working knowledge of business plans and the potential changes that may be driven by external conditions — such as a reduction in force due to a pandemic, for example.

In another example, 06 directs you to be able to:

"Evaluate credibility and relevance of external information to make decisions and recommendations (for example, salary data, management trends, published surveys and studies, legal/regulatory analysis)."

Here is an example of how this might break down on the exam. The question stem may identify you as the HR director for a large dairy farmer in Wisconsin faced with new food safety regulations. The question(s) could relate to collecting the data, interpreting the data, or applying it operationally:

>> **Collecting the information:** Consider where you would collect information related to industry practices if you were the HR manager for a large dairy farm. For example, you might decide to attend classes on food safety delivered by the Innovation Center for U.S. Dairy.

>> **Interpreting the information:** Now that you have plenty of information regarding food safety practices, you educate your management team on the best practices and help them identify any gaps between what is required and current practice.

>> **Applying the information:** After these gaps are identified, you help create an action plan to address the deficiencies. Your team identifies the need for new tools and equipment, employee training, and safety inspections to ensure ongoing compliance. You may also choose to hire a dedicated food safety specialist, driving the need for job descriptions and wage surveys.

Understanding the stages of planning

With the exception of business interruptions requiring a more agile approach, strategic planning generally follows a five-stage process.

1. Preparing to plan

The *pre-planning stage* requires decisions be made about the data that will be collected and how it will be collected. It includes factors such as who will participate, how long it should take, and what tools will be used.

As the nearby sidebar shows, the collection of data comes from multiple sources. They include industry trends, technological advances, the economic climate at a local and national level, the skill availability of the labor force, and, of course, the effort necessary for compliance with labor law or industry-specific regulations.

The pre-planning stage requires a strong data-mining effort on your part. Although you may not be responsible for collecting all the data, you may be called upon to spearhead the effort and will most certainly be required to help interpret and apply the information that is gathered.

2. Conducting an environmental scan

An *environmental scan* reviews the internal and external factors that influence an organization's ability to compete in its space. Internal strengths and weaknesses and external threats and opportunities are identified, and plans are then generated to respond to these conditions on a short-term and long-term basis. This process explores the technological, economic, social, and political factors that influence success.

REMEMBER

The SPHR requires working knowledge of the different types of environmental scanning formulas, including the following:

>> **PEST:** Political, economic, social, and technological analysis to collect data for the strategic planning process.

>> **PESTLE:** Political, economic, social, technological, legal, and environmental assessment of the business climate.

>> **Porter's five forces:** Michael E. Porter's description of the competitive influences of business success and failure listed as rivalry, supplier power, the threat of substitutes, buyer power, and the threat of new entrants into the market. A good business strategy collects this data and analyzes it for a better understanding of competitive position in the relevant market.

>> **SWOT:** A SWOT audit is a scan of the environment to identify internal strengths and weaknesses and external opportunities and threats. A strong strategic plan maximizes strengths and mitigates weaknesses, while capitalizing on opportunities and taking steps to reduce or eliminate threats.

3. Formulating the strategy

The mission statement, vision statement, and values statement (MVV) are at the foundation of *strategy formulation.* You probably already know what they mean, but here is what they can tell you about an organization:

>> The *mission statement* answers the question: Why do we exist?

>> The *vision statement* answers the question: Where do we want to be?

>> The *values statement* answers the question: What do we believe in?

REMEMBER

In addition to the MVV statements, a company's core competencies are often identified at this stage of the strategic planning process. *Core competencies* answer the question, "At the end of the day, what do we do?" For example, a car wash company's core competencies statement would be "at the end of the day, we wash cars." Or a construction company's statement would be "at the end of the day, we build things." Although these examples are simplified, they explain that the core competencies set the direction of action for a company in their strategic plan year. By reducing a company's thinking to the core, an organization can then identify, corral, and focus on the resources necessary to accomplish what, at the end of each day, is at the heart of their business — and the distractors.

Finally, no strategic formulation of a plan is complete without the identification of goals. If the MVV and core competencies are a 30,000-foot view of the organization as a whole, the goals bring them back to boots-on-the-ground action.

The SMART model is a useful way to remember how to write effective goals. The acronym stands for goals that are specific, measurable, attainable, relevant, and time-based. Clearly articulated goals are more likely to be achieved, and applying the SMART model will guide you through the process. From the perspective of the exam, you must be familiar with setting annual goals and objectives that correlate with the company's strategic direction, including the MVV. Other goals specifically mentioned in the exam objectives are growth targets, new programs and services, and net income expectations. After the goal-setting is complete, the implementation of the strategy can begin.

The SPHR exam requires you to have a thorough understanding of all stages of strategic planning. But a plan with no action becomes an exercise in futility. A helpful way to remember this is to visualize a regular piece of paper folded in half. Above the fold, you have listed all the steps in this process that occur while sitting in a conference room. Below the fold are the action steps that will require you to be in your office or on the production floor — it's time to get to work.

4. Implementing the action items

Strategy implementation is the execution of the business plan that is an outcome of the planning process. For human resources, it means taking the relevant portion of the plan and doing the work necessary to achieve the goals. Strategy implementation is a focus on the operational elements necessary to achieve the company goals. On a related note, SPHR candidates must be prepared for questions related to metrics. In fact, exam objective 04 specifies that senior HR leaders are able to "interpret and use" business metrics to drive achievement of the strategic initiatives.

5. Evaluating the outcomes

Strategy evaluation is the process of measuring how well or how poorly an organization is doing when compared to the strategic plan. The timing of the evaluations is important because they shouldn't be completed only at the end of the plan year. When the proper tools are identified and built, an organization can regularly collect data that will allow it to respond to deficiencies quickly and adjust course as necessary — thus the importance of finding the right tools for measuring success.

REMEMBER

You should be familiar with several evaluation tools in preparation for the exam. They include the following:

>> **Financial measures:** In simplest terms, these reports follow the money — how it comes in and where it goes out. An example is the company budget.

>> **Company overview:** A *company overview* is focused on performance and is often broken down by department. Examples include dashboards or a balanced scorecard.

>> **Quality initiatives:** These efforts exist both on a macro and micro level, meaning the focus can be on overall product/service quality or unit-by-unit quality. Quality is often cited as a company value, launching initiatives such as Total Quality Management (TQM) or the International Organization for Standardization (ISO).

>> **Productivity standards:** These standards measure the outputs of effort and include calls tended or time to receive.

>> **Sales targets:** These targets are set for several reasons, including identifying the break-even point and providing a plan for business growth. Sample reports include comparing year over year, month over month, and individual product growth or decline.

Managing Risk

Human resources activities are steeped in the practice of developing policy, procedures, and rules. At its base, this practice is driven by compliance with many labor laws that require written policies as a first step toward establishing a good-faith commitment to compliance. Most often housed in an employee handbook, these policies should be used as a guide for employee behavior and employer responsibilities.

Having a written policy is not enough to manage the multitude of risks presented in the business environment. These risks include wrongful termination, health and safety, data breaches, discrimination, harassment, pay disparity . . . if you have practiced HR for any period of time, you are most likely very familiar with this list and more. However, there are accepted methods of dealing with risks, regardless of the type. They include those listed in exam objective 03:

>> **Avoidance:** This risk management technique is used when a risk is to be avoided at all cost. An example in the workplace would be unlawful discrimination against a protected class individual, or quid pro quo sexual harassment by a supervisor.

>> **Mitigation:** While a labor attorney's primary reason for existence is to eliminate the target, HR is more often called upon to simply shrink the target. This can be accomplished by mitigating risk management strategies, such as requiring PPE for employees that are working in hazardous conditions that cannot be fully eliminated in other ways.

>> **Acceptance:** In some cases, it is a best practice to simply accept the risk. This can be difficult for some HR professionals to accept (we know what is "right"!), but it is important to remember that our role is to be neutral advisors to our leadership teams. This includes making them aware of the risk, helping to shape options, and implementing strategies where appropriate. An example would be developing a recommended wage survey using market data, but a supervisor deciding to pay below-market competitive conditions due to an employee's low level of experience.

That is not to say that HR should forget their ethical and legal responsibilities along the way. HRCI published a code of ethics and professional responsibility for all credential holders. It includes behaviors that mark ethical leadership such as

- Being ethical and acting ethically in every professional interaction

- Questioning pending individual and group actions when necessary to ensure that decisions are ethical and are implemented in an ethical manner

- Seeking expert guidance if ever in doubt about the ethical propriety of a situation

- Through teaching and mentoring, championing the development of others as ethical leaders in the profession and in organizations

>> **Transfer:** This is a simple risk management strategy in which all or a portion of the risk is transferred or shared. An example would be purchasing employment practices liability insurance (EPLI), or leasing employees through a professional employer organization (PEO).

As the examples show, having a written policy is simply a paper tiger. True risk management includes HR helping to build a culture of courtesy, dignity, and respect. This can be done by first having a written policy and then communicating that policy through training, promptly investigating complaints (including near-misses), and utilizing one of the preceding risk techniques for proper management.

Designing Interventions

The academic (evidence-based) domain of organizational development (OD) is worthy of entire textbooks and beyond the scope of your exam prep. Knowing some of the basics, though, can serve to inform you of how designing intentional strategic interventions can result in key business outcomes. At its simplest, OD is the practice of being intentional about the efforts necessary to ensure the effectiveness — and thus the competitive success — of a business. OD is driven by data, yet at its core sets off a series of planned interventions that allow an employer to effectively manage risk, take advantage of opportunities, and diversify, just to name a few. These interventions may be at the people, process, or project level, and may be further divided by organizational or departmental targets. This domain draws from the sciences of organizational behavior, social science, applied psychology, industrial-organizational psychology (I-O), and, of course, human resources and business.

To put this in context, reflect on information from the textbook *Industrial/Organizational Psychology* by Paul Levy (Worth Publishers). He suggests that the 21st-century competitive landscape for business will be characterized by "substantial and sporadic changes." He references research that gives a sense of what these changes will be related to, including technology and the globalization of the workforce. Senior leaders must be knowledgeable advisors to not only inform strategy but also design the interventions necessary to prepare.

The concept may seem daunting, and to be sure, it is not a "one and done" type of activity. HR must be familiar with the scanning tools on the front end and the measurement tools of the back end, with a large helping of change management techniques sprinkled in between.

Managing Change Strategies

Heading back to the sciences, many experts agree that changing adult behavior requires a complex approach of motivation techniques, knowledge of learning/unlearning, and biology (such as the study of the neuroscience behind change). In terms of the SPHR, exam objective 09 directs candidates to

> "Design and manage effective change management strategies to align organizational performance with the organization's strategic goal."

This is important information, for the objective gives us the framework from which to practice change management — it is not everything, all the time (harken back to the Porter quote at the beginning of the section "The Essence of Strategy"). Effective change management in the context of the exam focuses on the alignment of change with business strategy. While this is good news and suggests a somewhat finite activity, there are still a multitude of variables to consider, such as the PESTLE factors and the specific needs of the industry in which you practice. Regardless of the complexity, there are theories of change that can help. They include many "stage" models, three of which are explored here:

The three-stage model

Kurt Lewin's "Changing as three steps" (CATS) model is perhaps the most widely known, going back more than 60 years. A most simple formula, it describes the process of change as 1) unfreezing current behavior, 2) changing to desired behavior, and then 3) refreezing as the new norm. The unfreezing process must include not only the functional aspects of a process, but the underlying assumptions and beliefs of the team. Conversely, the refreezing step must include the adoption of new beliefs and patterns of behavior. Lewin's original theory has been criticized as an oversimplification of the change management process, a complaint sought to be overcome by the next model.

The eight-stage model

in 1996, John Kotter published his version of a stage model for change. He suggests that employers seeking to change organizational behavior must go through (in order) a series of steps. They include the following:

1. **Establish a sense of urgency.**

   What is the threat from the status quo?

2. **Create a guiding coalition.**

   Who has the unique knowledge and skill to guide change efforts?

3. **Develop a vision and strategy.**

   What does the future look like as a result of this change?

4. **Communicate.**

   What's in it for the employees and why does it matter?

5. **Empower employees.**

   What does the team need to do to make these changes?

6. **Generate short-term wins.**

   What is working?

7. **Consolidate gains and produce more change.**

   What else can we do or what else needs to be done for this to become normal?

8. **Anchor new approaches.**

   How are we different/more effective as the result of these changes?

Both Lewin and Kotter's models have been criticized for paying too little attention to the emotional side of change. The final stage model puts employee reactions to change at its center.

The five-stage model

Jeanie Duck's contribution to change models was first introduced in her book with the compelling title *The Change Monster*, published by Currency in 2002. In it she describes change as a curve made up of five stages:

>> **Stagnation:** Describes an environment of complacency that will not be "shaken up" without strategic leadership.

>> **Preparation:** Directs leaders to plan for the emotional reactions and barriers employees will experience when change is announced.

>> **Implementation:** As with the strategic plan, this is where the work begins.

>> **Determination:** A state necessary of leaders in order to assure employees that the "new way" is necessary and here to stay.

>> **Fruition:** The step of acknowledging and celebrating success while helping teams to avoid a new stage of stagnation.

These are just three examples of the myriad of change theories in management lore. Senior leaders should understand that these are simplified skeletons that serve as structural templates for managing the change process. The pattern remains consistent, but it is up to HR professionals to synthesize (put into a coherent whole) within these frameworks the unique variables of the business. It requires agility and an attitude of informed optimism based on the reality that very rarely does the work of business occur along a linear plane. Being rigid when trying to navigate yourself and teams through change is an irony that leads to HR's ineffectiveness and thus should be avoided.

Delivering through Technology

Perhaps nowhere else in HR professionals' environments does change manifest itself as rapidly as it does in technology. Foundational tech theory (such as Moore's law) suggests that our technological capabilities will double every two years. Often described as disruptions, techno-structural interventions have become a necessary part of the effectiveness of organizational leaders and the competitive success of the businesses they lead. While understanding how technology impacts business from a macro perspective is interesting, the exam focuses candidates' attention on the specific technology used to support HR activities.

Following trends in HR information systems

A 2020 Price Waterhouse Cooper (PwC) survey found that employers plan to continue investing heavily in HR technology through the year 2022. The number-one factor driving this investment? The ability to attract and retain talent (58 percent). This same study notes that HR cloud solutions lead the way in how these dollars are being spent, at about $150 million a year. Employers plan to spend other dollars on attracting talent, improving technology capabilities for employees (think employee self-service), and, of course, the growing-in-importance career pathing/skill development. Find the entire report at www.benefitnews.com/news/employers-plan-greater-investments-in-hr-tech-through-2022.

The exams more than likely will continue to address these trends by asking you to understand how to best apply HR technology on the job. One way is to consider the impact of tech on risk management (RM) activities. This includes data security and data retrieval — issues that exist for paper storage but must also be accounted for in the digital era. Other RM elements include the ability of a payroll system to track FMLA leave time, and hiring statistics related to protected class characteristics (EEO-1 reporting).

Managing the impact of data analytics

Predicting and reporting are not new activities for human resources. After all, what else is the hiring process other than using job-related tools to predict how an employee will fit within the organization? However, when placed within the context of data analytics, the potential (not to mention scale) of the process takes on a whole new dimension.

In addition to predicting behaviors, data analytics within the HR world may also be used to diagnose organizational challenges and, much like a physician, prescribe remedies (often within the domain of OD, discussed in the earlier section "Designing Interventions").

Data is collected from sources such as attendance records, the recruitment process, performance reviews, salary and promotion history, employee demographics, and more. Some of the more popular applications of analyzing this type of data include résumé analysis for best-fit candidates, collecting data to predict team members who are at high risk for turnover, and developing forecast models for future talent needs.

Challenges that senior leaders must be able to overcome include how to harness the messages embedded within the meta-collection of data. Human resource leaders must be able to form a simple, coherent narrative with clear calls to action in order for these efforts to produce positive results. It is also important that HR not replace face-to-face connection with the more impersonal aspect of only using data to make decisions. While we have learned in many cases that our "gut" is not legally defensible, there is both art and science to employee engagement, culture, and leadership. We must not lose sight of the importance of the human experience at work.

Avoiding the pitfalls of social media

It feels as though everyone is on social media. Professional associations, personal pages, business reviews, and more are the many ways that people can stay connected in today's world. This poses a few interesting issues for employers to address:

>> **Decreased productivity:** Statistics abound about how many workers peruse social media while on the clock. It's safe to say that regardless of the size of your employer, someone is surfing social media on company time. Limiting the use of mobile devices or company equipment to access social media or blocking specific websites while at work is appropriate for employers. Ways to do so include allowing it only while employees are on break and prohibiting mobile device use completely while driving a company vehicle or for company business. Some companies are going so far as to install slanted toilets — commodes designed to discourage prolonged use. Consider best practices when crafting these strategies and make sure that they're a business necessity and compliant with labor laws.

>> **Protected concerted activity:** An interesting twist in the evolution of social media is the National Labor Relations Board's (NLRB) position that an employee has a right to express her dissatisfaction with working conditions through social media. Another word for the NLRB term *concerted* is *collective*. Any time a group of employees is together — whether face-to-face or online — they have the right to discuss wages, hours, and other topics granted protection by the National Labor Relations Act (NLRA) for purposes of considering union organizing.

>> **Privacy:** Social media is an effective tool for many business applications, such as recruiting, marketing, and building the employer brand. The decision to use social media in these capacities should be thoroughly evaluated to ensure that your company's practices don't violate the privacy rights of affected individuals, such as posting pictures of children at a daycare. You also want to take care to avoid having to defend the use of candidate data that is protected, such as gender and family status. Although not illegal per se to know this information, you'll need to be able to show that you didn't use it to make any employment decision, such as hiring or promotion.

>> **Trade secrets and confidential information:** A business has the right to protect trade secrets and other competitive data, but doing so in a highly digitally connected age may be difficult. Think of protecting confidential information on social media by reverting to its antithesis — the power of the pen. Have strong *nonsolicitation agreements* (a signed contract prohibiting employees from approaching existing clients) signed by affected employees to protect customer lists. Write and enforce policies regarding the ownership rights of company

social media pages, with specific information about privacy settings. Use confidentiality agreements to define clearly what are considered to be trade secrets, and communicate to affected workers that the company will aggressively pursue legal remedies for failure to comply.

Building a virtual workplace

The use of collaboration tools online has never been more important due to globalization and the growing acceptance of virtual (remote) work. The needs that drive the selection of the proper technological solution include efficiency, ease of use, and, of course, building connections on a dimensional interface. Popular platforms such as Office 365 and Slack offer bundles of efficiency tools such as document editing, calendar sharing, instant messaging and the like. Employers may also consider customized solutions where appropriate, particularly if there are variables such as customer privacy or global restrictions. China, for example, will only allow approved platforms to be used for online collaboration between U.S.- and China-based businesses.

Speaking of China, you may remember the controversy surrounding Huwei and 5G. In 2020 Boris Johnson, the Prime Minister of the U.K., engaged in a negotiation with the China-based company to provide support for 5G capabilities to their government. Alarmed, the United States dispatched subject-matter experts to dissuade Johnson from this choice due in large part to fears of backdoor security breaches that could be used to spy on the United Kingdom and its partners such as the United States and Australia. Ultimately, the deal did not happen; however, it is a good lesson for all organizations that we must consider security on both a macro and micro scale when making decisions about technology.

TIP

Understanding the application of HR technology can be aided by considering the life cycle of the employee, and provides an opportunity to use your critical thinking skills. Challenge yourself to come up with an example of how technology impacts each stage of the employee life cycle such as:

>> Recruiting and selection

>> Orientation and onboarding

>> Employee acculturation and engagement

>> Learning and development

>> Total rewards

>> Separation

If you aren't sure, reach out to a subject-matter expert or peer within your organization and discuss the issue. This activity can help you take the *knowledge* of HR tech capabilities and *apply* it in the workplace — a major component to the level of SPHR exam difficulty.

Selecting and implementing project management software

Closely related to the preceding technology discussion is the ability of HR to support project management needs. The exam knowledge in Functional Area 01 relates the need for senior HR to understand project management goals, timetables, deliverables and procedures. Having said that, HR is not tasked with passing the PMP exam, so as with all of this, context matters, and models are an effective way to understand and support these organizational needs.

Selecting project management software can be systematic in that the software must have the capability to follow the five-stage process of project management. This includes the capability to initiate, plan, execute, manage, and close out a project. The initiation phase often includes establishing a project charter and scope. Planning for the project may include the identification of the internal and external resources necessary to achieve the scope, in addition to establishing timelines and accountabilities. Execution is where the work gets done, with each project team member contributing and delivering on his commitments. Managing the project often occurs concurrently with execution, with a project lead measuring and refining as the project environment evolves and shifts. Finally, the close of a project may include evaluating success and identifying next phases, depending on how the scope defined the project "end." Software capabilities to this end include establishing the goals and action plans of a specific project, having the ability to assign tasks and establish timelines, and providing data sharing and document control as well as visual progress charts (such as GANNT) and checklists of completion or hand-off. In short, exactly what the SPHR exam asks you to understand.

Similar to the human resource industry (HRBoK), project management has a body of knowledge (PMBoK) that guides best practices, knowledge, and competencies. Consider a short digression from your HR studies into a look at the PMBoK to gain a more robust understanding of this stand-alone practice.

Analyzing with metrics

Both objective and subjective tools that can help to determine the value of business activities are available to HR practitioners. Make sure that you're familiar with these as you prepare to take the SPHR exam.

A *cost-benefit analysis* (CBA) measures the effectiveness of collective intervention activities focused on company operations. Basically, a cost-benefit analysis takes a more global, whole-system view. Although a bottom-line dollar figure is used to communicate the results, a CBA seeks to measure both tangible and intangible outcomes in terms of money. Factors to evaluate include

>> **Alignment with the company's mission, vision, and values:** Does the suggested intervention strategy serve the MVV?

>> **Management engagement in the trenches (operational):** Is there sufficient buy-in of the managers for successful implementation of the activity, and if not, what does HR need to do to develop the management team?

>> **The direct costs of the program specifics:** Does the company's cash flow support the outcome, whether negative or positive?

>> **The indirect costs of implementation:** Have you considered the indirect costs of implementation, including wages, benefits, and lost productivity of the personnel involved?

>> **Risk factors of failing to implement:** What will happen if you don't implement this particular strategy?

>> **Revenue and profit:** What revenue will be generated as the result of these efforts, and what will be the profit margin?

CoolerCorks is a large-scale American manufacturer of wine storage cooling units, located in the mountains of Colorado. As part of this year's strategic plan, the company decided it would undertake a Lean Manufacturing transformation, where the focus is on streamlined operations and elimination of waste. Michaela, the quality manager, has questioned whether or not the inconvenience and cost of this transformation is really necessary. Which of the following statements is TRUE?

(A) Michaela should be given the option to step down, and a more committed replacement found.

(B) Michaela should be allowed to continue on as a manager; she'll come around eventually.

(C) Michaela should be coached through the process, seeking buy-in and commitment.

(D) Michaela should be fired.

The correct answer is (C). HR provides support to the management team during the change that often is the result of the strategic planning process. Choice (B) isn't a viable solution because it doesn't clearly communicate the performance expectations and solutions. Choices (A) and (D) may become necessary, but not until she has been given adequate time and support to perform successfully.

Forecasting

A crystal ball in human resources would come in handy at times, but the information may be less magic and more available than you may think. As I discuss in the earlier section "Understanding the stages of planning," data is collected both internally and externally for use in planning. If done properly, you now have at your disposal much of the information you need to properly forecast human resource needs at your place of employment. Consider the following examples (hopefully you recognize PEST at work):

>> **Political:** Who holds office at a national and local level can strongly influence organizational objectives. For example, in 2000 then-President Bill Clinton passed a national ergonomics safety standard. In 2001, when George W. Bush took office, he signed an order from Congress to repeal it. Based on the current political climate, immigration reform and diversity/inclusion will continue to be an emerging compliance issue for employers.

>> **Economic:** Swinging gas prices affect commerce on multiple levels, not the least of which is the cost of getting product from A to B. The economy is further deteriorated when companies must pass this cost along to consumers, increasing the cost of living. If wages don't keep up, American workers can't afford to buy. If workers can't afford to buy, company profits suffer, leading to negative outcomes such as furloughs or layoffs. Based on the current economic climate, employers should seek out tax and training credits for workforce expansion and training, as well as other government programs to get individuals back to work and to stimulate the economy.

>> **Social:** Cultural trends and patterns are often useful gauges toward the practice of human resources. One of the best examples is the 1960s civil rights era. The mood of the country was that of diversity, and Congress responded by passing the Civil Rights Act of 1964, which led to changes in workplace hiring practices and legal compliance, just to name a few. Similarly, in 2020, we saw the Supreme Court rule on the protected status of LGBT workers, protection that prior to the ruling was diluted and inconsistent. Based on the current social climate, anti-discrimination regulations will continue to emerge for groups not currently protected and provide depth in coverage for others. In light of the significant economic and social impact of the flu season, we should expect to see expanded health and safety regulations.

>> **Technological:** Employers can count on technological advances to emerge at a fairly fast pace. From enterprise resource planning (ERP) systems to radio frequency (RF) inventory scanners, multiple tools are available to increase quality and productivity. Based on the current technology climate, anticipate the need for virtual workspace and clearer telecommuting policies and procedures.

EXAMPLE

Which of the following statements is TRUE?

(A) Strategic planning is an executive-level activity.

(B) Analyzing the political climate is part of an environmental scan.

(C) Calls per hour is a type of quality measurement.

(D) The mission statement identifies where a company wants to be.

The correct answer is (B). PEST and PESTLE audits scan the environment for the political, economic, social, technological, legal, and environmental factors that must be addressed as part of an organization's strategic plan. Choice (A) isn't the best answer because midlevel managers are often part of the planning process and certainly become involved at the implementation stage. Choice (C) is incorrect because calls per hour are a measure of productivity. Mission statements, Choice (D), identify why a company exists.

Using scorecards

The use of scorecards in one form or another is a useful way to see a snapshot of how the company is doing as a whole when compared to the desired outcomes identified during the strategic planning process. One widely accepted approach is the use of a balanced scorecard.

REMEMBER

A *balanced scorecard* defines the accountability factors for each of these areas and collects data to measure how well or how poorly an organization is doing in addressing the deficiencies defined during the strategic planning process. The results allow for on-the-spot decision-making and adaptability, rather than waiting to see if the intervention measures worked at the end of some arbitrary period of time.

EXAMPLE

Which of the following measurement tools would best capture an overview of how well a company is doing when measured against the strategic plan?

(A) An ROI calculation

(B) A break-even analysis

(C) A balanced scorecard

(D) A financial dashboard

The correct answer is (C), a balanced scorecard, which pulls together data regarding the organization as a whole and compares it to the goals identified as part of the strategic planning process. Choices (A) and (B) are incorrect because these types of calculations are best used on a micro level for smaller interventions. Choice (D) is incorrect because it's specific to a function, not a company overview.

REMEMBER

One or two exam preparation resources aren't enough for you to ensure a passing score. Many of the exam objectives simply scratch the surface of business application. Reach out for more information on unfamiliar topics or on topics that represent the largest percentage of the exam. In the case of Leadership and Strategy, SPHR candidates need to create depth to these strategic concepts.

Chapter 2 highlights a list of authors recommended by HRCI. Many of these specialize in the content described in this chapter, particularly in that of strategic planning, change management, and other business philosophies. Make sure to account for a deeper dive into the work of these authors in your study plan.

Chapter 13

Bridging the Gap: SPHR 02 Talent Planning and Acquisition

alent Planning and Acquisition focuses on the beginning of the employee life cycle. This includes processes to source and measure the "fit" of a candidate to both the job and the organization. For purposes of the SPHR exam, this content is weighted at 16 percent. While the PHR exam has the exact same functional area title, the focus for SPHR candidates is on the strategic efforts — including forecasting, planning, and measuring results. This is reflected in HRCI's definition of Functional Area 02: "Forecast organizational talent needs and develop strategies to attract and engage new talent."

Preparing for Talent Planning and Acquisition

With only three business objectives and a low overall weighting, it would be easy for senior leaders to dismiss this area of the exam. Doing so, however, is at a cost of being a true organizational business partner. As mentioned in the previous chapter, the ability to attract qualified talent is the priority of an increased investment in HR technology. From this we can infer that a major pain point for businesses is the ability to acquire talent. A look at the exam responsibilities tells us that this area is solely focused on planning for and acquiring talent, saving components such as management and development for other content areas.

Responsibilities

HRCI defines 3 major areas of responsibilities of senior leaders in the area of Talent Planning & Acquisition. They include the following:

01 Evaluate and forecast organizational needs throughout the business cycle to create or develop workforce plans (for example: corporate restructuring, workforce expansion, or reduction)

02 Develop, monitor, and assess recruitment strategies to attract desired talent (for example: labor market analysis, compensation strategies, selection process, onboarding, sourcing and branding strategy)

03 Develop and evaluate strategies for engaging new employees and managing cultural integrations (for example: new employee acculturation, downsizing, restructuring, mergers and acquisitions, divestitures, global expansion)

Knowledge

In addition to the responsibilities above, SPHR candidates will answer questions from a baseline knowledge of these topics:

17 Planning techniques (for example: succession planning, forecasting)

18 Talent management practices and techniques (for example: selecting and assessing employees)

19 Recruitment sources and strategies

20 Staffing alternatives (for example: outsourcing, temporary employment)

21 Interviewing and selection techniques and strategies

22 Impact of total rewards on recruitment and retention

23 Termination approaches and strategies

24 Employee engagement strategies

25 Employer marketing and branding techniques

26 Negotiation skills and techniques

27 Due diligence processes (for example: mergers and acquisitions, divestitures)

28 Transition techniques for corporate restructuring, mergers and acquisitions, offshoring, and divestitures

29 Methods to assess past and future staffing effectiveness (for example: cost per hire, selection ratios, adverse impact)

Digging Deeper into the Exam Objectives

The three exam objectives give us a clue about the Talent Planning and Acquisition process. It begins with forecasting talent needs throughout the business life cycle, often sequenced as *infancy, growth, maturity,* and *decline*. Each of these phases presents unique resource needs. This in turn establishes the direction of the other human resource activities. For example, in a company's infancy stage, they may not have the cash flow available to pay premium wages for talent. Offering development activities through Learning and Development, structuring Total Rewards using equity or unlimited time off plans and offering virtual workdays are all examples of other HR activities that support the acquisition of talent. This requires a strategic view from which to begin the Talent Planning and Acquisition process.

Workforce Planning

The process of workforce planning is closely related to the exam objectives from Leadership and Strategy. Specifically, a workforce plan — defined as analyzing the number and skill sets of necessary employees — must align with organizational strategy such as growth targets or corporate restructures. In order to accomplish this, HR must have an in-depth knowledge of the organization's strategic plan. Ultimately, Talent Planning & Acquisition is about finding the right people, at the right time, and in the right place to execute business strategy.

Additionally, the workforce planning process is similar to the strategic planning process in that it begins with analyzing internal and external data and ends with measurements. HR may conduct a staffing needs analysis using budgets, growth targets, and the supply and demand of talent to forecast current and future staffing needs.

A skills inventory is a good first step to identify the qualifications and talents of the existing workforce. This can then be used to consider restructuring jobs or shuffling team members throughout the organizational chart. A skills inventory is also useful to build training and development strategies, particularly for hard-to-recruit positions such as engineers or nurses. Once gaps have been identified, HR is armed with the data necessary to take a look at the external labor market.

EXAMPLE

Which tool is primarily focused on gathering data about the internal talents of the employees?

(A) Labor market data

(B) Skills inventory

(C) Job analysis

(D) Performance appraisals

The correct answer is (B). A *skills inventory* is a tool used to gather data about the existing skill sets of current workers. It's an excellent resource to use during the workforce planning process, because it highlights the individual and collective strengths of the existing workforce, which can then be used to fill gaps during hiring or to eliminate redundancies if the company needs to lay off employees. Choice (A) is incorrect because it applies to the external labor market. Choice (C) refers to the tasks, duties, and responsibilities of the jobs, not the knowledge, skills, and abilities of the worker. Choice (D) is a tool used to provide feedback to employees, not to gather data about their skills.

Analyzing the labor market population

The labor force population is defined by many boundaries, including industry, geographic location, and skill set. Once these boundaries are clear, HR typically will access resources to measure the supply of qualified talent. These resources include state and local employment agencies, such as the Office of Employment Statistics or the Chamber of Commerce. While these resources exist on a national level, HR should seek as narrowly targeted data as possible for accurate analysis and informed decision-making.

An added dimension to this process is when an organization chooses to outsource non-core parts of its business. The advantage of outsourcing is that it can free up resources to focus on the organization's core competencies. It can also be helpful when staffing is difficult or the work is seasonal. In human resource departments, the most commonly outsourced functions include payroll and benefits administration, such as complying with COBRA regulations. When outsourcing becomes offshoring — the shift of a business unit outside the United States — the ability to analyze the labor market becomes much more complex, often requiring resources beyond a single HR department — another example of business strategy that drives the activities of talent planning.

Conducting wage surveys

In addition to supply and demand, HR supports the strategic plan of an organization by helping to forecast the cost of labor. Conducting wage surveys for particular positons in particular locations allows for budget forecasts that should include base wages and benefits as well as ancillary offerings such as time off, incentives, and commissions.

As can be expected, it may be difficult to gather accurate data directly from competitors. Another challenge is the reliability of data from websites such as www.salary.com, the Wikipedia (user-generated content) of salary sources. It is better to rely on state and local published information, such as the Office of Employment Statistics (OES) in California. This type of source data improves the integrity of the data and the defensibility of pay practices should they be called into question.

In some cases, it is best to purchase wage surveys. Often in exchange for participation, sponsored surveys have the advantage over government surveys in that they offer a level of detail not available in the state and local publications. Nonprofit industries are also unique in that their wages do not match the general labor market, so purchasing an industry-specific book of data is more reliable.

Pricing jobs is an ancillary function of the impact of wages on talent acquisition. This activity includes establishing the relative value of jobs when compared to similar work within and outside of the organization. More often than not, the result of this process is nondiscriminatory wage bands that establish the minimum and maximum salary range for a given position. Having this tool drives employee perceptions about pay equity, as well as provides legally defensible data for pay decisions that come under scrutiny.

Succession and replacement plans

There are two types of turnover — functional and dysfunctional. Functional turnover is the good kind, when an employee is promoted or a lower performing team member exits the organization. Dysfunctional turnover occurs when there is a loss of key personnel or high performers. There are many opportunities to improve retention efforts throughout all human resource functions. For example, paying competitive wages or offering generous family leave policies improves retention through Total Rewards. Building an open-door culture that fosters creativity and allows failure happens in the context of employee relations. Regardless of an employer's best efforts, both types of turnover do occur, and both types are costly. This means that senior HR leaders must build HR systems that support a reduction of turnover.

One way to manage the impact of turnover is to create succession and replacement plans. The key difference between succession plans and replacement plans is that succession plans are focused on longer-term needs and replacement plans are focused on more immediate needs. Both are considered to be a form of risk management. We can reinforce our learning by applying the four risk management techniques from Chapter 12 when thinking about application:

>> **Accept:** In this scenario, employers use hope as a strategy, reacting only if the need arises.

>> **Avoid:** When avoiding the risk of losing personnel, a multi-faceted approach is used. HR must spearhead efforts to retain employees and develop talent at all organizational levels.

>> **Mitigate:** Reducing the exposure of turnover includes a focus only on critical positions or difficult-to-recruit-for roles. Mitigating risk as a strategy may also include investing in development only for senior leaders, rather than at all levels within the organization.

>> **Transfer:** In a succession plan, this may include purchasing "key person" insurance or relying on temporary staffing solutions for unexpected turnover in less skilled positions.

Even if succession and replacement plans are successful, they still create an opening that must be filled. When this happens, the life cycle of the employee begins anew with the recruiting and selection process, collectively known as "staffing."

Overseeing the Staffing Function

Hiring qualified talent for a company is one of the most important contributions of a human resources department. Looking at recruiting and selection through this lens will (hopefully) change the mindset of it as a time-consuming task with more nos than yeses to the belief that it is this function from which we build competitiveness, culture, and job satisfaction. This process begins long before the first job ad is placed.

Employer branding

Recruiting in the current labor market is as difficult as it has ever been. The business environment has gone through many shifts as a result of politics, the economy and the collective skills and preferences of a new generation of workers. In many cases, candidates have significant student loan debt, can't afford homes in the area, need soft skills development or have a strong preference for remote work. These trends must be considered when an employer is communicating it's *employer brand,* which is defined as effectively communicating the employer value proposition (EVP) — a fancy way of answering the all-important candidate question, "Why should I come work for your company"?

So, what is HR to do? As with any business strategy, senior leaders in human resources must first identify the value of working for your team. This includes the tangible benefits such as competitive wages, tuition reimbursement, work flexibility, investment in training and development, retirement contributions, and generous leave policies. But it also includes the intangible benefits such as the organization's values (and adherence to said values), loyalty to their teams, trusted leadership, and ethical business practices, just to name a few. Once identified, HR should partner with other departments to communicate the employer brand not only within their recruiting efforts, but also as part of the company's overall marketing strategy. In short, communicating the EVP on a regular basis is part of a continuous recruitment plan.

The employer brand exists whether the business is aware of it or not. Just because a company doesn't actively manage the message of the EVP does not mean that message is not being communicated. Particularly with the dominance of social media, word gets out about how a company treats its employees. Scan the headlines today and you will likely find stories about corporate corruption, malfeasance, and unconscious bias. There are so many ways the employer brand can be miscommunicated (or properly communicated, depending on the ethics of the business).

Recruiting and selection

The recruiting process establishes a candidate's (and potential employee) expectations of how an organization treats its people, and what they value. And yet, the process is highly operational in nature. SPHR candidates should still be familiar with the operational systems used to attract qualified talent while also ensuring cultural values are embedded within the practices.

EMBEDDED BARRIERS

In a misguided attempt to improve recruiting efficiencies and the quality of talent, HR inadvertently creates significant barriers to the talent acquisition process. Many applicants describe the "black hole" that occurs when they send off a résumé in response to an online job posting. In other cases, such as the public sector, the selection process includes multiple interviews, multiple tests, and the patience of a saint. An example described by an SHRM article discloses some of the hiring practices of government agencies. They include vague job descriptions, snail-mail communication, and a time-to-hire that is upwards of many months. These types of barriers have a significant impact. While the generation of young professionals born between 1981 and the 1990s are projected to make up more than 75 percent of the general workforce population by 2025, only 27 percent are projected to go into public service. It is no surprise then that many government organizations are jumping on the bandwagon and plan to expend a significant investment on streamlining their hiring practices to be more applicant friendly. Check out the full article titled "Hiring Challenges Confront Public-Sector Employers" at www.shrm.org.

In the case of recruiting, the organizational structure matters. Where there is clarity on the organizational chart, there is clarity in the recruitment process. To be sure, this is not just the visual picture of the reporting hierarchy. Clarity includes the need to conduct thorough job analysis so the role is defined and HR can properly advertise and measure for the knowledge, skills, and abilities necessary for success. In some cases, HR may need to lead an organizational design (OD) intervention by redesigning jobs to meet business strategies; in others, HR may need to update job descriptions to reflect new responsibilities. Regardless, HR's ability to partner with other departments can help ensure there are multiple candidates to choose from when it comes time for selection.

TIP

Refer to Figure 8-1 in Chapter 8 for a visual look at the recruiting process.

Recruiting is about attracting qualified talent who desire to work for the organization. The selection process is about using tools that help to predict the fit of a candidate to the job and to the organization. These predictive tools must be compliant with labor laws by being nondiscriminatory in both intent and effect, and by being job related.

Tools that help to measure person-to-job fit include interview questions, realistic job previews, accurate job descriptions, and the applicant's work history and education. Predicting person-to-organization fit can be a bit more subjective, with a goal of finding ways to communicate the values, attitudes, and beliefs of the organization. Tools that help do this can include predictive personality assessments, panel interviews with peers, and, in some cases, offering new employees "quit-pay" if they are not happy — such as is the case at Zappos.

Other selection tools that are governed by the Uniform Guidelines on Employee Selection Procedures (UGESP) include applications, paper-and-pencil tests, interview questions, strength and agility tests . . . really, any task or procedure used during the selection process where the results are used to make a hiring decision.

Selection

The selection process requires the support of multiple departments (one of the many good reasons for developing strong relationships with internal stakeholders). Senior leaders will not necessarily be called upon to review applications or complete new-hire paperwork, but they are responsible for overseeing the selection process.

HIRING THE FORMERLY INCARCERATED

Many states have enacted legislation that disallows applications or interviews from asking about prior criminal convictions. This is due in large part to the underemployment rates of the formerly incarcerated, but it's also due to the demand for qualified labor in a tight labor market. While HR must comply with these laws, it must also be mindful of negligent hiring. For this reason, HR should audit its selection practices to create legally defensible methods (job related and nondiscriminatory) to staff the organization.

Conversely, some employers are embracing the formerly incarcerated as a labor-force population. Dave's Killer Bread Foundation headquartered in Oregon offers an employer toolkit that can be used to implement a strategy of employing those with a criminal history. Check out their Second Chance employment program at www.daveskillerbread.com/secondchances.

A good first step from a strategic perspective is to ensure that a thorough job analysis has been completed for every position within the organization. HR should also have a view of the next one to three years in mind so that any changes that will need to be made can be accounted for, such as making the decision to "build or buy" the talent to fill future needs. This choice drives decisions about budgets and learning and development activities, and underscores the need for clear career paths.

Training personnel who will be responsible for conducting employment interviews is also a wise step of senior leaders because interviewers may not be aware of the many forms of cognitive bias that can exist when assessing talent.

Take a look at Chapter 8 for a refresher on the different types of interviews and forms of bias if this is unfamiliar territory.

Integrating New Talent

The terms "orientation" and "onboarding" are often used interchangeably and harken back to the early days of human resources. As HR industry practices have evolved, the terms "acculturation" and "socialization" have emerged. This is significant in that it tells HR professionals that how they integrate the new talent within their organizations should have evolved as well. In fact, some studies find that a new hire makes the decision to stay or go within the first six months of employment, making this introductory time with the team a critical factor of long-term retention of talent.

Orientation is the operational component of bringing on a new team member. Heavy on the compliance side of HR, new employees are greeted with safety training, handbook acknowledgements, and the data that employers must collect and control. Orientation is also usually where employees receive the tools necessary to do their jobs. This may include the issuance of passwords, security badges, laptops, and so forth. As you may see from these examples, the orientation is highly administrative, and thus, represented more thoroughly in the PHR exam responsibilities.

Onboarding is more process-oriented than administrative. It involves taking a deeper dive with new team members, introducing them to the culture and helping them become familiar with the landscape — both physical and psychological. For this reason, many employers are starting the onboarding process post-hire, but separate from the day-to-day tasks and activities. For example, Facebook is famous for a two-month-long onboarding process for new engineers that shifts the employees through multiple departments so new hires get a sense of the business. This helps them meet other team members and can foster a collaborative approach from day one.

Acculturation and *socialization* are closely related terms. In the field of behavioral science, they refer to the process by which employees begin to absorb the attitudes, beliefs, knowledge, skills, and abilities to perform. This is not a new concept. In fact, a model from 1987 gives us a good look at how this process can be applied:

>> **Anticipatory socialization:** This is part of the recruiting and selection process and may include site tours, psychological testing, interviews, and testimonials from current workers. HR plays a significant role at this stage, often being the face of the company and thus, its ambassador.

>> **Entry and assimilation:** Messaging is a fundamental part of this step in the socialization process. Who do they hear from post-offer, pre-start date? How well do they understand the new role and what will be expected of them? Once they start the job, is what was promised true, such as work schedules and attitudes toward overtime or virtual work? Mentors and supervisor one-on-ones can help this transitional phase from applicant to employee be successful.

>> **Metamorphosis:** In this final stage, the employee begins to perform, contribute, and be productive. The timing of this stage is dependent upon the qualifications of the individual, and also the complexity of the job. In some cases, particularly for more complex jobs or those that require certification, this process can take years. The FAA, for example, notes that even after education and on-the-job experience, it can take air traffic controllers two to five years (in some cases, up to eight) to become fully certified. HR can help guide the conversations to understand the true learning curve for the organization's jobs. They can also help manage supervisor expectations and drive the performance-feedback process so the team member has the tools and resources for optimal performance.

TIP

For more detailed information on this process, check out "Organizational entry, assimilation, and exit" in *Handbook of organizational communication: An interdisciplinary perspective* by editors F. M. Jablin, L. L. Putnam, K. H. Roberts, and L. W. Porter (Sage Publications, Inc.).

As you may have noticed, a systems approach to socialization includes the elements of orientation and onboarding and culture acculturation; thus, it takes a more holistic approach that can result in more positive outcomes — such as a reduction in the turnover rate in an employee's first year of employment.

Engaging Employees

The term "employee engagement" has been thrown around a lot in recent years due to the widely publicized benefits of an engaged workforce.

Proven methods to improve engagement begin with senior leaders — including the CEO. This may require coaching and development so that a high-performing culture trickles down from the top.

Another method to improve employee engagement is to take special steps to communicate with team members. Engaged employees believe that they understand the general purpose of an organization's behaviors and, more importantly, how they contribute to the achievement of outcomes.

A DAY IN THE LIFE OF A DISENGAGED EMPLOYEE

Much is said about the value of an engaged workforce, but what about the negative effects of actively disengaged team members? "Disengaged" is defined by a Gallup survey as those employees who invest time but not energy or passion into their work. These employees are characterized by high absenteeism rates, low productivity, increased injuries/accidents, low quality output, and even destructive organizational citizenship behaviors. The Gallup poll in 2019 found that more than 50 percent of workers are not engaged, and worse, 13 percent of those are actively disengaged, costing employers billions of dollars each year in lost productivity. These numbers make a strong argument for putting employee engagement initiatives at the top of your strategic plan.

Actively engaged team members feel that their companies are invested in their success, a behavior heavily measured in the area of learning and development covered in the next chapter.

Finally, your engaged people are watching how you deal with the actively disengaged: specifically, what behaviors are disciplined, what behaviors are rewarded, and what behaviors are simply tolerated. Team members have an acute sense of the equity of expectations between high and low performers.

Termination in the Context of Talent Planning

As discussed in the chapter opening, the exam objectives in this area focus the responsibilities on the beginning of the employee life cycle. Two points to keep in mind:

>> The knowledge requirement in this content area directs us to understand termination approaches and strategies (23)

>> Employee separations are heavily represented on the PHR exam in content area 05, Employee Relations and Engagement

So why, then, is this knowledge present for SPHR candidates in the Talent Planning and Acquisition content area? The assumption here is that employee separations are highly operational and thus better oriented for the PHR candidate. It may also be inferred that separations in the sphere of the SPHR candidate's influence are related directly to strategic organizational interventions related to the business life cycle of *growth* or *decline*, such as mergers, acquisitions, and divestitures, so the focus of the content is related to terminations in this way.

TIP

If you would like to shore up your knowledge of terminations in the traditional sense, head on back to Chapter 11.

Corporate restructures

There are several examples of corporate restructures in the news today. From these, we can glean how HR may support the changes brought by this type of OD intervention.

In April of 2020, Univision announced major layoffs and furloughs as the result of the COVID-19. This included furloughs of four weeks or more, executive pay cuts, and suspension of retirement fund matching (notice these organizational behaviors were the responsibility of HR to implement).

Amazon invested $1.2 billion to acquire start-up Zoox, with a goal of developing self-driving taxis for major U.S. cities — not for package delivery, but for people. For now, Zoox will remain an independent subsidiary. This means that HR and other leaders at Amazon were probably called upon to exercise the practice of due diligence prior to the final purchase. This would include a thorough review by experts of the company finances, business practices, bench talent, employment contracts, employment practices, lawsuit history, and more.

These examples illustrate that senior HR leaders are very likely to be called upon to help their organizations navigate the vast land that is corporate restructuring. The most common types (in the context of employee separations) are discussed here.

Mergers and acquisitions

As the preceding Amazon example notes, mergers and acquisitions are highly complex and valuable business transactions. The benefits of a merger or acquisition include increased capacity, increased market share, taking out a key competitor, gaining talent that can be deployed in other areas, and so on. The value is inherent, but only if managed properly.

In addition to completing due diligence, HR is called upon to handle the cultural integration post-event. This means treating the acquired talent as new hires and spending significant time on the acculturation process. Some organizations go so far as to create integration teams or committees with representatives from each organization. These teams focus on building communication channels to help creatively solve problems and make decisions that will help the merger be successful. It can also help HR get in front of turf wars and restructure redundant work processes. This focus is time-consuming yet significant when you consider the cost of failure. Think of the merger between the New York Central and Pennsylvania Railroads who, in 1986, merged to become Penn Central and the sixth largest corporation in the United States. Just two years after the deal, the new business entity filed for bankruptcy.

Divestitures

The uncertainty of the global business environment over the last several years has demanded much attention. The trade war with China, for example, resulted in increased tariffs and disputes about ocean shipping lanes. The pandemic created bottlenecks in the supply chain. Shareholder activism, such as that between Sony and Third Point, has forced corporate leaders to take a look at who they are doing business with and how business gets done. With these and other pressures, it is no wonder that a Global Corporate Divestment Study in 2019 found that more than 80 percent of companies planned to divest some portion of their business in the next few years.

HRCI defines a divestiture as "the sale of a company's assets." This means that a company may sell off a business unit or brand. The benefits of a divestiture include freeing up capital for other, more profitable or less consuming parts of the business as well as increasing trust with shareholders. In the context of the SPHR exam, the phrase "freeing up capital" applies to the human capital, and it is up to HR to direct where these team members will go.

In many cases, these team members may need to be let go, and they go through the separation system already in place. HR can enhance this process by offering job placement services, such as résumé workshops and reverse job fairs. In other cases, the talent may be absorbed within other business units, which should prompt a savvy senior leader to "restart" the employee within the life cycle, including onboarding and acculturation.

TESTING YOUR KNOWLEDGE

The SPHR continues to be famous for its level of difficulty because senior leaders must be able to interpret and apply non-direct test questions. Here is an opportunity to test yourself on your ability to articulate how the *life cycle* is impacted by the HR *function*. Do this by thinking about how the exam objectives apply to each stage in the cycle. For example, can you answer the following question?

- Q. In what ways are strategic processes are supported by the *recruiting and selection* stage of the employee life cycle?

- A. Mergers and acquisitions, global expansion, national expansion, offshoring, PESTLE forces, and changes to products or services requiring different employee skill sets

With the exception of natural attrition, recruiting and selection are about growth. Exam content in this area likely will deal with the skill sets of the existing workforce when compared to strategic growth initiatives, and bridging gaps where necessary.

REMEMBER

The last chapter noted that the rapid pace of change for 21st-century employers will likely be in the areas of techno-structural interventions and globalization. Watch the headlines for corporate restructures related to these forces. Take a moment and think about how these forces may influence the organization that you work for.

IN THIS CHAPTER

» Discovering essential pieces for Learning and Development

» Developing tools to build resources

» Aligning Learning and Development activities with strategy

Chapter **14**

Shaping the Resources: SPHR 03 Learning and Development

ormerly referred to as "Human Resource Development," the functional area of Learning and Development on the SPHR exam has expanded. No longer considered only the training tasks of HR, Learning and Development encompasses the growth of people, processes, and the organization as a whole. When viewed using systems theory, this functional area builds on the idea that all human resource activities are connected — you can't change one element without affecting others. This is most reflected in content related to organizational design and development, and thus is closely tied to the function of Leadership and Strategy. For these reasons, don't be fooled by the simplicity of HRCI's description of this function as follows:

> "Develop training, development, and employee retention strategies."

There is a lot to unpack in those seven words, and this chapter begins that process of discovery.

Examining What You Need to Know for the Exam

Similar to the Talent Planning and Acquisition function of the SPHR exam, there are only three exam responsibilities in the functional area of Learning and Development (L&D). And like Total Rewards (the next chapter), this content only accounts for 12 percent of the exam, meaning you may expect to see about 18 questions out of the 150 scored items on your exam. While this book will hopefully serve as a reference guide for many years to come, the ultimate objective is to prepare you for exam day. For this reason, this chapter attempts to create a laser-light focus on the critical "must haves" for exam-day success.

Responsibilities

An organization's ability to compete rests squarely on their ability to attract and keep top talent. Learning and Development focuses on three key responsibilities that aid in the retention of qualified talent:

01 Develop and evaluate training strategies (for example: modes of delivery, timing, content) to increase individual and organizational effectiveness.

02 Analyze business needs to develop a succession plan for key roles (for example: identify talent, outline career progression, coaching and development) to promote business continuity.

03 Develop and evaluate employee retention strategies and practices (for example: assessing talent, developing career paths, managing job movement within the organization).

Knowledge of

As with all areas of the exams, HR professionals must call upon a baseline of knowledge when answering questions. For this reason, candidates should be familiar with these topics:

30 Training program design and development

31 Adult learning processes

32 Training and facilitation techniques

33 Instructional design principles and processes (for example: needs analysis, content chunking, process flow mapping)

34 Techniques to assess training program effectiveness, including use of applicable metrics

35 Career and leadership development theories and applications

36 Organizational development (OD) methods, motivation methods, and problem-solving techniques

37 Coaching and mentoring techniques

38 Effective communication skills and strategies (for example: presentation, collaboration, sensitivity)

39 Employee retention strategies

40 Techniques to encourage creativity and innovation

Analyzing Business Needs

As discussed throughout this book, to be an effective business partner is to be an effective manager of risk. These risks include the ability to staff for the current and future needs of the organization, which requires innovative problem-solving on a scale not seen for a long time. From the good news desk comes the fact that due to the economic crisis, many baby boomers are delaying retirement. An example from the bad news front is the increased cost of medical school that is causing students to opt out of the debt, creating a shortage of future medical professionals. These are just two examples of how HR must help to analyze business needs and then position the organization through HR best practices to succeed.

We can go deeper into the preceding two examples and take a look at how L&D activities can address the needs. When natural attrition through retirement doesn't occur, fewer positions are available for new college grads or entry-level performers. HR can create a stopgap by first assessing the needs, wants, and skill set of entry-level workers. Then they can review the organization's strategic plan and department structures to position team members as future replacements. From here, the replacement workers receive coaching, training, and increased job responsibilities so they are the obvious choice when the time is right. This example describes responsibilities 02 and 03 of this functional area in a nutshell.

Consider again the example of the rising cost of student debt. Beginning with analyzing the business needs, you know that there is a shortage of skilled medical staff to fill future industry needs. Kaiser Permanente in California opened its own School of Medicine and announced that the tuition costs of the first five graduating classes will be waived. An investment, to be sure, but less costly than not being able to staff for the core competency of medical care. On a simpler note, many employers are offering tuition reimbursement as part of their value proposition to attract and retain top talent. Similarly, companies such as Tesla are abandoning college degree requirements in order to remove barriers of finding exceptional talent.

Activating Training Systems

Training focuses on the skill sets necessary of the entire workforce as it relates to "current state." This also places particular emphasis on compliance, as most labor laws include a requirement that employees are trained on what to do — and not to do.

Instructional design

There are many options for training solutions that include purchasing off-the-shelf toolkits or customizing training. The correct choice is dependent on several factors, including budgets and content complexity. For safety training, off-the-shelf solutions are an efficient way to ensure consistency of the message among team members, an important element to demonstrating compliance with OSHA standards. For culture training, designing an in-house program is usually best. In order to know what selection to make, HR begins with a formal needs analysis.

Needs analysis

A training needs analysis is a formal process of identifying the gaps between current and desired state. It begins with the end in mind, working with stakeholders to identify the training objectives and then filling in the content around the desired results. When done correctly, this process makes evaluation of the training outcomes (and training ROI) much easier to complete and refine as needed.

Content chunking

The refinement process can be onerous when there are hours of videos or rigid itineraries that must be delivered in sequence. Additionally, many parts of a business are subject to rapid change, and training content must be flexible enough to adapt without having to start over every time an update needs to be made. Fortunately, the technique of content chunking can help.

Chunking content is the action of breaking up training material into micro learning–sized pieces. This may be as simple as using headings in written material to break up sections, or it may entail the more complex development of four-minute videos in an e-learning platform.

Not only does this practice make updating easier, but research shows that mastering smaller bits at a time aids in retention and drives learning — the focus of training efforts!

Process flow mapping

Process flow is a visual learning tool that translates data into sequences with symbols marking the way. This technique can be particularly helpful when highly complex processes need to be broken down. The result is a diagram of the steps necessary to achieve an outcome that can be used not only in training but also at the worksite for future reference.

Presenting content

HR is often called upon to use presentation skills in the course of their work. From making a business case for new resources, or training with the team, there are several techniques that will prove useful.

Presentation skills

The days of the Socratic seminar are over! Classroom-style lectures with a "sage on the stage" are no longer the most effective way to transfer knowledge. A review of adult learning styles can help reinforce this statement.

Andragogy is the science related to how adults learn. In addition to the tactile, visual, and auditory styles we are most familiar with, andragogy notes that adults learn best when they have control over their learning and they understand how it applies to their work. It is more specific than its counterpart, *pedagogy,* in which children are taught a more broad-based curriculum for future use.

Additionally, the traditional PowerPoint presentation continues to be an organized way to present data, and yet, it often inhibits true exchange of ideas. Ditching the PowerPoint and learning how to *facilitate* training is the best way to keep a connection with your team and invite input, a major component to adults having control over their learning outcomes.

TIP

Take a look at Chapter 9 for a refresher on the five different pieces that make adult learning unique.

Brainstorming techniques

One method to increase collaboration is to use formal and informal creative brainstorming techniques.

Formally, a Delphi technique is bringing a community of experts together and gathering input on a situation. It is an iterative process, with at least two rounds of the participants answering questions and justifying their answers. Adjustments are made until a satisfactory conclusion is reached.

Similar to the Delphi technique is the *nominal group* method, whereby the experts never actually meet. This is so the answers can't be contaminated by opinions. A group leader collects and collates the data and then sends it out for another review, until a consensus is reached.

Particularly in problem-solving, using questions is a simple and effective way to extract from the experts. Questions such as "In what ways can we _____?" or "What gets in the way of _____?" can help focus a group's attention on the problem at hand.

Note that these techniques are ways that HR leaders can engage in creative problem-solving that meets the needs of the workgroup. Putting together focus groups and committees can help ensure the systems and benefits of HR truly result in retention and engagement.

TIP

I am an introvert. I speak when called upon. Which means that in a brainstorming session filled with extroverts, you may not get all perspectives. For this reason, it is useful to ask participants to spend time in silence coming up with answers to the questions, and then using a round-robin facilitation technique to get input from all in the room. As Isabel Briggs-Myers said, "If you don't know what an extrovert is thinking, you haven't been listening. If you don't know what an introvert is thinking, you haven't asked." Keep this in mind when brainstorming.

Using Learning and Development for Retention

One of the major themes throughout the SPHR exam is the need to harness the power of HR systems to improve employee retention. L&D is highly strategic in that the activities in this domain can not only improve retention, but improve the quality and performance of team members. Both of these outcomes improve an organization's competitive advantage.

Assessing talent

HR activities designed to assess talent aren't limited to the dreaded annual review. In fact, senior leaders should keep in mind that assessing talent in L&D is different from assessing performance. This may be why the exam updates of 2018 moved the performance review process to the content domain of employee relations. The assessment process in L&D becomes strategic when you create and manage tools that assess *potential*. These tools should be focused on competencies within the context of the employee's current job and future goals.

"Stay, Groom, Go" is a method used by many employers to capture a snapshot of the workforce. This is based on the idea that 50 percent of employees should stay in their current positions, 25 percent of employees should be groomed for promotion, and 25 percent of team members need to exit. This approach has come under fire most recently because of the spotlight on large corporation "rank and yank" performance management practices. When used properly, however, comparative performance techniques can begin the process of assessing talent and creating learning and development strategies to be intentional about team member contributions.

Performance reviews are often used in workforce analytics. This is a blessing and a curse. Objectively, performance data can help shine a spotlight on highly productive workers. However, it can miss the value of narrative factors that do not fit neatly on a Likert scale (ratings from high to low on a scale of 1–5, for example). For this reason, strategic HR partners must find ways to assess talent with the objective of supporting organizational health, from achieving strategic goals to eliminating toxic behaviors. It can all be done through L&D behaviors.

AN HR DEPARTMENT OF ONE

Somebody somewhere a long, long time ago decided that HR can be handled by one person up until about the 80-employee mark. I disagree with this formula wholeheartedly, and yet it persists. For a single-employee HR department, just the idea of applying these elevated L&D strategies is exhausting. For this reason, senior leaders may need to look for alternatives to increase the capacity of the HR department. This may be done by arguing a business case to add experienced talent. It may also be accomplished by shifting to employee self-service functions, as well as training supervisors to take on traditional HR functions such as interviewing, discipline, and offering performance feedback. In the spirit of development, employment laws related to using student interns have been relaxed, so there is opportunity to find qualified talent while using job responsibilities to help an entry-level HR professional gain experience.

Regardless of the tool used to assess talent, HR must take care to properly train raters on how to offer constructive feedback that motivates rather than destroys initiative. Care must also be taken to remind raters of the presence of bias, those cognitive and often unconscious beliefs and attitudes that shape decision-making.

A strength summary is one tool HR can use in the context of development to objectively map out the existing skills and wants of its team. Take a look at Table 14-1 for an example. Note that you can modify this to reflect department planning or planning at an organizational level, such as senior leadership.

TABLE 14-1 Talent Summary

Position Title and Incumbent	Performance in Current Role	Next Position	Readiness	Replacement	Readiness
HR Generalist Erica Case	Exceeds expectations	HR Supervisor	Now	HR Assistant Tanya Carter	6–12 mos.
HR Intern Maggie Belle	Meets expectations	HR Assistant	Now	None	N/A

Adapted from Berger, L. A., & Berger, D. R. (2011). The Talent Management Handbook: Creating a sustainable competitive advantage by selecting, developing, and promoting the best people. New York: McGraw-Hill. Bench Strength Summary.

The decision to promote from within is one measure of an employer culture. As with any good management practice, HR can drive the practice of using the assessment phase of L&D to measure an employee's readiness to move on to the next phase in her career path.

Creating career paths

Careers are not an accident, and the young professionals coming up through the ranks are much more intentional than their Gen X and Boomer predecessors about who, what, where, when, and especially, the why of the work that they do. Career planning is the effort by HR to help team members identify, manage, and develop the skills necessary to take advantage of growth opportunities.

A career path first begins at a structural level. Up-to-date job descriptions with accurate (and not inflated) knowledge, skill, and ability requirements provide the clarity necessary for fluid movement. This is also an opportunity to tie wages to performance by simply defining job tiers such as Contributor Level 1, 2, and 3. As skills are developed or knowledge is gained, pay increases may follow. There often is an opportunity for cross-training here, which can help offset the risk of having only tribal knowledge to rely on.

Know also that some employees do not want to become managers and yet crave development to build skills and avoid stagnation. A useful solution is that of creating a *dual career ladder* system that represents a management track and a nonmanagement track. In the nonmanagement track, a team member is allowed to create depth in his role through subject-matter expertise as opposed to exchanging his skill set for one that demands more people leadership.

Coaching and development activities can be a highly effective way to improve employees' tangible skills and their less tangible job attitudes. A formal mentoring program is not the only way to create connections in the workplace. Instituting informal buddy systems and hiring outside coaches are both effective, provided the goals are established on the front end. If cash flow is tight, it's time for HR to get creative. Consider hosting a voluntary book club that taps into the wisdom of business leaders. Start a Lean In Circle (www.leanin.org) and invite up-and-coming women within and outside of the organization to network and learn from each other. These are just two examples of how HR can use L&D activities to fortify the ranks of current and future talent.

While career paths are important, organizations that can offer the "positions for life" of the 20th century are rare these days. This is often the argument made by less-aware COOs against offering generous learning and development activities. The fear is that either they will invest in team members who will leave for a better opportunity, or the company won't have capacity for upward mobility. Both of these things are true. But it doesn't matter as much as they think if HR can do what it does best and take a holistic approach. This means driving a culture where talent wants to stay because it is a psychologically safe place to be. It also means budgeting for competitive wages and making sure there are plenty of opportunities for team members to find purpose within their roles beyond just the job tasks. This can be done in the context of mentorships, volunteering in the community, work/life balance, and other flexible programs championed by HR. At the end of the day, the more talented and invested teammates are, the more productive and satisfied they are.

TIP

To understand the concept of psychological safety in application, search for the findings of Google's Project Aristotle. This study found that creating and sustaining an environment where employees feel psychologically safe is the number-one indicator of team success.

Allocating resources

There is an element of chess playing when choosing what to do with the talent of an organization. Timing matters along with the properties of the team members. While identifying employee superpowers is a function of the previous section on assessing talent, how you deploy those talents will determine success or failure — of the employee through retention and of the organization through competitiveness.

Many employees, particularly those who are high performers, don't want to be "handled." They want the opportunity to build the necessary skills through experience and increased trust that are career-defining as opposed to surviving in a job.

Another factor to consider is that of knowledge capital. This is the idea that an organization may predict future competitiveness based on the depth and accessibility of the knowledge of its employees. For this reason, HR must charge forward in the process of developing knowledge management programs, defined by HRCI as gathering, documenting, and sharing important information to improve employee performance.

Chapter 15

Harnessing the Value: SPHR 04 Total Rewards

Total rewards as a *strategy* is different from the operational components of it as a *function*. Processing payroll and complying with ERISA are certainly important tasks, and yet those remain firmly in the domain of PHR candidates. SPHR candidates must be able to navigate the complexity of compensation and benefits as both a cost and a motivator, their impact on perceptions of fairness, and the ability of these programs to shore up retention rates. This is done by understanding what these systems can — and can't — do. Senior leaders also must bear in mind the business needs to avoid overpaying for talent while at the same time rewarding valued team members. For SPHR candidates, Total Rewards are just as much art as they are science. HRCI defines this functional area that makes up 12 percent of the SPHR exam as follows:

> "Monitor the effectiveness of compensation and benefit strategies for attracting, rewarding, and retaining talent."

Total Rewards Exam Objectives

There are only two — that's right, two — exam responsibilities related to this domain. This requires a sharp focus only on what is most important for you to understand and be able to apply on game day. This chapter focuses on the strategies that drive positive outcomes from effective compensation and benefits systems.

Responsibilities

The operational responsibilities of Total Rewards are explained in the broadest of categories, compensation and benefits:

01 Analyze and evaluate compensation strategies (for example: philosophy, classification, direct, indirect, incentives, bonuses, equity, executive compensation) that attract, reward, and retain talent.

02 Analyze and evaluate benefit strategies (for example: health, welfare, retirement, recognition programs, work-life balance, wellness) that attract, reward, and retain talent.

Knowledge

In addition to the practical components listed above, there are additional knowledge requirements:

41 Compensation strategies and philosophy

42 Job analysis and evaluation methods

43 Job pricing and pay structures

44 External labor markets and economic factors

45 Executive compensation methods

46 Noncash compensation methods

47 Benefits program strategies

48 Fiduciary responsibilities

49 Motivation concepts and applications

50 Benchmarking techniques

Breaking Down the Content

Total Rewards is about much more than paying an employee a fair wage in exchange for a day's work. Total Rewards programs that are tied to the organization's strategic plan have influence in all the functional areas of the exams. Consider the function of Talent Planning and Acquisition. Chapter 8 discusses the objectives from the perspective of the employee life cycle that begins with recruiting and selection. Compensation influences a company's ability to compete for talent. The following section discusses some of the other main things you should know about the Total Rewards function of the exams.

Categorizing Total Rewards

As an SPHR candidate, consider the phrasing "attracting, rewarding, and retaining talent" in the description. Based on this, you may anticipate questions related to

AROUND THE WORLD: BENEFITS PRACTICES IN OTHER COUNTRIES

The United States isn't the leader in offering social or other welfare benefits to its workers. Examples of excellent benefits practices in other countries include the following:

- **Netherlands:** All employees are entitled to four weeks of paid holidays.

- **Argentina:** Employees receive ten continuous days of leave for the qualifying event of marriage, and overtime may not exceed more than 30 hours a month or 200 hours per year.

- **Slovakia:** New mothers are entitled to 34 weeks of maternity leave to care for a newborn, and they can request up to three years of time off to care for a new child.

Although the exams aren't likely to quiz you on these kinds of specifics, you should have a general understanding that compensation and benefits packages in other countries must take into account differences in minimum wages, holiday pay, social welfare benefits, and extended leave rights.

>> **A company's compensation philosophy:** The decision to lead, lag, or match the market with regard to compensation is directly related to supply and demand. You may have to recommend higher pay strategies for positions requiring in-demand or difficult-to-find skills. Other issues that arise from a company's compensation strategy include pay compression, red/green-circled employees, and the system for offering pay increases.

>> **Value-added benefits:** With the rising cost of benefits and the uncertainty of how the Patient Protection and Affordable Care Act (PPACA) will continue to change, the exam devotes a lot of attention to employee benefits packages. Being a resourceful business partner requires that you have knowledge of alternatives to traditional benefits and that you can recommend strategies to, at minimum, help employers keep their annual benefits offerings budget-neutral. That may include recommending financial options, such as increasing the employee shares of the burden or switching providers. Behavioral health options are also possible strategies, such as health and wellness programs for smokers or programs for employees who desire to lose weight.

Building compensation strategies

The purpose of strategic compensation and benefits packages is to support organizational outcomes, so paying attention to the company's strategic plan is important.

For example, say a company will be expanding into California from the Midwest. The company's current minimum wage is out of compliance with California's minimum wage laws, and its sick time policies will need to be updated to comply with the state's sick leave law that requires all employees to accrue one hour of paid sick time for every 30 hours worked. Cal Cobra is a bit different, and overtime is accrued on an 8- and 40-hour basis, not just a straight 40 per week. This HR department has a lot of work to do to support its company's strategic objective.

After a company's strategy is set, departmental goals in Total Rewards can be designed, implemented, and measured. One example is the use of *variable pay plans,* in which cash and noncash options are considered. For instance, customer service has been tasked with increasing its revenue generated from selling warranty services by 25 percent in the coming fiscal year. To do so, the company is offering a $100 spiff per month to the top-selling customer service representative.

These exams have a lot of information to digest regarding variable pay plans. A few items to understand are as follows:

>> **Bonuses:** Bonuses can be a win-win for all involved. Because *bonuses* are above and beyond the base pay rate, employers can offer these pay incentives without a long-term increase of payroll or overtime. When timed properly, employers can leverage the dollars for maximum effect, such as tying them to end-of-calendar-year performance paid to employees during the holidays.

>> **Team incentives:** *Team incentives* can be an effective way to motivate a group of workers that is required to achieve shared objectives. Examples include assembly stations in manufacturing or marketing groups working together on a project. They can be offered to nurture teamwork or increase productivity.

>> **Stock options:** The opportunity to own shares of a company is an equity compensation strategy. It can be effective for start-up companies that can't afford to pay market rates to attract (or keep) talent. It's also useful in fostering an *ownership culture* (where employees behave as though they own the company) and sharing the profitability where possible.

Regardless of the type of variable pay plans, the priority should be for the plans to be *self-funded,* which means that the benefit realized through the incentive is greater than or, at minimum, equal to the cost of the payout.

EXAMPLE

Which of the following compensation strategies would you recommend to a technology start-up in need of finding affordable yet highly qualified talent?

(A) Pay the average going rate within its industry to ensure pay fairness.

(B) Create a pay-for-performance system built to the average industry rates.

(C) Offer a C&B package that is above average to entice applicants to leave their existing employer.

(D) Use a combination of strategies including cash and noncash options, such as lower base pay with ownership equity options.

The correct answer is (D). The availability of cash is often a challenge for new start-ups, which means their compensation strategies often must be a blend of cash and noncash options. It's not unusual for technology companies to offer ownership equity options to find the talent they need to aggressively compete. Choices (A) and (B) are incorrect because matching the industry's pay practices isn't sufficient enough to motivate the highly qualified to leave their existing employers. Choice (C) is incorrect because most start-ups don't have the ability to pay above average.

Budgeting labor costs

Being able to predict the cost and affordability of labor strategies is an important function of senior leaders. It does not mean a taking a simple look at how much wages are as part of a profit and loss statement. Budgeting requires a holistic view of the past, present, and future needs for labor and should include the employee burden when all mandatory and voluntary benefits are factored in. Another HR behavior that can be helpful is to understand the return on investment of employee costs. For example, a company that pays a marketing professional $65,000 a year may need that employee to generate at least that much in new sales in order to break even. This requires HR to take a look at staffing levels to determine whether a company has too many human resources when compared to outputs and the achievement of strategic targets.

Understanding program limitations

As alluded to in the chapter intro, many employers place too much pressure on their compensation and benefits strategies, as though it is the one and only tool that can reward employees; improve job satisfaction; and improve attendance, productivity, and quality; but the truth is it is not a panacea.

Compensation is undoubtedly an important component to all the preceding benefits. Over-reliance, however, leads to complacency and decreases the quality of decision-making with regard to comp plans, which can increase the cost of labor or fail to produce desired outcomes. Here are a few things to keep in mind as you navigate compensation practices for your teams:

>> **Total rewards cannot improve employees' ethical behavior.** Power, authority, and the increased wages that come along with them do not change who people are at their core. As Adam Grant noted in his Audible book **Power Moves**, power does not corrupt; it only amplifies who a person already is.

>> **Higher pay rates do not always improve performance.** In fact, one study found that superstar performers believe they are worth higher pay (the belief that efficiency wages that pay higher produce high performance), and thus pay does not actually improve motivation or outputs. Additionally, there is a maximum threshold of pay that, once crossed, no longer improves employee performance at all.

>> **Pay does not greatly improve employee job satisfaction.** A 2010 study by Timothy A. Judge found that pay rates were only slightly correlated to higher levels of job satisfaction.

Find Judge's 2010 study, titled "The relationship between pay and job satisfaction: A meta-analysis of the literature," in the *Journal of Vocational Education Volume 77, Issue 2, October 2010.*

For these reasons, HR leaders must have a sense of what their total rewards strategies are expected to do and what they are actually doing. This can be done by evaluating their compensation plans and, more importantly, by approaching employee performance, job satisfaction and motivation using all functions of HR, not just compensation and benefits.

Creating the Framework

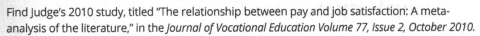

A true compensation and benefits system needs a framework from which to operate. While larger corporations may have compensation specialists who are educated in the ways of Total Rewards, many employers rely on their HR generalist teams, or partner with accounting or through outsourcing for the more complex tasks. Regardless of who holds the responsibility for execution, senior leaders must create and establish the bones of the practice. It begins by looking at the jobs.

Job analysis

Job analysis is part of the staffing function of human resources. It is the process of identifying the tasks, duties, and responsibilities of each job within the organization. From here, the jobs may be priced in accordance with relevance and importance to the entire workflow process and organizational competencies. This is done through job evaluation techniques.

Job evaluation and pricing

The ability to price jobs properly is important for many reasons, including creating a competitive wage range from which to attract talent. Fairness is another consideration. The concepts of distributive and procedural justice refer to whether or not employees believe that the outcome and processes of all pay decisions are fair. If an employee believes either one is skewed, it can affect their perception of the employer.

Evaluating jobs involves identifying the worth of each role using many factors. This may be done through comprehensive analysis, such as the point factor method (weighting each piece of each job), or the simpler task of ranking each job by order of importance.

In some cases, employers use the job evaluation process to calculate the cost of replacing (recruiting in the current labor market) the job should the incumbent leave. This requires knowledge of the external labor markets that the employers compete in for talent.

Benchmarking

As the name suggests, benchmarking is the practice of identifying a base from which to make pay decisions. HRCI defines a market salary survey as a review of median pay for specific positions in the same labor market. This is done by using state and local resources such as the *Occupational Outlook Handbook* from the Bureau of Labor Statistics as well as the Wages and Employment feature of the Department of Labor. You can find all kinds of data at www.onetonline.org. Jump online and run the same search for your location, and see how it compares to wages for HR specialists in other areas. It is the best way to understand how important salary benchmarking is when building diverse and market-appropriate compensation plans.

Legal issues

Compensation and benefits are arguably the most heavily regulated of all HR practices — and that's saying something! Laws such as the Fair Labor Standards Act (FLSA), the Older Workers Benefits Protection Act (OWBPA), and the Employee Retirement Income Security Act (ERISA), along with their amendments, must be factored into legally compliant rewards programs. The most pressing of issues are described here.

Job classification

Exempt or nonexempt? Independent contractor or employee? These are the main questions asked with regard to the legal classifications of those who produce work on your behalf.

The Fair Labor Standards Act (FLSA) is the federal law that covers wages and hours for employees. Most states have their own version; however, the SPHR exam tests your knowledge of federal law. In addition to requiring that employers pay a minimum wage and govern the employment of minors, the FLSA also has rules that require the payment of overtime to nonexempt (hourly) workers. This means employers must conduct a test to determine who is exempt from the overtime and meal- and rest-break requirements of the FLSA. Here is what the Department of Labor (www.dol.gov) has to say about exemptions:

> "Section 13(a)(1) of the FLSA provides an exemption from both minimum wage and overtime pay for employees employed as bona fide executive, administrative, professional, and outside sales employees. Section 13(a)(1) and Section 13(a)(17) also exempt certain computer employees. To qualify for exemption, employees generally must meet certain tests regarding their job duties and be paid on a salary basis at not less than $684 per week. Employers may use nondiscretionary

bonuses and incentive payments (including commissions) paid on an annual or more frequent basis to satisfy up to 10 percent of the standard salary level. Job titles do not determine exempt status. In order for an exemption to apply, an employee's specific job duties and salary must meet all the requirements of the Department's regulations."

It is an HR best practice to understand and be able to conduct regular exemption audits in accordance with federal law (for purposes of the exam) and based on state laws in the case of legally compliant practices.

TIP

Use the plumber's test to help determine whether an individual is an employee or independent contractor (IC). If you're the manager of a retail store who has a plumbing problem, you probably jump online and search for plumbers in the area; ICs advertise and are licensed. You make the call and the plumber tells you that he can be there between noon and 5 p.m. the next day — ICs set their own hours and schedule. When the plumber arrives, he brings with him his wrenches and hoses; ICs have their own tools and equipment. After he completes the repairs, he submits a bill. ICs keep their own finances and pay their own taxes. Finally, your core competency is retail sales, not plumbing, meaning that you couldn't have provided the same service that the plumber provided; ICs don't have skills that mirror the key aspects of the business.

THE FUTURE OF GIG WORKERS

Uber, Lyft and Postmates are perhaps the most well-known examples of companies in the newest version of the *gig economy,* a term used to describe the economic disruption of the independent workforce. While nothing new (songwriters and actors have been gig workers for a long time), what has changed is the emergence of a business model that simply connects gig workers to the customer through a digital platform. The HR practice that is coming under fire from regulatory agencies is whether or not these individuals are true independent contractors or should be classified as employees. Employee classification would make them eligible for protections and benefits.

The IRS definition offers some direction, but not enough. Here are their common law rules to use to determine independent contractor status. Review them and then apply your critical thinking skills — do you think Uber drivers are employees or ICs?

Facts that provide evidence of the degree of control and independence fall into three categories:

- **Behavioral:** Does the company control or have the right to control what the worker does and how the worker does his or her job? (www.irs.gov/businesses/small-businesses-self-employed/behavioral-control)

- **Financial:** Are the business aspects of the worker's job controlled by the payer? These include things like how the worker is paid, whether expenses are reimbursed, who provides tools/supplies, and so on. (www.irs.gov/businesses/small-businesses-self-employed/financial-control)

- **Type of Relationship:** Are there written contracts or employee-type benefits (such as a pension plan, insurance, vacation pay, and so on)? Will the relationship continue, and is the work performed a key aspect of the business? (www.irs.gov/businesses/small-businesses-self-employed/type-of-relationship)

To get more information on the controversy, take a look at the National Public Radio article titled "Uber, Lyft, Postmates Refuse to Comply with California Gig Economy Law" at www.npr.org or the court's decision in *Dynamex Operations West v. Superior Court of Los Angeles County,* which offers new classifications for workers in California. While currently being figured out on the West Coast, strategic HR people know that other states often quickly follow suit.

Transparency challenges

Many states and localities are adopting pay transparency laws that prohibit *employers* from pro-hibiting *employees* from discussing their pay with each other — in policy or in practice. This is for many reasons. One is that pay is considered a major factor in employees deciding to unionize. Another is that pay discrimination still exists in the workplaces of today, and limiting employee ability to share wages can mask unlawful pay practices.

On a related note, many states and localities are also adopting laws that prohibit employers from asking applicants about their salary history. This is due to systemic discrimination that will only be perpetuated if employers base salary offers on prior pay levels. States with some version of banning salary history include Alabama, Georgia, Hawaii, and Illinois. This list is growing every year, so while the exam will only ask you about national practices, you should know your state's requirements to properly advise your employer.

Pay disparity

Pay disparity occurs when employees that are doing the same or similar work are paid differently. This is not an issue if the reasons for the pay disparity are job or employee related, such as job duties or tenure. Where it becomes unlawful is if the disparity is based on a protected class char-acteristic, such as gender.

Another component of this is systemic discrimination built into job descriptions. For example, janitors are traditionally men, whereas maids are typically women. If there were pay disparity, it would most likely be that janitors were paid higher wages than maids. This may be legitimately job related (such as higher skill being necessary for repairs or machine-operating) and thus, a legal practice. If so, HR should take care to document these reasons using tools such as job and workforce demographic analysis. HR would be well advised to take immediate steps to remedy the situation if they find evidence of unlawful discrimination.

Fiduciary responsibilities

Fiduciary responsibility is the legal concept that certain persons have a higher degree of respon-sibility in matters related to finances and decision-making. This means that the fiduciary has a legal obligation to act in good faith on behalf of the organization and other stakeholders. In an organizational context, this includes all senior leaders as well as human resource personnel.

In human resources, this becomes abundantly clear when administering benefits. For example, the Supreme Court found that 401k plan fiduciaries have an obligation to continually "monitor and remove imprudent investments" in employee retirement plans *(Tibble vs. Edison Interna-tional)*. Fiduciary responsibility is also represented in the practice of building total rewards pack-ages that are the hallmark of executive compensation.

Shaping executive compensation

Executive compensation has a bad reputation, part of which has been earned. However, execu-tives do have unique needs that must be addressed when creating a total rewards package. Look-ing at this from the perspective of risk management may be a helpful way to understand the various components an executive package must consider. The risks include

>> **Turnover:** *Turnover* (which occurs when employees leave a company) packs a costly punch and is generally calculated as a percentage of salary. Take one to two times the executive base pay (an accepted number to calculate the cost of turnover), and a company is looking at a large expense. More impactful though is the law of supply and demand, in which wages are affected

by the availability of qualified talent. Qualified talent shrinks at the top of the talent pyramid, so keeping qualified executives happy is a core function of compensation packages. In reverse, not many executive-level positions are available when compared to other levels of management, so executives that leave one company for another are taking a risk.

>> **Retention:** The opposite of turnover, *retention* (keeping key employees) efforts are built into executive employment contracts, usually in the form of golden handshakes or golden handcuffs. A *golden handshake* (also referred to as a *parachute*) means that a *C-suite* (chief officers, such as chief executive officer or chief financial officer) executive is contractually guaranteed a severance package should the company be acquired or should she be fired or asked to retire early. A *golden handcuff* is also part of an executive contract, in which the individual is incentivized to stay in an executive position for a specified period of time in exchange for some financial reward.

>> **Taxes:** With high levels of compensation come higher tax obligations, costing executives a pretty penny when accepting a lucrative contract. This financial risk can be mitigated through *deferred compensation* in which an employee is paid a portion of his earnings at a later date. Deferred compensation is often built into an employee pension.

As with any other human resource activity, organizations should seek options in which the reward outweighs the risk, which translates into executive compensation that is tied to organizational and individual performance.

Building benefits systems

From a strategic perspective, HR must focus on building systems that manage cost while attracting and retaining talent. This includes finding ways to manage the rising costs of health insurance for both the employer and employee, such as identifying how much of the healthcare burden should belong to the employee. The Bureau of Labor Statistics (BLS) gives some indication of the trends. In 2019, BLS reported that private industry employers are paying 79 percent of the employee's health insurance premiums. From a talent planning and budgeting perspective, HR can forecast the cost to attract (and retain) talent using benefits plans. This includes the need to communicate the value of these plans to team members. Table 15-1 gives you a look at more of the BLS stats on this critical HR function.

TABLE 15-1 **2019 BLS Data on Employee Benefits, Private Industry**

Type of Benefit	Access Rate	Participation Rate
Medical care	69%	49%
Retirement	67%	52%
Life insurance	56%	55%
Type of Paid Leave	**Access Rate**	Critical Thinking:
Paid sick leave	73%	In what way(s) can HR use this data to design strategic benefits plans?
Paid vacation	79%	What is the value? What barriers may exist?
Paid holidays	79%	

Review the source data at www.bls.gov/news.release/pdf/ebs2.pdf

Regardless of the data, HR has been living the need to attract and retain team members using a holistic approach to employee benefits, the components of which are identified directly in TR exam objective 02.

Medical care

Many employers are competing in industries where offering healthcare is an expectation, not a benefit. Others are finding the need to tinker with their plans in order to be compliant with the Patient Protection and Affordable Health Act, also known as "Obamacare." The challenges with both of these strategic objectives is that the target seems to move every year! What is valued by some workers is not as valued by others. The law seems to change depending on the Supreme Court. States have their own stylized version of mandates, adding another dimension of complexity, especially for those employers who practice in multiple states. HR must stay up-to-date on the changes and advise senior leaders on the need to be flexible and adapt as needed.

HR also can lead the way in getting creative about their health benefit offerings. Offering concierge services is one such alternative. *Concierge medicine* (also called Direct Primary Care) is on the rise, the primary feature being that it is privately administered outside of the traditional insurance market. The advantages can be lower costs as insurance fees are virtually eliminated. Some claim that the quality of the healthcare is also improved, with benefits such as same-day appointments and 24-hour direct access to their personal physician.

Some employers are considering hybrid plans where the traditional insurance stays in place for catastrophic events, and concierge services are secured for regular care. This can be especially beneficial for the older workforce who are delaying full retirement in many cases due to healthcare costs. The American Association of Retired Persons (AARP) notes that the average appointment time with doctors under traditional insurance plans is about 15 minutes. This applies to both a young professional with no ongoing medical issues and an older worker, who may have underlying medical conditions and is more likely to be on multiple medications.

Health insurance Captives are also on the rise as an alternative to the traditional health insurance system. A *Captive* plan is an independent insurance company usually owned by a collaborative group of members. Captives are a form of self-insurance that used to be reserved mostly for larger employers who could afford to cover the start-up costs or a catastrophic event. As Captives evolve in response to market interest, providers are finding ways to offset these costs. This is making it a more affordable solution for mid-size employers that wish to opt out of the traditional insurance market and stop the annual increase in premiums.

There is no dispute that offering robust employee health benefits is important, but a true Total Rewards program must offer more than just medical, dental, and vision programs.

Retirement compensation

As noted in the preceding table, more than 67 percent of employers offer access to retirement plans, and more than half of employees are making contributions. The BLS statistics calculate these offerings using two types of plans, both of which are "defined." In a *defined contribution plan,* such as a 401k, the employee is allowed to contribute a flat amount or percentage of their salary to an investment account, with periodic employer matching. In a *defined benefit plan,* such as pension plans, the employer makes a set contribution to an employee retirement account based on factors such as tenure and salary.

SAVINGS HABITS IN AMERICA

Thinking about savings beyond retirement is a luxury for many American workers. A scan of the federal reserve found that the median amount of nonretirement savings of households in the United States is $4,960. This means that 50 percent have more than that and 50 percent have less than that saved for an emergency. This number bears further scrutiny, considering that these numbers only apply to those with any savings accounts at all! Savings-levels-as-a-crisis is further shored up by a 2017 report that four in ten Americans could not cover a $400 expense. This is due in large part to increased unemployment, the presence of enormous amounts of student loan debt, and unexpected emergencies. Scan the report from the reserve bank for more details to use in your decision-making at www.federalreserve.gov/publications/files/2017-report-economic-well-being-us-households-201805.pdf.

How are those percentages reflected at your place of work? Do you have wages that support employee savings beyond that threshold, or are they more likely to have less? How can you take proactive steps to teach your teams about the importance of savings, such as offering seminars on home purchasing or the cost of credit card debt? What percentage of your workforce has taken out a loan against their 401k account? These are all examples of markers that can be used to direct HR financial wellness initiatives. For example, some employers are expanding their benefits offerings to include short-term (versus retirement) savings benefits for employees and matching funds or bonusing workers who enroll to jump-start contributions. Another option is offering flexible spending accounts that decrease taxable income while earmarking funds for medical needs, including emergencies. Many resources such as local banks offer free on-site training for employees on financial matters. The key is to understand your workforce demographics and habits, and structure programs to improve their satisfaction.

Employee recognition programs

Total Rewards exam objectives include employee recognition plans in their description of the types of benefits that must be strategically managed. This is interesting, as recognition programs are often measured as part of an overall employee relations program such as promoting cultural values and treating employees with respect. So, in what context might HRCI be asking us to understand recognition?

The benefits of formal employee recognition programs are many. Sincere appreciation and acknowledgement of employee efforts can improve job satisfaction and build trust within teams. Lack of recognition has energy as well. Many employees in exit interviews tell HR that they left because they did not feel appreciated, which means employee recognition has a direct impact on retention. This may be the link to benefits HRCI asks you to find — using recognition through *rewards* to attract and retain talent.

Formal rewards programs utilized by employers that recognize outstanding effort include on-the-spot bonuses, length-of-service awards, additional paid time off, celebratory retreats or vacations, and cash payments for continuous improvement ideas that result in savings.

REMEMBER

It's a virtual world out there. HR must take steps to ensure its recognition and rewards programs do not leave behind virtual workers or expatriates working in other countries. Take a good look at what behaviors are rewarded and how they are identified and monitored to ensure the concept of justice is served (see the earlier section "Job evaluation and pricing").

Work-life balance

No longer a couple of buzzwords, the concept of work-life balance is a very real state that employees seek to achieve. Simply put, HRCI defines it as "the ability to effectively manage time at work with the time spent on leisure or with family members." It is a form of allocation of the precious time we have in a day. The benefits of these programs include increased job satisfaction, lower stress levels, and employee innovation.

Formal methods to help employees find balance include offering flexible work arrangements, including hybrid schedules that offer work-from-home solutions. Other employers offer unlimited time off plans. Employees seeking to develop expertise or live more creatively may also be able to take advantage of employee sabbaticals. Companies such as Google encourage employees to spend at least 20 percent of their work time on side projects to encourage innovation and give them more control over their work day/projects. This kind of autonomy can improve employee engagement.

USING OTHER RESOURCES TO STUDY

The case of for work-life balance provides us with an excellent example of how to elevate your studying efforts. Remember, Total Rewards is only 12 percent of your exam with only two responsibilities, so engaging in elevated studying must be extremely targeted to be useful. In this spirit, accessing other, credible resources can round out a study plan. The Society for Human Resource Management (SHRM) went through a strategic initiative where they had subject-matter experts build educational resources to offer free of charge. One such case study, written by G. Maxwell is titled "Case Study Series on Work Life Balance in Large Organizations." Find this and study it for the exam at www.shrm.org/Membership/student-resources/Documents/Worklife%20Balance%20Case%20Final_SW.pdf.

IN THIS CHAPTER

» **Recognizing the exam objectives**

» **Identifying strategies to increase engagement**

» **Making a difference in employee job attitudes**

» **Understanding the value of trust**

» **Committing to professional development**

Chapter **16**

Building Relationships: SPHR 05 Employee Relations and Engagement

The final functional area, Employee Relations and Engagement, brings us full circle. You may recall that one of the main keywords identified in Functional Area 01, Leadership and Strategy, was "alignment." In fact, the need for leaders to align HR systems with strategy is the common thread that binds together the framework for the SPHR. The company's strategic plan forms the basis for the workforce plan, which drives the activities in Talent Planning and Acquisition. The workforce plan identifies knowledge or skills gaps that may need to be addressed through the function of Learning and Development. Attracting and rewarding the talent of our teams is the focus of Total Rewards. In Employee Relations and Engagement, these HR functions are brought together to create the environment in which we ask our teams to achieve the strategic outcomes. The concept of strategic human resource management is built on the premise that high-performing HR systems that work well together result in high-performing organizations.

Charting Exam Content

Much has been written about the importance of the company climate and culture. These are two related conditions that create the psychological and physical work environment. They include many of the principles covered in Chapter 2, such as having a culture that welcomes diversity and includes multiple perspectives at all organizational levels. The climate and culture are created and supported by the use (or absence) of human relations and motivation principles. The physical environment is managed through compliance with health, safety, and security standards. In some cases, a union sets the standards through a collective bargaining agreement. Twenty percent of the total exam content is related to HR components that influence employee engagement with 1) the job, 2) each other, and 3) the organization and/or union.

This is reflected in HRCI's content description for this functional area:

"Develop and/or monitor strategies impacting employee satisfaction and performance including diversity and inclusion, safety and security, and labor strategies."

REMEMBER

Several areas of content overlap remain between the PHR and SPHR, particularly in the area of Functional Area 05. These include

>> Human relations

>> Motivation

>> Diversity and inclusion

>> Health, safety, and security

>> Collective bargaining

For this reason, make sure to complete a thorough review of Chapter 2, where these topics are discussed in great detail.

Responsibilities

As with each functional area, the exam responsibilities seek to define what is most important to a senior level HR professional's role:

01 Design and evaluate strategies for employee satisfaction (for example: recognition, career path) and performance management (for example: performance evaluation, corrective action, coaching).

02 Analyze and evaluate strategies to promote diversity and inclusion.

03 Evaluate employee safety and security strategies (for example: OSHA, HIPAA, emergency response plan, building access, data security/privacy).

04 Develop and evaluate labor strategies (for example: collective bargaining, grievance program, concerted activity, staying union free, strategically aligning with labor).

Knowledge

The ability to be successful in the above listed responsibilities requires a level of knowledge in these areas:

51 Strategies to facilitate positive employee relations

52 Methods for assessing employee attitudes, opinions, and satisfaction

53 Performance management strategies

54 Human relations concepts and applications

55 Ethical and professional standards

56 Diversity and inclusion concepts and applications

57 Occupational injury and illness prevention techniques

58 Workplace safety and security risks and strategies

59 Emergency response, business continuity, and disaster recovery strategies

60 Internal investigation, monitoring, and surveillance techniques

61 Data security and privacy

62 The collective bargaining process, strategies, and concepts (for example: contract negotiation, costing, administration)

REMEMBER

Your exam will have 175 questions but only 150 will be scored. Twenty-five are questions that are being validated by exam writers and thus, your answers will not count. You will not know which questions are unscored.

Making the Case for Engagement

"Culture eats strategy for lunch." —Michael Porter, Harvard University Professor and Business Strategy thought leader

There are multiple factors that create the climate and conditions under which we ask our teams to perform. These include the industry we are in, the general business environment, PESTLE conditions (see Chapter 12), and of course, business strategy. The degree to which our team members are performing is described as the level of *engagement*.

Many studies have been done on the impact of engagement. One such study found that only 26 percent of the workforce was engaged, whereas 28 percent were actively disengaged and nearly 50 percent were only partially engaged. That means that HR has the opportunity to increase the engagement levels of more than 70 percent of its team members!

The positive results that come from an actively engaged workforce are compelling. They include increased productivity, quality, customer satisfaction, and morale. It seems that higher engagement levels are directly correlated with improved results, not to mention creating a happier place to work.

REMEMBER

High-performing HR systems = high-performing organizations. A landmark study by Harvard Professor James Heskett and his team found that corporate culture may account for as much as 50 percent of a difference in operating profit and that more than one-half of a company's people would leave their current job for a more positive culture.

Top-down efforts are the most persuasive when seeking to improve employee engagement levels. Similar to compliance efforts, such efforts should begin with a statement in writing. This is most often packaged as a company's mission, vision, and values statement (MVV). This is fine; however, a written statement is only as valuable as how the MVV is practiced in the workplace. HR must model ethical behaviors, and in some cases, coach executives and managers who are not demonstrating behaviors consistent with the MVV.

The absence of the daily, practical application of the MVV and other statements of culture can lead to devastating results such as

» **Counterproductive work behaviors:** These include the fairly benign, such as tardiness, to the more alarming unlawful discrimination or embezzlement.

>> **A toxic work environment:** One in which employees actively work to undermine peers or organizational outcomes, characterized by destructiveness and hostility.

>> **Increased risk for labor law violations:** Examples include harassment or wrongful discipline/discharge.

Consider the example of a major newspaper which was already struggling to exist in a declining industry. In 2020, one of its opinion editors resigned with an open letter, describing the climate and culture as a "civil war inside . . . between the (mostly young) wokes [and] the (mostly 40+) liberals. . .." Her claims prompted criticism from staff members who disagreed with her characterization of the culture, furthering the idea that there was lack of alignment among teams with regard to the company's mission and values. The resigning writer further claimed that she was openly bullied publicly and on the company's in-house communication platform when she wrote views that were counter to the "narrative." Regardless of your thoughts on who or what is right or wrong, think about the effects of a cultural disconnect of this magnitude. A company that claims to strive for the free exchange of ideas yet allows an editor with an opposing opinion to be bullied is being destroyed from the inside out. Fixing issues such as these requires a shift — with significant HR support — to rediscover their values and purpose, and then coach senior leaders on how to lead with them.

TIP

Toxicity online can teach us a lot about the impact of negative behaviors to *any* environment. *League of Legend* online video game maker Riot Games found that if new players encounter toxic behavior in their very first game, they are 320 percent less likely to come back. Read more about their discoveries about toxic environments at `https://rework.withgoogle.com/case-studies/riot-games-assessing-toxicity/`.

PROJECT ARISTOTLE

A major function of applied Industrial-Organizational (I-O) Psychology is that of organizational research. Its bones can be traced back to the 1880s when Frederick Taylor first conducted a time study for his employer, Midvale Steel Co. This eventually led to his theory and system of *scientific management*, which is credited with influencing the way work is structured all around the world. Another well-known field study occurred at Western Electric Company (WEC) where the Hawthorne Effect was discovered. Researchers at WEC were surprised to find that increased productivity is not just a function of the physical environment or wages, but also supervisor attention.

A more recent example of research in the field of work is Google's Project Aristotle, a multi-year study seeking to understand the characteristics of strong teams. Some of their five findings were expected, such as "dependability" and "structure & clarity." "Meaning" and having "impact" were two other discoveries and were in line with Hackman and Oldham's Job Characteristics Model that found task significance helps to structure jobs that satisfy. The fifth finding was perhaps the most surprising and carried the distinction of being the most important predictor of high-performing teams. "Psychological safety" exists when team members feel able to take risks and be vulnerable with their team. Similar to the Hawthorne studies, it wasn't about the physical environment at all, or the ability to assemble team members with ivy league educations or decades of experience. Psychological safety is established when employers pay attention to the cultural and climate factors that affect employee health. This can be done by evaluating how mistakes are handled and whether employees are able to express disagreeing viewpoints in a constructive manner. Are errors and diversity of thought welcome or shut down?

Final note: Google has a dedicated team of organizational researchers that share their findings at the website `https://rework.withgoogle.com`. It is a fascinating lens through which to study our craft and take us beyond the seminal theories of scientific management, the Hawthorne effect and job characteristics model.

While these are certainly things HR seeks to avoid, making the case for engagement doesn't have to be about avoiding negative outcomes. A positive case for engagement begins by taking a look at the job attitudes HR systems can influence and manage.

Job attitudes

Your job as a human resource professional requires knowledge and competencies from many domains, including practices drawn from business management and from the psychologies of "what makes people tick." It is what makes your work so exciting! Three of the most studied concepts are those that make up employee job attitudes, summarized next.

Organizational commitment

This is the area that many HR professionals confuse with the definition of employee engagement. *Organizational commitment* is the job attitude that reflects the degree to which an employee is attached and identifies with a company, and the place to which loyalty is tethered.

The psychological contract — unwritten expectations and commitments — has changed over the last several years. The forces that changed how organizations compete are the same forces that have changed employee expectations. From the employee perspective, the idea that hard work and loyalty will result in a "job for life" simply doesn't exist anymore. Employers have had to adapt as well. They need to get used to the idea that the traditional 9 to 5, on-site job design no longer best serves their competitiveness. Understanding what employees need, designing systems to meet those needs, and acting with character and integrity matter when trying to increase the commitment level of employees.

Job satisfaction

Job satisfaction is an employee attitude that connects the job tasks themselves with the relational factors at work. Are employees allowed to use their strengths and apply their knowledge in a meaningful way? Does the nature of the tasks result in cognitive overload, such as roles with high levels of emotional labor (such as customer service jobs)? Does the work require a leader to take morally questionable actions? How are jobs designed for those employees who do not want large, complex tasks? Answering these questions requires HR practitioners to be flexible and creative, measuring for changes on a planned basis (such as annually or when an incumbent leaves).

As mentioned previously, J. Richard Hackman and Greg R. Oldham's job characteristic model found that high degrees of skill variety, task identity, task significance, autonomy, and feedback correlate with high degrees of job satisfaction. In short, how the work is structured makes a difference. While appropriate for jobs that were easily quantified and contained in a tidy set of tasks, duties, and responsibilities, the new world of work has different design needs that must be considered. For example:

>> Technology has made remote work a viable, productive option.

>> Knowledge is a form of capital that can be used for future success.

>> The labor market is rich with diverse knowledge, experience, and perspectives.

>> The increased use of teams has required more peer-to-peer engagement.

Job crafting is a practical technique that can address these changes to work. Job crafting is the ability for employees to design or modify their own jobs. The concept sprung from the need to adapt foundational theories as the environment (psychological and physical) changed. This practice allows for a continuous evolution of the job as changes or challenges are discovered.

The degree of autonomy when employing job crafting is a bit tricky. Autonomy increases an employee's ownership of the job outcomes. Yet carte blanche permission can significantly change the purpose of a job if not properly corralled. For this reason, HR should be involved to help teams and departments design jobs that accomplish the necessary tasks, duties, and responsibilities and thus, output.

Work engagement

Work engagement represents the degree to which employees have invested their physical, emotional, and mental resources into the tasks of the job itself — they find meaning in the work, not necessarily from the organization. The higher the investment, the more motivated and engaged employees are.

With a focus on jobs, the pandemic of 2020 resulted in many companies shifting to remote work in whole or in part. This demanded that HR begin to understand and evaluate the impact of remote work and virtual teams on workplace culture and relationships.

Engagement analytics company Humanyze took a look at the strength of relationships in a post-COVID remote world. The analytics team reviewed the information flow between relationships with "strong ties" and those with "weak ties." Strong ties existed between employees who interacted on a daily or weekly basis, and weak ties resulted between employees who rarely communicated. These ties are an indication of information flow, and information flow is related to productivity, engagement, trust, and more. When remote work surged, relationships with strong ties surged as well. And those with weak ties got weaker, in some cases by as much as 30 percent.

Creativity was affected as well. Chance encounters or informal collaborations can rarely occur remotely despite the clever use of technology. HR must closely monitor and respond to its own in-house communication trends and respond accordingly. HR must also take care to communicate the needs of all remote work teams and manage the tendency of small teams with strong ties to create sub-cultures of which HR is unaware.

Another issue of a remote world is that of *face-time bias*. This exists when team members who remain on-site are presumed to be more loyal simply because they are physically seen at work. Care must be taken that they are not disproportionately rewarded or promoted.

What drives the job attitudes of employee engagement, organizational commitment, and job satisfaction has generated much interest. Most thought leaders agree that only in some industries is "money" the number-one driver. More often than not, employees report that feedback and recognition are the important factors that drive job attitudes.

Performance feedback and recognition

Regular feedback, a simple thank-you, coaching for success, public acknowledgement, and recognition-with-reward are all effective at helping employees feel connected to the organization and the work itself. Effective feedback and recognition must be sincere and provide evidence so that it does not come across as false or manipulative.

While the benefits of giving positive feedback and recognizing employees seem clear, many supervisors still do not do it. This may be because they focus their engagement efforts on the low performers. The 80/20 rule may be useful here. These supervisors are living out the premise that 20 percent of employees cause 80 percent of challenges and thus, take up a disproportionate amount of feedback time. HR can help shift that leadership mindset by asking supervisors to flip the equation — 20 percent of their employees probably produce 80 percent of the widgets or drive 80 percent of their sales. Giving feedback and recognition to them will only multiply their results.

Other reasons supervisors fail to properly recognize or give feedback to their teams are the perception of lack of time, that some team members don't need it, or a reluctance to recognize employees for "just doing their jobs." HR must take steps to understand the barriers and benefits to bringing a robust feedback system that includes recognition to the workplace.

TIP

Recognition is one area that can yield immediate benefits even for teams that are not quite up to speed. Try an experiment with an underperforming department at your place of work. Involve the manager and make a plan to actively recognize the team for at least 30 days. Reflect on what worked and didn't work.

It's not just the power of positivity that can drive change, but also the impact of bullying and other toxic behaviors. Take a video trip to IKEA and see the results of their social experiment called "Bully a Plant: Say no to bullying" to see firsthand the power of words: www.youtube.com/watch?v=Yx6UgfQreYY.

Giving performance feedback is a critical step in the development of an engaged work force. The operational aspect of a performance management system is for PHR candidates. The strategic consideration for senior leaders is how to structure and manage the system that will drive employee behaviors toward results.

There is a general consensus that the annual review is no longer enough to keep up with the changes we have been discussing throughout this chapter. Performance-feedback systems must be styled to address the changes in workforce demographics, how jobs are designed, and the rise in telework. It may be time to unbind the annual appraisal from the annual pay increase as well. Depending on your organization's compensation philosophy, having these activities delivered together supports a more entitlement-oriented environment. If a business wants to pay for performance, its systems should be oriented toward rewarding results instead of loyalty.

There is also much to be said for the power of the one-on-one meeting between an employee and his manager. Some research has found that regardless of what is covered at a one-on-one, consistently having them has a cumulative effect on engagement, morale, and productivity. A factor of cultural hygiene, a best practice is to ask managers to hold these meetings at least once a month, with twice a month being better — in a pre-remote world. A study by O.C. Tanner found a significant shift when employers and employees were coping with remote work. In this case, weekly one-on-ones increased engagement levels by 58 percent, productivity by 31 percent, and a sense of purpose by 19 percent. HR must take steps to analyze its own workforce and structure feedback systems to be agile.

REMEMBER

An earlier study showed that HR has an opportunity to increase employee engagement in more than 70 percent of the workforce. One-on-ones go a long way toward this goal.

Many healthy teams require peers to offer feedback, so HR can help train teams on how to structure positive as well as constructive opinions that do not erode trust or create a hostile environment.

Gathering feedback is another way that leaders can influence employee job attitudes. Traditional methods include focus groups, surveys, and brainstorming exercises.

How companies respond to dissatisfaction is also important. Employees who are dissatisfied may react in one of two ways: actively or passively. Active behaviors include being highly vocal and, in some cases, acting with their feet by quitting. Passive behaviors include low levels of motivation and eventual burnout, which can lead to — you guessed it — quitting. In other words, how employees respond to dissatisfaction and how HR in turn responds to them makes a difference in retention.

NEEDS THEORY AND FEEDBACK/RECOGNITION

What motivates individual workers is a major consideration when structuring feedback for high-performing individuals. David McClelland's theory on motivation is an appropriate model for illustration of this idea:

- **Achievement:** Individuals who are achievement-oriented crave opportunities to perform and excel, usually independently! Giving them regular feedback is necessary so they can adapt in the moment and increase their chances of success. Recognition is dependent on personality type, although public recognition for a job well done may be appropriate for some achievement-driven individuals.

- **Affiliation:** Those motivated by affiliation would appreciate the opportunity to work closely with others. They value data that reinforces their impact on others, such as feedback or recognition from a customer or team (multi-rater).

- **Power:** Those motivated by individual or institutional power appreciate top-down feedback and feedback from those whom they respect. They want to be rewarded with titles and access to the higher-ups.

As you can see, knowing your people can really help shape feedback efforts that meet their needs.

Employee dissatisfaction is not actually something to be wholly avoided — nor is that even a realistic proposition. Those who are actively frustrated may be harnessed to help solve problems. Those passive workers may not quit if their experience with the employer has for the most part been positive. Both of these reactions require a commitment to building trust in the workplace.

The importance of trust at work

As mentioned in the earlier sidebar, Taylor's model of scientific management created the foundation of the workplace of the time. His focus on inputs, outputs, and the systems that process them was necessary at a time when work was characterized by industrial manufacturing. As workplaces have evolved over the last century, practices have had to evolve as well.

In addition to the hands-on industries such as manufacturing and healthcare, the 21st-century workplace is characterized by *knowledge workers*. This means that we must treat employee knowledge as a form of capital, both for current use and to position our teams for future opportunities. Additionally, the rise of uncertainty (political, economic, and global) as well as social unrest and cancel culture has had a significant effect on our teams' willingness to take risks (reference psychological safety at Google in the section "Project Aristotle"). Employees who do not trust their managers, their co-workers, or the organization as a whole are more reluctant to apply their knowledge, skills, and abilities toward creating an innovative workplace that can compete. A white paper published by Great Place to Work found that trust led to greater outcomes such as employee retention, customer satisfaction, organizational agility, and patient satisfaction.

Building trust requires that organizations (translation: HR) be intentional. Developing trust is a top-down activity, meaning it begins with the CEO modeling behaviors and executive teams making decisions that are in accordance with the company's mission, vision, and values. HR professionals can help measure the trust levels of their teams by conducting employee surveys and exit interviews, while at the same time ensuring they are hiring for culture factors as well as job factors. This is often accomplished by making a business case for trust as an intervention and maintenance strategy. HR is also responsible for modeling ethical behaviors and coaching leaders — even in the C-Suite.

Separations as an experience point

As seen throughout the entire SPHR exam content, so much of what senior leaders do is to structure the experience of the employee at all points of the life cycle. This, of course, is in balance with the strategic aims of the business and the contractual rights built by a collective bargaining agreement. And just as the experience begins before an individual becomes an employee, so also may it continue for those who remain after a downsizing event.

Handling layoffs and furloughs has unfortunately been a mainstay responsibility of HR departments across the world. Not only is the impact of companywide downsizing felt by those who separate, but the morale and turnover intentions of the remaining employees also change, resulting in increased disengagement, fears about job security, and decreased overall productivity and morale. Employees also watch how the company treats those who lose their jobs, and make assumptions about how they will be treated if they are separated. It is important that HR double the engagement efforts discussed previously to help the employees who stay and embed its values in the separation process for all team members.

It stands to reason that HR must develop compassionate yet functional best practices for those at the end of the employee life cycle. Ways to do this include being honest and transparent about the reasons for the downsizing. It is also helpful to team up with local job placement resources to help exiting employees find work. Offering severance packages can not only help offset the risk of terminations but can also offset the employee's loss of income until any available state benefits are received.

Human resource leadership development

So many theories of leadership, so little time. The truth is that there are master classes that debate ideas about leaders: Are they born or made? Behavioral or trait based? Static or state-like? Does gender matter in leadership outcomes? What about transactional versus transformational leadership styles? Regardless of the degree or qualities of leadership at your place of work, HR must engage in a form of professional self-care that is too often lost at the expense of others' needs. This section is dedicated to a few steps HR leaders can take to develop their own leadership competencies so they may be effective models for excellence.

Defining personal values

Perhaps my favorite author on leadership is Patrick Lencioni, who said, "If everything is important, then nothing is." Taking steps to identify what is most important to you can help you with difficult decisions. In some cases, values have already been established, such as with the code of ethics from HRCI and SHRM, or a company's code of conduct, or the obligations of fiduciaries. Assume that those values are a given. Think about what is most important to you as a leader and develop a personal leadership vision that will guide your behaviors. My leadership vision is to "be the leader I needed when I was younger." This drives many of my day-to-day behaviors and is the "why" behind many of my professional choices.

Modeling the way

Another on my favorites list is Simon Sinek, author of *Leaders Eat Last* (published by Portfolio). Simon's philosophy, born out of a conversation with a respected military officer, notes that the best leaders communicate to their teams that they care about them through their behaviors, not just words. Modeling leadership this way encourages others to consider the humanity of the people on their teams and shows others how to do so as well.

Asking for feedback

It's not enough to assume that your teams will tell you how you're doing, you must ask for meaningful feedback from all your stakeholders and then use the information to adapt.

Empowering others

It's very tempting to get turfy, especially when you're overworked in a VUCA environment (see Chapter 12). By empowering others to act — such as your HR teams and company managers — you create the bench depth necessary to grow the business in good times and keep the lights on when things get tough. Activate your team's talent by deputizing trusted individuals to act through training, feedback, recognition, and important responsibilities.

You have taken a major step toward achieving professional excellence by seeking your SPHR certification. Keep the commitment to yourself and stay the course even when the process seems daunting. The knowledge gained along the way as well as the example you are setting for the future leaders of HR is both timeless and priceless!

REMEMBER

Take the time to incorporate the information found on recognizing shared content in Chapter 2. This is where you can find additional content related to leading the charge in this important area of the SPHR exam.

5

Employing Your Knowledge: Practice Exams

Use the practice-makes-perfect principle by immersing yourself in practice tests with exam-style questions weighted as you'll see them on test day.

Interpret answers when you run up against *best* versus *right* options and discover how to set aside frustration and break down the question and answer options effectively.

Get to know exam answer logic and figure out why an answer is correct to enhance learning and retention for future use.

Feel the mind numbness of answering 175 questions in one sitting, so you can prepare you mind and body for exam-day conditions.

Chapter 17

Facing the Challenge: PHR Practice Exam

Any study material worth your dollars must include practice exams. Taking a test is, after all, the whole point of all of your efforts!

If you're a PHR candidate, remember that your exam is written from the perspective of operational activities. Get ready to see 175 exam-quality items about how the work of business and human resources gets done. Set aside three hours for the test included here, and limit all potential distractions such as your phone or the internet. Chapter 2 gives you a lot more advice on how to best use the prep resource of practice exams.

Use the bubble sheet that I include here to fill in the correct answers. You can mark the questions that you want to review after you complete the test. Don't forget, online you can find another PHR exam to supplement your efforts. (See the Introduction for more information.) The more exams you take, the better prepared you will be. Be mindful that the following exam is just one of the many you should prepare to take before the big day. Good luck!

Answer Sheet for PHR Practice Exam

1. _____	36. _____	71. Ⓐ Ⓑ Ⓒ Ⓓ	106. Ⓐ Ⓑ Ⓒ Ⓓ	141. Ⓐ Ⓑ Ⓒ Ⓓ
2. Ⓐ Ⓑ Ⓒ Ⓓ	37. Ⓐ Ⓑ Ⓒ Ⓓ	72. Ⓐ Ⓑ Ⓒ Ⓓ	107. Ⓐ Ⓑ Ⓒ Ⓓ	142. Ⓐ Ⓑ Ⓒ Ⓓ
3. Ⓐ Ⓑ Ⓒ Ⓓ	38. Ⓐ Ⓑ Ⓒ Ⓓ	73. Ⓐ Ⓑ Ⓒ Ⓓ	108. Ⓐ Ⓑ Ⓒ Ⓓ	143. Ⓐ Ⓑ Ⓒ Ⓓ
4. Ⓐ Ⓑ Ⓒ Ⓓ	39. Ⓐ Ⓑ Ⓒ Ⓓ	74. Ⓐ Ⓑ Ⓒ Ⓓ	109. Ⓐ Ⓑ Ⓒ Ⓓ	144. Ⓐ Ⓑ Ⓒ Ⓓ
5. Ⓐ Ⓑ Ⓒ Ⓓ	40. Ⓐ Ⓑ Ⓒ Ⓓ	75. Ⓐ Ⓑ Ⓒ Ⓓ	110. Ⓐ Ⓑ Ⓒ Ⓓ	145. Ⓐ Ⓑ Ⓒ Ⓓ
6. _____	41. Ⓐ Ⓑ Ⓒ Ⓓ	76. Ⓐ Ⓑ Ⓒ Ⓓ	111. Ⓐ Ⓑ Ⓒ Ⓓ	146. Ⓐ Ⓑ Ⓒ Ⓓ
7. Ⓐ Ⓑ Ⓒ Ⓓ	42. Ⓐ Ⓑ Ⓒ Ⓓ	77. Ⓐ Ⓑ Ⓒ Ⓓ	112. Ⓐ Ⓑ Ⓒ Ⓓ	147. Ⓐ Ⓑ Ⓒ Ⓓ
8. Ⓐ Ⓑ Ⓒ Ⓓ	43. Ⓐ Ⓑ Ⓒ Ⓓ	78. Ⓐ Ⓑ Ⓒ Ⓓ	113. Ⓐ Ⓑ Ⓒ Ⓓ	148. Ⓐ Ⓑ Ⓒ Ⓓ
9. Ⓐ Ⓑ Ⓒ Ⓓ	44. Ⓐ Ⓑ Ⓒ Ⓓ	79. Ⓐ Ⓑ Ⓒ Ⓓ	114. Ⓐ Ⓑ Ⓒ Ⓓ	149. Ⓐ Ⓑ Ⓒ Ⓓ
10. Ⓐ Ⓑ Ⓒ Ⓓ	45. Ⓐ Ⓑ Ⓒ Ⓓ	80. Ⓐ Ⓑ Ⓒ Ⓓ	115. Ⓐ Ⓑ Ⓒ Ⓓ	150. Ⓐ Ⓑ Ⓒ Ⓓ
11. Ⓐ Ⓑ Ⓒ Ⓓ	46. Ⓐ Ⓑ Ⓒ Ⓓ	81. Ⓐ Ⓑ Ⓒ Ⓓ	116. Ⓐ Ⓑ Ⓒ Ⓓ	151. Ⓐ Ⓑ Ⓒ Ⓓ
12. Ⓐ Ⓑ Ⓒ Ⓓ	47. Ⓐ Ⓑ Ⓒ Ⓓ	82. Ⓐ Ⓑ Ⓒ Ⓓ	117. Ⓐ Ⓑ Ⓒ Ⓓ	152. Ⓐ Ⓑ Ⓒ Ⓓ
13. Ⓐ Ⓑ Ⓒ Ⓓ	48. Ⓐ Ⓑ Ⓒ Ⓓ	83. Ⓐ Ⓑ Ⓒ Ⓓ	118. Ⓐ Ⓑ Ⓒ Ⓓ	153. Ⓐ Ⓑ Ⓒ Ⓓ
14. Ⓐ Ⓑ Ⓒ Ⓓ	49. Ⓐ Ⓑ Ⓒ Ⓓ	84. Ⓐ Ⓑ Ⓒ Ⓓ	119. Ⓐ Ⓑ Ⓒ Ⓓ	154. Ⓐ Ⓑ Ⓒ Ⓓ
15. Ⓐ Ⓑ Ⓒ Ⓓ	50. Ⓐ Ⓑ Ⓒ Ⓓ	85. Ⓐ Ⓑ Ⓒ Ⓓ	120. Ⓐ Ⓑ Ⓒ Ⓓ	155. Ⓐ Ⓑ Ⓒ Ⓓ
16. Ⓐ Ⓑ Ⓒ Ⓓ	51. Ⓐ Ⓑ Ⓒ Ⓓ	86. Ⓐ Ⓑ Ⓒ Ⓓ	121. Ⓐ Ⓑ Ⓒ Ⓓ	156. Ⓐ Ⓑ Ⓒ Ⓓ
17. Ⓐ Ⓑ Ⓒ Ⓓ	52. Ⓐ Ⓑ Ⓒ Ⓓ	87. Ⓐ Ⓑ Ⓒ Ⓓ	122. Ⓐ Ⓑ Ⓒ Ⓓ	157. Ⓐ Ⓑ Ⓒ Ⓓ
18. Ⓐ Ⓑ Ⓒ Ⓓ	53. Ⓐ Ⓑ Ⓒ Ⓓ	88. Ⓐ Ⓑ Ⓒ Ⓓ	123. Ⓐ Ⓑ Ⓒ Ⓓ	158. Ⓐ Ⓑ Ⓒ Ⓓ
19. Ⓐ Ⓑ Ⓒ Ⓓ	54. Ⓐ Ⓑ Ⓒ Ⓓ	89. Ⓐ Ⓑ Ⓒ Ⓓ	124. Ⓐ Ⓑ Ⓒ Ⓓ	159. Ⓐ Ⓑ Ⓒ Ⓓ
20. Ⓐ Ⓑ Ⓒ Ⓓ	55. Ⓐ Ⓑ Ⓒ Ⓓ	90. Ⓐ Ⓑ Ⓒ Ⓓ	125. Ⓐ Ⓑ Ⓒ Ⓓ	160. Ⓐ Ⓑ Ⓒ Ⓓ
21. Ⓐ Ⓑ Ⓒ Ⓓ	56. Ⓐ Ⓑ Ⓒ Ⓓ	91. Ⓐ Ⓑ Ⓒ Ⓓ	126. Ⓐ Ⓑ Ⓒ Ⓓ	161. Ⓐ Ⓑ Ⓒ Ⓓ
22. Ⓐ Ⓑ Ⓒ Ⓓ	57. Ⓐ Ⓑ Ⓒ Ⓓ	92. Ⓐ Ⓑ Ⓒ Ⓓ	127. Ⓐ Ⓑ Ⓒ Ⓓ	162. Ⓐ Ⓑ Ⓒ Ⓓ
23. Ⓐ Ⓑ Ⓒ Ⓓ	58. Ⓐ Ⓑ Ⓒ Ⓓ	93. Ⓐ Ⓑ Ⓒ Ⓓ	128. Ⓐ Ⓑ Ⓒ Ⓓ	163. Ⓐ Ⓑ Ⓒ Ⓓ
24. Ⓐ Ⓑ Ⓒ Ⓓ	59. Ⓐ Ⓑ Ⓒ Ⓓ	94. Ⓐ Ⓑ Ⓒ Ⓓ	129. Ⓐ Ⓑ Ⓒ Ⓓ	164. Ⓐ Ⓑ Ⓒ Ⓓ
25. Ⓐ Ⓑ Ⓒ Ⓓ	60. Ⓐ Ⓑ Ⓒ Ⓓ	95. Ⓐ Ⓑ Ⓒ Ⓓ	130. Ⓐ Ⓑ Ⓒ Ⓓ	165. Ⓐ Ⓑ Ⓒ Ⓓ
26. Ⓐ Ⓑ Ⓒ Ⓓ	61. Ⓐ Ⓑ Ⓒ Ⓓ	96. Ⓐ Ⓑ Ⓒ Ⓓ	131. Ⓐ Ⓑ Ⓒ Ⓓ	166. Ⓐ Ⓑ Ⓒ Ⓓ
27. Ⓐ Ⓑ Ⓒ Ⓓ	62. Ⓐ Ⓑ Ⓒ Ⓓ	97. Ⓐ Ⓑ Ⓒ Ⓓ	132. Ⓐ Ⓑ Ⓒ Ⓓ	167. Ⓐ Ⓑ Ⓒ Ⓓ
28. Ⓐ Ⓑ Ⓒ Ⓓ	63. Ⓐ Ⓑ Ⓒ Ⓓ	98. Ⓐ Ⓑ Ⓒ Ⓓ	133. Ⓐ Ⓑ Ⓒ Ⓓ	168. Ⓐ Ⓑ Ⓒ Ⓓ
29. Ⓐ Ⓑ Ⓒ Ⓓ	64. Ⓐ Ⓑ Ⓒ Ⓓ	99. Ⓐ Ⓑ Ⓒ Ⓓ	134. Ⓐ Ⓑ Ⓒ Ⓓ	169. Ⓐ Ⓑ Ⓒ Ⓓ
30. Ⓐ Ⓑ Ⓒ Ⓓ	65. Ⓐ Ⓑ Ⓒ Ⓓ	100. Ⓐ Ⓑ Ⓒ Ⓓ	135. Ⓐ Ⓑ Ⓒ Ⓓ	170. Ⓐ Ⓑ Ⓒ Ⓓ
31. Ⓐ Ⓑ Ⓒ Ⓓ	66. Ⓐ Ⓑ Ⓒ Ⓓ	101. Ⓐ Ⓑ Ⓒ Ⓓ	136. Ⓐ Ⓑ Ⓒ Ⓓ	171. Ⓐ Ⓑ Ⓒ Ⓓ
32. Ⓐ Ⓑ Ⓒ Ⓓ	67. Ⓐ Ⓑ Ⓒ Ⓓ	102. Ⓐ Ⓑ Ⓒ Ⓓ	137. Ⓐ Ⓑ Ⓒ Ⓓ	172. Ⓐ Ⓑ Ⓒ Ⓓ
33. Ⓐ Ⓑ Ⓒ Ⓓ	68. Ⓐ Ⓑ Ⓒ Ⓓ	103. Ⓐ Ⓑ Ⓒ Ⓓ	138. Ⓐ Ⓑ Ⓒ Ⓓ	173. Ⓐ Ⓑ Ⓒ Ⓓ
34. Ⓐ Ⓑ Ⓒ Ⓓ	69. Ⓐ Ⓑ Ⓒ Ⓓ	104. Ⓐ Ⓑ Ⓒ Ⓓ	139. Ⓐ Ⓑ Ⓒ Ⓓ	174. Ⓐ Ⓑ Ⓒ Ⓓ
35. Ⓐ Ⓑ Ⓒ Ⓓ	70. Ⓐ Ⓑ Ⓒ Ⓓ	105. _____	140. Ⓐ Ⓑ Ⓒ Ⓓ	175. Ⓐ Ⓑ Ⓒ Ⓓ

1. Match the staffing activity in Column A to its proper timing in Column B.

Column A	Column B
(A) Completing Form I-9	(1) Pre-offer
(B) Candidate interview	(2) Post-offer, pre-hire
(C) Completing Form W-4	(3) Post-hire

2. Which of the following would be an unfair labor practice?

    (A) Moving the work to a different plant with no union

    (B) Asking employees if they will vote for or against the union

    (C) Lecturing to employees how historical corruption caused problems with unions

    (D) Threatening to fire supervisors if they show support for the union

3. Which of the following is NOT an affirmative defense for a company being sued for quid pro quo sexual harassment?

    (A) Demonstrating that the employer exercised reasonable care to prevent unlawful behavior

    (B) Demonstrating that the employer promptly corrected unlawful behavior

    (C) Demonstrating that the employee failed to take advantage of any preventive or corrective opportunities provided by the employer

    (D) Demonstrating that the accused employee wasn't a supervisor

4. Jim accepts a contingent offer of employment from a new company and consequently gives notice. The employer eventually rescinds the offer after his drug screen came back positive for marijuana. Which of the common law doctrines did this employer violate?

    (A) Promissory estoppel

    (B) Duty of good faith and fair dealing

    (C) Fraudulent misrepresentation

    (D) None

5. A marketing function that reflects the concept of putting the right product, in the right place, for the right promotion at the right _____.

    (A) price

    (B) power

    (C) practice

    (D) percentage

6. Mary Jones is a full-time employee who has worked for a nationwide car manufacturer for more than 15 years. She needs time off of work to care for her child, who has recently been diagnosed with asthma. Match the activities in Column A with the order in which they should be taken in Column B.

Column A	Column B
(A) Notify Mary's supervisor that she will be off work.	Step 1
(B) Verify her eligibility for FMLA.	Step 2
(C) Request medical certification.	Step 3

7. Lori is a recruiter for a large marketing firm based out of New York City with multiple branches across the United States. Working out of the corporate offices is considered a career advantage, and she is determined to find a quality candidate. Which of the following recruiting activities should she do first?

   (A) Create an internal job posting.

   (B) Call a staffing agency with locations in multiple U.S. locations.

   (C) Research online recruiting resources.

   (D) Get the job posted on the company's website.

8. Which of the following decisions by an HR professional is the most ethical?

   (A) Allowing an employee to work a second job based on need, even though policy prohibits moonlighting

   (B) Staying with an occupational clinic because it sends her tickets to sporting events

   (C) Attending professional development meetings with subordinates

   (D) Giving preferred treatment to employees who are nice to her

9. The process of becoming part of an organizational team is called what?

   (A) Acculturation

   (B) Cultural integration

   (C) Onboarding

   (D) Affiliation

10. Jannah is a supervisor at ABC Speech Pathology with 14 direct reports. These employees are known as part of her what?

    (A) Management responsibility

    (B) Span of control

    (C) Management scope

    (D) Organizational structure

11. Data recall, confidential customer information, and the protection of digital assets must be reviewed according to which element of a PEST analysis?

    (A) Political

    (B) Economic

    (C) Social

    (D) Technological

12. Videoing an employee telling about his employment experience and then posting the video on the company recruitment website is an example of which of the following?

(A) Recruiting

(B) Documentation

(C) Communicating the employer brand

(D) Communicating the company culture

13. An employment arrangement in which an employee may quit at any time and the employer may terminate at any time is defined by which common law doctrine?

(A) Employment at-will

(B) Respondeat superior

(C) Implied contract

(D) Employment relationship

14. Which of these tools would best capture the reasons that employees leave an organization?

(A) Employee satisfaction surveys

(B) Exit interviews

(C) Turnover reports

(D) Labor market analysis

15. A group composed of members of the same race or the same heritage would be attributed as being what?

(A) Homogeneous

(B) Heterogeneous

(C) Patriot

(D) Fellows

16. An employee refused to go out on a date with her supervisor and was fired by him as a result. This is known as what type of harassment?

(A) Unlawful

(B) Discriminatory

(C) Quid pro quo

(D) Hostile

17. Which of the following visas may be extended to religious workers?

(A) R-1

(B) O-1

(C) L-1A

(D) P-1

18. A mass layoff of more than 500 employees would trigger which of the following acts protecting the affected individuals?

(A) The Consolidated Omnibus Budget Reconciliation Act

(B) The Health Insurance Portability and Accountability Act

(C) The Workforce Adjustment and Retraining Notification Act

(D) All of the above

19. Which of the following has had the most growth in online media recruiting?

    (A) Video branding

    (B) Mobile apps

    (C) Employee testimonials

    (D) Personal networks

20. Which of the following most accurately describes at-will employment?

    (A) The employer may terminate an employee at any time, for any reason.

    (B) The employee may quit without giving notice.

    (C) The employee serves at the will of the employer.

    (D) Both the employer and the employee can separate at any time without cause.

21. Conducting a pre-employment drug screen is most useful to prevent what?

    (A) Negligent hiring

    (B) Workplace violence

    (C) Injuries

    (D) All of the above

22. Why should a private-sector employer hire interns?

    (A) It's a great way to get free work done.

    (B) It's useful to prequalify potential candidates.

    (C) It invests in the communities in which the employer does business.

    (D) It's the right thing to do.

23. Which landmark case found that a seemingly neutral pre-employment test could result in unlawful discrimination if it has an adverse impact against a protected class group?

    (A) Griggs vs. Duke Power

    (B) The UGESPs

    (C) McDonnell Douglas vs. Green

    (D) Albermarle Paper vs. Moody

24. If an employee is found to be the victim of unlawful discrimination, he or she may be entitled to back pay under which landmark court decision?

    (A) Griggs vs. Duke Power

    (B) The UGESPs

    (C) McDonnell Douglas vs. Green

    (D) Albemarle Paper vs. Moody

25. Conducting employee exit interviews by a third party is most useful for which of the following?

    (A) Controlling the high emotions associated with separations

    (B) Obtaining honest feedback

    (C) Protecting the employer from a wrongful termination claim

    (D) Utilizing external resources to keep HR focused on operations

26. The Age Discrimination in Employment Act protects individuals over the age of what?

    (A) 40

    (B) 50

    (C) 63

    (D) All of the above

27. Which of the following activities are often outsourced to an external agency?

    (A) Payroll

    (B) Hiring

    (C) COBRA administration

    (D) All of the above

28. Consistent branding and the use of videos are combined for successful what?

    (A) Social media recruiting

    (B) Employee retention

    (C) Job satisfaction

    (D) Communicating benefits

29. Which of the following is an alternative staffing method?

    (A) Direct hires

    (B) Online recruiting

    (C) Job sharing

    (D) Temporary workers

30. How are ideas shared in a Socratic seminar?

    (A) Through adherence to an agenda

    (B) By the use of questions and answers

    (C) Through classroom lecture

    (D) As a fishbowl

31. If the passive method of teaching focuses on the instructor, the _____ method focuses on the learner.

    (A) active

    (B) engaged

    (C) participative

    (D) managed

32. Which of the following is an example of on-the-job training?

    (A) Vestibule

    (B) Lecture

    (C) Simulation

    (D) Job rotation

33. Banquet-style seating is most effective for which of the following training formats?

(A) Films

(B) Lectures

(C) Manuals

(D) Group discussions

34. An employee self-assessment is useful when _____.

(A) there are problems with teamwork

(B) the employee is new

(C) the job criteria aren't well established

(D) an employer wants to compare employees to each other

35. The presence of more than 50 percent of women in the workforce population may be an indication of what?

(A) The need for flexible work arrangements

(B) The need for employment practice liability insurance (EPLI)

(C) The likelihood of a sexual harassment lawsuit

(D) The need for a dating policy

36. Match the activity in Column A with its corresponding stage of the ADDIE model in Column B.

Column A	Column B
(A) Create standard operating procedures	(1) Evaluate
(B) Conduct a training needs assessment	(2) Analyze
(C) Design a training reaction survey	(3) Develop

37. The marketing department has been asked to create visual representations of SOPs to be used during the onboarding process of new hires. This is an example of which stage of the ADDIE model of instructional design?

(A) Analyze

(B) Design

(C) Develop

(D) Implement

38. Visual learners are best served through which style of training?

(A) Lecture

(B) Hands-on work

(C) On the job

(D) Handouts

39. A customer service representative isn't keeping up with the required call volume. For which of the following causes would training NOT be a solution?

(A) He is unfamiliar with the products.

(B) His headset is faulty.

(C) He has only been on the job for 30 days.

(D) The company installed a new ERP system.

40. When a job is designed to allow employees to apply multiple skill sets on the job, this job is likely high in what?

(A) Task identity

(B) Functional loading

(C) Skill variety

(D) Task significance

41. Statements that describe the measurable outcomes of training are known as what?

(A) Goals

(B) Interventions

(C) Targets

(D) Objectives

42. Maintaining the confidentiality of customer information is a function of what holistic risk management system?

(A) Enterprise risk management

(B) A response to a technological fail

(C) The establishment of a firewall

(D) The protection of human assets

43. It was discovered that an employee was able to siphon off cash from sales because she was responsible for both collecting the money and creating deposits. This failure is due to a lack of what?

(A) Training

(B) Documentation

(C) Standard operating procedures

(D) Internal controls

44. An emergency response plan is a required element of what safety compliance effort?

(A) A fire prevention plan

(B) The protection of information assets

(C) The establishment of IIPPs

(D) The identification of financial risks

45. Which of the following is the most important step in the implementation of an injury and illness prevention program?

(A) Hazard abatement procedures

(B) Management leadership and commitment

(C) Worker participation

(D) Program evaluation

46. Which of the following statements is true regarding state-run OSH programs?

(A) State programs aren't allowed under OSH.

(B) State programs are able to operate independently of the federal standards.

(C) State programs must exceed federal program standards.

(D) State programs must meet federal program standards.

47. An employee called OSHA to report a safety hazard that the employer had failed to address, resulting in a worksite inspection and fines. The employer found out and quietly demoted the worker. This is an example of which unlawful employment action?

   (A) Discrimination

   (B) Harassment

   (C) Wrongful discipline

   (D) Retaliation

48. Which statement regarding the FMLA is false?

   (A) FMLA leave focuses on wage replacement and job protection.

   (B) FMLA provides 12 work weeks of leave for eligible workers.

   (C) The certification requirements for leave are the same for all requests, including military.

   (D) An eligible employee is one who has worked 1,250 hours in the preceding 12-month period.

49. Employers are required to provide reasonable break time to nursing mothers for up to how many years after the child's birth?

   (A) None

   (B) One

   (C) Two

   (D) Three

50. Which of the following acts amended the FLSA to further define compensable time?

   (A) Davis-Bacon

   (B) McNamara-O'Hara

   (C) Portal-to-Portal

   (D) Equal Pay

51. _____ is/are the amount of money an employee will make on an hourly or salaried basis.

   (A) Minimum wage

   (B) Total compensation

   (C) Base pay

   (D) Incentives

52. Merit pay increases are what type of compensation?

   (A) Base

   (B) Total

   (C) Performance

   (D) Entitlement

53. Shift premiums are a type of what?

   (A) Pay differential

   (B) Hazard pay

   (C) Benefit

   (D) Entitlement

54. The CCPA _____ the amount of wages that can be garnished against an employee.

    (A) prohibits

    (B) doesn't address

    (C) limits

    (D) defines

55. If an employer is issuing evidence of past health insurance to an exiting employee, it is most likely complying with which law?

    (A) COBRA

    (B) Title VII

    (C) HIPAA

    (D) PPACA

56. If an employee is motivated by a high-level desire to achieve, which pay strategy is most likely to work?

    (A) Annual increases

    (B) Robust benefits

    (C) Variable pay

    (D) Group incentives

57. What pay practice is most nearly the opposite of base pay?

    (A) Piecework

    (B) Holiday pay

    (C) Benefits

    (D) Perquisites

58. In which of the following examples is there an experience rating to determine cost?

    (A) Unemployment claims

    (B) Workers' compensation

    (C) Company car insurance

    (D) All of the above

59. A pension plan that guarantees a set amount of benefits at the time of retirement is what kind of plan?

    (A) Cash balance

    (B) Contributory plan

    (C) Defined benefit

    (D) Defined contribution

60. Generally, a retirement plan may require that an employee be at least _____ years of age and have at least _____ year(s) of service before participating in a plan.

    (A) 18, one

    (B) 21, one

    (C) 18, two

    (D) 21, two

61. In selecting a payroll vendor, which of the following activities should you complete first?

    (A) Gain executive approval.

    (B) Gather an RFP.

    (C) Conduct a needs assessment.

    (D) Request a trial.

62. If an employer's social media policy violates the right of an employee to engage in coordinated discussion about wages or working conditions, what kind of a charge may be filed?

    (A) Discrimination

    (B) Unfair Labor Practice

    (C) Harassment

    (D) Whistleblower

63. What do union organizers do?

    (A) They assist union members in negotiating the CBA.

    (B) They serve as employer ambassadors to the union.

    (C) They're employees sponsored by a union who helps workers organize.

    (D) They serve as employee ambassadors to the union.

64. If an applicant intentionally applies for a job at a non-union shop specifically to begin an organizing drive, he is said to be engaged in what practice?

    (A) Salting

    (B) Featherbedding

    (C) Double breasting

    (D) Alter ego

65. The decline in union membership has been attributed to what?

    (A) Rights granted by varying national and state standards

    (B) Improved working conditions

    (C) Modernization of tools and equipment

    (D) All of the above

66. Brown bag lunches, word of mouth, and company intranet are all forms of what?

    (A) Training

    (B) Communicating with employees

    (C) Providing informal feedback

    (D) Reporting company information

67. An employee may quit at any time and for any reason is another way to describe which of the following?

    (A) Doctrine of free will

    (B) Doctrine of Lord Acton

    (C) Statutory exceptions

    (D) At-will employment

68. In which type of sexual harassment may the employer not establish an affirmative defense?

    (A) Quid pro quo with a tangible injury

    (B) Hostile environment

    (C) Vicarious liability

    (D) Workplace violence

69. A tangible employment action may be demonstrated by which of the following?

    (A) Documented in employment records

    (B) Evidence of retaliation

    (C) An official act of the company, such as firing or transfer

    (D) All of the above

70. Which court case decided that same-sex harassment is actionable under (anti-harassment) laws?

    (A) Medina Rene vs. MGM Grand Hotel

    (B) Burlington Industries vs. Ellerth

    (C) Oncale vs. Sundowner Offshore Services

    (D) Faragher vs. City of Boca Raton

71. Which agency is responsible for enforcing the standards related to unfair labor practices?

    (A) EEOC

    (B) NLRA

    (C) NLRB

    (D) DOL

72. Which act first defined a list of unfair labor practices by employers?

    (A) Labor-Management Relations Act (Taft-Hartley Act)

    (B) National Labor Relations Act (Wagner Act)

    (C) Labor-Management Reporting and Disclosure Act (Landrum-Griffith Act)

    (D) Railway Labor Act

73. If a union fails to properly hold a local leadership election every three years, which act is the union violating?

    (A) Labor-Management Relations Act (Taft-Hartley Act)

    (B) National Labor Relations Act (Wagner Act)

    (C) Labor-Management Reporting and Disclosure Act (Landrum Griffin Act)

    (D) Railway Labor Act

74. When President Ronald Reagan ordered striking air traffic controllers back to work, he was acting with authority granted by which of the following acts?

    (A) Labor-Management Relations Act (Taft-Hartley Act)

    (B) National Labor Relations Act (Wagner Act)

    (C) Labor-Management Reporting and Disclosure Act (Landrum-Griffith Act)

    (D) Railway Labor Act

75. Striking workers who seek higher wages or shorter working hours are engaged in what type of lawful strike?

   (A) Protest

   (B) Picketing

   (C) Unfair labor practices

   (D) Economic

76. Which of the following statements is true regarding unfair labor practice strikers?

   (A) They may be permanently replaced while on strike.

   (B) They are entitled to their jobs back after the strike has ended.

   (C) The striking workers are engaged in a ULP.

   (D) They cannot have their jobs back if it discharges another worker.

77. HazMat United has a policy that requires employees to clock out at the end of their shift prior to changing out of their hazardous material suits back into civilian clothing. Which of the following labor laws is the company violating?

   (A) Occupational Safety and Health Act

   (B) Service Contract Act

   (C) The Portal-to-Portal Act

   (D) None. This employer practice is legal.

78. Which element of a Human Capital Management Plan involves developing the necessary workforce and practices to achieve an organization's mission, vision, and values?

   (A) Strategic direction

   (B) Goal-setting

   (C) Project implementation

   (D) Sustainability

79. Electromation, Inc. was a small, non-union company with 200 employees experiencing financial difficulties. It decided to form committees in response to a change to employee bonuses and other employee concerns regarding policies, favoritism, and communication. Although these committees consisted of both employees and management, management had the final say on who was seated. Which of the following is one of the reasons the National Labor Relations Board ruled that this was an unlawful, company-dominated union?

   (A) Managers were on the committee.

   (B) The committees included discussions about conditions of employment.

   (C) Compensation committees without union representation are unlawful.

   (D) It wasn't recognized as a formal union.

80. Employees at Natural Bee Organics have to work on Saturdays because they are behind in production. The supervisor promises that if they catch up, they can go back to their regular schedules. This is an example of what type of operant conditioning?

   (A) Punishment

   (B) Extinction

   (C) Positive reinforcement

   (D) Negative reinforcement

81. Place the following in order of importance as they relate to managing risk for an employer:

    A. Safety hazards

    B. Disaster preparedness planning

    C. Customer confidentiality procedures

    D. Workplace violence policy

    (A) C, A, D, B

    (B) D, A, C, B

    (C) B, C, D, A

    (D) A, C, B, D

82. In which of the following examples does a positive correlation exist?

    (A) The longer employees are with a company, the fewer attendance problems they have.

    (B) Workplace harassment increases the likelihood of employee depression.

    (C) In the absence of random drug screening, employee drug use increases.

    (D) Positive coaching efforts result in decreased turnover.

83. Which of the following types of graphs best identifies the status of employees when succession planning?

    (A) Pareto chart

    (B) Forced distribution

    (C) Ranking

    (D) Fishbone diagram

84. Decentralized decision-making is more likely to occur in which of the following organizational structures?

    (A) Functional

    (B) Organizational

    (C) Product-based

    (D) Hierarchical

85. A retail distributor was suffering from a process that took the company too long to hire, particularly during the seasonal peaks associated with holidays. Which of the following should you recommend?

    (A) Continuous recruitment of salespeople

    (B) A human capital management plan

    (C) Promotions from within

    (D) The use of staffing agencies

86. Andragogy is best represented by which of the following statements?

    (A) The way adults learn

    (B) The way children learn

    (C) The way our brains unlearn information

    (D) A condition that exists in a learning organization

87. Job expansion and divestitures are examples of what type of organizational activity?

    (A) Restructuring

    (B) Downsizing

    (C) Mergers

    (D) Acquisition

88. What should occur prior to writing an organization's mission, vision, and values (MVV) statements?

    (A) Establish the company's budget.

    (B) Gain management buy-in to the process.

    (C) Conduct an environmental scan.

    (D) Evaluate the corporate strategy.

89. Engagement is to the employee life cycle what the employee's _____ is to the company.

    (A) job

    (B) responsibility

    (C) impact

    (D) performance

90. James, an employee at your company, was recently told that he must continue to work the Saturday/Sunday shift even though his co-worker Sally will be working a preferred shift as an accommodation of her disability. James sues for reverse discrimination. What is the most likely outcome of his claim?

    (A) James wins his suit because he is the victim of reverse discrimination under the ADA.

    (B) James loses his lawsuit because he isn't a qualified individual with a disability.

    (C) James's lawsuit is thrown out because charges of reverse discrimination are prohibited.

    (D) The employer changes James's shift to settle the dispute without having to go to court.

91. If an employment test is found to not predict what the employer thought it was going to predict, it may be low in what type of validity?

    (A) Content validity

    (B) Criterion-related validity

    (C) Face validity

    (D) Discriminant validity

92. Which of the following is one of the five disciplines of Peter Senge's learning organization?

    (A) Systems thinking

    (B) Drive for results

    (C) Strategic planning

    (D) Employee training

93. Using dimensions to identify the requirements of the job that are supported by anchor statements of behavior will best be transferred to which type of performance evaluation?

    (A) BARS

    (B) Narrative

    (C) Comparison

    (D) Ranking

94. The school of medicine for which you work has partnered with a national university to create a leadership development program. Which of these outcomes might this program serve?

   (A) Initiating a companywide patient care program

   (B) Building a motivated and engaged workforce

   (C) Identifying the technical skills required for physicians

   (D) All of the above

95. Erica's Corner Café employs servers who are considered tipped employees under the FLSA. She pays them a base salary of $2.13 an hour and allows them to keep all of their tips. Some employees make below the federal minimum wage. Which of the following statements is true?

   (A) Erica may be violating their rights under the FLSA if their base pay plus tips doesn't meet the minimum wage standard.

   (B) Erica may be violating the FLSA because the base pay is too low, regardless of tip earnings.

   (C) Erica should be paying a base pay of the federal minimum wage of $7.25 per hour, plus overtime.

   (D) There is nothing wrong with the café claiming a tip credit against its minimum wage obligation.

96. How are incentives a type of variable pay?

   (A) They are part of a total compensation package.

   (B) They are based on individual or organizational performance.

   (C) Incentives aren't calculated as part of base pay.

   (D) They are not guaranteed.

97. Which of the following is the best reason an employer may choose to pay below-market rates for a certain position?

   (A) The competitors are paying below-market rates.

   (B) The job is only worth a below-market rate.

   (C) The rates are in line with the company budget.

   (D) There is an abundance of talent for the position.

98. The company you work for would like you to recommend a gainsharing plan that rewards the manufacturing workers when they exceed productivity requirements. Which program should you recommend?

   (A) Improshare

   (B) Profit sharing

   (C) An ESOP

   (D) An ESPP

99. An employee has been called back to military status but has an unresolved employment dispute with his employer. His attorney may request the arbitrator to _____ the statute until he returns from duty.

   (A) Toll

   (B) Dismiss

   (C) Dispute

   (D) Interrupt

100. The executive management team at Harbor Marina needs to know how long it will take for the value of a training activity to be equal to the cost. Which of the following approaches should the HR professional use?

   (A) Cost-benefit analysis

   (B) Return on investment

   (C) Break-even analysis

   (D) Training investment factors

101. Which of the following is an example of a key performance indicator (KPI) in a sales department?

   (A) Employee attendance

   (B) Sales growth

   (C) Sales commissions

   (D) Number of injuries

102. Hazel Billings has been working for the company for the last 12 months. She is still struggling to acclimate to the organization. She feels alienated from her work group, often eating lunch alone. As such, she begins calling out sick to work. In which of Maslow's hierarchical stages of needs is Hazel?

   (A) Physiological

   (B) Safety

   (C) Social

   (D) Esteem

103. Why should an employer have a return-to-work program?

   (A) To reduce the overall cost of workplace injuries

   (B) To comply with OSHA

   (C) To avoid the lost productivity of injured workers

   (D) To do the right thing

104. An employee puts money in a vending machine, expecting to receive a soda. When the soda is not forthcoming, he pushes the button again with much greater force. This is an example of which of the following theories of motivation?

   (A) Hierarchy of needs

   (B) Achievement, affiliation, and power

   (C) Theory X and Theory Y

   (D) Operant conditioning

105. Match the item in Column A with its corresponding type of benefit in Column B.

Column A	Column B
(A) Health insurance — small employer	(1) Voluntary
(B) Workers' compensation	(2) Mandatory
(C) Retirement contribution	
(D) Social security contribution	
(E) Time off for active military duty	

106. The Society of Executive Management publicly criticized a member of the SEC for suggesting that publicly traded companies with profits of more than $2 million should be mandated to report their executive compensation packages. The society's goal is to stop a bill that would make this information part of the public record. This is an example of which of the following activities?

    (A) Appropriating
    (B) Lobbying
    (C) Conferencing
    (D) Petitioning

107. A Catholic church placed a job ad for a new secretary with a requirement that the new hire must be Catholic. A Protestant woman applied and was denied. She filed a charge of unlawful discrimination based on her religion. Which of the following statements is true?

    (A) The woman was correct. It's unlawful to make a hiring decision based on a protected class characteristic.
    (B) The church was correct. In this case, the applicant's religion was a bona fide occupational qualification.
    (C) The church was correct because it is exempt from Title VII.
    (D) There isn't enough information because it is unclear whether she was otherwise qualified for the job.

108. Keeping an employee's personnel file up-to-date is most likely in response to which of the following?

    (A) Attorneys recommend doing so.
    (B) It allows you to demonstrate compliance with labor law.
    (C) If it isn't documented, it never happened.
    (D) It gives supervisors the ability to terminate an employee for cause.

109. Why would you use a staffing agency to fulfill key positions within your organization?

    (A) It allows you to prequalify workers on the job.
    (B) It establishes the agency as the employer of record.
    (C) It allows you to focus on other company core competencies.
    (D) It's less expensive than direct recruiting.

110. GrandMart LLC is being sued for multiple charges of unlawful discrimination and begins to analyze the political climate in the states where it operates to see where there may be favorable court conditions toward business. This practice is known as what?

    (A) Predictive analysis
    (B) Court selection
    (C) Scanning the environment
    (D) Forum shopping

111. Which of the following was not originally identified for protection under Title VII of the Civil Rights Act of 1964?

    (A) Age
    (B) Sexual orientation
    (C) Gender
    (D) All of the above

112. For which group may a written Affirmative Action Plan (AAP) be required?

(A) Companies with a court-ordered mandate

(B) Construction companies under contract with the federal government

(C) Supply and service contractors to the federal government

(D) All of the above

113. Freddy's Family Farmacy in Vermont is a locally grown, holistic distributor of prescription and over-the-counter medications. The owners recently asked you to line up a polygraph exam for prospective employees as part of the hiring process. What act would you violate if you were to comply?

(A) The Privacy Act of 1974

(B) The Employee Polygraph Protection Act of 1988

(C) The Fair Credit Reporting Act

(D) None. Lie detector tests aren't illegal if used under these circumstances.

114. The company you work for has recently decided that it must lay off an entire management tier as part of a recent merger. The executive team asks you for recommendations on how to reward the departing employees for years of service. Which strategy would be best?

(A) Offer outplacement services.

(B) Design severance agreements.

(C) Educate them on any available unemployment benefits.

(D) Offer to cover their COBRA insurance for an extended period of time.

115. To what does the natural disaster exception apply?

(A) Exclusion from WARN requirements

(B) Exclusion from Title VII compliance

(C) Coverage for work-related injuries if they're a result of the natural disaster

(D) None of the above

116. Which of the following activities is the most acceptable in the storage of Form I-9?

(A) Electronic copy stored on a shared drive

(B) Scanned documents, then the shredding of the original

(C) At an offsite storage location with limited access

(D) Paper storage with the employee's personnel file

117. Jasmine Jones, a manager at your organization, was recently diagnosed with severe asthma. She may qualify for what?

(A) Job protection under the ADA

(B) Wage replacement under FMLA

(C) Health certification under HIPAA

(D) Paid family leave

118. What technique or tool should you use to expose a potential employee to a typical day on the job for which he or she is applying?

(A) Job description

(B) Job analysis

(C) Realistic Job Preview (RJP)

(D) Peer interview

119. Why should a company use a professional employer organization (PEO)?

    (A) To reduce the risks associated with being the employer of record

    (B) To eliminate the costs associated with employee benefits

    (C) To avoid having to pay for workers' compensation

    (D) To streamline management processes

120. If an employee believes she has been discriminated against based on her race, which of the following statements is true?

    (A) The employee must file a charge with the EEOC before she can file a lawsuit against her employer.

    (B) The employee should hire an attorney to help her navigate the court system.

    (C) The employee has one year to file a claim.

    (D) The employee should first attempt to resolve the dispute with her employer.

121. Which strategy may be used if an organization finds that it needs to downsize?

    (A) Work furloughs

    (B) Layoffs

    (C) Reductions in force

    (D) All of the above

122. Geography, technology, and education are examples of which of the following?

    (A) Forces affecting the competitive landscape

    (B) SWOT audit sources

    (C) Segments of the labor market

    (D) Internal departments

123. What is an ethnocentric staffing strategy?

    (A) Filling key international openings with parent-country nationals

    (B) Filling key international openings without regard to home country

    (C) Using host-country nationals to fill key management positions

    (D) Using host-country nationals or regional nationals to fill key positions

124. In the _____ phase of training evaluation, participants are immediately asked questions about their thoughts on the training.

    (A) reaction

    (B) learning

    (C) behavior

    (D) results

125. In the _____ phase of training evaluation, participants are evaluated based on the amount of knowledge that has been transferred to the job.

    (A) reaction

    (B) learning

    (C) behavior

    (D) results

126. In the _____ phase of training evaluation, participants are evaluated based on how the employees apply the training to their jobs.

   (A) reaction

   (B) learning

   (C) behavior

   (D) results

127. A negatively accelerated learning curve is characterized by which of the following?

   (A) Early growth that slows over time

   (B) Slow beginning with gradual increases

   (C) A combined up-and-down demonstration of performance

   (D) Erratic performance that slowly improves

128. A positively accelerated learning curve is characterized by which of the following?

   (A) Early growth that slows over time

   (B) Slow beginning with gradual increases

   (C) A combined up-and-down demonstration of performance

   (D) Erratic performance that slowly improves

129. An S-shaped learning curve is characterized by which of the following?

   (A) Early growth that slows over time

   (B) Slow beginning with gradual increases

   (C) A combined up-and-down demonstration of performance

   (D) Erratic performance that slowly improves

130. The management team at Rowdy Mfg. wants you to design training that allows the new hires to work on production equipment, but without disrupting the production output. What type of training should you recommend?

   (A) On the job

   (B) Vestibule

   (C) Classroom simulation

   (D) Offsite

131. An employee at Clara's Toes shoe store has the skills to be a superstar, but she seems to lack motivation. Which of the following training strategies should be engaged?

   (A) Discipline

   (B) Job shadowing

   (C) Coaching

   (D) Simulation

132. The company you work for is struggling with a quality issue that it thinks is the result of lack of training and outdated equipment. Which of the following tools would be best to help the company brainstorm about the issue?

   (A) Fishbone diagram

   (B) Pareto chart

   (C) Stratification chart

   (D) Histogram

133. The auto parts store you work for distributes 1,000 products per day, of which angry customers reject approximately 195 because of poor packaging. These customers are threatening to stop doing business with you. This defect is representative of which of the following quality phenomenon?

(A) Vendor weakness

(B) Pareto chart

(C) Lack of quality assurance

(D) The Peter Principle

134. Grant Packaging LLC has a flat line structure with very few opportunities for advancement. What strategy would BEST retain a high-potential employee worker?

(A) Offering her more challenging work

(B) Paying her a higher salary

(C) Fast-tracking her into an executive role

(D) Allowing her additional time off

135. Taylor Turkeys has its busiest time of year coming up in three months and needs to design a training program that gets a temporary workforce up and running as quickly as possible. Which of the following training evaluations would best serve this purpose?

(A) Reaction evaluation

(B) Behavior evaluation

(C) Pilot program

(D) Summative evaluation

136. Tanya is the HR manager tasked with a strategic initiative to make the performance-feedback system more meaningful and effective. Which of the following activities should she do first?

(A) Compare the current program to external benchmarks.

(B) Interview the executives to find out what they want.

(C) Train the evaluators on how to conduct a review.

(D) Interview both the employees and managers to find out what they need.

137. Hearing executives say, "Women won't stay long at a company because they will have to leave for family reasons" is evidence that there is a need for what type of training?

(A) Education on work/life balance

(B) Diversity training

(C) Teaching of the leave benefits that the company offers

(D) Better new-hire onboarding

138. Defining what is confidential and identifying how long it must remain so are two objectives to writing what?

(A) An arbitration agreement

(B) A noncompete agreement

(C) A nondisclosure agreement

(D) A policy to comply with the FCRA

139. In which scenario is a random drug screen the best solution?

   (A) When compelled to random drug screen by law

   (B) Before an employee returns to work after an injury

   (C) When there is reasonable suspicion that someone is under the influence

   (D) To test all employees for drug use on a regular basis

140. Which of the following statements is true regarding workers' compensation?

   (A) Workers' compensation isn't required for federal employees.

   (B) Workers' compensation is within the scope of individual states.

   (C) Workers' compensation is the result of a common law doctrine.

   (D) OSHA requires workers' compensation.

141. For every dollar spent on an injury and illness prevention plan, employers can expect a _____ time return on that investment.

   (A) two-

   (B) four-

   (C) six-

   (D) eight-

142. In an effort to eliminate workplace hazards, jobs with the highest injury and illness rates would benefit most from which of the following safety intervention strategies?

   (A) A job hazard analysis

   (B) A hired safety consultant

   (C) Lockout/tag-out procedures

   (D) Outsourced employees

143. Management at Arbini Winery is in the process of updating its risk management plans and efforts. The management needs to decide what to do about the potential liability in unlawful discrimination claims. In which of the following solutions does the employer decide to transfer the risk?

   (A) The company purchases EPLI.

   (B) The company prohibits unlawful discrimination through policy and training.

   (C) The company develops investigative steps should a claim of discrimination be reported.

   (D) The employer decides that it's unlikely that these types of claims will occur and tables it for the next fiscal year.

144. Two supervisors completed work for the day and began to change out of their uniforms. A friendly argument began but quickly escalated, resulting in one employee stabbing the other in the leg, causing an injury that required stitches. Which statement is true?

   (A) The injury isn't recordable because it was just horseplay gone awry.

   (B) The injury isn't recordable because it wasn't work related.

   (C) The injury is recordable because it was work related and required treatment beyond first aid.

   (D) The injury is recordable because it escalated into an act of workplace violence.

145. Jobs in which employees come into contact with hazardous materials should include what safety precautions?

   (A) Hires who have experience working with the material

   (B) Very close supervision by management

   (C) The use of PPE

   (D) All of the above

146. According to the FLSA, an employee's work week is a fixed and regular recurring period of _____ hours.

   (A) 40

   (B) 56

   (C) 160

   (D) 168

147. An employee must be _____ years of age to work in most non-farm jobs, and _____ years of age to work in hazardous non-farm jobs.

   (A) 12, 14

   (B) 14, 16

   (C) 16, 18

   (D) Children under 18 may never work in hazardous non-farm jobs.

148. The bank you work for has partnered with the local university to offer a front-line supervision course for any employee who wants to attend. The classes are held every Saturday morning from 8 a.m. to noon. Which statement is true?

   (A) The time is considered compensable under the FLSA.

   (B) The time is considered compensable under the Portal-to-Portal Act.

   (C) The time is compensable because the employer established the program.

   (D) The time is not compensable because attendance is voluntary and not directly related to an employee's work.

149. An employer established a training program to be delivered after hours and, although voluntary, implied that Chris's position at work would be enhanced should he attend. What did the employer violate?

   (A) The employee's rights under Title VII

   (B) The compensable time requirements of the Portal-to-Portal Act

   (C) The overtime requirements of the FLSA

   (D) Nothing. The program was voluntary and not required as a condition of employment.

150. Which of the following is a characteristic of a top-hat plan?

   (A) It establishes a baseline for organizational productivity.

   (B) The employee completely funds it.

   (C) It may allow executives to defer compensation into the next year.

   (D) It allows employees to own company stock.

151. When a new job is created and the wage range established, what activity is most likely completed?

  (A) Job analysis

  (B) Job pricing

  (C) Job ranking

  (D) Point factoring

152. The labor market had an abundance of service technicians in years past, allowing your company to pay below-market rates. Now that the skill set is in high demand, you are being forced to pay more for the same talent. What is most likely occurring?

  (A) Pay compression

  (B) Green-circled employees

  (C) Red-circled employees

  (D) COLAs have not kept up.

153. Using the scenario in the previous question, what strategy should you recommend to your employer going forward?

  (A) Regularly audit the market and match pay rates for all employees, not just new hires.

  (B) Give pay raises to all green-circled employees.

  (C) Freeze pay increases for red-circled employees.

  (D) Offer COLAs annually on a go-forward basis.

154. A company offers equity compensation to new employees. In which stage of the life cycle is this organization?

  (A) Infancy

  (B) Growth

  (C) Maturity

  (D) Decline

155. Workers' compensation insurance is to _____ as retirement plans are to _____.

  (A) Required, desired

  (B) Obligated, generous

  (C) State-run, national

  (D) Compliance, optional

156. If the CEO's pay is 354 times that of the average worker within your company, which problem do you have?

  (A) Ethical

  (B) Internal equity

  (C) Discriminatory

  (D) Illegal

157. The most general cause of employee dissatisfaction with pay is what?

  (A) The supervisors are unfair in their ratings.

  (B) Employees think that they are worth more.

  (C) A negative perception occurs in the fairness of outcomes.

  (D) The job is not paid what it is worth.

158. Which of the following statements is true about vesting?

    (A) Employees are immediately vested in their own contributions.

    (B) Employees must wait to access all funds until they have met the vesting requirements.

    (C) Employees must be 100 percent vested after two years in a plan.

    (D) Employees may be 20 percent vested after three years of service in the plan.

159. For which of the following positions does compensation outsourcing make the most sense?

    (A) Executives

    (B) Sales staff

    (C) Piece-rate workers

    (D) Exempt-level employees

160. Open enrollment support, summary plan description creation, and COBRA administration are all examples of what?

    (A) HR generalist responsibilities

    (B) Functions of a large HR department

    (C) Responsibilities of an insurance broker

    (D) Potential outsourced functions

161. The company you work for, Health Systems Management, Inc., has a blanket policy that prohibits any employee from speaking negatively about the employer on social media. This policy may be unlawful based on which of the following?

    (A) It may violate an employee's right to engage in protected concerted activity under the NLRA.

    (B) It's a violation of an employee's right to freedom of speech.

    (C) It violates an employee's right to privacy.

    (D) It's only unlawful if it isn't consistently applied.

162. A large retail store has a social media policy that, in part, urges employees to develop a healthy sus-picion of other employees or customers who try to trick them out of confidential information. Which statement is true?

    (A) The policy may be discriminatory.

    (B) The policy violates an employee's right to privacy.

    (C) The policy may create a hostile work environment.

    (D) The policy is lawful.

163. A construction company fired five workers after they appeared in a YouTube video to complain about the potential handling of hazardous materials without proper training. These employees were illegal immigrants, and the company was non-union. Which of the following statements is true?

    (A) The employees have no rights under the NLRB because they were illegally in the United States.

    (B) The employees have no rights under the NLRB because the company was non-union at the time.

    (C) The employees have every right to complain because the complaint was about safety.

    (D) The employees have every right to complain because social media policies that prohibit negative press are valid.

164. Which of the following techniques would be most effective in avoiding union organizing?

   (A) Having an open-door policy

   (B) Prohibiting leaflet distribution on company premises

   (C) Fostering an open, inclusive work environment

   (D) Offering higher pay rates

165. An HR manager in Arizona fired an employee in New Mexico whom she had never met based on the reports of the employee's direct supervisor. She was unaware that this supervisor had a history of treating African-American employees differently than others. The company may be liable for unlawful discrimination under which doctrine?

   (A) Respondeat superior

   (B) Constructive discharge

   (C) EO 11246

   (D) Cat's paw

166. In arbitration law, it is generally impermissible for a decision maker to communicate with a party to a disagreement when the other party is absent. This is known as what?

   (A) Toll

   (B) Ex parte

   (C) In absentia

   (D) Precedent

167. Which statement is best when giving an employment reference of a past employee who was terminated for excessive absenteeism?

   (A) The employee missed five days in three months.

   (B) The employee was terminated for excessive absenteeism.

   (C) The employee missed too much work.

   (D) The employee had an attendance problem.

168. An employee was terminated because she was talking with her co-workers about trying to get pregnant. The employer told her that she was separating under the at-will doctrine of employment. To challenge this separation in court, which of the following exemptions to at-will employment will the employee most likely use?

   (A) Contract

   (B) Statutory

   (C) Public policy

   (D) Duty of good faith and fair dealing

169. A supervisor changed an employee's schedule, forced him to commute to a farther location than usual, and otherwise made his working conditions unpleasant in the hopes that the employee would quit, which of course he eventually did. What charges did he file against the company?

   (A) Discrimination

   (B) Harassment

   (C) Constructive discharge

   (D) Respondeat superior

170. Of the following answer choices, which represents the best example of the main purpose of employment policies?

   (A) Complying with labor law

   (B) Changing the behavior of employees

   (C) Establishing standard operating procedures

   (D) Improving employee performance

171. Select the option that best demonstrates an employer's commitment to true performance management.

   (A) Accountability to company policy

   (B) Annual performance reviews that aren't late

   (C) Systems for regular formal and informal communication

   (D) A commitment to hiring right the first time

172. Employee engagement is best demonstrated through which of the following individual behaviors?

   (A) Zero tardies

   (B) Regular attendance at meetings

   (C) A demonstrated desire to learn

   (D) A feeling of job security

173. One of your superstar employees just gave notice and is leaving for the competition. When asked his reason for leaving, he stated that although he loved the work and the company, the travel schedule was affecting his ability to be home with his family. Which strategy would most likely result in preventing this from happening with similar employees?

   (A) A formal system to complain about working conditions

   (B) Regular employee surveys

   (C) Annual performance reviews

   (D) Job rotation between otherwise qualified employees

174. The primary difference between a performance improvement plan (PIP) and discipline is what?

   (A) A PIP is more legally defensible.

   (B) A PIP is focused on success rather than termination.

   (C) Employees are more accepting of a PIP.

   (D) Discipline provides documentation.

175. Behavior management is a science, and therefore it can be both observed and _____.

   (A) corrected

   (B) measured

   (C) changed

   (D) modified

Chapter 18

Answers and Explanations to PHR Practice Exam

All right, one test down. You may want to take a moment before scoring your exam to focus on the areas that you felt gave you a bit of trouble. Write down what topics or question format felt tricky or the content that you had never seen before in your studies. Do so quickly, without regard for grammar or formatting so you can refer back to it after you score the test to see if your gut feelings or concerns are accurate.

After you complete your scoring, you can convert the numbers into a percentage by dividing the number of correct answers by the total number of items. Say, for example, that you missed 20 questions. Your score would be 89 percent (155 correct items divided by 175 items). While I recommend a thorough review of the answer explanations to maximize retention, take advantage of the abbreviated answer key at the end of this chapter if you're in a hurry.

Refer to Chapter 3 for more tips and tricks on how to handle the question format and what to do if you have to guess an answer on exam day.

1. **A → 2; B → 1; C → 3.** Post-hire activities are those that are done after an offer has been made and accepted and often have legal implications. Employers cannot require an applicant to complete Form I-9 (A) until a formal offer of employment has been accepted, and Form I-9 must be completed no later than 72 hours after an employee's first day of work; if the candidate cannot provide the required documents, he cannot be formally hired. The candidate interview (B) is a form of pre-employment test that predicts an applicant's fit for the job; candidates who are selected will receive an offer of employment. Form W-4 (C) is a required payroll document that is only necessary if the candidate begins work for wages.

2. **B.** Choice (B) is the correct answer because it violates Section 8 of the National Labor Relations Act (Wagner Act).

   Choice (A) is incorrect because companies can do it for economic reasons. Choice (C) is incorrect because it's called a *captive audience meeting* and is protected if done on company time. Choice (D) is incorrect because supervisors can be fired if they show support for a union. They must take a company position as a supervisor or risk being fired.

3. **D.** Supervisory status will rarely be used (although recent Supreme Court rulings may change this). Choices (A), (B), and (C) are all acceptable affirmative defenses established by case precedent.

4. **D.** In this case, the employer was well within its right to rescind the conditional job offer of employment based upon an employee's pre-employment drug screen results, making Choice (D) the correct answer.

   The other answers are all examples of common law doctrines. *Promissory estoppel* (Choice [A]) would have occurred if the employer promised something and the individual acted on that promise. The *duty of good faith and fair dealing* (Choice [B]) would have been compromised if the employer had acted in an unfair manner, and *fraudulent misrepresentation* (Choice [C]) would have occurred, for example, if the employer had given false information to entice the employee to leave his current position.

5. **A.** Often referred to as the 4 Ps of marketing — product, place, promotion, and price — are decisions that must be made regarding a company product or service. The other answers aren't part of the 4 Ps of marketing.

6. **B → Step 1; C → Step 2; A → Step 3.** Step 1 is (B). By verifying that Mary is eligible for Family Medical Leave Act (FMLA), you're ensuring that her rights are protected and that you comply with the standard if required. After you have verified her eligibility, you may request medical certification from her physician (C) and work with the supervisor to determine replacement needs and sources (A).

7. **A.** Promoting from within capitalizes on the resources already expended in an earlier recruiting effort, and the question stem states that working at corporate is an attractive option. Choices (B), (C), and (D) are all good efforts, but not the best answer to this scenario.

8. **C.** Attending professional development activities with subordinates isn't unethical. Choices (B) and (D) are clearly inappropriate, and Choice (A), although compassionate, isn't appropriate when considering ethical behavior.

9. **A.** *Acculturation*, also called *socialization*, is part of the onboarding process that includes becoming part of a team and learning the group dynamics.

   Cultural integration (Choice [B]) may occur as the result of a merger or acquisition, whereas *onboarding* (Choice [C]) is a step to getting the new hire acquainted with the job. *Affiliation* (Choice [D]) is a term associated with the need theory of motivation.

10. **B.** *Span of control* refers to the number of employees a manager directly supervises. Choices (A) and (C) refer to much more than just direct reports, and Choice (D) is a visual representation of the organizational hierarchy.

11. **D.** Technological factors, such as the ability to recall data and protection of assets, must be reviewed as part of a thorough PEST analysis. The political (Choice [A]), economic (Choice [B]), and social (Choice [C]) landscapes don't address the items in the question.

12. **C.** *Employer branding* serves to tell the public about why people should come and work for the organization. Establishing the employer brand is the broader scope of two of the other answers — Choices (A) and (D). Videoing and then posting the video doesn't serve as a compliance document, Choice (B).

13. **A.** *Employment at-will* allows either party to terminate the employment relationship at any time and for any reason.

Choice (B) is another common law doctrine, dealing with the employer being responsible for the actions of its employees. Choice (C) is an exception to the at-will doctrine, and the *employment relationship*, Choice (D), exists when both parties agree to work with each other.

14. **B.** Employee reasons for leaving are captured prior to their last day of work in *exit interviews*.

Employee satisfaction surveys, Choice (A), are designed to measure employee opinions before they make a decision to leave. *Turnover reports*, Choice (C), are designed to identify what positions are unfilled, and a *labor market analysis*, Choice (D), is too broad in scope to capture specific information about why people choose to leave a specific employer.

15. **A.** A *homogeneous* group, Choice (A), includes people who share the same background or heritage. Choice (B) is the opposite. Choice (C) is a devoted citizen, and Choice (D) is the recognition of academic merit.

16. **C.** *Quid pro quo* harassment occurs when a supervisor requires a romantic or sexual behavior in exchange for something else, such as not being fired.

Choices (A) and (B) aren't the correct terms, although the harassment certainly may be found to be unlawful and discriminatory. Choice (D) is another type of harassment in which an employee's working conditions are altered due to abuse based on a protected class characteristic.

17. **A.** An *R-1* is a nonimmigrant visa that may be extended to religious workers to be in the United States for up to five years. Choice (B) is for workers with extraordinary abilities, Choice (C) is a visa for executives, and Choice (D) may be extended to athletes or entertainers.

18. **D.** Separation of employment is a trigger for multiple worker protection acts, including all listed here, which makes Choice (D) correct.

COBRA, Choice A, allows separated workers to continue to purchase healthcare. HIPAA, Choice B, allows them to get future coverage despite pre-existing conditions. WARN, Choice (C), requires notice because the layoff affects more than 99 workers.

19. **B.** The explosion of mobile job apps within the last testing window makes Choice (B) the correct answer.

Also increasing, but at a slower pace, are the use of videos for the employer brand, Choice (A), and employee testimonials, Choice (C) (similar to a product or service review). Choice (D) has been growing at a more steady pace since its birth several years ago.

20. **D.** At-will employment is a common law doctrine that allows either party to employment to separate at any time and for any reason, making Choice (D) the best answer.

21. **D.** Many benefits to pre-employment drug screening include a defense against a negligent hiring claim (Choice [A]), the prevention of potential violence on the job (Choice [B]), and workplace injuries (Choice [C]), making Choice (D) the correct answer.

22. **B.** Using student interns is an excellent source of hiring for companies that allows both the candidate and the employer to qualify each other for the position.

Choice (A) could get the employer in trouble if not properly managed, and both Chioces (C) and (D), although correct, aren't the focus of student internships.

23. **A.** The correct answer is (A), which found that a high school diploma requirement was excluding African Americans. (B) requires that all employment tests be valid predictors of behavior. (C) places the burden on an employer to show why it failed to hire someone who was otherwise qualified. In (D), an employee who had been the subject of unlawful discrimination may be eligible for back pay.

24. **D.** *Albemarle Paper vs. Moody* found that an employee who had been the subject of unlawful discrimination may be eligible for back pay.

    In Choice (A), a high-school diploma requirement excludes African Americans, making it discriminatory. Choice (B) requires that all employment tests be valid predictors of behavior. Choice (C) places the burden on an employer to show why it failed to hire someone who was otherwise qualified.

25. **B.** Using a third party to conduct the exit interview allows the exiting employee to provide more honest, meaningful feedback as to why he or she is leaving.

    It may not have an impact on how an employee feels about the separation (Choice [A]), and it won't protect an employer from a charge of wrongful termination (Choice [C]). Choice (D) may be necessary for the busy HR professional, but it's not the best answer.

26. **D.** The Age Discrimination in Employment Act applies to all individuals older than the age of 40.

27. **D.** Outsourcing is a very useful way to accomplish many of the functions of HR in the absence of a robust HR department. Activities include processing payroll (Choice [A]), hiring (Choice [B]), and complying with COBRA (Choice [C]).

28. **A.** Successful social media use in recruiting has a consistent message communicated via the brand, and videos are one way to do that. The employer brand isn't used for retention (Choice [B]) or satisfaction efforts (Choice [C]), nor does it help communicate the benefits (Choice [D]).

29. **C.** Job sharing highlights an alternative to traditional staffing sources, such as direct hires (Choice [A]) and temporary workers (Choice [D]) and the use of the internet to find talent (Choice [B]).

30. **B.** In a *Socratic seminar*, conclusions are drawn and ideas shared through questions and answers, so Choice (B) is correct.

    An agenda (Choice [A]), classroom lecture (Choice [C]), or room setup such as a fishbowl (Choice [D]) aren't key factors to this instructional method.

31. **A.** Choice (A) is the best answer because active teaching addresses the needs of the training participant. The active method of teaching results in engaged (Choice [B]) and participative (Choice [C]) attendees. Choice (D) is an answer distractor and doesn't apply.

32. **D.** The correct answer is Choice (D) because on-the-job training occurs in real time at the workstations.

    Meanwhile, off-the-job training pulls employees out of the environment in which they will eventually apply their knowledge. In *vestibule training*, Choice (A), work is simulated at a different location from where the work would normally be done. A *lecture*, Choice (B), is a method used in a classroom setting, and *simulation training*, Choice (C), is training that mimics actual conditions of the job but is not done where the work is regularly completed.

33. **D.** *Banquet-style seating* helps facilitate training that requires discussion because it has already organized people into groups. Films (Choice [A]) and lectures (Choice [B]) are best facilitated using theater-style seating, and the use of manuals (Choice [C]) or other hands-on activities is best served by a traditional classroom setup.

34. **B.** The best answer to this question is Choice (B). New employees should be asked to conduct a self-assessment after the first 90 days of employment in order to help facilitate the constructive feedback that is often necessary to get them up to speed. An employee assessment isn't the best way to address teamwork issues, Choice (A), because most employees won't point the finger at themselves. Choice (C) won't be served by an assessment of the employee's behavior, and Choice (D) is incorrect for similar reasons.

35. **A.** *Flexible work arrangements* can help retain key workers of both sexes, allowing for better work-life balance. EPLI insurance (Choice [B]) and a dating policy (Choice [D]) aren't the direct result of women in the workplace. The question doesn't adequately predict a sexual harassment lawsuit (Choice [C]).

36. **A → 3; B → 2; C → 1.** The *development* stage of training (3) is where the collateral materials to be used in the training are created (A), and the analysis stage (2) of the instructional design model of ADDIE is a function of data collection to assess the need (B). The *evaluation* phase (1) occurs after the sessions have been completed (C).

37. **C.** The correct answer is Choice (C) because the development stage of ADDIE is when training material is created or *developed*.

    The *design* stage, Choice (B), is concerned with designing training around tasks and participants. The *analysis* stage, Choice (A), occurs when the needs to be addressed through training are identified. After documents have been developed, they can be implemented, Choice (D).

38. **D.** Visual learners learn by seeing the material in print or graphic form, making Choice (D) the correct answer. Lectures (Choice [A]) work well for auditory learners, whereas tactile learners are best served through hands-on (Choice [B]) or on-the-job (Choice [C]) training.

39. **B.** Training won't solve a problem with tools or equipment, so Choice (B) is correct. Training may have impact on being unfamiliar with the products (Choice [A]), being a new hire (Choice [C]), or becoming proficient with software programs (Choice [D]).

40. **C.** The correct answer is skill variety, one of the criteria of the job characteristics model that allows employees to use more than one skill in their work.

    Choice (A) is the ability to identify how the employee's task contributes to the final product. *Horizontal loading*, Choice (B), refers to assigning tasks that share similar skill sets. Task significance is an intrinsic motivator when the job has a larger purpose or meaning, Choice (D).

41. **D.** In instructional design, the objectives of learning should be clearly defined prior to the development of training. In training design, objectives state the outcomes that will shape the learning content and final effectiveness evaluations.

    Goals, Choice (A), tend to be stated on the operational level, trickling down from the strategic plan. Interventions are also linked to business strategy and are used to fill the gap between actual and desired states, Choice (B). Choice (C) is a generic term used both at a strategic and operational level.

42. **A.** Enterprise risk management (ERM) is a system to address all aspects of organizational risk, including protecting the confidentiality of customer information, which makes Choice (A) correct.

Responding to a technological fail (Choice [B]) and establishing firewalls (Choice [C]) are aspects of the system. The protection of human assets (Choice [D]) doesn't address information, but rather the physical well-being of employees.

43. **D.** Establishing internal controls such as those defined by the generally accepted accounting principles (GAAP) helps avoid potential conflicts such as the one described in the question, making Choice (D) the correct answer. In this case, separating the functions so that the responsibilities are shared would not prevent something like this from happening, whereas Choices (A), (B), and (C) serve only to prohibit it.

44. **C.** Injury and illness prevention plans (IIPPs) are designed to communicate information to employees about workplace hazards. Many of these plans share elements, whereas others, such as fire prevention plans (Choice [A]), are specific to the hazard. The need isn't an element of protecting information or financial assets as in Choices (B) and (D).

45. **B.** Without leadership and management commitment, a company's IIPP will struggle to allocate resources to abate hazards (Choice [A]), engage workers (Choice [C]), or evaluate program outcomes (Choice [D]).

46. **D.** State-run programs must meet the federal safety standards established by the Occupational Safety and Health Act and Administration, making Choice (D) the correct answer.

47. **D.** Retaliation occurs when an employer punishes a worker for exercising a right under the law — in this case, the right to blow the whistle — making Choice (D) the correct answer.

Discrimination, Choice (A), occurs when an employee is unlawfully treated based on a protected class characteristic. Harassment, Choice (B), may be present if the employee is forced to endure taunting or abusive conduct from co-workers or supervisors. In Choice (C), a claim of wrongful discipline may have merit; however, it's secondary to the correct answer.

48. **A.** The Family Medical Leave Act (FMLA) provides unpaid, job-protected leave to eligible employees.

49. **B.** The Patient Protection and Affordable Care Act amended the Fair Labor Standards Act in 2010, requiring employers to accommodate nursing mothers' need to express breast milk for a year following the birth of a child.

50. **C.** The Portal-to-Portal Act amended the FLSA in 1947 to clarify what was compensable time. One of the primary outcomes was that regular commute time — from one portal or doorway to another — wasn't compensable under the FLSA.

Davis-Bacon, Choice (A), required prevailing wages for public works projects. McNamara-O'Hara, Choice (B), addressed minimums for service workers. The Equal Pay Act, Choice (D), addressed disparity in pay between men and women doing the same jobs.

51. **C.** *Base pay* is the amount of money an employee receives as the result of performing work.

Minimum wage (A) is set by law, total compensation (B) includes variable pay and benefits, and incentives (D) are a type of variable pay based on performance.

52. **C.** *Performance-based pay* is earned based on effort.

   Base pay, Choice (A), is paid as part of the work agreement, and total compensation, Choice (B), includes all facets of remuneration. Entitlement pay, Choice (D), is based on years of service or cost of living increases; an employee is entitled to the increase because she works there.

53. **A.** Shift premiums are considered a pay differential because they're different from the regular hourly rate.

   Hazard pay, Choice (B), is also a type of pay differential, paying a higher premium for difficult or dangerous work. A benefit, Choice (C), is generally a part of an overall compensation plan, and entitlement, Choice (D), is a compensation philosophy.

54. **C.** The Consumer Credit Protection Act limits the amount of pay that can be garnished on a weekly basis; thus, Choice (C) is correct.

55. **C.** The Health Insurance Portability and Accountability Act (HIPAA) prohibits the exclusion of pre-existing conditions when an employee had previous coverage of said condition.

   The Consolidated Omnibus Budget Reconciliation Act (COBRA), Choice (A), is the right of employees to continue to purchase the employer plan when there is a qualifying event. Title VII, Choice (B), is part of the Civil Rights Act of 1964 that prohibits discrimination in employment and doesn't govern health insurance. Future coverage of pre-existing health conditions isn't the focus of the Patient Protection and Affordable Care Act (PPACA), Choice (D).

56. **C.** Because *variable pay* is based on individual and/or organizational performance, Choice (C) is the best answer. Annual increases (Choice [A]) and benefits (Choice [B]) don't directly reward achievement, and group incentives (Choice [D]) reward team rather than personal effort.

57. **A.** The opposite of base pay is pay based on merit. Choices (B), (C), and (D) aren't performance driven.

58. **D.** In all of the answers, an experience factor is generated based on claims experience, making Choice (D) the correct answer.

59. **C.** A *defined benefit plan* guarantees an employee a set amount of money at the time of retirement, usually as a monthly payment.

   A *cash balance plan*, Choice (A), is a retirement program where employers deposit a percentage of the employee's pay into a retirement account, and the employee isn't required to contribute. A *contributory plan*, Choice (B), is one in which a percentage of earnings are deposited into a retirement account. A *defined contribution*, Choice (D), doesn't define the benefit; rather, it defines the amount an employer/employee may contribute to the plan, such as a 401k.

60. **B.** The Employee Retirement Income Security Act (ERISA) established that a plan may require an employee to be at least 21 years of age with at least one year of service before being eligible to participate.

61. **C.** *Conducting a needs assessment* helps identify what the company's need is in managing payroll.

   After that has been completed, you can then write a Request for Proposal (RFP) (Choice [B]) that addresses the needs, request a trial run (Choice [D]) of the selected software, and then present executives with options to approve it (Choice [A]).

62. B. The National Labor Relations Board (NLRB) may file an Unfair Labor Practice (ULP) charge against the employer if its social media policy is too broad. The question doesn't discuss any discriminatory elements such as protected class conditions (Choice [A]), nor does it describe a situation of sexual or hostile workplace harassment (Choice [C]). A *whistleblower* (Choice [D]) is someone who reports a company for corrupt or unsafe business practices.

63. C. Union organizers are sponsored and trained by unions to travel and help workers organize. With the AFL-CIO, they select their union-organizing training participants from union members or elected union representatives; others are from college campuses or community groups.

A bargaining agent assists members with the collective bargaining agreement (CBA) (Choice [A]), and union stewards serve as employee ambassadors to the union (Choice [D]). Any person with decision-making authority may act on behalf of the employer when bargaining (Choice [B]).

64. A. The term *salting* refers to the process of padding the applicant pool with those in sympathy with union aims, making Choice (A) the correct answer.

Featherbedding, Choice (B), is the hiring of more workers than are necessary to perform a job. *Double breasting,* Choice (C), refers to a common owner of two businesses, one of which is union. The *alter ego doctrine,* Choice (D), is a term used to describe an employer who is trying to dodge its collective bargaining responsibilities by setting up another company with substantially the same operations.

65. D. Union issues such as safety and fair pay have been granted as rights by statute (Choice [A]), while working conditions (Choice [B]) and updated tools and equipment (Choice [C]) have improved, making unions less necessary than in earlier times.

66. B. You can communicate with employees several different ways, and they include informal brown bag lunches in which employees voluntarily bring their lunches to a meeting, a company intranet where business issues and announcements are posted, and word of mouth, where supervisors and other employees are used to pass information among employees.

Word of mouth isn't a type of training, making Choice (A) incorrect. Both Choices (C) and (D) are types of information an employer would need a mode of communication for.

67. D. *At-will employment* is the right for an employer to terminate or an employee to quit at any time for any reason, making Choice (D) correct.

There is no such thing as the doctrine of free will, Choice (A). The doctrine of Lord Acton, Choice (B), refers to an author of freedom essays unrelated to employment issues. Statutory exceptions, Choice (C), are conditions under which a labor law or employment doctrine may not apply.

68. A. The Supreme Court established that in cases where an adverse employment action was made by a supervisor via quid pro quo harassment, an employer may not build an affirmative defense. An example of a tangible injury includes denial of a promotion or wage, or a demotion.

In the other three answer choices, an employer may have the opportunity to provide an affirmative defense demonstrating that they took all possible preventive efforts.

69. D. A tangible employment action, such as hiring, firing, and demoting, can only be caused by someone — such as a supervisor — acting on behalf of the employer. The EEOC states that this action can be demonstrated by documentation, higher-level review, and execution of the action, making Choice (D) correct.

70. **C.** The Supreme Court found in *Oncale vs. Sundowner Offshore Services* that Title VII is violated anytime the work environment is permeated with hostile or discriminatory behavior that alters the work environment, regardless of sex.

71. **C.** The National Labor Relations Board (NLRB) is responsible for enforcing the standards set forth in the National Labor Relations Act (Choice [B]). The Equal Employment Opportunity Commission (EEOC), Choice (A), enforces Title VII, and the Department of Labor, Choice (D) is responsible for many other labor laws including safety and wage and hour.

72. **B.** The trifecta of labor law governs unions, and the National Labor Relations Act (NLRA) was the act that first defined unfair labor practices.

    The Labor-Management Relations Act (LMRA), Choice (A), followed, which protected employers from union abuses. The third act was the Labor-Management Reporting and Disclosure Act (LMRDA), Choice (C), which established controls for unions in response to corrupt union practices against their members. The Railway Labor Act of 1926, Choice (D), was a cooperative effort between labor unions and railway employers to minimize the impact that striking workers had on U.S. transportation.

73. **C.** The Labor-Management Reporting Act (Landrum-Griffith Act) established rules for unions in an effort to protect members from corrupt practices. The National Labor Relations Act (Wagner Act), Choice (B), gave employees the right to unionize, and the Labor-Management Relations Act (Taft-Hartley), Choice (A), protected employers from union abuses. The Railway Labor Act, Choice (D), was one of the first efforts between unions and employers to find alternative dispute methods to strikes.

74. **A.** The Labor Management Relations Act sought to balance the power between unions and employers.

    The National Labor Relations Act, Choice (B), first granted union power in 1935. The Labor-Management Reporting and Disclosure Act, Choice (C), which established controls for unions in response to corrupt union practices against their members, also curbed union power. The Railway Labor Act, Choice (D), was a collaboration between unions and railway employers to minimize the likelihood of strikes and thus avoid the disruptions to transportation they cause.

75. **D.** *Economic* strikers are those workers who are protesting conditions of employment such as wages or hours. *Picketing*, Choice (B), may be an activity used by strikers to communicate their dissatisfaction. Unfair labor practices strikers, Choice (C), are protesting unlawful acts by the employer. There is no such thing as a protest strike, Choice (A).

76. **B.** Absent serious misconduct on the part of the worker, unfair labor practice strikers are entitled to their jobs back, even if it means discharging a replacement worker.

77. **C.** The correct answer is Choice (C) because compensable time was first established as a concept under the Fair Labor Standards Act, and later clarified through the Portal-to-Portal Act.

    It requires that "preparatory and concluding activities" that are integral to the job function be paid. The OSH Act, Choice (A), communicates safety standards, whereas the Service Contract Act, Choice (B), requires affected employers to pay prevailing wage and fringe benefits under certain conditions.

78. **A.** Because HCMPs are used as a strategic planning tool to guide a company's responses to emerging workforce and organizational needs, the correct answer is Choice (A). Goal-setting, Choice (B), may be a tool used for plan implementation, and project implementation, Choice (C), is an activity described within the plan. Sustainability, Choice (D), is a corporate responsibility concept that helps organizations avoid resource depletion.

79. **B.** The National Labor Relations Act (NLRA) guarantees workers the right to organize independent of their employer. Having managers appoint employees who were then allowed to discuss conditions of employment makes Choice (B) the correct answer. Also, the committee could make recommendations that had job security and economic implications for current workers. These decisions, outside the normal collective bargaining domain, would violate NLRB rules.

The presence of management on the committees and the committees themselves, Choices (A) and (C), aren't unlawful; Choice (D) is irrelevant because all company committees don't have to be declared part of an official union.

80. **D.** *Negative reinforcement* occurs when something unpleasant is removed in response to employee behavior. *Positive reinforcement,* Choice (C), provides a reward when behavior occurs, for example, incentives for speeding up production.

Punishment, Choice (A), would exist if the supervisor told the workers they would be fired if production weren't caught up. *Extinction,* Choice (B), is similar to negative reinforcement; however, it refers to extinguishing the behavior, not removing the consequence.

81. **D.** In the absence of an emergency, existing safety hazards should be the first item addressed. Customer confidentiality procedures describe action steps designed to protect confidentiality, and disaster preparedness planning includes communicated plans to use in the event of a disaster. Workplace violence policy is last in this scenario because a policy won't directly protect a stakeholder.

82. **B.** When two sets of data are strongly linked together, a high correlation is said to exist, referred to as a *co-relationship.* A *positive correlation* demonstrates that when one variable increases, the second variable also increases, or if one variable decreases, the second likewise decreases, so Choice (B) is correct. Choices (A), (C), and (D) are examples of negative correlations because when one variable increases, the other decreases.

83. **B.** Similar to a bell curve, *forced distribution* identifies the top 25 percent of employees within a department, 50 percent of workers who can stay in their current position, and the bottom 25 percent of employees in need of intervention.

A *Pareto chart,* Choice (A), and a *fishbone diagram,* Choice (D), are tools used in problem-solving. Choice (C) is a simpler version of forced distribution and isn't a chart.

84. **C.** In a *product-based structure,* Choice (C), divisions are formed based on lines of products, customers, or geography.

While lending itself to either centralized or decentralized, it's more likely to be decentralized than the traditional *functional* (Choice [A]) or *hierarchical* (Choice [D]) corporate structure. In Choice (B), the term *organizational* is a distractor.

85. **B.** A *human capital management plan* is part of the strategic planning process in which talent needs are forecasted and addressed. Continuous recruitment (Choice [A]) won't solve seasonal peaks, and making promotions from within (Choice [C]) still leaves gaps. The use of staffing agencies (Choice [D]) may be a solution, but only after the needs are predicted.

86. **A.** Andragogy refers to the way adults learn, whereas pedagogy, Choice (B), is the science of how children learn. The process of unlearning information is related to the neuroscience of change, Choice (C), and andragogy is not a condition of a learning organization, Choice (D).

87. **A.** Choice (A) is correct because it may include both expansion and reduction to address a strategic initiative. Choice (B) is an example of reduction, whereas Choices (C) and (D) are more about the joining of assets than simple restructures.

88. **B.** The best answer to this question is Choice (B). Having management committed to the process will help shape and influence a meaningful MVV.

    Establishing a budget, Choice (A), is a transactional activity that shouldn't influence the MVV. Scanning the environment, Choice (C), is helpful to collect data, but not in advance of management engagement. Choice (D) is an evaluation step, usually occurring after the MVV is in place.

89. **D.** Employee performance, Choice (D), is the correct answer because the engagement stage in the employee life cycle is related to the worker's performance management.

    Choice (A) is communicated at the onboarding stage of the life cycle, as are responsibilities, Choice (B). Choice (C) isn't relevant.

90. **C.** The correct answer is Choice (C), because the amended version of the ADA prohibits reverse discrimination claims under the ADA. This answer makes the other answer choices irrelevant.

91. **B.** A test is said to be low in *criterion-related validity* if it doesn't predict the behaviors that an employer thought it was going to predict. Choice (A) refers to the test being reflective of all relevant job responsibilities. Choice (C) refers to the appearance of the successful prediction of outcomes. In Choice (D), uncorrelated items stay uncorrelated.

92. **A.** *Systems thinking* refers to a holistic view of the inter-relatedness of an organization.

    Choices (B) and (C) aren't one of the five disciplines. Choice (D) is a distractor because a learning organization is not just about employee training; it's the science of how a company works.

93. **A.** The Behaviorally Anchored Rating Scale (BARS) uses anchor statements to support job requirements, so Choice (A) is the correct answer. Choice (B) is descriptive, and both Choices (C) and (D) use other employees to measure performance.

94. **B.** A *leadership development program* first serves the broader needs and desired outcomes of an organization. Focused development programs typically are designed to serve narrower needs such as quality or job competencies for a specific role.

    Choice (A) isn't the best answer simply because the focus of leadership development is not on one single outcome, but rather many. Identifying technical skills for physicians, Choice (C), is too narrow of a focus to be served by a leadership development program.

95. **A.** Companies are allowed to claim a tip credit against the minimum wage earnings, provided they pay the difference when base pay plus tips does not meet the minimum wage standards.

96. **B.** Because the focus of variable pay is performance, Choice (B) is the best answer. The other answers, although true, aren't the best options for this question because they aren't critical to the existence of a variable pay system.

97. **D.** Employers have many reasons for paying below-market rates, but when evaluating compensation rates, they should first consider the abundance of talent.

    Regardless of what competitors are doing (Choice [A]), job worth (Choice [B]), or the budget requirements (Choice [C]), the absence or abundance of talent drives results.

98. **A.** *Improshare* is a gainsharing plan that rewards efforts that exceed past production standards.

Improshare is more narrowly focused than a profit-sharing plan (Choice [B]). It also doesn't offer employee stock as do Employee Stock Ownership Plans (Choice [C]) and Employee Stock Purchase Plans (Choice [D]).

99. **A.** A *toll* temporarily suspends the counting of time in a legal action for various reasons, making Choice (A) the correct answer in this example.

Dismissing the statute, Choice (B), would close out the case permanently from a legal perspective. The case is already in dispute, so Choice (C) wouldn't make sense, and Choice (D) is a distractor, a term that doesn't apply to the described situation.

100. **C.** In this question, the key word is *equal*. Although all answers may provide the executive team members with some degree of the information they seek, Choice (C) is the most specific; a *break-even analysis* will determine at what point total revenue equals total return.

Choices (A), (B), and (D) speak to an overall return on the investment dollars but are broader than the initial request.

101. **B.** *Sales growth* is a key indicator of performance in a sales department. KPI helps a company measure progress toward organizational goals, is generally long term in nature, and must be adaptable to changing realities. These goals are most often established through the strategic planning process.

Choices (A) and (D), although important, speak to operational issues that shouldn't be fluid. Choice (C) doesn't adequately capture the sales information necessary to determine whether a change of strategy is required.

102. **C.** Abraham Maslow stated that employees have needs at different stages that must be met in order for them to stay motivated. The *social stage* speaks to the desire of individuals to belong to a workgroup, so Choice (C) is the correct answer.

Choices (A) and (B) refer to the most basic needs of an individual, such as food, shelter, and safe working conditions. Choice (D) is a higher level in the hierarchy, referencing the idea that people are motivated by achievement and recognition.

103. **A.** A *return-to-work program* helps get injured workers back to work in a modified capacity and on payroll, rather than having their wages replaced through the insurance, thereby reducing the overall cost of the injury.

OSHA doesn't require return-to-work programs, Choice (B), and avoiding lost productivity, Choice (C), isn't a primary goal of these programs. Choice (D) isn't the best answer because it's subjective.

104. **D.** B.F. Skinner's *operant conditioning* is what happens to an employee when he executes one behavior and receives a consistent result, reinforcing the behavior and future expectation.

Choice (B) is McClelland's *three-factor theory of motivation*, identifying an employee's needs to achieve, belong, and/or lead. In Choice (C), McGregor addresses a manager's view of how employees are motivated. Choice (A) is Maslow's *hierarchy of needs*.

105. **A and C → 1; B, D, and E → 2.** Health insurance for small employers (A) and contributions to retirement accounts (C) are voluntary employment benefits. Employers are required to offer workers compensation insurance (B), make contributions through payroll tax to the employee's Social Security account (D), and provide time off for active military service (E).

106. **B.** *Lobbying* is the effort of a group to influence legislation.

Appropriating (Choice [A]) is the process of setting funds aside for a specific purpose. *Conferencing* (Choice [C]) is the gathering together of individuals to discuss specific issues, and *petitioning* (Choice [D]) is a formal plea to a lawmaker to make desired changes to existing or proposed laws.

107. **B.** Under very narrow circumstances, an employer may claim a protected class characteristic is a bona fide occupational qualification (BFOQ) and use it as a condition of employment.

Choice (C) is incorrect because churches aren't exempt from Title VII, and Choices (A) and (D) are irrelevant as religion is a BFOQ.

108. **B.** Compliance with labor law is the fundamental reason for maintaining a personnel file, making Choice (B) the best choice in this scenario.

Choices (A), (C), and (D) are by-products of compliance, helping to manage employer risk as recommended by attorneys. Managing risks includes the employer having the documentation necessary to defend a wrongful termination charge.

109. **C.** HR professionals must wear multiple hats, and outsourcing is an effective way to marshal resources. It allows you to focus on other areas of core competencies, making Choice (C) the correct answer.

Prequalifying workers (Choice [A]) is part of the recruiting process, not the post-hire process, and establishing the agency as the employer of record (Choice [B]) is irrelevant because there may be co-employment issues regardless. The notion that it's less expensive than direct recruiting (Choice [D]) isn't always true.

110. **D.** The correct answer is *forum shopping*, the practice of trying to get a trial held in a court that is more likely to produce a favorable outcome.

Predictive analysis, Choice (A), is a data-mining process, and *scanning the environment,* Choice (C), is part of the strategic planning process. Choice (B), *court selection,* is a generic term that can be applied to multiple behaviors.

111. **D.** Although age, sexual orientation, and gender are currently granted protected class status, Title VII of the Civil Rights Act of 1964 originally prohibited discrimination based on race, ethnicity, national origin, and religion, making Choice (D) correct.

112. **D.** Companies with past discriminatory practices may be compelled by the court to have a written affirmative action plan (AAP). Construction companies and supply and service contractors may also be required to have written plans, depending upon the value of their contracts.

113. **D.** The correct answer is (D) because the use of a polygraph in this example is an exception.

Choice (B) prohibits the use of lie detector tests with certain exceptions. One exception is the limited use in hiring of individuals with access to storage of or sale of controlled substances. Choices (A) and (C) don't address polygraphs.

114. **B.** Severance packages are often structured based on years of service.

Outplacement services (Choice [A]) and unemployment benefit counseling (Choice [C]) are helpful, but they don't result in the requested outcome. Choice (D), covering COBRA insurance, may be built into a severance agreement.

115. **A.** If a plant's closing is due to a natural disaster, such as an earthquake or flood, otherwise obligated employers are exempt from the notification requirements of WARN. They aren't, however, exempt from discrimination laws (Choice [B]) or workers' compensation (Choice [C]).

116. **B.** The best answer is Choice (B). As long as other measures are taken to ensure the integrity, readability, and access of the records, the original documents can be destroyed after they're stored electronically. Storing Form I-9 on a shared drive (Choice [A]) doesn't adequately address confidentiality issues. Choice (C) may inhibit presentation on demand, and Choice (D), although acceptable, isn't recommended.

117. **A.** Because breathing is considered a major life activity under the Americans with Disabilities Act (ADA), the correct answer is Choice (A).

    FMLA, Choice (B), doesn't offer wage replacement, and HIPAA, Choice (C), will become necessary only if her employment is terminated. Choice (D) doesn't exist at a national level.

118. **C.** The best answer is Choice (C), because an organization may use a Realistic Job Preview to communicate both the positive and negative aspects of the job as part of the interview process.

    An organization does a *job analysis,* Choice (B), to identify the key tasks, duties, and responsibilities and then uses the job analysis to write job descriptions, Choice (A). A peer interview, Choice (D), could be used, but it's not the best answer.

119. **A.** A PEO reduces exposure to the risks associated with being an employer, making Choice (A) the correct answer.

    Choices (B) and (C) are examples of those risks and are often built into the billing rate. Whether or not a PEO would have a positive effect on Choice (D) is dependent upon many unique employer factors, such as the total number of workers and labor burden.

120. **D.** The EEOC encourages employees to first address the issue with their employer prior to filing a formal complaint.

    In most cases, an employee must file a discrimination charge with the EEOC prior to filing a lawsuit, Choice (A). Choice (B) must be considered on a case-by-case basis. In Choice (C), the employee has 180 days to file a charge with the EEOC.

121. **D.** An organization can downsize in several ways, and they don't all have to be permanent, making Choice (D) the correct answer.

122. **C.** The correct answer is Choice (C) because they're subsets of the labor market that may be used to identify targeted recruiting efforts.

    The forces referred to in Choice (A) are competitive in nature, such as new entrants to the market or supplier power. SWOT audit sources, Choice (B), scan the external environments for threats and weaknesses. Internal departments, Choice (D), aren't catalogued or recorded by the question criteria.

123. **A.** An *ethnocentric staffing* strategy is one that uses home-country expatriates to staff global positions.

    Choice (B) is a geocentric strategy, Choice (C) is a polycentric strategy, and Choice (D) is a regiocentric staffing policy.

124. **A.** Donald Kirkpatrick described four methods of training evaluation. The correct answer is Choice (A) because in *reaction evaluations*, participants are queried on their feelings about the training immediately afterward.

In *learning evaluations*, Choice (B), the amount of knowledge is measured, often through a quiz. In *behavior evaluations*, Choice (C), employees are observed applying the newly acquired behaviors on the job. In *results evaluations*, Choice (D), the effects of the training are measured.

125. **B.** Donald Kirkpatrick described four methods of training evaluation. The correct answer is Choice (B) because what participants have learned is measured, often through a quiz.

In *reaction evaluations*, Choice (A), participants are queried on their feelings about the training immediately afterward. In *behavior evaluations*, Choice (C), employees are observed applying the newly acquired behaviors on the job. In *results evaluations*, Choice (D), the effects of the training are measured.

126. **C.** Donald Kirkpatrick described four methods of training evaluation. The correct answer is Choice (C) because in behavior evaluations, employees are observed applying the newly acquired behaviors on the job.

In *reaction evaluations*, Choice (A), participants are queried on their feelings about the training immediately afterward. In *learning evaluations*, Choice (B), the amount of knowledge is measured, often through a quiz. In *results evaluations*, Choice (D), the effects of the training are measured.

127. **A.** Employees learn and apply information from training at different paces. A *negatively accelerated learning curve* shows early performance that gradually declines over practice.

A *positively accelerated learning curve*, Choice (B), is one in which early performance outcomes are low, but they gradually improve. An *S-shaped learning curve*, Choice (C), is characterized by a combined up-and-down graph of learning. Choice (D) isn't an example of the formal types of learning curves.

128. **B.** Employees learn and apply information from training at different paces. A *positively accelerated learning curve* is one in which early performance outcomes are low, but they gradually improve.

A *negatively accelerated learning curve*, Choice (A), shows early performance that gradually declines over practice. An *S-shaped learning curve*, Choice (C), is characterized by a combined up-and-down graph of learning. Choice (D) isn't an example of the formal types of learning curves.

129. **C.** Employees learn and apply information from training at different paces. An *S-shaped learning curve* is characterized by a combined up-and-down graph of learning.

A *negatively accelerated learning curve*, Choice (A), shows early performance that gradually declines over practice. A *positively accelerated learning curve*, Choice (B), is one in which early performance outcomes are low, but they gradually improve. Choice (D) isn't an example of the formal types of learning curves.

130. **B.** Choice (B) is correct because in *vestibule training*, employees are removed from the main production line and trained on real equipment.

On-the-job training (Choice [A]) wouldn't solve the workflow issue, and classroom simulation (Choice [C]) or offsite training (Choice [D]) may not allow for equipment simulation.

131. **C.** The correct answer is Choice (C) because the employee is given the opportunity to work through her motivation issues and apply her talent.

Discipline, Choice (A), is a form of training, but it may not lead to successful retention of said talent. Choices (B) and (D) address her abilities, which isn't the training need.

132. **A.** A *fishbone diagram* is a helpful problem-solving tool that captures common issues, such as man, material, or machines, which makes Choice (A) the correct answer.

A *Pareto chart* (Choice [B]) graphically represents the 80/20 rule, which states that 20 percent of the defects cause 80 percent of the issues. A *stratification chart* (Choice [C]) breaks down a problem into its components. A *histogram* (Choice [D]) seeks to find patterns of issues.

133. **B.** A *Pareto chart* graphically represents the 80/20 rule, which approximates that 20 percent of the defects cause 80 percent of the issues.

Vendor weakness (Choice [A]) is unknown without more information, as is a lack of quality assurance (Choice [C]). The Peter Principle (Choice [D]) states that employees are promoted up to their highest levels of inefficiencies, which doesn't apply here.

134. **A.** Offering your high-potential employees more challenging work gives them the opportunity to use their talents.

Choices (B) and (D) can be replicated elsewhere and therefore don't serve a retention need. Choice (C) isn't available due to the company's flat-line structure with low opportunity for advancement.

135. **C.** Running a pilot program allows the training designers to evaluate the relevance of the content.

Summative evaluations, Choice (D), occur after training and include Choices (A) and (B).

136. **D.** Interviewing the employees and managers will give Tanya a good idea of what to do and what not to do in the design of performance management.

Choices (A) and (C) both are incorrect as first steps, although they may prove to be helpful later in the process. Choice (B) would be redundant because she already has executive direction in the form of the strategic initiative.

137. **B.** Stereotypes such as these that executives have said may be present and unaccounted for in the workplace. Although careful navigation is recommended to avoid the appearance of discriminatory practices, serving to change the attitudes of the workforce will help.

Choices (A), (C), and (D) don't adequately address the stereotype.

138. **C.** A *nondisclosure agreement* binds an employee to protect confidential information for a period of time.

An *arbitration agreement* (Choice [A]) binds an employee to an alternative dispute resolution, whereas a *noncompete agreement* (Choice [B]) requires an employee to not directly compete with the business should she leave. The examples aren't objectives of the Fair Credit Reporting Act (Choice [D]).

139. **A.** Random drug screening is advisable when required by law (such as for commercial drivers), making Choice (A) the best answer.

Choice (B) is known as a return-to-work test and isn't unannounced. Reasonable suspicion testing, Choice (C), is used when a trained supervisor suspects an employee is under the influence. *Blanket testing*, Choice (D), is used to regularly test all employees.

140. B. Although public workers are entitled to workers' compensation benefits, state laws mostly govern private employers regarding coverage.

Choices (A), (C), and (D) are false.

141. C. The Occupational Safety and Health Administration (OSHA) estimates that an employer can expect a six-time return on the investment of a single dollar into an IIPP, making Choice (C) the correct answer.

142. A. Employers who have high injury rates will more effectively eliminate hazards if they're properly identified, making Choice (A) the correct answer.

Hiring a safety consultant (Choice [B]) or outsourcing the employees (Choice [D]) doesn't eliminate the risk. Lockout/tag-out (Choice [C]) may be an appropriate solution for some, but not all, hazards.

143. A. Arbini Winery transfers the risk to the insurance company by purchasing Employment Practices Liability Insurance (ELPI).

In Choices (B) and (C), the company attempts to minimize or avoid the risk altogether. In Choice (D), the company decides to accept the risk.

144. C. Because the injury occurred in the work environment while changing from uniforms, which was a condition of employment, and the treatment received went beyond first aid, this injury is recordable.

Choices (A), (B), and (D) are false statements.

145. C. OSHA standards require that employers provide gear and training to workers that come into contact with hazardous conditions at work. It isn't always necessary to hire workers with experience, Choice (A), and close supervision by management, Choice (B), isn't realistic.

146. D. The FLSA defines an employee's workweek as seven consecutive 24-hour periods.

147. C. The option that answers both parts of the question is Choice (C). According to the Fair Labor Standards Act, 16-year-olds may work in most non-hazardous jobs, whereas for jobs declared hazardous by the Secretary of Labor, the individual must be at least 18. Younger workers from the age of 12 to 15 are able to work on a limited basis under the FLSA.

148. D. The Portal-to-Portal Act has four factors to use when determining compensable time in attending training programs. These factors are

Attendance is outside of regular working hours.

Attendance is truly voluntary.

The course or seminar isn't directly related to an employee's job.

The employee doesn't produce any work as the result of attendance.

149. B. The Portal-to-Portal Act requires payment for time spent in training if an employee is led to believe that his work or status would be affected by not attending.

Employee rights under Title VII (Choice [A]) are related to protected class characteristics. The question doesn't give you enough information for Choice (C) to be correct because you don't know how many hours Chris worked that week. Choice (D) is simply false.

150. **C.** A *top-hat plan* is a type of executive retirement plan, making Choice (C) the correct answer.

It isn't based on organizational performance, Choice (A). Depending on the type of plan offered, it may be funded completely by the employer, making Choice (B) incorrect, and it isn't a part of stock ownership, Choice (D).

151. **B.** *Job pricing* occurs when a new job is created or an existing job is changed to establish wage ranges that are in line with the market.

Job analysis (Choice [A]) is part of creating a job in general, and *job ranking* (Choice [C]) compares the value of jobs to one another. *Point factoring* (Choice [D]) is a method used to classify jobs on an organizational basis.

152. **A.** *Pay compression* occurs when there is a small difference in pay between employees despite tenure, education, or skills, making Choice (A) the correct answer.

The question referred to the external labor market, not the internal pay scales, making Choices (B) and (C) incorrect. Cost-of-living adjustments, Choice (D), aren't based on skill sets or the availability of talent.

153. **A.** To avoid pay compression, you should recommend to your employer regular wage surveys to increase retention and ensure equity to market conditions, making Choice (A) the correct answer.

Pay raises (Choice [B]), pay freezes (Choice [C]), and cost-of-living adjustments (Choice [D]) won't adequately address the avoidance of pay compression in the future.

154. **A.** Young companies often don't have the cash to pay top wages for talent, and as such, make good use of equity ownership as a recruiting and retention strategy.

Companies in a growth stage (Choice [B]) are more likely to focus on pay/benefits that improve retention of key workers. Companies in the maturity stage (Choice [C]) are better positioned cash-wise to offer higher base wages without the need to sacrifice equity. Equity compensation when an organization is in decline (Choice [D]) wouldn't be an attractive option for new employees.

155. **D.** Workers' compensation insurance is required by law, whereas retirement plans are voluntary, not regulated until they're offered.

156. **B.** The best answer is Choice (B). Issues of compensation equity focus on both the perceived and actual fairness of outcomes.

Ethics in this case is a matter of debate depending on the job worth (Choice [A]), and the question doesn't have enough information to determine whether the practice is either discriminatory (Choice [C]) or illegal (Choice [D]).

157. **C.** Perceptions of fairness, although not reality, often drive whether or not employees are satisfied with their pay.

Choices (A), (B), and (D) are all examples of fairness in outcomes based on job- or self-worth.

158. **A.** The Employee Retirement Income Security Act (ERISA) requires that employees be allowed immediate access to their own contributions but does allow a vesting schedule for employer-contributed funds, depending upon the type of plan selected.

159. **B.** Sales commissions can be especially difficult to track and manage for large organizations, making the use of incentive compensation outsourcing a viable option.

The board of directors or a compensation committee often determines executive compensation (Choice [A]). *Piece-rate pay* (Choice [C]) is a measure tied to manufacturing productivity. *Exempt* (Choice [D]) is an attribute of responsibilities more than pay practices.

160. **D.** Outsourcing compensation and benefits responsibilities is becoming increasingly popular. Duties commonly outsourced include supporting open enrollment, creating summary plan descriptions (SPD), and complying with COBRA requirements.

161. **A.** The National Labor Relations Board (NLRB) considers the use of social media by employees to discuss wages and working conditions a concerted (coordinated) protected activity.

It isn't a violation of an employee's freedom of speech, Choice (B), because employers can prohibit some discussion as it relates to trade secrets or other confidential information, nor is it a violation of their right to privacy, Choice (C). Choice (D) is false.

162. **D.** The National Labor Relations Board (NLRB) found that cautioning employees about being tricked into divulging confidential information doesn't violate employee rights to engage in protected activity.

163. **C.** Because the complaint was about safety conditions, Choice (C) is correct. The construction company settled and offered back pay and reinstatement, which all employees declined.

164. **C.** Fostering an open, inclusive work environment that takes into account employee opinions and needs is the foundation of union-avoidance strategies.

Although an open door policy (Choice [A]) would help, it doesn't guarantee that policy is in practice, making it not as strong as Choice (C). A prohibition against distributing leaflets (Choice [B]) must be very broad to avoid a ULP charge, and offering higher pay rates (Choice [D]) doesn't address the root cause of union organizing.

165. **D.** An employer may be liable for a subordinate's bias even if it's unaware of it under the *cat's paw* doctrine. As such, it's advised that HR conduct its own independent investigation prior to taking employment action.

Respondeat superior Choice (A), is a common law doctrine that stands for the company being responsible for the actions of its supervisors. In constructive discharge, Choice (B), an employee quit his job due to a hostile work environment. Executive order (EO) 11246, Choice (C), is the benchmark presidential order prohibiting employment discrimination.

166. **B.** Known as *ex parte*, it's generally impermissible for a party to a disagreement to be deprived of its ability to defend its position, making Choice (B) the correct answer.

A *toll*, Choice (A), means that the time on the statute of limitations has run out or has been suspended. *In absentia*, Choice (C), refers to a decision being made in the absence of a relevant party to a contract or dispute. A *precedent*, Choice (D), is set based on previous court decisions.

167. **A.** Although many attorneys recommend only giving dates of employment, title, and salary history, the best defense against a claim of defamation is factual information. For this reason, Choice (A) is the most suitable.

168. **B.** The statutory exception to at-will employment protects employees from being terminated for a discriminatory reason as set forth in equal opportunity legislation.

A *contract exception* (Choice [A]) occurs when there is a violation of an employment agreement. The *public policy exception* (Choice [C]) suspends at-will employment for employees who refuse to break the law or for filing a workers' comp claim. The duty of good faith and fair dealing (Choice [D]) excepts at-will employment when an employer terminates an employee for an unfair or unethical reason, such as wanting to avoid the payment of a sales commission.

169. **C.** In *constructive discharge,* a supervisor makes working conditions so hostile or unpleasant that the employee feels he or she has no other choice than to quit.

Discrimination (Choice [A]) occurs when an employee is treated adversely based on a protected class condition. *Harassment* (Choice [B]) exists when an employee is subjected to sexual or hostile working conditions. *Respondeat superior* (Choice [D]) is a legal condition in which employers are held responsible for their employees' actions.

170. **A.** The best answer is Choice (A). Having a written policy that communicates standards of behavior is often an employer's effort at compliance with labor law.

A policy doesn't change employee behavior, Choice (B), directly or improve performance, nor is it the place for written standard operating procedures (SOP), Choice (C). Employment policies, Choice (D), may provide general guidelines for employee behavior, but it's not the main purpose for having these policies.

171. **C.** True performance management occurs on a regular basis both on the job and through formal reviews, making Choice (C) the correct answer. The other options, although important facets to a total performance management system, are less important in the behavior management of people.

172. **C.** Employees who feel valued and engaged will have a desire to learn, both on the job and through more formal training programs.

This leads to looking forward to being at work and on time (Choice [A]), regular attendance at meetings (Choice [B]), and a feeling of job security (Choice [D]).

173. **B.** In this example, Choice (B) is most likely to retain employees.

Having a crystal ball is impossible for employers; therefore, HR professionals need to have tools at their disposal to help address issues before employees leave. In this case, a survey of department employees may have identified the travel issue, allowing for creative problem-solving and a solution, such as job rotation (Choice [D]). An annual review (Choice [C]) or complaint system ([A]) wouldn't adequately address this issue.

174. **B.** A *performance improvement plan* gives employees tools and feedback that are geared toward successful behavior modification.

A PIP and discipline both provide legally defensible documentation when done properly (Choices [A] and [D]), and it isn't necessarily true that employees are more receptive to performance feedback via a PIP, as in Choice (C).

175. **B.** The best answer is Choice (B). The ability to observe and measure behavior allows for intervention strategies to be developed but doesn't in and of itself correct (Choice [A]), change (Choice [C]), or modify (Choice [D]), the behavior.

Answer Key for Practice Exam I

1.	A2, B1, C3	31.	A	61.	C	91.	B	121.	D	151.	B
2.	B	32.	D	62.	B	92.	A	122.	C	152.	A
3.	D	33.	D	63.	C	93.	A	123.	A	153.	A
4.	D	34.	B	64.	A	94.	B	124.	A	154.	A
5.	A	35.	A	65.	D	95.	A	125.	B	155.	D
6.	B1, C2, A3	36.	A3, B2, C1	66.	B	96.	B	126.	C	156.	B
7.	A	37.	C	67.	D	97.	D	127.	A	157.	C
8.	C	38.	D	68.	A	98.	A	128.	B	158.	A
9.	A	39.	B	69.	D	99.	A	129.	C	159.	B
10.	B	40.	C	70.	C	100.	C	130.	B	160.	D
11.	D	41.	D	71.	C	101.	B	131.	C	161.	A
12.	C	42.	A	72.	B	102.	C	132.	A	162.	D
13.	A	43.	D	73.	C	103.	A	133.	B	163.	C
14.	B	44.	C	74.	A	104.	D	134.	A	164.	C
15.	A	45.	D	75.	D	105.	AC1, BDE2	135.	C	165.	D
16.	C	46.	B	76.	B	106.	B	136.	D	166.	B
17.	A	47.	D	77.	C	107.	B	137.	B	167.	A
18.	D	48.	A	78.	A	108.	B	138.	C	168.	B
19.	B	49.	B	79.	B	109.	C	139.	A	169.	C
20.	D	50.	C	80.	D	110.	D	140.	B	170.	A
21.	D	51.	C	81.	D	111.	D	141.	C	171.	C
22.	B	52.	C	82.	B	112.	D	142.	A	172.	C
23.	A	53.	A	83.	D	113.	D	143.	A	173.	B
24.	D	54.	C	84.	C	114.	B	144.	C	174.	B
25.	B	55.	C	85.	B	115.	A	145.	C	175.	B
26.	D	56.	C	86.	A	116.	B	146.	D		
27.	D	57.	A	87.	A	117.	A	147.	C		
28.	A	58.	D	88.	B	118.	C	148.	D		
29.	C	59.	C	89.	D	119.	A	149.	B		
30.	B	60.	B	90.	C	120.	D	150.	C		

Chapter 19

Using Your Skill Set: SPHR Practice Exam

L ike a professional athlete, you can train all year, but the moment of truth is all about game day. Practice exams are one of the most important tools for studying, and this chapter includes 175 questions of exam-level items to use as a dry run.

These questions are designed to be difficult because the SPHR exam is for a senior HR leader. Be mindful of the time constraints of about a minute per question, but also be sure to be thoughtful about your answers.

You may want to use a blank piece of paper to log your answers so you can take the test more than once, or you can use the following bubble answer sheet. Check out Chapter 2 for more ideas on how to use practice exams for maximum effect. You can also go online at www.dummies.com/go/ phrsphrexam for an additional SPHR practice test.

Answer Sheet for SPHR Practice Exam

1. Ⓐ Ⓑ Ⓒ Ⓓ	36. Ⓐ Ⓑ Ⓒ Ⓓ	71. Ⓐ Ⓑ Ⓒ Ⓓ	106. Ⓐ Ⓑ Ⓒ Ⓓ	141. Ⓐ Ⓑ Ⓒ Ⓓ
2. Ⓐ Ⓑ Ⓒ Ⓓ	37. Ⓐ Ⓑ Ⓒ Ⓓ	72. Ⓐ Ⓑ Ⓒ Ⓓ	107. Ⓐ Ⓑ Ⓒ Ⓓ	142. Ⓐ Ⓑ Ⓒ Ⓓ
3. Ⓐ Ⓑ Ⓒ Ⓓ	38. Ⓐ Ⓑ Ⓒ Ⓓ	73. Ⓐ Ⓑ Ⓒ Ⓓ	108. Ⓐ Ⓑ Ⓒ Ⓓ	143. Ⓐ Ⓑ Ⓒ Ⓓ
4. Ⓐ Ⓑ Ⓒ Ⓓ	39. Ⓐ Ⓑ Ⓒ Ⓓ	74. Ⓐ Ⓑ Ⓒ Ⓓ	109. Ⓐ Ⓑ Ⓒ Ⓓ	144. Ⓐ Ⓑ Ⓒ Ⓓ
5. Ⓐ Ⓑ Ⓒ Ⓓ	40. Ⓐ Ⓑ Ⓒ Ⓓ	75. Ⓐ Ⓑ Ⓒ Ⓓ	110. Ⓐ Ⓑ Ⓒ Ⓓ	145. Ⓐ Ⓑ Ⓒ Ⓓ
6. Ⓐ Ⓑ Ⓒ Ⓓ	41. Ⓐ Ⓑ Ⓒ Ⓓ	76. Ⓐ Ⓑ Ⓒ Ⓓ	111. Ⓐ Ⓑ Ⓒ Ⓓ	146. Ⓐ Ⓑ Ⓒ Ⓓ
7. Ⓐ Ⓑ Ⓒ Ⓓ	42. Ⓐ Ⓑ Ⓒ Ⓓ	77. Ⓐ Ⓑ Ⓒ Ⓓ	112. Ⓐ Ⓑ Ⓒ Ⓓ	147. Ⓐ Ⓑ Ⓒ Ⓓ
8. Ⓐ Ⓑ Ⓒ Ⓓ	43. Ⓐ Ⓑ Ⓒ Ⓓ	78. Ⓐ Ⓑ Ⓒ Ⓓ	113. Ⓐ Ⓑ Ⓒ Ⓓ	148. Ⓐ Ⓑ Ⓒ Ⓓ
9. Ⓐ Ⓑ Ⓒ Ⓓ	44. Ⓐ Ⓑ Ⓒ Ⓓ	79. Ⓐ Ⓑ Ⓒ Ⓓ	114. Ⓐ Ⓑ Ⓒ Ⓓ	149. Ⓐ Ⓑ Ⓒ Ⓓ
10. Ⓐ Ⓑ Ⓒ Ⓓ	45. _____	80. Ⓐ Ⓑ Ⓒ Ⓓ	115. Ⓐ Ⓑ Ⓒ Ⓓ	150. Ⓐ Ⓑ Ⓒ Ⓓ
11. Ⓐ Ⓑ Ⓒ Ⓓ	46. Ⓐ Ⓑ Ⓒ Ⓓ	81. Ⓐ Ⓑ Ⓒ Ⓓ	116. Ⓐ Ⓑ Ⓒ Ⓓ	151. Ⓐ Ⓑ Ⓒ Ⓓ
12. Ⓐ Ⓑ Ⓒ Ⓓ	47. Ⓐ Ⓑ Ⓒ Ⓓ	82. Ⓐ Ⓑ Ⓒ Ⓓ	117. Ⓐ Ⓑ Ⓒ Ⓓ	152. Ⓐ Ⓑ Ⓒ Ⓓ
13. Ⓐ Ⓑ Ⓒ Ⓓ	48. Ⓐ Ⓑ Ⓒ Ⓓ	83. Ⓐ Ⓑ Ⓒ Ⓓ	118. Ⓐ Ⓑ Ⓒ Ⓓ	153. Ⓐ Ⓑ Ⓒ Ⓓ
14. Ⓐ Ⓑ Ⓒ Ⓓ	49. Ⓐ Ⓑ Ⓒ Ⓓ	84. Ⓐ Ⓑ Ⓒ Ⓓ	119. Ⓐ Ⓑ Ⓒ Ⓓ	154. Ⓐ Ⓑ Ⓒ Ⓓ
15. Ⓐ Ⓑ Ⓒ Ⓓ	50. Ⓐ Ⓑ Ⓒ Ⓓ	85. Ⓐ Ⓑ Ⓒ Ⓓ	120. Ⓐ Ⓑ Ⓒ Ⓓ	155. Ⓐ Ⓑ Ⓒ Ⓓ
16. Ⓐ Ⓑ Ⓒ Ⓓ	51. Ⓐ Ⓑ Ⓒ Ⓓ	86. Ⓐ Ⓑ Ⓒ Ⓓ	121. Ⓐ Ⓑ Ⓒ Ⓓ	156. Ⓐ Ⓑ Ⓒ Ⓓ
17. Ⓐ Ⓑ Ⓒ Ⓓ	52. Ⓐ Ⓑ Ⓒ Ⓓ	87. Ⓐ Ⓑ Ⓒ Ⓓ	122. Ⓐ Ⓑ Ⓒ Ⓓ	157. Ⓐ Ⓑ Ⓒ Ⓓ
18. Ⓐ Ⓑ Ⓒ Ⓓ	53. Ⓐ Ⓑ Ⓒ Ⓓ	88. Ⓐ Ⓑ Ⓒ Ⓓ	123. Ⓐ Ⓑ Ⓒ Ⓓ	158. Ⓐ Ⓑ Ⓒ Ⓓ
19. Ⓐ Ⓑ Ⓒ Ⓓ	54. Ⓐ Ⓑ Ⓒ Ⓓ	89. Ⓐ Ⓑ Ⓒ Ⓓ	124. _____	159. Ⓐ Ⓑ Ⓒ Ⓓ
20. Ⓐ Ⓑ Ⓒ Ⓓ	55. Ⓐ Ⓑ Ⓒ Ⓓ	90. Ⓐ Ⓑ Ⓒ Ⓓ	125. Ⓐ Ⓑ Ⓒ Ⓓ	160. Ⓐ Ⓑ Ⓒ Ⓓ
21. Ⓐ Ⓑ Ⓒ Ⓓ	56. Ⓐ Ⓑ Ⓒ Ⓓ	91. Ⓐ Ⓑ Ⓒ Ⓓ	126. Ⓐ Ⓑ Ⓒ Ⓓ	161. Ⓐ Ⓑ Ⓒ Ⓓ
22. Ⓐ Ⓑ Ⓒ Ⓓ	57. Ⓐ Ⓑ Ⓒ Ⓓ	92. Ⓐ Ⓑ Ⓒ Ⓓ	127. Ⓐ Ⓑ Ⓒ Ⓓ	162. Ⓐ Ⓑ Ⓒ Ⓓ
23. Ⓐ Ⓑ Ⓒ Ⓓ	58. Ⓐ Ⓑ Ⓒ Ⓓ	93. Ⓐ Ⓑ Ⓒ Ⓓ	128. Ⓐ Ⓑ Ⓒ Ⓓ	163. Ⓐ Ⓑ Ⓒ Ⓓ
24. Ⓐ Ⓑ Ⓒ Ⓓ	59. Ⓐ Ⓑ Ⓒ Ⓓ	94. Ⓐ Ⓑ Ⓒ Ⓓ	129. Ⓐ Ⓑ Ⓒ Ⓓ	164. Ⓐ Ⓑ Ⓒ Ⓓ
25. Ⓐ Ⓑ Ⓒ Ⓓ	60. Ⓐ Ⓑ Ⓒ Ⓓ	95. Ⓐ Ⓑ Ⓒ Ⓓ	130. Ⓐ Ⓑ Ⓒ Ⓓ	165. Ⓐ Ⓑ Ⓒ Ⓓ
26. Ⓐ Ⓑ Ⓒ Ⓓ	61. Ⓐ Ⓑ Ⓒ Ⓓ	96. Ⓐ Ⓑ Ⓒ Ⓓ	131. Ⓐ Ⓑ Ⓒ Ⓓ	166. Ⓐ Ⓑ Ⓒ Ⓓ
27. Ⓐ Ⓑ Ⓒ Ⓓ	62. Ⓐ Ⓑ Ⓒ Ⓓ	97. Ⓐ Ⓑ Ⓒ Ⓓ	132. Ⓐ Ⓑ Ⓒ Ⓓ	167. Ⓐ Ⓑ Ⓒ Ⓓ
28. Ⓐ Ⓑ Ⓒ Ⓓ	63. Ⓐ Ⓑ Ⓒ Ⓓ	98. Ⓐ Ⓑ Ⓒ Ⓓ	133. Ⓐ Ⓑ Ⓒ Ⓓ	168. Ⓐ Ⓑ Ⓒ Ⓓ
29. Ⓐ Ⓑ Ⓒ Ⓓ	64. Ⓐ Ⓑ Ⓒ Ⓓ	99. Ⓐ Ⓑ Ⓒ Ⓓ	134. Ⓐ Ⓑ Ⓒ Ⓓ	169. Ⓐ Ⓑ Ⓒ Ⓓ
30. Ⓐ Ⓑ Ⓒ Ⓓ	65. Ⓐ Ⓑ Ⓒ Ⓓ	100. Ⓐ Ⓑ Ⓒ Ⓓ	135. Ⓐ Ⓑ Ⓒ Ⓓ	170. Ⓐ Ⓑ Ⓒ Ⓓ
31. Ⓐ Ⓑ Ⓒ Ⓓ	66. Ⓐ Ⓑ Ⓒ Ⓓ	101. Ⓐ Ⓑ Ⓒ Ⓓ	136. Ⓐ Ⓑ Ⓒ Ⓓ	171. Ⓐ Ⓑ Ⓒ Ⓓ
32. Ⓐ Ⓑ Ⓒ Ⓓ	67. Ⓐ Ⓑ Ⓒ Ⓓ	102. Ⓐ Ⓑ Ⓒ Ⓓ	137. Ⓐ Ⓑ Ⓒ Ⓓ	172. Ⓐ Ⓑ Ⓒ Ⓓ
33. Ⓐ Ⓑ Ⓒ Ⓓ	68. Ⓐ Ⓑ Ⓒ Ⓓ	103. Ⓐ Ⓑ Ⓒ Ⓓ	138. Ⓐ Ⓑ Ⓒ Ⓓ	173. Ⓐ Ⓑ Ⓒ Ⓓ
34. Ⓐ Ⓑ Ⓒ Ⓓ	69. Ⓐ Ⓑ Ⓒ Ⓓ	104. Ⓐ Ⓑ Ⓒ Ⓓ	139. Ⓐ Ⓑ Ⓒ Ⓓ	174. Ⓐ Ⓑ Ⓒ Ⓓ
35. Ⓐ Ⓑ Ⓒ Ⓓ	70. Ⓐ Ⓑ Ⓒ Ⓓ	105. Ⓐ Ⓑ Ⓒ Ⓓ	140. Ⓐ Ⓑ Ⓒ Ⓓ	175. Ⓐ Ⓑ Ⓒ Ⓓ

TIME: 3 hours for 175 questions

DIRECTIONS: Answer the following questions by selecting the correct answer from the options. You may only select one correct answer.

1. What is the median number of the following series of values?

   13, 13, 14, 16, 18, 21, 24
   (A) 13
   (B) 14
   (C) 16
   (D) 18

2. A company decides to video employee testimonials, asking them why they love working for the business. These videos will be posted on the company intranet for use as a recruiting tool. They are engaged in which business practice?
   (A) Marketing
   (B) Sales
   (C) Branding
   (D) Social media

3. Tailgate safety training conducted by a supervisor is the best example of which of the following?
   (A) Downward communication
   (B) Upward communication
   (C) Cross-functional communication
   (D) Compliance training

4. An HR professional is using a staffing agency exclusively because it gives her tickets to major sporting events four times a year. This is an example of what?
   (A) A discriminatory practice
   (B) Unethical behavior
   (C) Illegal activity
   (D) Conflict of interest

5. An ice cream company that has vendor criteria for the humane treatment of dairy cows is practicing what?
   (A) Compliance with the FDA
   (B) Food safety standards
   (C) Social responsibility
   (D) Corporate governance

6. How is a nominal group technique different from a Delphi group?
   (A) Nominal groups never meet face-to-face, whereas Delphi members do.
   (B) Delphi groups never meet face-to-face, whereas nominal members do.
   (C) Delphi members share their findings together, whereas nominal groups keep their information private.
   (D) Nothing. Nominal is another term for Delphi.

7. The CEO and CFO of a major computer equipment manufacturer in Florida were charged by the SEC for lying to auditors and shareholders about their internal financial controls. Under which of the following were they most likely charged?

   (A) Sherman AntiTrust

   (B) GAAP

   (C) Sarbanes-Oxley

   (D) Rule of law

8. A company with a cost-leadership strategy will MOST likely engage in which of the following HR activities?

   (A) Recruit robustly for R&D personnel

   (B) Have a long planning horizon

   (C) Offer less training than its counterparts

   (D) Promote from within

9. What calculation will tell you when a training initiative will begin to pay off?

   (A) Cost-benefit analysis

   (B) Break-even analysis

   (C) Return on investment

   (D) All of the above

10. The amount of time a company will look forward when building a strategic plan is called what?

    (A) Scanning timeline

    (B) Future forecast

    (C) Projection schedule

    (D) Planning horizon

11. Which of the following is LEAST likely to occur as the result of downsizing?

    (A) Lower operating costs

    (B) Improved productivity

    (C) Lower employee morale

    (D) Layoffs

12. Calculate the turnover rate for a company with 500 employees that had 50 FTE separate over the course of one year.

    (A) 5%

    (B) 10%

    (C) 15%

    (D) 50%

13. RFC Producers has decided to move its operations to a new city. It was able to find a warehouse location that had been the site of a previous distributor, but it's going to require some major capital improvements. Which of the following statements is TRUE?

    (A) This is a brownfield operation.

    (B) This is a greenfield operation.

    (C) The company will have to pay less in city taxes because it is making improvements.

    (D) The company will have to pay more in city taxes because it will need more infrastructure.

14. A manufacturer decides to offer its items for sale through a network of distributors. Which of the 4 Ps of marketing does this represent?

    (A) Product

    (B) Placement

    (C) Price

    (D) Promotion

15. The more employees a supervisor manages, the wider the _____?

    (A) span of control

    (B) sphere of influence

    (C) job responsibilities

    (D) pay gap

16. A system that is designed to integrate multiple business functions, such as HR, product planning, and sales, is called a what?

    (A) HRIS

    (B) ERP

    (C) HRMS

    (D) IMS

17. An HR manager develops a document that outlines the merit of transferring corporate training to an LMS. She includes market data, a cost-benefit analysis, and a list of the relevant training topics that the system would deliver. She is presenting which of the following?

    (A) Business case

    (B) Business plan

    (C) Balanced scorecard

    (D) Training assessment

18. Which element of the strategic planning process involves determining threats in the external environment?

    (A) Planning

    (B) Implementation

    (C) Evaluation

    (D) Scanning

19. What is the purpose of a transition stay bonus?

    (A) To reward employees who aren't laid off as the result of a merger

    (B) To offset the financial pressure of a layoff for a predetermined period of time

    (C) To reward longevity to exiting employees

    (D) To encourage workers in eliminated positions to remain for a period of time

20. ABC Industries has decided to start a new business in a foreign country. In addition to the new building, the company will be adding hundreds of long-term jobs. This is known as what?

    (A) Joint venture

    (B) Enterprise risk management

    (C) Greenfield investment

    (D) Corporate task

21. The DOD is the primary customer of defense contractors. This is an example of which of Porter's five forces?

   (A) Buyer power

   (B) Supplier power

   (C) Threat of new entrants

   (D) Rivalry

22. Buyer and supplier power are examples of what type of strategic force that affects a company's ability to compete?

   (A) Internal

   (B) Driving

   (C) Critical

   (D) External

23. What number in the following sequence is the mode?

   4 3 5 4 4 3 2

   (A) 4

   (B) 3

   (C) 5

   (D) 2

24. What is the average number of the following series of values?

   4 3 5 4 4 3 2

   (A) 4.25

   (B) 3.57

   (C) 4.17

   (D) 2

25. In which of the following ways might a company save money through a merger?

   (A) The elimination of duplicate jobs

   (B) Shared marketing materials

   (C) Co-branding

   (D) The merging of budgets

26. Outsourcing the recruiting function of human resources BEST serves which organization?

   (A) A small start-up

   (B) A company in a growth phase

   (C) An established company with a robust recruiting budget

   (D) A nonprofit organization

27. Which of the following is correlated to high employee morale?

   (A) A small number of temporary staffers

   (B) A well-used employee suggestion system

   (C) A high number of employee referrals

   (D) Low injury rates

28. Corporate America, Inc. is seeking to expand into the Pacific Rim starting with an outpost in Japan. The company wants to staff this location with the MOST qualified talent. This is an example of which type of staffing strategy?

(A) Ethnocentric

(B) Geocentric

(C) Polycentric

(D) Country-neutral

29. What are host-country nationals?

(A) Employees who are hired for jobs in their own country

(B) Employees working outside of their home country

(C) Employees who are from neither the host nor the home country

(D) None of the above

30. What is another term for a parent-country national?

(A) Inpatriate

(B) Expatriate

(C) Local national

(D) Patriot

31. Which of the following activities is a strategy for managing a company that must downsize?

(A) Attrition

(B) Hiring freezes

(C) Early retirement buyouts

(D) All of the above

32. A new hire received a TNC email from the USCIS. What does he need to do next?

(A) Provide approved documentation within 72 hours.

(B) Contact the employer for a Further Action Notice.

(C) Contact USCIS to contest the notification.

(D) Visit the necessary offices to correct documentation.

33. The fundamental factor of the Uniform Guidelines on Employee Selection Procedures is that all tests must be what?

(A) Job related

(B) Nondiscriminatory

(C) Predictive of success

(D) Legally defensible

34. What option would be the MOST effective at measuring an applicant's aptitude for mathematical reasoning?

(A) A high-school diploma

(B) An online general math test

(C) Interview questions that ask applicants to solve equations

(D) A paper-and-pencil test that asks math questions of the type likely to be found on the job

35. Which of the following statements about the ADA is TRUE?

   (A) The ADA requires essential functions of the job to be identified.

   (B) The ADA applies to employers with 25 or more employees.

   (C) The Office of Disability Employment Policy enforces the ADA standards.

   (D) Any person with a disability is entitled to accommodation under the ADA.

36. Which of the following statements is TRUE if an employer asks a female applicant in an interview, "How many children do you have?"

   (A) The employer has discriminated against the applicant based on her family status.

   (B) The employer has violated gender discrimination laws.

   (C) The question is only a problem if the employer doesn't also ask men the same question.

   (D) The employer has not technically violated anti-discrimination laws, but the question may be evidence of intent to discriminate.

37. "This job requires that you like working with people. Do you like working with people?" This interview question is an example of what interviewer error?

   (A) Leading question

   (B) Snap judgment error

   (C) Negative emphasis

   (D) Halo effect

38. Saving money and travel costs while still being effective techniques are advantages to which of the following recruiting methods?

   (A) Virtual interviewing

   (B) College recruiting

   (C) Job fairs

   (D) Online advertising

39. Working at a popular fast-food chain is less attractive now that the chain's food has been linked to overprocessing its menu items. This is an example of what?

   (A) Employer brand

   (B) Product perception

   (C) Marketing efforts

   (D) Unethical business practices

40. Which of the following groups is required to complete an EEO-1 report?

   (A) All private employers

   (B) All public employers

   (C) Private employers with more than 100 employees

   (D) The EEO-1 report is voluntary for employers.

41. A school-to-work transition program is what type of training?

   (A) On-the-job training

   (B) Cooperative training

   (C) Classroom-based training

   (D) An apprenticeship

42. Blended learning is a mix of traditional classroom training and what?

    (A) On-the-job features

    (B) Simulations

    (C) Vestibules

    (D) Online classes

43. If an HR specialist wants to take three months off to teach career skills at inner city schools, which program should you recommend?

    (A) A leave of absence

    (B) A sabbatical leave

    (C) A layoff

    (D) A voluntary resignation with option to rehire

44. A supervisor within your organization gave all of his employees a 3 on a scale of 5 in his performance reviews. Which error did he MOST likely commit?

    (A) Halo

    (B) Horn

    (C) Central tendency

    (D) Bias

45. Match the training term in Column A with its correct example in Column B.

Column A	Column B
(A) Synchronous	(1) The participant watches videos on their own time.
(B) Asynchronous	(2) The participant must be online at a specific time each week.
(C) Self-paced	
(D) Instructor-led	

46. A continuing education strategy for an employee is part of what kind of planning?

    (A) Succession

    (B) Strategic

    (C) Workforce

    (D) Career

47. A student who is able to access online training via videos and discussion boards is engaged in what kind of learning?

    (A) Asynchronous

    (B) Synchronous

    (C) Distance

    (D) Independent

48. Which of the following indicators of employee job satisfaction is present when a retail store clerk is allowed to issue refunds of up to $100 without management approval?

   (A) Job enrichment

   (B) Self-direction

   (C) Autonomy

   (D) Job enlargement

49. Which of the following BEST represents task significance as a job satisfier?

   (A) The level of importance of the job

   (B) The degree to which a job has impact on others

   (C) The amount of authority a worker has in his position

   (D) All of the above

50. What does the vertical axis of the learning curve represent?

   (A) Experience

   (B) Education

   (C) Learning

   (D) Time lapse

51. The system designed to develop, implement, and measure employee performance is called what?

   (A) Human resource development

   (B) Performance appraisal

   (C) Feedback

   (D) Performance management

52. Which demographic does flexible scheduling BEST serve?

   (A) Older workers

   (B) Employees with families

   (C) Women

   (D) All of the above

53. Which of the following is NOT a goal of a performance review?

   (A) Discussing past performance

   (B) Disciplining the employee

   (C) Discussing future performance through development needs/wants

   (D) Tying performance to pay increases

54. A learning management system is BEST described as what?

   (A) A learning portal

   (B) Training receptacle

   (C) Company intranet

   (D) Human resource information system

55. An employee's desire to be well respected by others is an example of which of Maslow's levels on his hierarchy of needs?

   (A) Physiological

   (B) Self-esteem

   (C) Belonging

   (D) Self-actualization

56. An employee believes that he is the master of his own destiny. He very likely has a high what?

   (A) Opinion of his talents

   (B) Level of confidence

   (C) Internal locus of control

   (D) Context

57. A group of forklift drivers who had been with a company for five years recently discovered that their salary rates are only 5 percent higher than the newly hired. HR explains that it's because the market rates have substantially increased due to the shortage of qualified workers. What has occurred?

   (A) Pay disparity

   (B) Age discrimination

   (C) Pay compression

   (D) Broadbanding

58. Executive perquisites are generally _____ items.

   (A) noncash

   (B) taxable

   (C) transportation-related

   (D) deferred compensation

59. The Lilly Ledbetter Act established that the time period of 180 days for filing a charge of pay discrimination must what?

   (A) Begin on the initial day the wage discrimination occurs

   (B) Renew every time an employee is paid

   (C) Begin on the employee's last day of work for wages

   (D) Begin on the employee's first day of work

60. A worker who sets her own hours, works for multiple customers, and has a business license is MOST likely a what?

   (A) Exempt employee

   (B) Nonexempt employee

   (C) Independent contractor

   (D) Business owner

61. A company that has a wide range of employee benefits needs should consider which of the following benefits packages?

   (A) The lowest priced

   (B) The option with the best ratio of cost to benefits

   (C) A cafeteria plan

   (D) A cash incentive to not take the company plan

62. A company is experiencing issues with employee attendance on Mondays and Fridays. Which pay-for-performance strategy is MOST likely to help with this problem?

   (A) Make a component of pay-for-performance tied to attendance.

   (B) Discipline employees who violate the attendance policy.

   (C) Reduce the team-based incentive for groups with less than perfect attendance.

   (D) Eliminate gainsharing as a possible option until overall attendance improves.

63. Which of the following is one of the primary reasons the FLSA was passed?

   (A) To provide employees with safe work

   (B) To discourage employers from requiring or abusing overtime

   (C) To streamline timecard reporting

   (D) To regulate payroll taxes through paycheck deductions

64. An employer requiring employees to sign nondisclosure agreements in order to prevent them from disclosing their pay rates does not have a high degree of what?

   (A) Ethics

   (B) Pay equity

   (C) Pay openness

   (D) Pay honesty

65. A severance benefit that gives an executive two to four times her annual salary in the event of termination is also known as a what?

   (A) Golden boot

   (B) Retirement proposal

   (C) Golden handcuffs

   (D) Golden parachute

66. A company wanting to share ownership with employees to encourage accountability should use which of the following bonus plans?

   (A) Stock options

   (B) Annual bonuses

   (C) Performance incentives

   (D) Perquisites

67. Which of the following benefits is voluntary?

   (A) Workers' compensation

   (B) Retirement

   (C) Social Security

   (D) Disability

68. What is an advantage for employers that utilize lump-sum increases?

   (A) LSIs do not increase overtime costs.

   (B) LSIs can accelerate base wage progression.

   (C) LSIs are easier to track than hourly increases.

   (D) LSIs can increase pension payments.

69. Which of the following types of drug/alcohol screening is both reliable and legally defensible?

   (A) Urine

   (B) Hair

   (C) Breath

   (D) Blood

70. Which strategy would BEST protect worker and customer privacy?

   (A) Appointing a chief privacy officer

   (B) Limiting access to electronic and paper documents

   (C) Training employees on proper use of information

   (D) Having employees and vendors sign confidentiality agreements

71. An employee in good standing who has worked for a company for 20 years may not be separated under the employment at-will doctrine for what reason?

   (A) Public policy exception

   (B) Duty of good faith and fair dealing

   (C) Statutory rights

   (D) Implied employment contract

72. The duty to bargain in good faith is required of which party?

   (A) The employer

   (B) The union

   (C) The employee

   (D) Both the employer and the union

73. In the *NLRB vs. Weingarten*, what was the outcome?

   (A) The Supreme Court ruled that union members had a right to representation in a disciplinary session.

   (B) The Supreme Court held that no union presence was required at meetings that are designed to only investigate employee wrongdoing.

   (C) The Supreme Court ruled that all employees — union or otherwise — are entitled to representation at disciplinary and investigatory meetings.

   (D) The Supreme Court found that Weingarten had done nothing wrong.

74. During a union campaign, a supervisor told his employees that they were not allowed to talk about the union organizing during work, even though they are allowed to talk about other non-work-related items. This is an example of what ULP from the TIPS doctrine?

   (A) Threatening

   (B) Interfering

   (C) Spying

   (D) Promise

75. In a case filed with the EEOC, management repeatedly used a derogatory word to describe the mental illness of a disabled worker, and the worker was eventually terminated as a result of his disability. Which of the following did the EEOC eventually find?

(A) Discriminatory treatment

(B) Wrongful termination

(C) Violation of the ADA

(D) All of the above

76. Which of the following tools is BEST for an employee who needs an easy reminder of product codes when entering orders into the system?

(A) Standard operating procedure

(B) Reference guide

(C) Policy

(D) Work rule

77. How can HR BEST support a positive organizational climate?

(A) Hiring the MOST qualified workers for the job

(B) Surveying employees to gain input on needs

(C) Avoiding unnecessary policies, procedures, and rules

(D) Implementing executive coaching activities

78. A company picnic sign posted on top of an exit safety sign is an example of what OSHA violation?

(A) Serious

(B) Willful

(C) De minimus

(D) Other than serious

79. An employer who wants to avoid a claim of negligent hiring should conduct which of the following?

(A) A background check on applicants

(B) Reference checking of potential workers

(C) School records check to verify education

(D) All of the above

80. An employer with _____ or fewer employees does not have to keep injury and illness records.

(A) three

(B) five

(C) ten

(D) fifteen

81. Which of the following positions is considered an HR generalist?

(A) Safety technician

(B) LOA coordinator

(C) HR manager

(D) Forklift trainer

82. An employee at an insurance brokerage house is a cancer survivor. As a result, she is a strong believer in the products and services that the company offers, especially its survivor benefits and cancer insurance. She is highly invested in her clients. Which of Hofstede's dimensions exists?

    (A) Degree of identification

    (B) Degree of acceptance

    (C) Employee versus work orientation

    (D) Local versus professional orientation

83. Licensing and certification regulations of jobs may be linked to which of the following outcomes?

    (A) Slower economic recovery

    (B) Difficulties finding jobs

    (C) Higher pay rates

    (D) All of the above

84. Which statistical analysis would be MOST useful to calculate the need for employees if sales increase by a set dollar amount?

    (A) Regression analysis

    (B) Staffing ratios

    (C) Simulation models

    (D) Productivity ratios

85. A large dairy organization has a dedicated team that closely follows BEST business practices in quality assurance. Team members must have advanced degrees in dairy or quality, analyze processes, make recommendations, and implement solutions. This team is MOST likely a what?

    (A) Lean team

    (B) Community of experts

    (C) Community of practice

    (D) Center of excellence

86. The MOST important feature to the theory of economic valuation is what?

    (A) Individual preferences and choices

    (B) Market value of a nontangible item

    (C) Supply and demand

    (D) Cost to build

87. A company that uses a corporate code of conduct that includes rules for nonsegregation, fair pay, and global human rights MOST likely has adopted which of the following?

    (A) Nondiscriminatory treatment practices

    (B) Title VII of the Civil Rights Act

    (C) The Global Sullivan Principles

    (D) A greenfield operation

88. What is the relationship between the FMLA and the ADA?

    (A) Both require all employers to offer job-protected leave to affected employees.

    (B) Both govern leave laws for pregnant workers.

    (C) Neither prohibits discrimination based on race or ethnicity.

    (D) Both offer wage replacement for displaced workers.

89. An employee was passed over for a promotion because she had exercised her leave rights under the Family Medical Leave Act. What is the BEST example of the employer's unlawful act?

(A) Retaliation

(B) Interference

(C) Discrimination

(D) Harassment

90. An organization expanding into the Middle East is offering highly competitive salaries for employees who are willing to transfer for a period of three years. Based on the requirements of the foreign country, single women and homosexuals aren't eligible for transfer. What statement is TRUE?

(A) Based on American labor law, this company is in danger of an unlawful discrimination lawsuit.

(B) This company practice is correct because American labor law does not apply in other countries.

(C) Congress allowed for a foreign business exception in which American discrimination laws are suspended if compliance would violate foreign country laws.

(D) This company should not do business in this region due to violations of civil rights.

91. Which statement is TRUE regarding partial public workers such as those paid through Medicaid to care for disabled family members?

(A) They are still required to join the union.

(B) They are not considered government workers.

(C) They may only opt out of paying for purely political union activities.

(D) They do not have to pay union dues.

92. A person who has "an ear to the people" is known as what?

(A) Advocate

(B) Steward

(C) Ombudsman

(D) Arbitrator

93. Of the following, which should be the FIRST response in an organizational crisis?

(A) Protecting a company's financial assets

(B) Responding to media inquiries

(C) Communicating to stakeholders status of response

(D) Reporting to regulatory agencies

94. Reducing expenses and protecting company financial assets are the outcomes of which of the following risk management activities?

(A) Establishing corporate credit policies and objectives

(B) Providing oversight of departmental expenses

(C) Establishing an employee code of conduct

(D) Managing the company budget

95. A medical diagnosis is MOST likely a legitimate request for which HR documentation?

(A) A listing of employee medications for purposes of complying with the company substance abuse program

(B) Documenting history of workers' compensation claims

(C) Certifying leave for a family emergency

(D) Requesting a doctor's certification for ADA LOA of more than three days

96. According to Bennis, which of the following elements is the LEAST important for visionary leadership?

(A) A passion for their work

(B) A focus on the bottom line

(C) The ability to embrace errors

(D) Willingness to take risks

97. Which answer is MOST reflective of a collaborative work environment?

(A) Knowledge workers create, and manual workers execute.

(B) Information flows downward from the executive team.

(C) Each teammate makes knowledge contributions and participates in decision-making.

(D) Access to confidential information is restricted.

98. According to Mintzberg, mentor, disseminator, and spokesperson are examples of which management role?

(A) Interpersonal

(B) Decisional

(C) Informational

(D) Leader

99. Which of the following BEST contributes to the success of an organization that is entering a new competitive market?

(A) The presence of a strategic plan

(B) Executive competencies

(C) HRM policies that align with the corporate mission, vision, and values

(D) The existence of relevant and up-to-date SOPs

100. Shared basic assumptions are BEST described as what?

(A) Tribal knowledge

(B) Brain drain

(C) Cultural forces

(D) Shared responsibilities

101. A culture of problem-solving is a characteristic of what?

(A) Quality programs

(B) Learning organization

(C) Good management

(D) Employee intelligence

102. Although succession plans are necessary for all types of businesses, on which of the following options would the lack of a succession plan have the MOST negative impact?

(A) Small, family-owned businesses

(B) Publicly traded corporations

(C) Multinational corporations

(D) Joint ventures

103. Organizational development activities should focus first and foremost on what?

(A) Financial realities

(B) Employee development

(C) Management development

(D) Respect and inclusion

104. When change occurs in an organization, resistant employees often increase the old, undesirable behaviors. Why does this happen?

(A) All employees fear change.

(B) The company may not have communicated the expectations properly.

(C) The employees have been conditioned (or rewarded) to behave a certain way.

(D) The company did not hire the right people with the right attitudes.

105. An employee is required to work around a hot furnace that heats tools up to above 500 degrees. When he puts on safety gloves, he can handle the hot tools without getting burned. This is an example of which of the following types of reinforcement?

(A) Negative reinforcement

(B) Positive reinforcement

(C) Conditioning

(D) Safety reinforcement

106. Which of the following measures the amount of employee performance improvement as the result of an organizational intervention?

(A) Utility analysis

(B) Cost-benefit analysis

(C) Return on investment

(D) Economic value add

107. Measuring the alignment of nonfinancial performance measurements with a company's strategic plan is BEST reported using which of the following tools?

(A) Quarterly reports

(B) Annual budget

(C) Balanced scorecard

(D) Profit and loss statement

108. Calculate the pay and benefits cost as a percentage of operating expense using this information:

Total number of employees: 30

Annual revenue: $90,000,000

Annual operating expenses: $3,600,000

Total pay and benefits cost: $1,300,000

(A) 20%

(B) 24%

(C) 36%

(D) 38%

109. A company with a decentralized approach to organizational structure is MOST likely to have which of the following?

(A) Foreign subsidiaries

(B) Flat-line structures

(C) Strategic business units

(D) A board of directors

110. You have been tasked with utilizing the Delphi technique to forecast business in the coming fiscal year. What are you MOST likely going to be doing?

(A) Interviewing management and employees

(B) Facilitating information-gathering meetings

(C) Developing a series of questionnaires

(D) All of the above

111. An employer investigating a claim of harassment before terminating an employee and a company collecting financial data to use in a divestiture are examples of which of the following processes?

(A) Legal

(B) Ethical

(C) Due diligence

(D) Disclosure

112. The parent company of a foreign business must have what percent of control in order for it to be considered a subsidiary?

(A) More than 25 percent

(B) More than 50 percent

(C) More than 75 percent

(D) 100 percent

113. A gap analysis is MOST similar to which of the following terms?

(A) Needs assessment

(B) Core competencies

(C) Training needs

(D) Strategic plan

114. MartPro General is a retail giant that has such buying power that suppliers have no choice but to agree to the company's terms. This isn't the case for MartPro's smaller competitors. What is said to exist?

(A) Monopoly

(B) Monopsony

(C) An unfair business practice

(D) Discrimination

115. Which of the following statements about corporate social responsibility is TRUE?

(A) American labor law requires social responsibility.

(B) Ethical leadership creates profit.

(C) Considering all stakeholder needs creates value.

(D) Social responsibility has the MOST impact on the global landscape.

116. Strategy is to change as mission statements are to what?

(A) Fluidity

(B) Consistency

(C) Necessary

(D) Evolving

117. The HR manager of a multinational corporation has been tasked with developing a global training program that creates a shared corporate culture. She begins by surveying top management members at all locations to ask their opinions on what factors would contribute to this outcome. She is engaged in which of the following practices?

(A) Communicating from the top down

(B) Conducting an occupational assessment

(C) Measuring corporate cultural intelligence

(D) Conducting a needs assessment

118. Which of the following is the MOST important critical competency when selecting virtual team members?

(A) Independent

(B) Technically proficient

(C) Cost sensitive

(D) Shared time zones

119. A candidate for an open IT position has successfully completed the first interview. She is now being asked to participate in a series of tests, which includes handling mock troubleshooting calls, coaching others on IT issues, and taking a programming quiz. She is MOST likely going where?

(A) To a staffing agency

(B) To a PEO

(C) To an assessment center

(D) To an occupational clinic

120. Marvin, a Latino VP at an elementary school, was arrested after being accused of inappropriately touching students. While out on bail, the school board decided to place him on administrative leave without pay, which subsequently led to his dismissal. Ultimately the courts found that inappropriate conduct had in fact occurred. Because he had been placed on leave prior to being found guilty, Marvin filed a charge of discrimination with the EEOC. Which of the following is the MOST likely outcome?

(A) The school board's decision was nondiscriminatory because the decision to suspend was based on the underlying conduct, not on the arrest.

(B) The school board's decision was nondiscriminatory because there was no disparate impact.

(C) The school board's decision was found to be discriminatory because employers may not base decisions on arrest records.

(D) The school board's decision was discriminatory because it did result in disparate impact based on national origin.

121. The company you work for is planning a large reduction in force beginning in January. You suggest to the executive team that the company host job fairs, résumé writing workshops, and career counseling for those losing their jobs. These activities are examples of what HR activity?

(A) Compassionate leadership

(B) Legal compliance with WARN

(C) Outplacement services

(D) Recruiting

122. In the wake of September 11, 2001, many companies pulled together a group of HR professionals and executives to make quick decisions about how the terrorist attacks would affect their employees. Decisions were made about generous leave policies for the day and communicating critical information to employees. What kind of meetings and solutions occurred?

(A) A rapid response

(B) Ad hoc

(C) Emergency response

(D) Disaster recovery

123. What is the balance of probabilities in civil law?

(A) It is the level of likelihood that a party to a dispute committed a crime.

(B) It is when the burden of proof is upon the accused.

(C) It is the concept that it's more likely than not that the accused caused harm.

(D) It is when the burden of proof is upon the complainant.

124. Match the court case in Colum A with its outcome in Column B.

Column A	Column B
1. *Faragher v. City of Boca Raton*	A. A claim of hostile work environment is actionable under Title VII of the Civil Rights Act.
2. *Meritor Savings Bank v. Vinson*	B. Ruled that gay and transgender workers are protected under Title VII of the Civil Rights Act.
3. *Harris v. Forklift Systems*	C. Determined that harassment may be actionable even without an explicit threat of adverse action because employees inherently know that this threat exists.
4. *Bostock v. Clayton County*	D. Defined behaviors of a hostile work environment as that which falls between what is merely offensive and what results in tangible physical injury.

125. Dial Corp. used a physical strength test to screen applicants for their entry-level workforce. Prior to using the strength test, 46 percent of the new hires were women. After its implementation, the hiring rate for women dropped to 15 percent. In addition, more than 90 percent of male applicants passed the test whereas less than 40 percent of female applicants were successful. What was the MOST likely finding of the EEOC?

   (A) Adverse impact against women had occurred.

   (B) The physical strength tests weren't job related.

   (C) The tests were appropriate because they simulated the job.

   (D) Dial intentionally discriminated against women.

126. A retail store offered Laura a position as a night salesclerk contingent upon her passing a urinalysis screen for drugs. Laura informed management that she could not produce urine because she had end stage renal disease. The drug testing offered alternative drug screening methods if requested by the company. The company refused, and Laura wasn't hired. What did the store violate?

   (A) The Family Medical Leave Act

   (B) Title VII of the Civil Rights Act of 1964

   (C) The Americans with Disabilities Act

   (D) None because blood or hair screening violates privacy laws

127. What is the BEST way to avoid a defamation lawsuit when giving employee references?

   (A) Have a policy that doesn't verify employment of past employees.

   (B) Don't allow management to give personal references.

   (C) Only verify employment with truthful information.

   (D) Give separating employees a document with final pay rate, dates of employment, and reason for termination to show future employers.

128. The purpose of the back-pay remedies of the OFCCP are to do what?

   (A) Punish an employer for unequal pay practices.

   (B) Recover damages if an employee is harmed by pay discrimination.

   (C) Make workers "whole" from discrimination.

   (D) Pay interest on lost wages.

129. High inter-rater reliability can be shown when?

   (A) Multiple interviewers reach the same or similar conclusion about an applicant.

   (B) A single interviewer reaches the same conclusion about an applicant over multiple interviews.

   (C) A test predicts a different outcome over a period of time.

   (D) The person hired has successful performance on the job.

130. Who is the employer of record in a PEO that conducts all the administrative elements of HR, such as recruiting, processing payroll, and recordkeeping?

   (A) The business where the work is done is the employer of record.

   (B) The employees are independent contractors.

   (C) The PEO is the employer of record.

   (D) It's a joint employment agreement.

131. You notice that an employee attending training does not take notes, focusing instead on what the trainer is saying. Which training technique will be MOST effective for him?

(A) An auditory recording of the class

(B) Graphs and charts that show pictures of the content

(C) Hands-on training that allows him to practice

(D) An on-the-job showcase of the training techniques

132. A company in the maturity stage of the business life cycle is MOST likely to employ which employee development activity?

(A) Technical training

(B) Mentorships

(C) Lifelong learning opportunities

(D) Work-life balance

133. Which statement is TRUE about the development of high-potential employees?

(A) High-potential employees will find a way to increase their own job satisfaction.

(B) Every department has at least one high-potential employee.

(C) Having natural gifts is not enough to make high-potential employees worth an investment.

(D) High-potential employees are usually supervisors or managers.

134. An insurance company that begins to offer human resource consulting and risk management consulting services is establishing itself as a what?

(A) Preferred provider organization

(B) Professional employer organization

(C) Business process outsource service

(D) Enterprise risk manager

135. What strategy would MOST benefit an organization for employees who have reached a career plateau?

(A) Make a change into another department to learn new skills.

(B) Find work at another company in a similar field.

(C) Go back to school to improve their education.

(D) Take a sabbatical to re-energize.

136. What should you do for a supervisor who is modeling the negative behaviors of his manager?

(A) Discipline or demote him.

(B) Coach the manager.

(C) Assign the supervisor another mentor.

(D) Offer development classes for the supervisor.

137. Psychological tests are high on what type of validity?

(A) Content

(B) Construct

(C) Reliability

(D) Predictive value

138. A 360-degree review is MOST useful when _____.

    (A) The position supports multiple departments.

    (B) The employee cannot be counted on to give himself a fair self-rating.

    (C) There is a performance deficiency.

    (D) The supervisor is perceived as being unfair.

139. Of the proposed training room configurations, which is the LEAST likely to encourage discussion?

    (A) Modular

    (B) Circular

    (C) Classroom

    (D) Conference

140. Why would employers choose vestibule training?

    (A) They are limited on the space available for training.

    (B) They want to avoid the overproduction of inventory.

    (C) Time constraints drive the training efforts.

    (D) They do not have a dedicated trainer.

141. In forced distribution, supervisors may be required to do what?

    (A) Distribute 100 percent of their employees into three categories: 10 percent superstars, 80 percent at benchmark, 10 percent needing improvement

    (B) Rate the employees against each other on a curve

    (C) Eliminate the bottom 10 percent of their employees each year

    (D) All of the above

142. What is the first step in designing a performance-feedback process?

    (A) Analyzing the job

    (B) Aligning it to the mission

    (C) Developing the measurables

    (D) Observing employees

143. An employee refused to fill out a 360-degree assessment on his peers, feeling that it is "outside of his pay grade." What is MOST likely the problem?

    (A) The employee has low morale.

    (B) The employee does not know what is expected of him.

    (C) The employee has not accepted the process as meaningful or relevant.

    (D) The employee is not being properly supervised.

144. An employer has just completed a reduction in force and the tasks that were the responsibility of two employees have now become the tasks of one. This is an example of what?

    (A) Job enrichment

    (B) Job enlargement

    (C) Autonomy

    (D) Doing more with less

145. An employee has reported being bored in his job. His position has been adjusted to take on new responsibilities for which he will have to develop new skills that should make the job more interesting and challenging. This is known as what?

    (A) Job enrichment

    (B) Job enlargement

    (C) Job rotation

    (D) Mentoring

146. Which of the following is the BEST example of how learning occurs in a high-context culture?

    (A) Learning is focused on productivity outcomes.

    (B) Learning occurs by following SOPs.

    (C) Learning occurs through on-the-job training and modeling.

    (D) Learning is focused on the technical aspects of the position.

147. If a supervisor is giving feedback to an employee about her productivity outputs, she is MOST likely measuring what?

    (A) Traits

    (B) Behaviors

    (C) Results

    (D) Characteristics

148. A manager has communicated to his production line supervisors that they must get their labor-to-sales ratio at or below 11 percent by the end of the fiscal year. Which of the following does this BEST represent?

    (A) Performance measure

    (B) Performance objective

    (C) SMART goal

    (D) Team objective

149. An employee is unable to pay his utility bill at home due to his low wages, and the strain is showing on the job. His supervisor tells him that if he would just learn to be a team player, others would respond more favorably to him and he could begin to apply for the higher-paying, supervisory positions. This strategy is not likely to work because the employee is at what level of Maslow's hierarchy of needs?

    (A) Psychological

    (B) Physiological

    (C) Esteem

    (D) Safety

150. The company you work for places heavy emphasis on tasks, duties, and responsibilities. What kind of culture is said to exist?

    (A) Transactional

    (B) Low-context

    (C) High-context

    (D) Managerial

151. A company with varying degrees of employee diversity such as age, gender, and family status should consider offering what type of employee benefit plan?

   (A) PTO programs

   (B) Cafeteria plans

   (C) Flexible spending accounts

   (D) Cash-in-lieu of benefits

152. Which of the following is one challenge of pay-for-performance systems?

   (A) Employees may reject the criteria used to measure performance.

   (B) Pay-for-performance can only be adopted for management or executives.

   (C) Employees don't care how their performance impacts pay.

   (D) Pay-for-performance programs are very difficult to calculate.

153. How can a company resolve a long-term issue of pay compression?

   (A) Freeze raises for red-circled employees.

   (B) Regularly collect market wage data on all positions.

   (C) Terminate workers who are paid above the pay range.

   (D) Bump supervisors so the spread between supervisors and employees is greater.

154. What of the following is an example of collusion under the Sherman Antitrust Act?

   (A) A group of competitors agreeing to not offer free shipping for online merchandise

   (B) A group of construction companies deciding who will submit the winning bid in exchange for subcontracts

   (C) A group of hospitals in Connecticut getting together to fix the pay rates of healthcare industry workers

   (D) All of the above are prohibited examples of collusion

155. Your employer wants you to visually correlate employee work experience and skill development with pay increases. Which approach should you use?

   (A) Offer seniority-based pay.

   (B) Plot a maturity curve.

   (C) Review cost-of-living adjustments.

   (D) Recommend a pay-for-performance system.

156. Which of the following is TRUE of executive top-hat retirement plans?

   (A) They are funded entirely by the employer.

   (B) They are funded entirely by the employee via deferred compensation.

   (C) They must be the same plans as those offered to employees.

   (D) They are taxable at the time the money is paid in rather than when distributed.

157. Executive pay based on performance criteria that is approved by a board of directors allows companies to do what?

   (A) Include discretionary bonuses to the total reward package.

   (B) Gain a neutral perspective on what should be measured.

   (C) Deduct executive compensation in excess of $1 million.

   (D) Hold executives accountable to performance outcomes.

158. Variable pay is to voluntary as minimum wage is to what?

(A) Performance

(B) Deliberate

(C) Discretionary

(D) Compelled

159. The marketing manager's annual salary is $82,000. The range for this position is low $31.30, mid $47.91, and high $59.58. What is this employee's compa-ratio?

(A) 55%

(B) 74%

(C) 82%

(D) 121%

160. Breaking jobs down into compensable factors and then assigning weights to these factors is part of which job evaluation method?

(A) Ranking

(B) Classification

(C) Point

(D) Benchmarking

161. An employer may listen to employee phone conversations provided that what occurs or has occurred?

(A) The employee provides signed permission.

(B) The employer stops listening if he realizes the call is personal.

(C) The employer notifies the employee and customers that all calls will be monitored.

(D) All of the above

162. Which activity should be completed prior to the establishment of a peer review panel for discipline?

(A) Have panel members sign a confidentiality agreement.

(B) Hold a vote with the employees to select this dispute method.

(C) Conduct a wage survey to determine how much extra pay the panelists should receive.

(D) Select a neutral arbitrator to lead the team.

163. An employee was suspended for being found smoking in the bathroom. It was his first offense, and he appealed to the union because the punishment seemed unduly harsh. What is MOST likely driving his attitude?

(A) Favoritism

(B) Procedural justice

(C) Distributive justice

(D) Discrimination

164. A progressive discipline policy runs the risk of negating which of the following common law doctrines?

(A) Employment at-will

(B) Respondeat superior

(C) Duty of good faith and fair dealing

(D) Rights granted by statute

165. One example of transferring organizational risk of wrongful termination or sexual harassment law-suits is for HR to recommend what?

(A) The employer provides annual supervisor training.

(B) The company adopts a policy of zero tolerance for harassment.

(C) The HR manager researches and recommends the purchase of EPLI insurance.

(D) The company regularly investigates claims of harassment and only terminates for cause.

166. A union member recommended to his co-workers that they decertify the union because of lack of support from the union's elected officials. A union representative subsequently threatened that the employee was going to lose his job if he continued to try and get the union decertified. This is a violation of which of the following acts?

(A) The National Labor Relations Act (Wagner Act)

(B) The Labor-Management Reporting and Disclosure Act (Landrum Griffin Act)

(C) The Labor-Management Relations Act (Taft-Hartley Act)

(D) The Railway Labor Act

167. What is one of the primary purposes of the National Labor Relations Act?

(A) To protect members from their union

(B) To protect companies from union ULPs

(C) To encourage collective bargaining

(D) To regulate union activity

168. Having an open-door policy can help in which of the following HR activities?

(A) Training and development

(B) Union avoidance

(C) Productivity improvements

(D) Improved job satisfaction

169. Union-avoidance strategies should fundamentally focus on activities that do what?

(A) Educate workers on why unions are bad.

(B) Weed out bad management.

(C) Increase pay and benefits for workers.

(D) Decrease employee dissatisfaction.

170. Which of the following statements is TRUE of employee handbooks?

(A) A handbook protects employees from unfair business practices.

(B) The law requires a handbook.

(C) A handbook helps employers comply with various labor laws.

(D) All of the above

171. Which of the following influencers has the MOST effect on an organizational climate?

(A) Managers

(B) Executives

(C) Employees

(D) Human resources

172. A legally binding method for solving disagreements between an employee and his employer is the definition of which of the following?

(A) Mediation

(B) Grievance proceedings

(C) Arbitration

(D) Alternative dispute resolutions

173. There has been a sharp decline in a previously productive employee's performance as the result of his divorce. Which of the following intervention strategies should HR recommend?

(A) Documentation of performance to ensure consistent application of the discipline policy

(B) Referral to the company EAP

(C) Additional time off with pay until the issue is finalized

(D) A layoff so he can collect unemployment while dealing with the divorce

174. Which of the following is an employee right if he is suspected of using illegal drugs on the job?

(A) Protection under the ADA

(B) Confidentiality

(C) Time off to seek rehabilitation

(D) Job protection if he successfully completes treatment

175. Which scenario is LEAST likely to be covered under workers' compensation insurance?

(A) An injury at work due to employee intoxication

(B) A mental stress claim due to supervisor harassment

(C) An injury from a car accident while conducting company banking

(D) All of the above would be covered.

Chapter 20

Answers and Explanations to SPHR Practice Exam

Now it's time to see how you did. This chapter allows you to keep score, but it also provides you with a justification of the correct answer and explanations of the incorrect choices.

You may want to convert your score into a traditional percentage. You can easily do it by dividing the total number of correct answers by the total number of questions. For example, say that you missed 25 questions. Your score would be an 86 percent (150 divided by 175).

A best practice for these simulations is to take your time reviewing both the correct and incorrect answers to maximize your retention and enhance learning. If you are time crunched, however, I have included an abbreviated answer key at the end of this chapter.

As an SPHR candidate, consider also taking the PHR exam included in Chapter 17. You really need a strong foundation, and taking practice exams can ensure that you're doing as much as you can to build your knowledge.

1. **C.** The *median* number is the one that is found in the middle. To find it, count the total number of units and add 1. Divide this number by 2 and then find the answer by counting up. In this case, there are seven units — 7 + 1 is 8. Eight divided by 2 is 4. Sixteen is the fourth number on the list and therefore is the median.

2. **C.** The employer *brand* is how a company presents itself to the public, employees, future employees, and customers, making Choice (C) the correct answer.

   The company often uses *social media* (Choice [D]) to accomplish it. *Marketing* (Choice [A]) is the operational function of identifying what the public wants and getting the word out about a company's products and services. The *sales function* (Choice [B]) is responsible for selling the goods or services indirectly through distributors or directly to the consumer.

3. A. Organizational communication that flows down from management is called *downward communication*, making Choice (A) the correct answer.

Upward communication (Choice [B]) is when information flows up the organizational hierarchy, such as through a suggestion system. *Cross-functional communication* (Choice [C]) exists when multiple departments work together or have support responsibilities. *Compliance training* (Choice [D]) is a specific type of training.

4. D. HR professionals are expected to refrain from using their position for material or financial gain. When this occurs, the competing desires of the employee and the company create a *conflict of interest.*

Her action isn't a discriminatory practice (Choice [A]), which is an unlawful action taken based on a protected class status, nor is the behavior necessarily an illegal activity (Choice [C]). The decision could be an unethical behavior (Choice [B]), but intent does matter, making Choice (D) the best answer to this question.

5. C. *Social responsibility* practices focus company efforts on practices that do no harm or that positively affect the customers and communities where they live and work.

The FDA is focused on food safety standards, more so than treatment of animals (Choices [A] and [B]). *Corporate governance* (Choice [D]) is the balancing of the needs of the stakeholders affected by business practices.

6. B. The primary difference between a nominal group and Delphi group is that participants in a Delphi group never meet, whereas nominal groups do.

7. C. The Sarbanes-Oxley act sets the financial reporting standards for publicly traded companies.

The Sherman AntiTrust Act (Choice [A]) prohibits monopolies (exclusive control over an industry). Its primary purpose is to encourage competition. GAAP (Choice [B]) are the generally accepted accounting principles that guide the establishment of internal accounting controls and are not a law under which an individual may be charged. While the SEC requires publicly traded corporations to follow GAAP standards, they are issued by the Financial Accounting Standards Board (FASB). Rule of law (Choice [D]) refers to the rights of individuals that cannot be changed or compromised, such as those found in the Bill of Rights in the United States or the Charter of Fundamental Rights of the European Union.

8. D. An organization with a *cost-leadership strategy* is focused on building a stable workforce, which requires training (contrary to Choice [C]) and promoting from within.

Choice (A) is a characteristic of a company with a differentiation strategy, not cost-leadership. A long planning horizon, Choice (B) is the amount of time a company looks ahead in its planning process and may not be the best strategy to support cost leadership.

9. B. The best answer is Choice (B). A *break-even analysis* is used to calculate when an effort will begin to make money or the break-even point at which time the activity's results have paid for the initial investment.

Cost-benefit analysis (Choice [A]) and *return on investment* (Choice [C]) are used to calculate the return and benefit when compared to the initial investment.

10. D. A *planning horizon* is how far into the future a company will look when strategic planning, making Choice (D) the correct answer.

Often, it's a one-, three-, or five-year view. A scanning timeline (Choice [A]), future forecast (Choice [B]), and projection schedule (Choice [D]) are false terms for this forecasting activity.

11. **B.** *Downsizing* is a strategy for companies that need to realign their workforce through employee separations and job restructuring. The loss of employees often results in lower productivity for a period of time, not higher.

    It may lower short-term operating costs (Choice [A]), it's accomplished by layoffs (Choice [D]), and there is low morale among the employees who survive the cuts (Choice [C]).

12. **B.** You calculate the turnover rate by dividing the total number of separations by the total number of employees.

13. **A.** A *brownfield operation* is one that reuses land or buildings for business, contrasted with *greenfield* (Choice [B]), which is a new location where no building had previously existed. There is not enough information in the question to determine if their tax burden will be impacted (Choices [C] and [D]).

14. **B.** The placement of products refers to how the products will be offered to the consumer, making Choice (B) the correct answer.

    The *product* (Choice [A]) refers to what items or services will be sold, *price* (Choice [C]) is the amount a customer will pay for a product, and *promotion* (Choice [D]) is how the items will be marketed.

15. **A.** *Span of control* refers to the number of employees, functions, or processes for which a manager is responsible.

    Sphere of influence (Choice [B]) isn't the correct term for the definition in the example. Job responsibilities (Choice [C]) and pay levels (Choice [D]) aren't solely reliant upon the number of direct or indirect reports.

16. **B.** *Enterprise resource planning* (ERP) is a software platform designed to integrate many functions of business.

    Human resources information systems (HRISs) (Choice [A]) and *human resources management systems* (HRMSs) (Choice [C]) are more focused on the life cycle of the employee, from recruiting to separation. An *information management system* (IMS), Choice (D), is a form of organizing the storage and retrieval of information.

17. **A.** A *business case* is the activity of putting together a proposal for a business activity that includes the scope, cost, and benefit.

    A *business plan* (Choice [B]) is a company document that reviews the purpose of the organization and its goals and plans on how to achieve those goals. The *balanced scorecard* (Choice [C]) is a set of business metrics that measures objectives, and a *training assessment* (Choice [D]) measures the effectiveness of a training program.

18. **D.** *Scanning* involves a review of the external threats and opportunities as well as other forces, such as competition that may have an impact on a company's success within the strategic plan period.

    Scanning is a function of the *planning* process (Choice [A]). *Implementation* (Choice [B]) involves applying the elements of the plan to operations, and the *evaluation* stage (Choice [C]) involves measuring whether or not the plan is working.

19. **D.** A *transition stay bonus* is used to help organizations that are closing facilities or eliminating jobs. It's a method of offering a financial incentive to employees to stay on until the process is complete.

It isn't generally used as a recognition or reward (Choices [A] and [C]), nor to offer wage replacement to displaced workers (Choice [B]).

20. **C.** A *greenfield investment* exists when a company builds a new facility in a new location.

A *joint venture* (Choice [A]) is a partnership between two or more organizations. *Enterprise risk management* (Choice [B]) is addressing the financial and operational risks of doing business. A *corporate task* (Choice [D]) is a generic term for many of the activities associated with the day-to-day tasks of work.

21. **A.** *Buyer power* is increased when the number of consumers is low compared to the number of suppliers of goods or services — the buyer is able to bargain for better pricing or favorable treatment.

Supplier power (Choice [B]) is increased when there are a lot of buyers, but few providers. The *threat of new entrants* (Choice [C]) refers to new competitors in a market, and *rivalry* (Choice [D]) refers to the overall competitive landscape of an industry or product.

22. **D.** Michael Porter's five forces include *external* components, such as the level of both buyer and suppler power.

Internal (Choice [A]) forces affecting an organization's ability to compete include the presence of key people. *Driving* (Choice [B]) and *critical* (Choice [C]) aren't the correct terms for these strategic forces.

23. **A.** The value that occurs most frequently in a series of numbers is called the *mode*; therefore, Choice (A) is the correct answer.

24. **B.** You find the average of a set of numbers by adding all the numbers and then dividing the total by the number of values. In this case, it's 25/7, equaling 3.57.

25. **A.** The best answer is Choice (A). A common side effect of a merger is redundancy in support functions such as accounting or human resources. For this reason, it becomes necessary to eliminate roles that are redundant.

Shared marketing materials (Choice [B]) or a unified brand (Choice [C]) and the merging of budgets (Choice [D]) don't directly have an impact on cost savings.

26. **B.** A company in a growth phase may need access to talent fairly quickly and may not have the dedicated HR resources for the time-consuming task of hiring multiples as Choices (C) or (D) may. A small start-up, Choice (A), may not have the finances to pay for outsourced services.

27. **C.** If employees are happy with their boss and company, they're more likely to refer qualified individuals from their personal network for open jobs.

A small number of temporary staffers doesn't directly influence employee morale (Choice [A]), nor is a suggestion system (Choice [B]) a strong measure of employee satisfaction levels. Injury rates (Choice [D]) are better correlated to a company's safety programs than to the company climate.

28. **B.** A *geocentric* staffing strategy seeks to hire the most qualified talent for key positions, regardless of nationality.

Ethnocentric staffing (Choice [A]) fills key positions with parent-country nationals. In Choice (C), *polycentric* staffing, the company would use Japanese talent to fill key positions at the outpost and American talent at corporate headquarters. Choice (D) is a distractor because there is no such staffing strategy.

29. **A.** *Host-country nationals* are employees working in the country of their birth.

Employees working outside of their country of origin, Choice (B), are known as *expatriates,* and *third-country nationals,* Choice (C), are employees who aren't from either the home or host country.

30. **B.** If corporate headquarters are in the country of an employee's birth, and this employee is working at a global site, the employee is known as an *expatriate* or a *parent-country national.*

Inpatriates (Choice [A]) are actually out of their *patria* (fatherland). *Local nationals* (Choice [C]) are those employees who work in their home country. A *patriot* (Choice [D]) is one who passionately defends his country, not a term that applies to global staffing strategies.

31. **D.** Companies that decide to downsize may do so by not replacing employees who quit or retire, known as *natural attrition,* freezing all hiring for current openings and offering early retirement buyouts to reduce employee headcount.

32. **B.** A *tentative nonconfirmation (TNC) email* will be sent to an employer and new employee if there is a record mismatch on Form I-9 documents. The employee should receive and review a Further Action Notice from the employer and make a decision about what to do to correct the findings. New hires have 72 hours to provide required documentation to employers (Choice [A]) to complete Form I-9/eVerify. The employee shouldn't contact the USCIS (Choice [C]) or visit the necessary offices for correction (Choice [D]) until he knows what further action to take.

33. **A.** The *Uniform Guidelines on Employee Selection Procedures* (UGESP) require that any pre-employment requirement be linked to the necessary knowledge, skills, and abilities of the job.

Doing so ensures that the tests are nondiscriminatory (Choice [B]) predictors of success (Choice [C]) on the job, which will increase the likelihood of being legally defensible (Choice [D]).

34. **D.** The closer pre-employment tests match the job, the more likely they are to be an effective predictor of future performance success. The UGESP require that pre-employment tests be job related.

A high-school diploma (Choice [A]), online general math test (Choice [B]), and interview questions (Choice [C]) aren't the most reflective of the type of work to be done on the job.

35. **A.** The Americans with Disabilities Act (ADA) doesn't require that employers have written job descriptions. However, it does require the essential functions of the job to be identified and documented. Written job descriptions that exist prior to a charge of employment discrimination can be used to demonstrate compliance with the standards.

36. **D.** Technically, the employer hasn't done anything wrong by simply asking the question as in Choices (A) and (B); however, if the employer uses the information to make a hiring decision, it will have unlawfully discriminated based on a protected class status. In addition, the EEOC has found that asking these types of questions may be used as evidence of intent to discriminate. For this reason, employers should avoid asking questions about protected class status in interviews of either men or women (Choice [C]).

37. **A.** This is an example of a leading question, in which the interviewer *leads* the applicant down the path of the correct answer.

A *snap judgment error,* Choice (B), occurs when the interviewer jumps to a conclusion about an applicant without probing for further information. *Negative emphasis,* Choice (C), occurs when the interviewer places more decision-making weight on a negative aspect of an applicant. The *halo effect,* Choice (D), is the opposite; the interviewer places heavy emphasis on a candidate's positive traits.

38. **A.** The internet has opened a host of lower-cost recruiting options such as virtual interviewing. A first interview using an online program such as Skype allows for a quasi face-to-face interview without the investment of a full travel commitment.

College recruiting (Choice [B]) and job fairs (Choice [C]) often require onsite efforts. Online advertising isn't characterized by its cost savings (Choice [D]).

39. **A.** The image of the employer within the community can drive recruiting efforts. People don't want to work for companies that have a negative image or that are perceived to have a poor reputation within the community.

Product perception (Choice [B]) and marketing efforts (Choice [C]) both relate directly to the company's products or services more so than company reputation. This scenario isn't an example of an unethical business practice (Choice [D]).

40. **C.** Employers with more than 100 employees excluding state and local governments and primary and secondary school systems, institutions of higher education, Indian tribes, and tax-exempt private membership clubs other than labor organizations generally must file the EEO-1 report.

41. **B.** *Cooperative training* occurs when schools align their curriculum and activities with practical, real-world scenarios of work.

On-the-job training (Choice [A]) is learning that happens on the job. *Classroom-based training* (Choice [C]) happens in a formal classroom setting, not necessarily in partnership with a vocation. An *apprenticeship* (Choice [D]) is a paid position in which the person learns while on the job.

42. **D.** *Blended learning* is growing because it utilizes both traditional classroom time and virtual or online options, making Choice (D) the correct option.

On-the-job training (Choice [A]) is paid training that occurs while doing the actual work. *Simulations* (Choice [B]) are practice runs of the work off the line or by using examples. *Vestibule training* (Choice [C]) is a production training method that uses simulation techniques off the line.

43. **B.** *Sabbaticals* are underutilized tools that can help employers retain key employees who want to develop or apply their skill set toward socially or personally rewarding activities. Used often in the academic world, they're becoming a more popular option in the business community as well.

Formal sabbatical leave as part of a benefit package is paid, whereas leaves of absence (Choice [A]) are generally unpaid. Choices (C) and (D) are more a form of company downsizing.

44. **C.** Rating all employees right down the middle is a strategy often used by supervisors who want to avoid conflict, or by new supervisors who haven't had adequate time to assess employee performance. This strategy is an error because it doesn't accurately distinguish between employee work behaviors.

In the *halo effect* error (Choice [A]), the rater places heavier value on an employee's positive characteristics, and the *horn* effect (Choice [B]) is just the opposite. All of these rater errors are a form of rater bias (Choice [D]).

45. **A → 2, B → 1, C → 1, D → 2.** *Synchronous learning* (A) is any method of training that occurs in real time — such as training that is led by an instructor (D) or where a participant is required to be online at a certain time (2). Training that occurs independent of the instructor or other participants, such as watching a video online (1) on their own or being self-paced (C), is a form of *asynchronous* (B) learning.

46. **D.** There are several options to creating a successful career plan. These options include formal and informal education opportunities, on-the-job training, and new job responsibilities.

    Succession plans, Choice (A), are used by organizations to develop employees while planning for replacement of key positions. *Strategic plans,* Choice (B), are a tool used by companies to manage threats and maximize opportunities. *Workforce planning,* Choice (C), evaluates the current skill set of the workforce and compares it to future needs to fill in any possible gaps.

47. **A.** *Asynchronous learning* occurs when students are able to access the training material at their own pace. It doesn't require logging in at the same time as the instructor or participating in real-time discussions like *synchronous training,* Choice (B).

    The participant not being at the same location as the instructor characterizes *distance learning,* Choice (C), and *independent learning,* Choice (D), isn't a formal term for the different types of learning methods.

48. **C.** *Autonomy* is a job satisfier because employees are granted the authority to act in certain situations, making Choice (C) the correct answer. One advantage of autonomy is that trusting the employees often results in ownership over the outcomes.

    Job enrichment (Choice [A]) involves an expansion of job responsibilities, not necessarily an expansion of employee judgment or decision-making. *Self-direction* (Choice [B]) isn't the proper term for job satisfiers, and in *job enlargement* (Choice [D]), work tasks are added to an employee's existing job.

49. **B.** *Task significance* is measured by the impact the work has on the lives of others. Examples include working with the ill or in a socially responsible position. Employees with high levels of task significance report higher levels of job satisfaction and are less likely to leave their work.

    Job importance within the organization, Choice (A), is similar, but it's not the primary characteristic of task significance. Authority, Choice (C), doesn't play an important role.

50. **C.** A *learning curve* is a graphical representation of the rate of learning and its impact on outputs.

    It doesn't represent the experience (Choice [A]) or education level (Choice [B]) of participants, nor is it representative of a time lapse (Choice [D]).

51. **D.** A *performance management system* is the framework from which performance feedback is given.

    Human resource development (Choice [A]) is the name for the functional area of human resources. Activities include training, development, discipline, and formal appraisals. A performance appraisal (Choice [B]) is a feedback (Choice [C]) tool for use within the system.

52. **D.** Job sharing, phased retirement, and working from home are all flexible-scheduling options that may serve a broad demographic in a workforce made up of a highly diverse group of individual needs.

53. **B.** Although a *performance review* is designed to communicate both positive and negative information about past performance, it isn't a tool for discipline. Employees should have a basic understanding of their performance status prior to being given a formal appraisal.

54. **A.** A *learning portal* is a place where training participants are able to access training program materials and track progress.

Choice (B), training receptacle, isn't a training term. A company intranet, Choice (C), and HRI system, Choice (D), are both vehicles for accessing training rather than a build-out of learning content.

55. **C.** Maslow described a hierarchy of needs that serves to drive employee behavior.

After the lower needs of physiological (Choice [A]) or safety are met, the higher needs declare themselves. Being respected by peers creates a sense of belonging, which in turn serves as a motivator. This includes the need to feel confident, Choice (B). Self-actualization, Choice (D), is the highest point of Maslow's pyramid, representing achievement of one's full potential.

56. **C.** An *internal locus of control* is defined by an individual's belief in his ability to affect the outcomes of his job and career. Individuals with a high internal locus of control believe that they can positively affect their level of success both in life and on the job.

The question doesn't speak to opinion (Choice [A]) nor does being the master of one's destiny necessarily correlate to a high degree of confidence (Choice [B]). *Context* (Choice [D]) is a term used to describe cultures, not individuals.

57. **C.** *Pay compression* occurs when a company's existing pay rates don't keep pace with the market.

Choices (A) and (B) are forms of discrimination based on protected class characteristics. Choice (D) is a pay strategy used to group like jobs into ranges.

58. **A.** *Perquisites* are generally noncash items that aren't taxed as income.

They include cars, housing, executive memberships, and other status items, not just transportation, Choice (C). Choice (B) is tricky because it could also be correct, but perks are more characterized as noncash items than being taxable. Perks aren't a form of deferred compensation, Choice (D).

59. **B.** The Lilly Ledbetter Act, also known as the Fair Pay Act, established that the 180-day statute of limitations for filing a charge of pay discrimination resets every time an employee is paid.

60. **C.** Several factors can help HR professionals determine whether a worker is an independent contractor or employee. Consider a plumber, for example. To find a plumber, you'll probably look for his advertisement. When you call, the plumber will tell you when he will arrive. The plumber will have a license number, set his own schedule, and be allowed to work for multiple customers at once. These factors all indicate the worker is a legitimate independent contractor.

Exempt (Choice [A]) and nonexempt (Choice [B]) are pay classification categories for employees who generally don't work for others, similar to a business owner (Choice [D]).

61. **C.** A *cafeteria plan* allows employees to select and therefore customize a benefits package that suits their needs. Older workers may be more interested in prescription coverage, whereas a family with young children may desire a lower deductible.

    Therefore, Choice (C) best serves a broad range of needs based on employee demographics. Any option that focuses on price (Choice [A]) instead of scope may not be broad enough to meet the needs of the employees (Choice [B]). A cash incentive (Choice [D]) doesn't meet the benefits needs of the workers.

62. **A.** Transparency and clear expectations are critical to successful pay-for-performance systems. In an environment with narrowly focused attendance problems, such as high absenteeism on Mondays or Fridays, the issues are best addressed through direct and honest action.

    Discipline as a form of training isn't a pay strategy, making Choice (B) incorrect. Reducing team-based incentives (Choice [C]) and eliminating gainsharing (Choice [D]) payments for individual infractions will be perceived as unfair and don't address the individual issue.

63. **B.** The Fair Labor Standards Act (FLSA) was passed to accomplish three things: discourage the use of child labor, discourage the use of overtime, and establish a minimum wage.

64. **C.** *Pay openness* refers to the degree of transparency employers have as it relates to employee pay rates, making Choice (C) the right answer. Other elements of pay openness include communicating pay policies and having procedures on how pay rates are decided.

    Confidentiality in pay isn't an ethical issue (Choice [A]). *Pay equity* (Choice [B]) refers to the perceived or real fairness of pay between employees. *Pay honesty* (Choice [D]) is an answer distractor and not a legitimate term.

65. **D.** A *golden parachute* is used in executive contracts to offset risks inherent to higher-level positions. These risks include the availability of similar high-paying jobs and termination due to a company acquisition.

    There is no such thing as the golden boot (Choice [A]). A retirement proposal (Choice [B]) isn't a type of severance benefit. Golden handcuffs (Choice [C]) keep executives via payment of bonuses; they don't offer wage replacement upon separation.

66. **A.** Employee stock options grant employees ownership shares of publicly traded companies. Because they now own shares in the company, it's a form of equity compensation.

    Annual bonuses (Choice [B]), performance incentives (Choice [C]), and perks (Choice [D]) aren't equity rewards.

67. **B.** Retirement benefits such as IRAs and pensions are offered at the discretion of the employer and are not required by federal or state law. After the plans are offered, however, the government regulates these plans.

68. **A.** Giving employees a lump-sum increase at the end of each year rather than a wage can hold down costs related to hourly pay, including overtime and pension payment calculations.

    LSIs don't accelerate base pay growth (Choice [B]), nor are they necessarily easier to track (Choice [C]). An increase in pension payments (Choice [D]) isn't an advantage for employers.

69. **A.** These tests are able to focus on detecting a broad panel of drug use without unintentionally revealing genetic information or other irrelevant information.

Hair screening (Choice [B]) can't be used to test for alcohol, and breath testing (Choice [C]) is most commonly used to determine alcohol impairment. The use of blood tests (Choice [D]) is more invasive and therefore more likely to result in privacy issues than the other types of testing.

70. **B.** In risk management, the best solution is the one that eliminates or restricts an employee behavior, making (B) the correct answer.

    A chief privacy officer, Choice (A), isn't the most realistic solution for many companies. Choices (C) and (D) are viable options in protecting privacy, but they are behavior-based, which makes them less reliable as a safeguard than removing the risk altogether.

71. **D.** An *implied employment contract* can be created when an employee has longevity with a company if a supervisor promises continued employment as long as she does her job well or if she receives favorable performance reviews.

    The *public policy exception* (Choice [A]) to employment at-will protects workers from being fired for complying with the law. The *duty of good faith and fair dealing* (Choice [B]) is the concept that parties to a contract must deal honestly with each other. *Statutory rights* (Choice [C]) are rights granted by law, such as the right to vote.

72. **D.** Both the employer and the union are required to bargain in good faith during negotiations of an agreement, which includes coming prepared to the meetings and sending participants who have the authority to act on behalf of the company and union members.

73. **A.** Known as *Weingarten rights*, union members have the right to representation if they're asked to participate in a meeting that they reasonably believe may lead to discipline.

74. **B.** The TIPS doctrine is an acronym used to describe unfair labor practices. *Interfering* with an employee's right to engage in union organizing is an unfair labor practice.

    Interference includes prohibiting the employee from discussing the union on work time if they're allowed to talk about other non-work-related subjects. Employers also may not *threaten* (Choice [A]) employees with termination or shop closing, *spy* (Choice [C]) on employees to gain information, or *promise* (Choice [D]) workers more pay or benefits in exchange for keeping the union out.

75. **D.** In *EEOC vs. Swissotel Employment Services, LLC*, the EEOC ordered Swissotel to pay $90,000 to a disabled worker who was discriminated against under the ADA and wrongfully terminated.

76. **B.** A *reference guide* is a tool used to communicate concentrated, highly relevant information for employees to do their jobs.

    Standard operating procedures (Choice [A]) are used to document and train on formal processes. A *policy* (Choice [C]) is used to communicate employee and employer rights and responsibilities and often includes work rules (Choice [D]), such as employee codes of conduct.

77. **C.** The organizational climate is easily described as the temperature of the workplace. Surveys, focus groups, and staff meetings are all ways HR can best gather input from employees and measure how well or how poorly the company is doing.

    Hiring the most qualified workers (Choice [A]) is a sound business practice to ensure employee fit and product quality. Surveying employees to gain input (Choice [B]) is an important activity to measure the organizational climate. Executive coaching activities (Choice [D]) may not always be necessary or appropriate, and they're often used as an intervention rather than prevention strategy.

78. **C.** *De minimus* violations are those that are technically out of compliance with OSHA standards but not a direct threat to employee safety or health.

Serious violations (Choice [A]) are those that are likely to cause employee injury, and willful violations (Choice [B]) are those in which the employer knew of a threat to employee safety, but didn't take steps to correct it. Other than serious (Choice [D]) are violations of standards that aren't likely to cause death or serious injury but are still a hazard to employees.

79. **D.** Claims of negligent hiring arise when an employer hasn't taken due diligence to screen potential hires.

Background checks (Choice [A]), reference checking (Choice [B]), and verification of education credentials (Choice [C]) all help minimize claims of negligent hiring.

80. **C.** Employers with ten or fewer employees are partially exempt from maintaining injury and illness records. However, any fatality or illness requiring hospitalization of three or more employees must be reported.

81. **C.** An HR manager is generally responsible for more than one HR function.

There are many types of safety specialists, including technicians (Choice [A]), injury and other types of leave coordinators (Choice [B]), and safety trainers (Choice [D]).

82. **A.** Hofstede described the degree to which an employee identifies with her organization as characterized by feeling connected with a company's values, products, services, and clients.

The *degree of acceptance* (Choice [B]) is focused on leadership styles. *Employee versus work orientation* (Choice [C]) is a management perspective that is focused on the completion of tasks, and the dimension of *local versus professional orientation* (Choice [D]) refers to the degree to which an employee identifies with her business unit or location rather than the company as a whole.

83. **D.** Jobs that require specific licensing or certifications may have impact on the rate of economic recovery because not enough qualified workers meet the requirements (Choice [A]). It can be argued, however, that qualifying the workforce through licensees and certifications better controls the type of recovery that occurs.

Regulations also may make it more difficult for those without licenses or certifications to find work (Choice [B]) and require higher pay rates (Choice [C]) to recruit qualified talent.

84. **A.** A *regression analysis* makes a comparison of past relationships to other components. In this example, the analysis would compare number of employees to gross sales.

Staffing ratios (Choice [B]) are used to identify labor support needs, such as the number of sales reps per customer. *Simulation models* (Choice [C]) attempt to mimic a situation in order to anticipate outcomes, and *productivity ratios* (Choice [D]) calculate output per employee.

85. **D.** A *center of excellence* is a team of experts brought together to achieve a specific business objective.

Lean (Choice [A]) refers to a quality program that focuses on the elimination of process waste. *Community of experts* (Choice [B]) refers to a group of cross-functional subject-matter experts on a broad topic such as organizational development. *Community of practice* (Choice [C]) is a group of people who share a profession, grouped together inside or outside of the organization.

86. **A.** In valuating items, an individual choice or preference drives the value. High preferences of one item over another increase the value.

The *market value of a nontangible item* (Choice [B]) is the attempt to measure the worth of a nonphysical item, such as holding a patent. *Supply and demand* (Choice [C]) refers to the availability of a good or service (supply) compared to the desire for that good or service in the market (demand). *Cost to build* (Choice [D]) is a tangible financial measure that calculates the cost to build a product (raw material, labor, ancillary expenses).

87. **C.** The Global Sullivan Principles were enacted to promote economic, social, and political justice by companies that do business globally.

Nondiscriminatory treatment practices (Choice [A]) are required by Title VII (Choice [B]) as efforts of compliance with American labor law. A *greenfield operation* (Choice [D]) refers to the start-up of a new operation at another location.

88. **C.** Neither the Family Medical Leave Act (FMLA) nor the Americans with Disabilities Act (ADA) prohibit discrimination on the basis of race or ethnicity. Both FMLA and the ADA require covered employers to grant medical leave to an employee under certain circumstances. Choice (A) is incorrect because the ADA applies to employers with 15 or more employees, and the FMLA applies to employers with 50 or more workers. The ADA doesn't cover pregnant workers (Choice [B]) because pregnancy by nature is a temporary state. The FMLA is unpaid leave, making Choice (D) an incorrect answer.

89. **B.** The best answer is Choice (B). Under the Family Medical Leave Act, *interference* occurs when an employer restrains, denies, or retaliates against an employee who exercises his rights under the law.

Retaliation (Choice [A]) occurs when an employer punishes an employee for exercising his rights under a law. *Discrimination* (Choice [C]) happens when an employment decision is based on a protected class condition. *Harassment* (Choice [D]) is hostile behavior on the part of an employee or co-worker in the workplace.

90. **C.** Discrimination prohibitions of Title VII, the Americans with Disabilities Act, and the Age Discrimination in Employment Act may be different for businesses operating in foreign countries.

In general, companies aren't required to comply with these laws if doing so would violate the laws of another country, making Choice (A) incorrect. Some labor laws do apply in other countries, so Choice (B) is incorrect. Choice (D) is an opinion.

91. **D.** In *Harris vs. Quinn*, the Supreme Court found that partial public workers may opt out of joining a union and not be required to pay union fees, making Choice (D) the correct answer.

92. **C.** An *ombudsman* is a neutral employee who serves as an impartial problem-solver within organizations.

An employee *advocate* (Choice [A]) can be anybody within the company, including an HR professional. A *union steward* (Choice [B]) is both an employee of the company and a union official representing union members. An *arbitrator* (Choice [D]) is a neutral individual used in alternative dispute resolution proceedings.

93. **A.** Choice (A) is the first response.

Protecting a company's financial assets allows the company to continue business operations, which will frame its responses to the media (Choice [B]), communicate status to the stakeholders (Choice [C]), and help to provide thorough information to regulatory agencies (Choice [D]).

94. **A.** Establishing company credit policies and objectives can help to reduce expenses by looking at loan or credit fees and establishing credit use rules.

    Providing oversight of department expenses (Choice [B]) and managing the company budget (Choice [D]) are overreaching examples of HR's authority. An employee code of conduct (Choice [C]) isn't primarily a risk-management activity.

95. **D.** A general diagnosis isn't considered an unlawful medical inquiry under the ADA, provided that it's consistently applied and only requests information about the nature of the illness.

    Inquiring about current meds (Choice [A]) or medical history (Choice [B]) may be an unlawful inquiry, and the FMLA limits the amount of information that an employer can request in a medical certification (Choice [C]).

96. **B.** Warren Bennis believed that visionary leaders have a passion for their work, are able to embrace mistakes, and are willing to take risks, making Choice (B) the least important piece of visionary leadership.

97. **C.** A *collaborative workforce* is characterized by the idea that all workers are knowledge workers, regardless of their production capacity.

    Organizations that segment employees by thinkers and doers (Choice [A]) and a downward flow of direction from management (Choice [B]) are indicative of a less collaborative workplace. Restriction to confidential information (Choice [D]) isn't a characteristic of a collaborative work environment.

98. **C.** Mintzberg classified management into three categories. *Informational* leaders are tasked with the processing of information, both inbound and outbound.

    Interpersonal (Choice [A]) leaders are focused on the relationships between people, and *decisional* (Choice [B]) leaders use information and relationships to make decisions. Choice (D) isn't one of Mintzberg's management roles.

99. **A.** The presence of a strategic plan, especially when entering a new competitive market, is the best option to contribute to the company's success.

    Executive competencies (Choice [B]) impact a company's success, but without a strategic plan that includes company performance metrics, they may be difficult to measure. The strategic planning process is often where the mission, vision, and values are developed (Choice [C]) and where the external market is scanned for potential threats and opportunities. From this plan, policies may be developed, and operationally, SOPs established to meet the goals of the strategic plan (Choice [D]).

100. **C.** Schein best describes shared basic assumptions as beliefs and behaviors that are deeply embedded into organizational culture, making Choice (C) the best answer.

    Tribal knowledge (Choice [A]) exists when most work is done from the intelligence of the workers, not from written procedures. A *brain drain* (Choice [B]) is said to occur when talent leaves a company or a country, particularly on a regional scale. *Shared responsibilities* (Choice [D]), often present in a team environment, are the obligation of two or more employees to complete a task or duty.

101. **B.** A *learning organization* is characterized by a culture of problem-solving by subject-matter experts, which includes learning and growing from mistakes.

It takes a whole system view of the work, including the existence of a quality management program (Choice [A]) and a strong management team to support these objectives (Choice [C]). Employee intelligence (Choice [D]) isn't a factor in developing a culture of problem-solving and learning.

102. **A.** Although having succession plans in place is important for all businesses, the best answer is Choice (A).

    Larger companies (Choices [B] and [C]) and joint ventures (Choice [D]) are more likely to have talented individuals in place should death or disability occur in the top ranks. This may not be the case for small, family-owned businesses.

103. **D.** Organizational development (OD) is about making changes through people, process, or companywide interventions. A successful OD program is built on a foundation of respect and inclusion.

    Financial realities (Choice [A]) may not support OD actions even though they may be necessary. Choices (B) and (C) are part of an overall OD strategy, but they aren't necessarily the foundation of OD efforts.

104. **C.** The best answer is Choice (C). An *extinction burst* occurs when an employee increases the frequency and force of the older, undesirable behavior because she has been conditioned to expect certain outcomes using that behavior. Some employees actually welcome change, making Choice (A) incorrect. Although communication, Choice (B), and hiring right, Choice (D), are keys to successful change management, employees will still need time to embrace the new behaviors.

105. **A.** *Negative reinforcement* is the process of removing something when an employee behaves in a certain way. It also occurs when a behavior prevents something from occurring, as in the example.

    Positive reinforcement (Choice [B]) occurs when an employee is rewarded by the addition of a desirable incentive for the correct behavior. *Conditioning* (Choice [C]) is the overall theory of motivation under which positive and negative reinforcement are components and isn't the best answer for this question. *Safety reinforcement* (Choice [D]) isn't part of the theory of operant conditioning.

106. **A.** *Utility* is a term that can mean useful or satisfactory. It's this description that makes a utility or *usefulness* analysis the appropriate tool when measuring the amount of movement an intervention affected in employee performance.

    A *cost-benefit analysis* (Choice [B]) measures the value of inputs when compared to outputs, as does *return on investment* (Choice [C]). An *economic value add* (Choice [D]) refers to the economic model used to calculate profit when compared to the cost of capital.

107. **C.** A *balanced scorecard* helps a company look at nonfinancial measurements. It can be designed to report on many factors, such as customer service, employee training, and development and process efficiencies.

    Reports that are on a timed schedule, such as quarterly (Choice [A]), annual (Choice [B]), and end-of-year P&L (Choice [D]), generally report on financial criteria to measure success.

108. **C.** The correct answer is 36 percent. You calculate it by dividing the total operating expenses by the total pay and benefits cost.

109. C. *Strategic business units* (SBU) are specialized divisions of an organization that make their own decisions about their products, services, and finances, which makes Choice (C) the correct answer. Although still responsible to top management, the business unit has a higher degree of control over most business elements. It often has an independent mission statement and strategic plan.

A decentralized structure isn't directly linked to foreign subsidiaries (Choice [A]) or the existence of a board of directors (Choice [D]). A *flat-line structure* (Choice [B]) is another way to organize leadership and can exist in both centralized and decentralized structures.

110. C. The *Delphi technique* involves creating a series of questionnaires that are circulated among experts.

In a traditional approach to this system, the experts don't meet so you won't need to directly interview individuals (Choice [A]) or facilitate meetings (Choice [B]).

111. C. *Due diligence* is best described as an investigation to collect information, making Choice (C) correct.

Due diligence will satisfy legal (Choice [A]) and often ethical (Choice [B]) or financial disclosure requirements (Choice [D]) as well.

112. B. A *foreign subsidiary* is defined as a company that is more than 50 percent owned or controlled by a parent company in another country.

113. A. A *needs assessment*, also referred to as a *gap analysis,* is used to compare the current state to a desired future state. It may be used to review a company's core competencies (Choice [B]) as part of the strategic planning (Choice [D]) process. Training needs (Choice [C]) are identified through a training needs assessment.

114. B. A *monopsony* exists when there is a large buyer of goods and services, whereas a *monopoly* (Choice [A]) exists when there is a single seller. Discrimination (Choice [D]) isn't occurring, and an unfair business practice (Choice [C]) is dependent on multiple factors.

115. C. When the needs of stakeholders such as customers, vendors, and the communities from which companies operate are considered, value — including profit — is created.

American labor law (Choice [A]) doesn't require specific efforts toward social responsibility per se, but rather offers guidance in areas, such as global (Choice [D]) practices in the area of wages and working conditions as part of compliance efforts. No direct correlation exists between ethical leadership and profits (Choice [B]).

116. B. Unlike company strategies, a corporate mission statement communicates the purpose of the organization and is unlikely to change often, making *consistent,* Choice (B), the correct answer.

Fluidity, Choice (A), and *evolving,* Choice (D), imply movement rather than a stable guide. The term *necessary* in Choice (C) is irrelevant, because it's neither stable nor moving.

117. D. This HR manager is most likely conducting a training needs assessment, so the correct answer is Choice (D).

Top-down communication (Choice [A]) occurs when information flows from upper management down through the ranks. An *occupational assessment* (Choice [B]) screens for required job competencies, and *cultural intelligence* (Choice [C]) refers to a person's ability to function in culturally diverse situations.

118. **A.** The need for virtual team members to be highly independent is in the very nature of their work. A virtual team can be spread out among different time zones, and there is very little day-to-day direction, which means team members must be able to work independently and manage their own goals and outcomes.

Technical proficiency (Choice [B]), being aware of costs (Choice [C]), and existing in the same time zone (Choice [D]) are all important, but less likely to influence positive performance than an ability to work independently.

119. **C.** An *assessment center* is less of a place and more of a series of activities designed to measure a candidate's job-related competencies through tests and simulations.

Staffing agencies (Choice [A]) and professional employer organizations (PEO) (Choice [B]) are employers of record and most likely to process new-hire paperwork than they are to assess for proficiencies. An occupational clinic (Choice [D]) is used at the pre-hire stage to conduct employee physicals and drug screens.

120. **A.** The EEOC found that the school board's decision was based on the underlying conduct, not the fact of the arrest (Choice [C]) or his national origin (Choice [D]), and the EEOC concluded that no discrimination had occurred.

Disparate impact occurs when a seemingly neutral employment decision results in a discriminatory outcome against a protected class group, not an individual, so Choice (B) is incorrect.

121. **C.** *Outplacement services* are a strategy that HR uses to help exiting employees make the transition into job seekers. Activities include allowing unemployment departments or other organizations to come in and interview skilled workers and help them build their résumés.

Outplacement assistance is less a factor of compassionate leadership (Choice [A]) or a function of recruiting (Choice [D]). The Worker Adjustment and Retraining Notification Act (Choice [B]) doesn't require outplacement assistance when laying off workers.

122. **B.** *Ad hoc* meetings or solutions aren't planned and are generally in response to a specific issue or event. A helpful way to remember this is that the term *ad hoc* means *for this.*

Rapid response (Choice [A]), emergency response (Choice [B]), and disaster recovery (Choice [D]) are all terms that refer to action plans in light of an emergency.

123. **C.** Civil law differs from criminal law in the level of proof that must be present. In civil law, if there is a dispute between parties to an employment contract, the case is decided based upon the balance of probabilities; if it's more likely than not that the accused caused the harm, the court can uphold a civil claim.

124. **A → 2; B → 4 (combined cases); C → 1; D → 3.**

125. **A.** In this scenario, the EEOC found that adverse impact against women had occurred as the result of a pre-employment test that, although job related, was significantly more difficult than the job itself. On a side note, Choice (A) is the only answer for which the question gave you enough information to decide.

126. **C.** The EEOC found that the retail store violated Laura's rights under the Americans with Disabilities Act for failing to reasonably accommodate an otherwise qualified applicant's needs.

She wasn't eligible for protection under the FMLA (Choice [A]) because she had not worked for the employer for 1,250 hours in the previous 12 months, and you don't know whether she was a member of a different protected class to determine if (Choice [B]) is correct. Choice (D) isn't a true statement.

127. **C.** The best defense against a defamation lawsuit is the truth, making Choice (C) the correct answer. Employers can avoid defamation lawsuits by keeping accurate records and providing objective information when giving an employment reference on a past employee.

    Although many lawyers would say Choice (A) is the best way to handle these calls, doing so isn't always realistic, especially if it conflicts with required reference information such as background checks for childcare workers or substance abuse records for commercial drivers. Choices (B) and (D) aren't bad strategies, but Choice (C) is the best answer.

128. **C.** The goal of orders of back pay to remedy past discrimination is to make the affected employee *whole*, which may include awarding interest, benefits, lost overtime, or hourly pay rates. The Office of Federal Contract Compliance (OFCCP) is one such group under the Department of Labor that may use back pay to remedy discriminatory pay practices.

129. **A.** When more than one person interviews a candidate and everyone agrees or shares similar opinions about the qualifications of the candidate, a strong *inter-rater reliability* is said to exist.

    It isn't shown if one interviewer feels the same way after multiple interviews (Choice [B]), nor is it related to the actual test reliability as in Choice (C). The interview is considered valid if the person hired has successful performance on the job (Choice [D]).

130. **C.** In a true professional employer organization (PEO) relationship that is primarily administrative in scope, the PEO remains the employer of record.

    Joint employment (Choice [D]) may become a reality if the businesses share employees to get work done or the PEO has the right to hire, terminate, or manage the actions of the employee. Where the work is done (Choice [A]) isn't the primary factor of determining the employer of record. Independent contractors (Choice [B]) are self-employed.

131. **A.** *Auditory learners* learn best by hearing the information.

    Although graphs and charts (Choice [B]) and hands-on training (Choice [C]) are useful tools, this employee would best be served by a recording. *On-the-job training* (Choice [D]) is more of a tactile and visual learning method.

132. **B.** *Mentorships* are useful for a company that has a depth of talent from which to draw. A formal internal or external program can help develop high-potential employees and serve a corporate succession plan.

    Technical training (Choice [A]) may be more necessary for business start-ups and companies in growth mode. *Lifelong learning* (Choice [C]) is a state of existence that can occur at any business life-cycle stage, as is the need for *work-life balance* (Choice [D]), which is the ability of workers to find harmony between their work and off-duty time.

133. **C.** Having natural talent isn't enough of a reason to identify and develop high-potential employees (HiPo). A strong work ethic, level of motivation, presence of a support team, and other factors must be considered when selecting high-potential employees to invest in.

    HiPo can actually get bored and move on if not properly managed and developed (Choice [A]). They can exist anywhere in the organization, not necessarily by department (Choice [B]) or in the ranks of management (Choice [D]).

134. **C.** BPOs are becoming a more popular option for outsourcing back office functions such as HR and accounting. Some professional organizations serve as a BPO, and companies simply expand upon their current offerings, such as insurance providers and IT groups.

    A *preferred provider* (Choice [A]) is a medical group that is within an insurance company's network. A *professional employer organization* (Choice [B]) is a form of employee outsourcing by using a third-party employer of record. An *enterprise risk manager* (Choice [D]) isn't a term used to describe general management positions.

135. **A.** Individuals who have reached a career plateau have a decision to make: Should I stay or should I go? Often, finding a way to re-energize and motivate seasoned workers who still have more to give is best, so transferring the employee into another department reinforces the organizational commitment on both sides and most benefits the company.

    Without a win-win strategy, the employee may choose to find work in another field (Choice [B]), and the talent will exit. The worker may also go back to school to improve his education, which may or may not benefit the organization (Choice [C]). Taking a sabbatical leave (Choice [D]) isn't the best choice from the company's perspective, because it leaves a temporary void to be filled.

136. **B.** The best answer in this scenario is to provide coaching to the supervisor's manager. All employees learn from behavior modeling to some extent, so providing coaching to those in leadership positions is a quality investment for overall employee behavior.

    Discipline or demotion, Choice (A), shouldn't be the first step because the employee may be trainable. Assigning the employee another mentor, Choice (C), doesn't support a long-term outcome of developing both the employee and manager. Choice (D) eventually may be necessary, but it's best to use the situation as an opportunity to develop and enhance the relationship between the worker and his manager.

137. **B.** A *construct* is a psychological concept that can't be traditionally measured, such as in pounds or inches. An example is employee motivation. Because psychological tests regularly measure what they say they're going to measure, they have high construct validity.

    Content validity (Choice [A]) differs in that it doesn't review the outcome of a psychological test, but rather that the tool is comprehensive enough to capture all angles of a concept. *Reliability* (Choice [C]) is said to be high when the test — over a period of time — consistently measures what it says it's going to measure. *Predictive value* (Choice [D]) is the degree to which a positive or negative test correlates to the predicted future behavior.

138. **A.** A *360-degree review* gathers data from the multiple stakeholders dependent on job performance. It allows for an accurate and relevant view from those most affected by employee behavior.

    Because multiple raters are involved in giving a 360-degree review, the decision shouldn't be dependent upon an employee's ability to judge his own performance (Choice [B]). Any review format should be able to adequately respond to employee performance deficiencies (Choice [C]), and supervisor bias should be addressed with the supervisor, not by changing methods (Choice [D]).

139. **C.** Traditional *classroom-style* seating (Choice [C]) is best used for lecture training in which minimal participation is required.

    A *modular set-up* (Choice [A]) encourages small group discussion, and the *circular set-up* (Choice [B]) invites face-to-face participation, similar to the conference room setting (Choice [D]).

140. B. Training on the line can result in an overproduction of inventory, causing cash flow and other production issues. *Vestibule training* occurs in a simulated environment, independent of real-time production. Vestibule training isn't characterized by space (Choice [A]), time (Choice [C]) or trainer issues (Choice [D]).

141. D. *Forced distribution* is a ranking tool that evaluates employees within a department against each other. It's generally represented as a bell curve. Often, supervisors must discipline or eliminate the bottom 10 percent of employees who are at the "needs improvement" level of performance.

142. A. Knowing what each job entails and the subsequent identification of the roles and responsibilities is an important first step to designing an accurate, relevant, and meaningful feedback system.

Alignment to the mission (Choice [B]) of the organization is a secondary priority of a feedback system, after it's patterned off the job requirements. Creating performance measurables (Choice [C]) would be difficult until the job analysis is complete. Observing employees (Choice [D]) is a method that can be used to complete the job analysis.

143. C. Employees must accept the methodology of the performance-feedback process. If it lacks relevance or meaning to their day-to-day job, they will be more reluctant to fully engage in the process.

Choices (A), (B), and (D) aren't related to the assessment, making them incorrect.

144. B. *Job enlargement* differentiates itself from job enrichment (Choice [A]) in that it's driven by the quantity of work, not necessarily the quality of work. *Autonomy* (Choice [C]) is the degree of decision-making authority an employee has. Choice (D) isn't an example of job satisfiers/dissatisfiers.

145. A. In *job enrichment,* the quality of the work is improved or serves the employee's career development versus the job-specific tasks required on a day-to-day basis, as is the case with job enlargement (Choice [B]).

Job rotation (Choice [C]) is when employees are cross-trained in multiple jobs and rotate through them on a regular basis. *Mentoring* (Choice [D]) is a development activity that involves performance coaching another employee or subordinate.

146. C. A *high-context culture* is characterized by shared knowledge and outcomes; therefore, behavior modeling on the job is the best answer.

A focus on productivity (Choice [A]), standardized procedures (Choice [B]) or the technical aspects of a job (Choice [D]) are more closely related to low-context cultures.

147. C. Several different types of behaviors are measured when giving performance feedback. *Results-based feedback* is often focused on quantifiable elements of the job such as productivity. Choices (A), (C), and (D) are measures of people or jobs rather than output.

148. C. SMART goals are specific, measurable, attainable, relevant, and time-based. Although goals may be used to measure performance, in this example multiple factors beyond a single employee's performance will be necessary to achieve this goal. Examples include overtime management and proper workforce planning.

A performance measure (Choice [A]) or objective (Choice [B]) is identified as part of the SMART goal. In this case, the objective is to hit the 11 percent target. The question doesn't focus on team goals (Choice [D]).

149. **B.** Maslow theorized that until an employee's lower needs were met, the employee couldn't be motivated by higher needs, such as safety (Choice [D]), esteem (Choice [C]), belonging, or self-actualization. In this scenario, the supervisor's efforts to address the employee's deficiencies addressed the symptom, not a root cause, thereby making the strategy less likely to succeed. Maslow's hierarchy doesn't have a psychological need (Choice [A]).

150. **B.** A *low-context culture* is characterized by dependence on standard operating procedures and accomplishing goals.

   This is in contrast to a *high-context culture* (Choice [C]), where the emphasis is placed on collaboration and the relationships that must exist to get things done. Choice (A) is a style of leadership, and Choice (D) serves as a distractor.

151. **B.** The best choice is (B). *Cafeteria plans* allow employees to select benefits that best suit their needs.

   Paid time off (PTO) programs (Choice [A]) and cash-in-lieu of benefits (Choice [D]) may be valued more by some than by others, so they aren't good answers. Flex spending accounts (Choice [C]) don't address the diversity component of the question, so they're not a good option.

152. **A.** Employees spend a lot of time in a pay-for-performance environment trying to actively work the criteria to their advantage or to focus on the job outputs that best serve the incentive. Choices (B), (C), and (D) are not necessarily true statements.

153. **B.** Employers who regularly survey and respond to market pay rates are less likely to experience an issue of pay compression. Building this in as a regular activity helps to avoid the issue altogether and ensure pay equity when compared to market rates.

   Red-circled employees (Choice [A]) are paid above the pay grade for positions, but freezing their raises only addresses the immediate issue. Terminating workers who are paid above the grade may result in disparate impact if they're older workers (Choice [C]). Increasing supervisors without market data or based on performance creates higher overhead without long-term resolution to the issue (Choice [D]).

154. **D.** The Sherman Antitrust Act prohibits wage fixing, price fixing, bid fixing, and other types of activities that negatively affect another person such as the consumer or employee. For employers, this means that wage surveys must be strategically designed to avoid inadvertent collusion.

155. **B.** A *maturity curve* is closely related to seniority; however, it has the advantage of increasing employee pay based on skill development, not length of service. It isn't a true pay-for-performance system because it also rewards years of service through work experience.

156. **A.** *Top-hat executive retirement plans* are nonqualified plans that are funded entirely by the employer. They offer retirement benefits above and beyond those of traditional plans such as IRAs or 401(k)s.

157. **C.** The Omnibus Budget Reconciliation Act of 1993 sought to eliminate the ability of organizations to deduct executive compensation in excess of $1 million unless it was qualified as performance-based.

   Discretionary bonuses (Choice [A]) aren't tied to performance, and a board isn't necessarily the most neutral body to determine performance criteria (Choice [B]). Choice (D) is trickier, but it's a more subjective answer than Choice (C).

158. **D.** Variable pay such as bonuses and incentives are part of a total compensation package that is negotiated between an employer and employee. Employers are compelled to pay employees only a minimum wage for work. Minimum wage isn't tied to employee performance, (Choice [A]), nor is it deliberate (Choice [B]) or discretionary (Choice [C]).

159. **C.** This manager's compa-ratio is 82 percent of the midpoint range for the position. You find the compa-ratio by dividing the employee pay by the midpoint of the range for the position. In this example, you need to convert the annual salary to an hourly rate by dividing it by 2,080 working hours in a year. The formula then becomes $39.42 divided by $47.91 multiplied by 100 to get a percentage.

160. **C.** Identifying the degree of importance of job factors and assigning relevant weights are activities of the *point* method of pricing jobs, making Choice (C) the correct answer.

    Ranking (Choice [A]) is the easiest form of job classification methods, simply requiring ordering the jobs by level of importance. The *classification* method of job evaluation (Choice [B]) is more difficult, requiring employers to group jobs with similar tasks into job classes for comparison. In *benchmarking* (Choice [D]), employers attempt to categorize jobs by similar characteristics.

161. **B.** Employers aren't fully restricted from listening to employee phone calls at work with one exception. If the employer is monitoring a call and realizes the call is personal, the employer must immediately stop listening.

162. **A.** *Confidentiality agreements* are an important step to engaging a peer review panel as an alternative to traditional corporate disciplinary action. These agreements ensure that the data reviewed at the meetings will be treated as confidential information.

    A vote (Choice [B]) isn't necessary to approve a method for discipline unless it's part of the collective bargaining and ratification process. Additional pay (Choice [C]) for sitting on a peer review panel isn't required by law, so it can be determined at the discretion of the employer. A peer review panel doesn't have to have a neutral arbitrator (Choice [D]).

163. **C.** In *distributive justice,* employees have issues with the perceived fairness of the distribution of outcomes, making Choice (C) the correct answer. If the employee believed that the punishment fit the crime, he would have been more likely to respond by modifying his behavior in response to the discipline.

    Favoritism (Choice [A]) would be the correct answer if the question pointed you in the direction of mistrust of the supervisor. Choice (B) would be correct if the employee felt the procedure used to decide his punishment was the focal point. Unfair treatment based on a protected class status would have to be present in order for Choice (D) to be correct.

164. **A.** This common law doctrine allows for any parties in employment to terminate the relationship at any time and for any reason. Policies that promise a series of disciplinary actions dilute the employer's ability to terminate at will.

    Respondeat superior (Choice [B]) stands for *let the master answer*. It's a legal principle that holds the employer responsible for the behavior of supervisors. The *duty of good faith and fair dealing* (Choice [C]) is the doctrine that requires parties to a contract to act in an honest manner with each other. *Rights granted by statute* (Choice [D]) refers to the definition of a law.

165. **C.** Purchasing employment practice liability insurance is the only example given that transfers the risk to another agency — in this case, the insurance company. The other answers relate to avoiding or mitigating the risk of harassment and other types of adverse employment actions.

166. **B.** Union members are allowed to dissent with their union and engage in protected activities, such as expressing their view on the activities of union officials. The Labor-Management Reporting and Disclosure (Landrum-Griffith) Act protects these rights.

The National Labor Relations Act (Wagner Act), Choice (A), granted workers the right to organize and have rights established through the collective bargaining process. The Labor-Management Relations Act (Taft-Hartley Act), Choice (C), sought to balance the power of unions with employer rights. The Railway Labor Act, Choice (D), was a cooperative effort between existing unions of the times and the railroads (eventually adding airlines) to minimize disruptions to transportation caused by striking workers.

167. **C.** The NLRA was passed to protect an employee's right to organize. This right included protecting the collective bargaining process from companies that would refuse to bargain in good faith.

The Labor Management Reporting and Disclosure Act was designed to safeguard members from union corrupt practices (Choice [A]) and to identify union unfair labor practices (Choice [B]). The Labor Management Relations Act sought to regulate union activity (Choice [D]).

168. **B.** Having a well-utilized open-door policy in which employees are encouraged to talk to management about their concerns is one way to avoid the unionization of the workforce.

Training and development activities (Choice [A]) aren't directly related to open-door policies, nor are productivity improvements (Choice [C]). Improved job satisfaction (Choice [D]) is a trickier answer because job satisfaction and unionization are often linked; however, it's a subset of union avoidance, making Choice (B) the best choice.

169. **D.** Employees join unions because they believe a union can improve their working conditions — pay, benefits, hours, and managers. Therefore, union-avoidance strategies should focus on listening to what employees need and responding accordingly.

Educating workers, Choice (A), should focus on why the company wants to remain union-free. Choices (B) and (C) are viable options, but both are efforts linked to the correct answer.

170. **C.** Although not directly required by a single labor law, a handbook helps employers comply with multiple requirements of having certain policies and communicating said policies to employees.

171. **A.** Managers have the greatest effect on organizational climate because they work directly with the human talent. As a result, they're responsible for multiple climate factors including improving employee morale, celebrating successes, and avoiding dysfunctional turnover.

Executives (Choice [B]) and human resources (Choice [D]) exist at more of an arm's length from the day-to-day operations of an organization, making them less influential on climate than managers. Employees (Choice [C]) are the subject of the question, not a direct influencer.

172. **C.** *Arbitration* is a binding legal proceeding in which both parties agree to engage should a dispute arise.

Along with nonbinding mediation (Choice [A]), it's a type of alternative dispute resolution (Choice [D]). Grievance procedures (Choice [B]) are nonbinding.

173. **B.** The best answer is Choice (B). *Employee assistance programs* are used to help employees who are experiencing personal issues.

Preparing for the discipline process (Choice [A]) is too soon, because this employee is normally a productive worker. Paying the employee to take time off (Choice [C]) is unreasonable, and manufacturing a layoff (Choice [D]) is an unethical solution to this issue.

174. **B.** The best answer is Choice (B). Even if the suspicions are proven, all employees have the right to have their medical information kept private. The Americans with Disabilities Act (Choice [A]) specifically excludes current users of illegal drugs from its protections.

Time off to seek rehabilitation (Choice [C]) is the right of the employer to decide, and employees who use illegal substances at work have no job protection requirement under the ADA (Choice [D]).

175. **A.** In general, an injury that occurs at work due to employee behavior such as drinking, fighting, or other horseplay may be denied coverage under the employer's workers' comp insurance.

Mental stress claims (Choice [B]) and car accidents (Choice [C]), while under the control of the employer, are both most likely covered if they're proven to be work related.

Answer Key for Practice Exam I

1.	C	22.	D	43.	B	63.	B	84.	A
2.	C	23.	A	44.	C	64.	C	85.	D
3.	A	24.	B	45.	A2, B1, C1, D2	65.	D	86.	A
4.	D	25.	A	46.	D	66.	A	87.	C
5.	C	26.	B	47.	A	67.	B	88.	C
6.	B	27.	C	48.	C	68.	A	89.	B
7.	C	28.	B	49.	B	69.	A	90.	C
8.	D	29.	A	50.	C	70.	B	91.	D
9.	B	30.	B	51.	D	71.	D	92.	C
10.	D	31.	D	52.	D	72.	D	93.	A
11.	B	32.	B	53.	B	73.	A	94.	A
12.	B	33.	A	54.	A	74.	B	95.	D
13.	A	34.	D	55.	C	75.	D	96.	B
14.	B	35.	A	56.	C	76.	B	97.	C
15.	A	36.	D	57.	C	77.	C	98.	C
16.	B	37.	A	58.	A	78.	C	99.	A
17.	A	38.	A	59.	B	79.	D	100.	C
18.	D	39.	A	60.	C	80.	C	101.	B
19.	D	40.	C	61.	C	81.	C	102.	A
20.	C	41.	B	62.	A	82.	A	103.	D
21.	A	42.	D			83.	D	104.	C

105.	A
106.	A
107.	C
108.	C
109.	C
110.	C
111.	C
112.	B
113.	A
114.	B
115.	C
116.	B
117.	D
118.	A
119.	C
120.	A
121.	C
122.	B
123.	C
124.	A2, B4, C1, D3

125.	A	134.	C	143.	C	152.	A	161.	B	170.	C
126.	C	135.	A	144.	B	153.	B	162.	A	171.	A
127.	C	136.	B	145.	A	154.	D	163.	C	172.	C
128.	C	137.	B	146.	C	155.	B	164.	A	173.	B
129.	A	138.	A	147.	C	156.	A	165.	C	174.	B
130.	C	139.	C	148.	C	157.	C	166.	B	175.	A
131.	A	140.	B	149.	B	158.	D	167.	C		
132.	B	141.	D	150.	B	159.	C	168.	B		
133.	C	142.	A	151.	B	160.	C	169.	D		

6

The Part of Tens

IN THIS PART . . .

Avoid the common mistakes that other test takers make.

Anticipate the challenges you'll face on exam day.

Identify what you need to gear up to study for the test and then implement some helpful study tips.

Chapter **21**

Ten PHR/SPHR Exam Pitfalls and How to Avoid Them

The exam format can ambush even the best-laid plans. Factor in exam choice, test-taking anxiety, and your individual knowledge, skills, and competencies, and it is no wonder that many learners report that this is one of the most difficult tests they have ever taken! However, know that both the PHR and the SPHR exams are designed to test your knowledge and ability to apply that knowledge, not to design questions to intentionally confuse you or make you fail. Having said that, you should be aware of several exam-specific pitfalls. Being prepared is key to confidence, so this chapter focuses on a few of the most common snags you should prepare to avoid.

Sitting for the Wrong Exam

Success begins with selecting the right exam. Just as pre-employment tests are used to predict an individual's future success on the job, so can you use assessment exams to ensure you sit for the best exam for you!

If you are unsure of which exam to take, go ahead and start with both the PHR and SPHR assessments and see which has content that seems most familiar. Take your time with each; this is an important step and should not be taken lightly. Keep in mind that your goal in taking these assessment exams is not to *pass* them. Your goal is to identify your current knowledge levels and use that information to decide which exam to take and then to create a study plan and timeline based on the assessment results.

If you're planning on taking the SPHR, be aware that you should consider measuring your baseline knowledge with the PHR content. The PHR is about the operational fundamentals from which an SPHR candidate will form strategy. If you don't have a strong foundation, your tactics will crumble.

Similarly, PHR candidates without the proper amount of practical work experience and senior leadership should avoid taking the SPHR exam. Wisdom truly does come from time spent in the trenches, and the SPHR will severely test your abilities to interpret and apply HR principles from an expert-oriented viewpoint. Facts and data are important, but the SPHR exam is just as much art as it is science in its content presentation.

The investment of both your time and dollars can motivate some individuals to leap right into the SPHR exam water, but the resource investment shouldn't be the primary driver of your final exam choice. Think of the certification process as a marathon, not a sprint — a long-term career goal that may take a few years to achieve.

TIP

Check out the online cheat sheet at www.dummies.com/cheatsheet/phrsphrexam for more help and information on choosing the right exam to boost the odds in your favor.

Underestimating Exam Preparation Time

Test takers often misjudge how much time they need to prepare for taking the test. Unfortunately, there is no way to pinpoint exactly how much or how little prep time you may need. I can only offer you an educated perspective based on my own exam preparation experience, the reports of other exam survivors, and industry best practices:

>> **My own experience:** I sincerely wish that I had my own *For Dummies* resource when I sat for the PHR and the SPHR exams. Understanding the 50,000-foot view would have helped me drill down into the boots-on-the-ground exam prep and better understand what I was up against. Here is a short list of what I did to prepare:

- The first textbook I used was the *PHR/SPHR Professional in Human Resources Study Guide* by Anne Bogardus (Sybex/John Wiley & Sons, Inc.), mainly because the $30 or so price tag was just about what I had to spend in my prep budget. I had the privilege of writing the 4th and 5th editions for the 2012 and 2018 content updates. Bogardus reviewed many of the main points covered in the exam objectives, and in most cases, she helped illuminate concepts for which I needed more resources.

- The second textbook resource was *Human Resource Management* by Robert L. Mathis and John H. Jackson (Southwestern Cengage Learning). I credit their work with teaching me about business management and strategy. Here is where I first discovered the life cycle of the employee and Michael Porter's five forces, concepts I use still today in my work as a consultant and author. If you want baseline knowledge similar to what you would find in an HR course, start here. For those individuals on a budget, consider the previous edition rather than the current one, but don't go back more than one edition.

- When I sat for the PHR in the days of the dinosaur, the internet wasn't the viable resource that it is today. In fact, computer-based testing was not even available yet! So, I was not able to access many of the useful websites that I reference in this book when prepping for the PHR, and relied instead on a used copy of the SHRM Learning System. When I took the SPHR the online world was much more robust; I accessed government websites and became a SHRM member so I could access their rich online database of all things human resources.

- I reviewed flash cards while eating breakfast. I recorded myself reading exam prep material and listened to it while driving. I made myself worksheets and matching games and worked them while waiting for dinner to cook. In all, I spent between 12 to 14 hours studying per week, but I spent many more hours immersing myself in the subject material. For both exams, I finished well under the time limit and passed on the first try. Regardless of the outcome, I recognized that this accelerated-immersion approach taught me more than I ever thought there was to know about the field of human resources, and I'm a better professional as a result of the dedicated study time.

>> I must confess that I did not know about the Exam Content Outline (ECO) from HRCI when I sat for either of my exams. This seems like such a simple miss that I am almost embarrassed to share that. The ECO is the number-one tool I wish that I had available to me because it gives shape and establishes the boundaries of what will be measured. Without this guide, I felt like I had to study anything and everything related to human resources from the dawn of time, instead of going deep into the concepts that really matter. While I appreciated the broad view, it created an unnecessary level of stress and uncertainty. I cannot emphasize this enough — print a copy of the relevant Exam Content Outline and use it to target your studying.

>> **Reports of exam survivors:** Several different online forums are available of people sharing their prep experience. I also have firsthand reports from individuals who have taken my prep classes. Their time commitment varied from the superstars of 20-plus hours per week to those who came at it when they had a chance. The average seemed to be about 12 to 14 hours per week over a four-to-six-month period. In addition, all of the successful exam takers couldn't emphasize enough the importance of taking practice exam after practice exam. They shared in frustration that *none* of their study materials covered *all* of what was asked on their exam, which is why practice exams from multiple resources can help increase your chances of seeing familiar material on the tests.

REMEMBER

Exam takers are required to sign an Exam Confidentiality Statement that prohibits them from sharing exam content. Be careful with what you discuss with other certification-seekers after you take the exam so that you do not violate this agreement and subject your credential to cancellation.

>> **Certification courses:** As a general guideline, most exam preparation programs run about 14 weeks. They can be found at many local colleges and universities, both in person and online, as well as offered by many private companies. Chapter 2 also gives you pointers on how to build a custom study plan designed around your strengths and weaknesses should you prefer to prep solo.

How much time each week to dedicate to your studies is largely dependent on your comfort level and initial assessment scores. Understanding your time/assessment score data and applying it to your study plan is critical because no single resource is customized to your existing knowledge levels; you must be the captain of your ship. Remember, authors of exam prep material aren't granted special access to exam content. We build the material from years of experience, thought leader interviews, industry best practices, and most importantly, the exam content outlines.

Unlearning State-Specific Applications

Both the PHR and SPHR exams are written to federal law. State laws in similar areas must meet or exceed the federal guidelines, and as an HR practitioner in California, I had to practice setting aside my West Coast ways and relearn some of the HR basics. Differences in areas such as minimum wage, overtime, and safety were very real obstacles to applying my baseline knowledge. Creating a cheat sheet of labor laws in your state that are different from the federal standards is worth your study time. Taking your time navigating these test questions can also help you spot multiple-choice answers that are correct in your state, but not at a federal level.

Getting Tripped Up: The Perils of Overthinking

Overthinking both the question stem and the options is a very real threat to a passing score. The answers are intentionally written with *distractors*, which means more than one answer could be correct, and that all answers make sense. When you come up against these issues, keep the following in mind:

>> **Don't linger on the answer choices.** If you understand what the question stem is asking, you should be able to quickly narrow down the answers to the two most likely correct options. Spend your minute-or-so-time-per-question strategy noodling through those two choices rather than trying to interpret and compare all four options.

>> **Go back and re-read the question, focusing on the verbs.** Are they asking you to design a solution? Or act on a complaint? Perhaps they want you to diagnose a problem or assess a need? The verbs are your *call to action* and the best answer will usually be the tool to do so.

>> **Focus also on the subject of the question stem.** Is it written from the perspective of a boss or an employee? A regulatory agency may even be driving the issue. The expectations of people and agencies you serve in your day-to-day activities are different, depending on the origin of need.

These strategies may work in the scenario-based questions, but they aren't necessarily the best option on the questions that are testing your knowledge. The good news is that these questions tend to be easier, because the answers are often objective, right-or-wrong types of choices. Subjective judgment or critical thinking is less important for those types of questions.

Playing the Guessing Game

As someone who writes test questions, I can tell you that I spend a ridiculous amount of time reviewing my answers to ensure that the proper mix of multiple-choice options are presented on the practice exams. Don't listen to the so-called experts who say that Choice (C) is most often the correct choice, because it's just not true. The only way to successfully guess on these exams is to properly eliminate the obvious incorrect answers first.

If you have narrowed down your answer to the two best choices and still aren't sure, try using the answer in a sentence. Draw upon the question stem and plug in the answers to see which one fits best. Look for the option that fully addresses what the question is asking.

Your final option is to mark the question for review and hope that as you move through the rest of the exam, your memory will be jogged or, better yet, you'll find the answer in another related question. Whatever you do, don't leave a question blank. Make your best guess, mark it for review, and come back to it later. If you run out of time before you have a chance to review, you lose the opportunity entirely to get the answer correct.

Trusting Your Instinct

Read each question once or twice to ensure that you know what it's asking. Before looking at the multiple-choice options, answer the question in your mind. Then review the answers for the one that most closely aligns with your first instinct. If you have scratch paper or a whiteboard available, consider writing down your answer before you review the options and work through the question as though it were a puzzle. Why did you answer it the way you did? What logic or criteria did you call upon to find your answer? As with most of these strategies, the first time to practice them should not be on test day. Take a practice exam or chapter review questions while practicing this approach to see if it works for you.

Many test takers report having a gut feeling about which answer is correct. Trust this feeling when you have exhausted the other options that I recommend here. You have spent many hours studying this material and are a seasoned HR professional, so go with your intuition when necessary.

Changing Answers

When you take the PHR or the SPHR, you have the ability to mark questions for review at the end to go back and take a second look. This strategy is extremely valuable when you aren't sure of an answer but you need to move on. Reviewing questions is also handy if more than one exam question is related to the one on which you're stuck, and you can find the answer somewhere else in the exam. Changing answers works for some, but not for others, so you need to know where you stand with this strategy before your exam date. Here are a few perspectives from both sides.

Speaking from experience, I can't change my answers. I get flummoxed too easily. Although I did pass my exams when I took the PHR and SPHR, I certainly didn't ace them. I was also finished more than an hour before the time limit. For this reason, if I had to do it again, I would use the mark-for-review feature more often. You don't want to be in the position of failing this exam by only a few points, and one or two questions may tip the scales in your favor.

On the other hand, a research study that appeared in the *Journal of Personality and Social Psychology* conducted over a 70-year period suggests that exam takers who change their answers go from wrong to right 51 percent of the time, so if you feel compelled to make the switch you should do so.

TIP

I also recommend that you read an excellent article about other multiple-choice, test-taking tips at www.socialpsychology.org/testtips.htm#taking. Among many of its points of wisdom, they remind you "don't psych yourself out"! You will be just fine regardless of the test outcome; breathe through it and do your best.

If you do decide that you need to change an answer, be very thoughtful before clicking the radial button and making a change. Try to link the question and options back to the exam objectives and make the argument both for and against the change to be certain that you want to do so.

Focusing Too Much on the Clock

You have a little more than a minute per question, and some questions take longer to answer than others. Many test takers fall victim to watching the clock too closely, which distracts them from answering questions, so you need to figure out how closely you manage that timer.

The best advice is to take at minimum two simulation exams. In one, watch the clock. In the other, don't watch the clock. At the end of both exams, ask yourself the following questions:

>> Did you feel more pressure when you were watching the clock?

>> Did watching the clock make you work faster?

>> Were you more likely to mark an answer for review and move on when watching the clock?

>> How much review time did you have left on both exams?

I'm a huge fan of balance, and this advice will serve you well. A healthy blend of keeping your eye on the hourglass without overthinking it allows you to react quickly if you need to speed up without dominating your thought process. Don't let the clock force you into making riskier choices than are necessary, but also don't linger on questions that stump you.

Be sure and select an answer for every question; don't leave one blank. If you have to make an educated guess, mark it for review later, but take your best guess just in case you run out of time and can't go back. Refer to Chapter 1 for more information about the exam scoring and Chapter 3 for more tips on dealing with the unknown.

Managing Distractions

Part of your studying efforts should be figuring out how to tune out your personal distractors. The first step is to discover what bothers you and then figure out ways you can block out those distractions.

For me, my distractors are my phone and hunger. The phone isn't allowed in the exam room, so if your phone is one of your distractors, then you won't have to deal with that distractor while taking the test. If you study or take practice exams with your phone on, you aren't properly applying yourself to exam-day conditions. Turn it off, hide it, do whatever you have to do so that you're training yourself to live without it on game day.

Hunger is also solvable. Although your nerves may not allow you to eat a large meal prior to the test, I encourage you to be prepared. Low blood sugar or just a growling stomach can detract you from the total mind focus that these exams demand of you. You can't take food into the exam room, but you can have a healthy snack in the locker. Know that the clock will not stop for snack or bathroom breaks.

WARNING

HRCI partnered with Pearson VUE to administer these exams remotely during the COVID-19 outbreak. As of this writing, it is unclear if this will become a permanent practice. If you are scheduled to take your certification exam online from home or work, know that no one can enter the room while your test is in progress, and you cannot leave the workspace unless a break is scheduled. For more on what to expect for a remotely proctored exam experience, check out Pearson VUE's short video at https://home.pearsonvue.com/Test-takers/OnVUE-online-proctoring.aspx.

Room temperature can also be a major distractor because being too hot or too cold is uncomfortable. Plan accordingly and dress in layers on exam day so that you can adapt quickly and easily. Be sure to bring a light sweater that you can take off, and wear bottoms that are comfortable to sit in for a three-hour stretch.

Plan to take a quick break at the halfway point to eat some raw almonds or choke down a string cheese and bottle of water. Protein is your best choice for a quick brain boost, and the reprieve will allow you a moment to reset your mind and body for the final hour and a half. The clock is still ticking, so don't dillydally, and be sure *not* to check your phone in case the proctors think that you're cheating. Your phone isn't allowed and could cost you the exam.

Some test takers report the other test takers as distractions. People come and go, coughing, sneezing, and emitting all of the other lovely body sounds of a large group of people in a small room. Part of your training should be figuring out how to concentrate with a lot of movement around you. Plan to take an exam simulation at the public library or at a local coffee shop. Practice using headphones — the noise-cancelling kind, not the ear buds — to see if they help or hinder. On exam day, keep your mind on the task at hand and be courteous to other test takers by not becoming a distraction yourself.

Resist the temptation to be distracted by others who finish their exam earlier. They may be taking a different test. If you plan to sit for the exam with a study partner, chat ahead of time about what you'll do if the other finishes early. Don't give up if your partner finishes before you; use all of the time allotted to maximum effect.

TIP

If you need a reasonable accommodation for any of these items that were just mentioned, don't hesitate to ask for it! Both HRCI and Pearson VUE testing locations have many options available to ensure each candidate has a fair opportunity to successfully pass the exam, including extra testing time, a separate testing room, and breaks.

Avoiding Mind Tricks

It's easy to panic, especially if you're hit with difficult or unknown test questions right out of the gate. You must train your mind to avoid negative self-talk or self-defeating statements. I have heard from many failed exam takers that they "knew they were going to fail after the first question" and that "halfway through the exam they realized there was no way they could finish all of the questions in time." These types of thoughts can cripple even the most prepared and confident individual, so be on alert for them while you take practice exams and *shut them down* on exam day.

While you're taking practice exams, work on replacing negative thoughts by reminding yourself to take it one question at a time. Mark for review the ones that cause you anxiety and then move on. Don't worry about what's coming; simply stay focused on the question in front of you. In other words, stay in the present moment.

REMEMBER

A failing score doesn't mean that you aren't good at your job. As with most goals people set for themselves, it may take one or two tries to master the beast, but you're well worth it. Successful certification can happen for you, and the credential will result in career highs. Kudos to you for putting yourself out there and adding the credibility to your profession that the business you serve and employees that you represent so desperately need. Your employer is counting on you to be the best HR practitioner that you can be, and the studying, application, and commitment are well worth your positive attitude as you go through this career-defining process.

Chapter **22**

Ten (or So) Study Tips for the Exam Bodies of Knowledge

One of the biggest oversights of people planning to take the PHR or SPHR exam is that they don't properly utilize the road map that is the exam content outline (ECO). This document is straight from the horse's mouth — the Human Resource Certification Institute (HRCI). Although many excellent preparation resources are on the market that have successfully prepared exam takers for decades, the ECO should be the foundation of all of your efforts. This chapter describes organizational tools and textbook-alternative resources you can create using the ECO as your guide. Doing so ensures that you have a well-balanced approach to tackling the exams that goes beyond simply reading a textbook.

REMEMBER

There really is no wrong way to study. What works for you may not work for someone else, so don't get caught up in form at the expense of content. The only constant for *all* exam takers is the ECO. Seek to understand what the road map is asking of you by applying the objectives to every facet of your studying efforts. If you can't align a topic with an objective, work harder and do some research. If you still can't relate it, check out the knowledge requirements and see if you can make sense of it there. If you *still* can't match the topic to the objective, ask a question of an expert.

Being Organized and Planning

Having a plan and then knowing what you need to do with the right materials can be the difference between streamlined studying that produces results and disorganized chaos that is stressful. The following items share a common thread. They're all tools that you can use to get ready to study:

>> **Binders:** I'm a binder freak. For exam prep, you need one place to put all of the detritus that will collect during the preparation process. Store fact sheets, notes, and other data related to the exam objectives. Follow this important process before you even first pick up your study guide:

1. **Print out the exam objectives from HRCI.**

2. **Divide them out by exam functional area.**

3. **Insert the documents under the proper functional area.**

Refer to these objectives every time you crack open a book or log in to study. In fact, attempt to match up what you read to the relevant exam objective or knowledge requirement to ensure that you're properly aligning your knowledge with what may be presented on the test. Note that you can organize this digitally as well, using apps such as GoodNotes.

>> **Index cards:** Index cards are useful for breaking down complex pieces of information into manageable concepts. Consider color-coding your index cards with highlighters and using single colors for key exam concepts. Assign one color per exam objective or be more selective and use certain colors for difficult topics. For instance, I had trouble understanding strategy concepts during my exam prep, so all my notes for those exam objectives were in pink: pink paper, text highlighted in pink, and flash cards made on pink index cards. Using the same color adds another dimension of sorting, ordering, and cataloguing the data, making visual connections to eventually piece together.

TIP

I am a highly visual learner. Auditory learners may apply a similar concept to the previous advice: Just play music by a single artist while studying (I listen to Billy Joel when writing). Recall of the music will create a pathway to recall the data you were studying at the time you listened to it. Tactile learners should consider studying while moving — reading out loud while walking or listening to an audio resource while exercising.

>> **Recordings:** Reading or speaking aloud into a recording device is a valuable technique that allows you to study the same material in different ways, first by reading it aloud and then by listening to it later. A client of mine once told me that a person's favorite word in the whole universe is his own name. Similarly, auditory learners seem to retain information better when they hear content in their own voice. I highly recommend reading aloud into your phone's recording device and playing it back. For non-auditory learners, consider this approach for especially difficult concepts. One student would read her prep book aloud to her infant son — he didn't know the difference nor did he care as long as he heard her voice. The point is, get creative!

>> **Peppermint gum:** Peppermint has been shown to be a gentle brain stimulant that increases both recall and memory. Peppermint *gum* has an added benefit for tactile learners. Chewing gum while studying is a physical activity and can help your brain create deep grooves for information recall.

REMEMBER

Long-term retention of information occurs over time. You must engage in activities that help you carve out pathways to the place where your brain stores information so that you have an indestructible path to travel back to retrieve it on test day. Think of your exam preparation activities as a trail of breadcrumbs, guiding you back when you need it.

Using Outlines

An *outline* is a great way to condition your mind to build frameworks out of complex information. Examples of complex information on these exams include academic theories or processes that have multiple threads that must be followed to successful completion. An outline is a tool that forces you to extract the main point of a theory or process and then fill in the blanks as you further review the data.

TIP

Try to write your outline from the *end* to the *beginning* of a concept rather than from beginning to end. Starting with the end will at first be confusing, but as you work your way up, your mind will be required to pay attention to the items that naturally help you fill in the blanks and make the necessary connections for understanding.

On the other hand, using outlines for whole chapters or exam functions has limited value. Outlining entire chapters/exam areas is a tactile tool to touch information through writing or typing it out. You can get greater value in selecting two or three related exam objectives, bringing in the knowledge components, and then filling in the blanks by making connections with research.

Consider creating a mind map to show the relationships between important exam concepts. Figure 22-1 shows an example of one I made at GoConqr.com to understand Geert Hofstede's cultural dimension of Power Distance. This type of visual is much more valuable than simply transferring information from a textbook or other resource because it requires you to do the homework, think, and synthesize, and then apply what you've studied to finish information related to critical exam objectives.

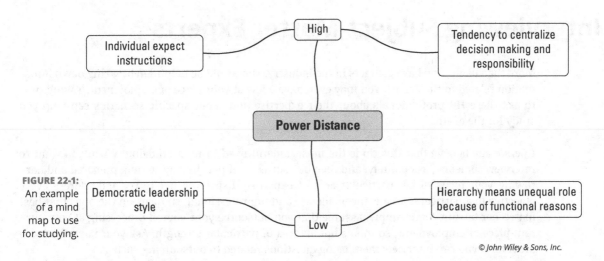

FIGURE 22-1:
An example of a mind map to use for studying.

© John Wiley & Sons, Inc.

Challenge yourself to pick one topic per functional area and use the outline format to study. Remember that it's not enough just to transfer data; you need to give yourself a call to action to research, just as you would if the topic came up on the job.

TIP

And don't forget to mix it up! For example, candidates may use a mind map for labor laws, auditory recordings for Total Rewards, and reading to understand the practices of recruiting and selection.

Going Online

As I mention repeatedly throughout this book, particularly in Chapter 2, the internet has tons of resources that you can tap into to drill further into the exam objectives. Be careful because the internet is full of potential distractions and rabbit holes through which you can fall (such as Facebook, Instagram — the list is endless) and emerge an hour later not having accomplished anything related to studying for the exam.

When you go online to gather more information about a specific topic, I recommend that you stay extremely focused. When creating your study plan, pick two or three exam objectives per functional area, and then plan to use online videos to support your studying.

Two credible YouTube channels that I recommend are

>> **World at Work TV:** World at Work (www.youtube.com/user/WorldatWorkTV) is a nonprofit organization that studies HR practices from the perspective of Total Rewards. This free channel regularly posts videos about all things related to compensation and benefits, including sales compensation and other pay-for-performance programs.

>> **SHRM Official:** SHRM Official (www.youtube.com/user/SHRMofficial) is the YouTube channel of the Society for Human Resource Management. Its video list includes a broad selection of many topics that are identified in the exam ECO, so this site is well worth regular visits as you prepare for the exams.

Interviewing Subject-Matter Experts

More than likely, you have contacts in the industry who would be helpful in breaking down information related to the exams. You may even have a few at your place of employment. Taking time to ask these HR professionals about their expertise and about specific scenarios can help you study for the exam.

I personally believe that this tip is the most underutilized form of studying. When you want to interview someone, ask politely, and then be courteous of her time by coming prepared and narrowing your focus to her particular area of expertise. Expecting her to try and address every objective in a particular area is inconsiderate and unprofessional, so focus on the ones that best match her talents. For example, assume that you outsource your payroll processing at your current place of employment, so this is not an area of particular strength. Ask your payroll service provider if you can interview them using questions related to outsourcing such as

>> What kind of information needs to be collected and tracked for compliant payroll processing?

>> What are some of the advantages and disadvantages for employers that outsource their payroll?

>> What types of employee self-service technologies are you seeing emerge, and how can they be adapted?

>> What are some common misconceptions about payroll outsourcing?

>> What forms of training do you use for your employees, and would you recommend them to me as I prepare for this exam?

Presenting Unfamiliar Exam Objectives

One technique to master difficult concepts that I like to recommend is what I refer to as *teach-to-learn.* You more than likely have training responsibilities on your job. With the variety of exam objectives in all functions of HR, there is probably a topic in which your employees could use a training class. Pick an item that you aren't extremely familiar with and create a training presentation that forces you to go into research mode. Some examples include preventing harassment, coaching employees, or increasing production using employee motivation techniques.

If you don't have the opportunity in your job to train, look online for a local HR association and volunteer to present at a monthly or quarterly meeting. Preparing for a group of your peers may be just enough pressure to ensure that you master a difficult concept backward and forward, so you'll know it when test day arrives.

If neither of those options are appealing to you, take a difficult concept and try to explain it to your spouse or a friend who is unfamiliar with the topic. Note what questions he or she has and where you are unable to articulate a point. You can then plan to study those areas more in-depth to ensure that you understand the exam item.

Comparing HR Best Practices to Your Work Experience

Take some time to review the exam responsibilities and knowledge requirements for each functional area and compare them to how they apply to your workplace. You may not be surprised to note that you do things a bit differently where you work. However, HRCI conducts studies and interviews subject-matter experts (SMEs) to identify best practices in the field of HR. Knowing where your workplace veers off of the exam objectives will raise your awareness on where you may struggle on your exam. For example, your employer may not place a high value on the strategic planning process. By doing this exercise, you can identify that you need to do some extra legwork to understand why the strategic planning process is a valuable tool for employers.

TIP

If you work in the type of environment where it's acceptable, take this strategy a step further and educate your bosses on why they should be doing things a different way. Practice building a *business case* (data-driven justification for a work activity) and use it to sway your employer to the best business practice of the exam objective(s).

Discerning Action Objectives from Knowledge Objectives

Closely look at each exam responsibility to spot action words such as *design, implement,* and *measure,* which are in contrast to the knowledge components that use phrasing such as *techniques, methods,* and *types.* Understanding *what* the exam objectives are asking of you will define the *how,* as in how you need to study the concepts and the *what,* as in what should be studied (techniques, methods, types).

Establishing both context and form is important. Understanding that you need to know how to develop (action) and test (action) business continuity plans (exam objective) is different from the knowledge of data storage and back-up.

Work to spot these links and differentiate between what is actionable versus knowledge based. Doing so can help you interpret what the exam items are asking of you when you face them on the test.

Remember that many of the functional areas share content — at least it appears so on the surface. Here is an example in the functional area of Talent Planning and Acquisition:

> PHR knowledge requirement 16: Interviewing and selection techniques, concepts, and terms
>
> SPHR knowledge requirement 21: Interviewing and selection techniques and strategies

In this example, PHR candidates would focus their interpretation of recruiting and selection studying on the practical practices of recruiting sources and types of interviews. SPHR candidates, while still needing to know about sourcing and interview types, would go deeper and think about the application and use of these tools to achieve strategic objectives.

Spacing Practice for Success

Spaced practice is the studying of material over a longer period of time, which is the opposite of *massed practice*, which is more commonly referred to as cramming. Giving yourself 12 or 14 weeks to study allows your brain to absorb not only pieces of information, but also how the information applies as a whole. On a smaller scale, consider using spaced practice on a weekly basis.

For example, if you have ten hours per week to study, space that practice over five two-hour sessions rather than two five-hour sessions. Everyone has what I refer to as the *saturation point* when studying, and after about two hours your ability to absorb (and thereby retain for future recall) more information begins to diminish.

Knowing Where to Focus When Studying Labor Laws

These exams do have a few studying techniques that work better than others, particularly in the area of going over the labor laws. Concentrate on the following when studying labor laws:

>> **Labor law names:** Particularly with the union labor laws, studying both the formal act name and the author names is necessary. These laws include the National Labor Relations Act (Wagner Act), Labor Management Relations Act (Taft-Hartley Act), and the Labor Management Reporting and Disclosure Act (Landrum-Griffith Act). Use the acronym WTL (standing for Wagner, Taft-Hartley, and Landrum-Griffith), which refers to the authors' names in the chronological order the acts were passed.

>> **Dates when laws passed:** Instead of memorizing the dates, shape your knowledge in context. Focus on when laws passed, such as in the 1960s, 1970s, 1980s, and so on. Align the decades with social cues, and you're more likely to critically apply your knowledge on the exams.

>> **The numbers:** You need to know the number of employees threshold that triggers labor law compliance. Also, be sure to review the number of months that activates certain activities, such as the Consolidate Omnibus Budget Reconciliation Act (COBRA) coverage and union elections.

Refer to the appendix for a more complete listing of the various labor laws you should understand for both exams.

REMEMBER

HRCI is very clear that you will be tested on the labor laws in effect at the time of your exam. You must take responsibility to go outside of any study resource to make sure you have the most up-to-date information. This is why I always recommend that you rely first on the fact sheets from the Department of Labor when studying.

Appendix

Federal Employment Law

In order to effectively manage risk, HR professionals at all stages of their career must be up-to-date on the major labor laws that affect each functional area represented on the exam. Hence, make sure that you're prepared for the PHR or SPHR exam and know these laws. Rote memorization isn't sufficient though; you need to understand the implications of application and what to do When major laws conflict (such as state versus federal). When studying, focus on the following:

TIP

>> **The number of employees that triggers coverage:** Regardless of the size of the employer you work for, a labor law applies. Some of the test questions attempt to distract you with incorrect information based on the number of employees required to trigger protection.

Make yourself a table that has a few columns, as shown in Table A-1. Head each of the columns with the number of employees and fill in the blanks with the labor laws that are triggered by that number of employees.

Resist the temptation to download a complete table from the internet. You need to do the legwork here. The practice of doing the research to find the numbers takes you deep into the material, a sure way to reinforce the concept for recall on the exam.

>> **Who the law is designed to protect:** Some of these laws protect the worker, some grant the employer certain rights, and a few others protect a union. Know who the law is protecting so you can interpret exam questions more effectively.

>> **Why the law was passed in the first place:** Adult learners tend to retain information best when they understand *why* something is relevant. If this describes you, pay attention to a bit of the history surrounding the law or court case to improve your ability to recall the details on test day.

>> **The employment context:** Many of these laws apply to more than one legal domain. Be sure and focus your studying on how the law defines the employment context.

TABLE A-1 **Test Preparation Sample**

1	15	20	50
Workers compensation laws	Americans with Disabilities Act	Age Discrimination in Employment Act	Executive order 11246
Fair Labor Standards Act	Title VII of the Civil Rights Act of 1964		Family Medical Leave Act

TIP

Most of these labor laws in Table A-2 have some form of a frequently asked question (FAQ) or Fact Sheet document online. Take the time to access these documents (use credible sources such as the Department of Labor or the Equal Employment Opportunity Commission), and then use the documents to create digital flash cards or quizzes on free websites such as www.goconqr.com or www.quizlet.com. You can also use the information in Table A-2 to create flash cards.

TIP

In day-to-day practice and also on the exams, the first piece of information to consider from a compliance perspective is the size of the employer. Table A-3 shows you the major labor laws that apply based on the number of employees. Use this table to test your knowledge.

TABLE A-2 Important Employment Laws and Bureaus

Name	Year	Description
Payne vs. The Western & Atlantic Railroad Company	1884	Defined employment at-will.
Bureau of Labor Statistics (BLS)	1869	Established to study industrial accidents and maintain accident records.
Sherman Antitrust Act	1890	Controlled business monopolies; allowed court injunctions to prevent restraint of trade. Used to restrict unionization efforts.
Clayton Act	1914	Limited the use of injunctions to break strikes; exempted unions from the Sherman Antitrust Act.
Federal Employees Compensation Act (FECA)	1916	Provided benefits similar to workers' compensation for federal employees injured on the job.
Longshore and Harbor Workers' Compensation Act	1927	Provided workers' compensation benefits for maritime workers injured on navigable waters of the United States or on piers, docks, and terminals.
Railway Labor Act	1926	Protected unionization rights; allowed for a 90-day cooling-off period to prevent strikes in national emergencies. Covers railroads and unions.
Norris-La Guardia Act	1932	Protected the right to organize; outlawed yellow-dog contracts.
National Labor Relations Act (NLRA); also referred to as the Wagner Act	1935	Protected the right of workers to organize and bargain collectively; identified unfair labor practices; established the National Labor Relations Board (NLRB) to regulate the relationship of employers and unions.
Federal Insurance Contributions Act (FICA)/Social Security Act	1935	Required employers and employees to pay Social Security taxes.
Federal Unemployment Tax Act (FUTA)	1936	Required employers to contribute a percentage of payroll to an unemployment insurance fund.
Public Contracts Act (PCA); also referred to as the Walsh-Healey Act	1936	Required contractors to pay prevailing wage rates.
Fair Labor Standards Act (FLSA)	1938	Defined exempt and nonexempt employees; required and set the minimum wage to be paid to nonexempt workers; required time-and-a-half to be paid for nonexempt overtime hours; limited hours and type of work for children; established recordkeeping requirements.
Labor-Management Relations Act (LMRA); also referred to as the Taft-Hartley Act	1947	Prohibited closed shops; restricted union shops; allowed states to pass "right to work" laws; prohibited jurisdictional strikes and secondary boycotts; allowed employers to permanently replace economic strikers; established the Federal Mediation and Conciliation Service; allowed an 80-day cooling-off period for national emergency strikes.
Portal-to-Portal Act	1947	Clarified the definition of "hours worked" and "compensable time," such as time spent putting on PPE, for the FLSA.
Patent Act	1952	Established the U.S. Patent and Trademark Office to protect inventions and the rights of the inventors.
Labor-Management Reporting and Disclosure Act (LMRDA); also referred to as the Landrum-Griffin Act	1959	Controlled internal union operations; provided a bill of rights for union members; required a majority vote of members to increase dues; allowed members to sue the union; set term limits for union leaders.
Equal Pay Act	1963	Required that women performing substantially similar or identical work to men be paid the same wage or salary rate.

Name	Year	Description
Title VII of the Civil Rights Act	1964	Established the Equal Employment Opportunity Commission (EEOC); prohibited employment discrimination on the basis of race, color, religion, national origin, or sex.
Executive Order (EO) 11246	1965	Prohibited employment discrimination on the basis of race, creed, color, or national origin; required affirmative steps for all terms and conditions of employment; required a written Affirmative Action Plan (AAP) for contractors with 50 employees.
Immigration and Nationality Act (INA)	1965	Eliminated national origin, race, and ancestry as bars to immigration; set immigration goals for reunifying families and preference for specialized skills.
Service Contract Act	1965	Required government contractors to pay prevailing wages and benefits.
Age Discrimination in Employment Act (ADEA)	1967	Prohibited discrimination against persons 40 years of age or older; established conditions for bona fide occupational qualification (BFOQ) exceptions.
EO 11375	1967	Added sex to the protected classes in EO 11246.
Consumer Credit Protection Act (CCPA)	1968	Limited garnishment amounts on employee wages; prohibited discharge of employees for a single garnishment order.
EO 11478	1969	Included disabled individuals and those 40 years of age or older in the protected classes established by EO 11246.
Black Lung Benefits Act (BLBA)	1969	Provided benefits for coal miners suffering from pneumoconiosis due to mine work.
Occupational Safety and Health Act (OSH Act)	1970	Required employers to provide a safe workplace and comply with safety and health standards; established the Occupational Safety and Health Administration (OSHA) to enforce safety regulations; established the National Institute for Occupational Safety and Health (NIOSH) to research, evaluate, and recommend hazard reduction measures.
Fair Credit Reporting Act (FCRA)	1970	Required employers to notify candidates that credit reports may be obtained; required written authorization by the candidate and that the employer provides a copy of the report to the candidate before taking an adverse action.
Griggs vs. Duke Power	1971	USSC: Required employers to show that job requirements are related to the job; established that lack of intention to discriminate isn't a defense against claims of discrimination.
Equal Employment Opportunity Act (EEOA)	1972	Established that complainants have the burden of proof for disparate impact; provided litigation authority for the EEOC; extended the time to file complaints.
Rehabilitation Act (RA)	1973	Expanded opportunities for individuals with physical or mental disabilities; provided remedies for victims of discrimination.
Privacy Act	1974	Prohibited federal agencies from sharing information collected about individuals.
Vietnam Era Veterans Readjustment Assistance Act (VEVRAA)	1974	Provided equal opportunity and affirmative action for Vietnam veterans.
Employee Retirement Income Security Act (ERISA)	1974	Established requirements for pension, retirement, and welfare benefit plans including medical, hospital, accidental death and dismemberment (AD&D), and unemployment benefits.
Albemarle Paper vs. Moody	1975	USSC: Required that employment tests be validated; subjective supervisor rankings aren't sufficient validation; criteria must be tied to job requirements.

(continued)

APPENDIX **Federal Employment Law** 363

Name	Year	Description
NLRB vs. J. Weingarten, Inc.	1975	USSC: Established that union employees have the right to request union representation during any investigatory interview that could result in disciplinary action.
Washington vs. Davis	1976	USSC: Established that employment-selection tools that adversely impact protected classes are lawful if they have been validated to show future success on the job.
Copyright Act	1976	Defined fair use of copyrighted work; set the term of copyright effectiveness.
Mine Safety and Health Act (MSHA)	1977	Established mandatory mine safety and health standards and created the Mine Safety and Health Administration (MSHA).
Automobile Workers vs. Johnson Controls, Inc.	1977	USSC: "Decisions about the welfare of the next generation must be left to the parents who conceive, bear, support, and raise them, rather than to the employers who hire those parents."
Uniform Guidelines on Employee Selection Procedures (UGESP)	1978	Established guidelines to ensure that selection procedures are both job related and valid predictors of job success.
Pregnancy Discrimination Act (PDA)	1978	Required that pregnancy be treated the same as any other short-term disability.
Civil Service Reform Act	1978	Created the Senior Executive Service, the Merit Systems Protection Board (MSPB), the Office of Personnel Management (OPM), and the Federal Labor Relations Authority (FLRA).
Revenue Act	1978	Established Section 125 and 401(k) plans for employees.
EO 12138	1979	Created the National Women's Business Enterprise Policy; required affirmative steps to promote and support women's business enterprises.
Guidelines on Sexual Harassment	1980	Assisted employers to develop antiharassment policies, establish complaint procedures, and investigate complaints promptly and impartially.
Retirement Equity Act	1984	Lowered the age limits on participation and vesting in pension benefits; required written spousal consent to not provide survivor benefits; restricted conditions placed on survivor benefits.
Consolidated Omnibus Budget Reconciliation Act (COBRA)	1986	Consolidated Omnibus provided continuation of group health coverage upon a qualifying event.
Tax Reform Act	1986	Reduced income tax rates and brackets.
Immigration Reform and Control Act (IRCA)	1986	Prohibited employment of individuals who aren't legally authorized to work in the United States; required I-9s for all employees.
Drug-Free Workplace Act	1988	Required federal contractors to develop and implement drug-free workplace policies.
Employee Polygraph Protection Act (EPPA)	1988	Prohibited the use of lie-detector tests except under limited circumstances.
Worker Adjustment and Retraining Notification Act (WARN Act)	1988	Required 60 days' notice for mass layoffs or plant closings; defined mass layoffs and plant closings; identified exceptions to the requirements.
Americans with Disabilities Act (ADA)	1990	Required reasonable accommodation for qualified individuals with disabilities.
Older Worker Benefit Protection Act (OWBPA)	1990	Amended ADEA to prevent discrimination in benefits for workers 40 years of age and older; added requirements for waivers.

Name	Year	Description
Immigration Act	1990	Required the prevailing wage for holders of H1(b) visas; set H1(b) quotas.
Civil Rights Act (CRA)	1991	Allowed compensatory and punitive damages; provided for jury trials; established defenses to disparate impact claims.
Glass Ceiling Act	1991	Established a commission to determine whether a glass ceiling exists and identify barriers for women and minorities. As a result, the Office of Federal Contract Compliance Programs (OFCCP) conducts audits of the representation of women and minorities at all corporate levels.
Unemployment Compensation Amendments	1992	Reduced rollover rules for lump-sum distributions of qualified retirement plans; required 20 percent withholding for some distributions.
Energy Policy Act of 1992	1992	Allowed employers to provide a nontaxable fringe benefit to employees engaged in qualified commuter activities such as bicycling and mass transit.
Family and Medical Leave Act (FMLA)	1993	Required qualifying employers to provide 12 weeks of unpaid leave to eligible employees for the birth or adoption of a child or to provide care for defined relatives with serious health conditions or to employees unable to perform job duties due to a serious health condition.
Taxman vs. Board of Education of Piscataway	1993	Found that in the absence of past discrimination or underrepresentation of protected classes, preference may not be given to protected classes in making layoff decisions.
Harris vs. Forklift Systems	1993	USSC: Defined an actionable hostile work environment as that which falls between merely offensive and that which results in tangible psychological injury.
Omnibus Budget Reconciliation Act (OBRA)	1993	Revised rules for employee benefits; set the maximum deduction for executive pay at $1 million; mandated some benefits for medical plans.
Uniformed Services Employment and Reemployment Rights Act (USERRA)	1994	Protected the reemployment and benefit rights of reservists called to active duty.
Congressional Accountability Act (CAA)	1995	Required all federal employment legislation passed by Congress to apply to congressional employees.
Illegal Immigration Reform and Immigrant Responsibility Act (IIRIRA)	1996	Reduced the number and types of acceptable documents used to prove identity and employment eligibility, and launched the eVerify pilot programs.
Mental Health Parity Act (MHPA)	1996	Required insurers to provide the same limits for mental health benefits that are provided for other types of health benefits.
Health Insurance Portability and Accountability Act (HIPAA)	1996	Prohibited discrimination based on health status; limited health insurance restrictions for pre-existing conditions; required a Certificate of Group Health Plan Coverage upon plan termination.
Personal Responsibility and Work Opportunity Reconciliation Act	1996	Required employers to provide information about all new or rehired employees to state agencies to enforce child-support orders.
Small Business Job Protection Act	1996	Redefined highly compensated individuals; detailed minimum participation requirements; simplified 401(k) tests; corrected qualified plan and disclosure requirements.
Small Business Regulatory Enforcement Fairness Act (SBREFA)	1996	Provided that a Small Business Administration (SBA) ombudsman act as an advocate for small business owners in the regulatory process.

(continued)

Name	Year	Description
EO 13087	1998	Expanded coverage of protected classes in EO 11246 to include sexual orientation.
Burlington Industries vs. Ellerth	1998	USSC: Established that employers have vicarious liability for employees victimized by supervisors with immediate or higher authority over them who create an actionable hostile work environment.
Faragher vs. City of Boca Raton	1998	USSC: Established that employers are responsible for employee actions and have a responsibility to control them.
Oncale vs. Sundowner Offshore Services, Inc.	1998	USSC: Extended the definition of sexual harassment to include same-sex harassment.
NLRB: Epilepsy Foundation of Northeast Ohio	2000	Extended Weingarten rights to nonunion employees by allowing employees to request a co-worker be present during an investigatory interview that could result in disciplinary action.
NLRB: M. B. Sturgis, Inc.	2000	Established that temporary employees may be included in the client company's bargaining unit and that consent of the employer and temp agency aren't required to bargain jointly.
Needlestick Safety and Prevention Act	2000	Mandated recordkeeping for all needlestick and sharps injuries; required employee involvement in developing safer devices.
Energy Employees Occupational Illness Compensation Program Act (EEOICPA)	2000	Provided compensation for employees and contractors subjected to excessive radiation during production and testing of nuclear weapons.
EO 13152	2000	Added "status as a parent" to protected classes in EO 11246.
Circuit City Stores vs. Adams	2001	USSC: Arbitration clauses in employment agreements are enforceable for employers engaged in interstate commerce except for transportation workers.
EO 13201	2001	Applies to federal contractors and subcontractors.
Sarbanes-Oxley Act (SOX)	2002	Mandated improved quality and transparency in financial reporting and increased corporate responsibility and the usefulness of corporate financial disclosure; required companies to establish and maintain an adequate internal control structure and procedures for financial reporting.
Pharakhone vs. Nissan North America, Inc.	2003	Established that employees who violate company rules while on FMLA leave may be terminated.
NLRB: IBM Corp.	2004	NLRB reversed its 2000 decision in Epilepsy, withdrawing Weingarten rights from nonunion employees.
Jespersen vs. Harrah's Operating Co.	2004	Established that a dress code requiring women to wear makeup doesn't constitute unlawful sex discrimination under Title VII.
Smith vs. City of Jackson, Mississippi	2005	USSC: Established that ADEA permits disparate impact claims for age discrimination comparable to those permitted for discrimination based on sex and race.
Pension Protection Act (PPA)	2006	Amended ERISA financial obligations for multiemployer pension plans; changed plan administration for deferred-contribution plans.
Burlington Northern Santa Fe Railway Co. vs. White	2006	USSC: Established that all retaliation against employees who file discrimination claims is unlawful under Title VII, even if no economic damage results.
Sista vs. CDC Ixis North America, Inc.	2006	Established that employees on FMLA may be legally terminated for legitimate, nondiscriminatory reasons, including violations of company policy if the reason is unrelated to the exercise of FMLA rights.

Name	Year	Description
Bates vs. United Parcel	2006	Established that when employers apply an unlawful standard that bars employees protected by the ADA from an application process, the employees don't need to prove they were otherwise qualified to perform essential job functions. The employer must prove the standard is necessary to business operations.
Taylor vs. Progress Energy, Inc.	2007	Established that the waiver of FMLA rights in a severance agreement is invalid. FMLA clearly states that "employees cannot waive, nor may employers induce employees to waive, any rights under the FMLA."
Repa vs. Roadway Express, Inc.	2007	Established that when an employee on FMLA leave is receiving employer-provided disability payments, he may not be required to use accrued sick or vacation leave during the FMLA absence.
Phason vs. Meridian Rail Corp.	2007	Established that when an employer is close to closing a deal to sell a company, WARN Act notice requirements are triggered by the number of employees actually employed and the number laid off on the date of the layoff, even if the purchasing company hires some of the employees shortly after the layoff.
Davis vs. O'Melveny & Myers	2007	Established that arbitration clauses in employment agreements won't be enforced if they're significantly favorable to the employer and the employee doesn't have a meaningful opportunity to reject the agreement.
Velazquez-Garcia vs. Horizon Lines of Puerto Rico, Inc.	2007	Established that the burden of proof that a termination wasn't related to military service is on an employer when an employee protected by USERRA is laid off.
Genetic Information Nondiscrimination Act (GINA)	2008	Prohibits employment discrimination on the basis of genetic information. Prohibits employers from requesting, requiring, or purchasing genetic information, and describes exceptions.
Patient Protection and Affordable Health Care Act	2010	Created new requirements for employer-sponsored healthcare plans. Amended the FLSA to require large employers to provide lactation breaks and facilities for employees who are breast-feeding.

TABLE A-3 **Laws Sorted by Employer Size**

Law	1 or more employee	15 or more employees	20 or more employees	50 or more employees	100 or more employees
Age Discrimination in Employment Act (ADEA)			X		
Americans with Disabilities Act (ADA)		X			
Consolidated Omnibus Budget Reconciliation Act (COBRA)			X		
Fair Credit Reporting Act (FCRA)	X				
Family & Medical Leave Act (FMLA)				X	
Genetic Information Nondiscrimination Act (GINA)		X			

(continued)

TABLE A-3 *(continued)*

Law	1 or more employee	15 or more employees	20 or more employees	50 or more employees	100 or more employees
Immigration Reform & Control Act (IRCA)	X				
Occupational Safety & Health Act (OSHA)	X				
Older Workers Benefit Protection Act (OWBPA)			X		
Pregnancy Discrimination Act (PDA)		X			
Title VII of the Civil Rights Act of 1964		X			
Uniformed Services Employment and Reemployment Rights Act (USERRA)	X				
Worker Adjustment and Retraining Notification Act (WARN Act)					X

Index

retirement, 222

   strategies, building, 215–217

compensation reports, 49

competing for talent, 158

complaints, 90, 173

complexity in business environments, 78

compliance, 90, 145, 266, 286. *See also* labor laws; *specific laws*

computer-based training (CBT), 145, 151

conciliation, 53

conditioning, 44, 148, 251, 255, 276, 278, 307, 332

confidence, importance on test day, 69–70

confidentiality, 45, 188–189, 318, 341, 347

confidentiality agreements, 48, 316, 339

conflicts of interest, 126, 292, 320

Consolidated Omnibus Budget Reconciliation Act (COBRA), 161, 269, 273, 364, 367

construct validity, 312, 336

constructive discharge, 265, 285, 286

constructive feedback, 82, 83

Consumer Credit Protection Act (CCPA), 248, 273, 363

content chunking, 207–208

content theories of motivation, 43

content validity, 139

continuing education, 80, 298, 325

contract learning, 145

cooperative training, 297, 324

core competencies, 90, 182

core knowledge requirements, 17–18, 40

core subject areas, 15–17

corporate citizenship, 90, 124

corporate culture, 90, 167–168, 225–228, 306, 314, 331–332, 338

corporate governance, 124

corporate restructures, 201–202, 253, 277

corporate social responsibility, 90, 124, 309, 333

correlation, positive, 252, 276

cost leadership, 158, 293, 320

cost-benefit analysis (CBA), 91, 190, 320, 332

COVID-19 pandemic, 180

CRA (Civil Rights Act), 135, 138, 273, 365

cramming, 66, 358

creative brainstorming, 208–209

creative interview questions, 139, 140

credentials, 71, 91

credit policies and objectives, 305, 331

criterion validity, 139, 253, 277

critical thinking, 153

C-suite, 221

culture, 91, 167. *See also* corporate culture

customer service, understanding of, 123

customs, in organizational culture, 168

D

data analytics, 187–188

data collection, 181–182

data management, 130–131, 149–152

de minimus violations, 303, 329

defamation claims, 265, 285, 311, 335

deferred compensation plan, 92, 221

defined benefit (contribution/retirement) plan, 92, 222, 248, 273

degree of identification, 304, 329

Delphi technique, 92, 208, 292, 308, 320, 333

Department of Homeland Security (DHS), 39

Department of Labor (DOL), 35, 38

design of training, 145–146, 149–150, 271

development, 92, 144. *See also* Learning & Development; *specific development types*

differentiation strategy, 157

digital badge, 71

direct compensation, 156

direct questions, 56–57

disability, 67, 92. *See also specific labor laws related to disability*

disaster preparedness, 46, 48

discipline, 171–172, 173, 266, 272, 286

discrimination. *See also specific labor laws*

   defined, 286, 330

   PHR practice exam, 258, 265, 272, 280, 285

   SPHR practice exam, 297, 300, 305, 310, 323, 326, 330, 334

disparate impact (adverse impact), 42, 138

dispute resolution, 53, 92

distractions, during exam, 350–351

distractors, answer, 59–60

distributive justice, 171, 218, 316, 339

diversity, 41–43, 92

diversity training, 260, 282

divestitures, 92, 202–203

downsizing, 93, 233, 258, 280, 293, 296, 321, 323

downward communication, 93, 292, 320

drills, 47

drug/alcohol screening, 302, 327–328

dual career ladder system, 211

Duck, Jeanie, 186–187

due diligence, 93, 308, 333

duty of good faith and fair dealing, 53, 268, 302, 328, 339

dysfunctional turnover, 196

E

EAPs (employee assistance programs), 93, 318, 340–341

eating before test, 67

EAW. *See* employment at will

ECO (exam content outline), 347, 353

economic environment, 77, 121

economic forecasting, 191

economic strikes, 50, 251, 275

economic valuation, 93, 304, 330

educated guesses, 62

educational trends in HR, 76–77

EEO-1 reporting, 131, 141, 297, 324

EEOA (Equal Employment Opportunity Act), 93, 363

EEOC (Equal Employment Opportunity Commission), 35, 258, 280, 303, 310, 311, 328, 334

EEOC vs. Swissotel Employment Services, LLC, 328

eight-stage model of change, 186

80/20 rule, 230, 260, 282

e-learning, 93, 145

eligibility, exam, 8–9

Emergency Paid Leave Act, 162

emergency preparedness, 46

emergency response plans, 246, 272

Employee and Labor Relations (PHR functional area 05). *See also specific related topics*
  exam objectives, 165–167
  important areas of, 167
  overview, 16, 21, 165
  SPHR overlap, 167

employee assistance programs (EAPs), 93, 318, 340–341

employee benefits. *See also specific benefits;* Total Rewards
  building systems for, 221–224
  credible internet resources, 38
  defined, 88, 93
  mandatory, 255, 278
  in other countries, 215
  outsourcing, 264, 285
  as percentage of operating expense, 308, 332
  selecting and communicating, 159–163
  voluntary, 115, 255, 278

employee engagement
  building, 169–171
  defined, 93
  demonstration of, 266, 286
  early techniques for, 169
  improving, 200–201
  making case for, 227–229
  practice exam questions related to, 253, 277

employee handbooks, 93, 172–173, 184, 317, 340

employee recognition programs, 223

employee references, giving, 265, 285, 311, 335

employee referrals, 137, 295, 322

Employee Relations and Engagement (SPHR functional area 05). *See also specific related topics*
  credible internet resources, 39–40
  exam objectives, 225–227
  overview, 17, 225
  PHR overlap, 167

employee retention, 93, 110, 145, 207, 209–211, 221, 260, 282

Employee Retirement Income Security Act (ERISA), 158, 160–161, 273, 363

employee stock options, 301, 327

employee suggestion systems, 173–174

employee surveys, 169, 266, 286

employee turnover, 93, 196, 220–221, 293, 321

employees. *See also specific related topics*
  age of, 262, 283
  behavior of, in organizational culture, 168
  developing, 147–149, 211
  dissatisfaction of, 231–232
  IRS definition of, 38–39
  life cycle of, 135, 189, 197, 203
  listening to phone conversations of, 316, 339
  number triggering labor law coverage, 361

employer
  asking to pay for certification, 33
  behavior of, in organizational culture, 168
  of choice, 94
  demonstrating knowledge to, 81–82

employer branding
  defined, 94
  effect of negative image or reputation, 297, 324
  external relationships, 124
  in recruitment process, 136–137, 197, 242, 268, 292, 319
  social media recruiting, 244, 270

employment at will (EAW)
  defined, 94
  implied employment contract, 302, 328
  overview, 53–54
  practice exam questions related to, 242, 243, 249, 269, 274, 316, 339
  statutory exception to, 265, 286

employment offers, 140

employment practice liability insurance (EPLI), 261, 283, 317, 339

employment tests, 60, 138–139

employment-related decisions, 161

merit pay, 247, 248, 273

Meritor Savings Bank v. Vinson, 310, 334

metamorphosis stage, socialization, 200

metrics, 104, 142, 190–191

mind maps, 152, 355

minimum wage, 104, 254, 277, 316, 339

Mintzberg, Henry, 28, 306, 331

mission, vision, and values (MVV) statements, 54, 227, 253, 277

mission statement, 105, 182, 309, 333

mitigation, risk, 184, 196

mLearning, 146

mobile job apps, 243, 269

mode, 105, 295, 322

modeling leadership, 233

monopsony, 309, 333

motivation, 31, 43–44, 105, 124, 232, 255, 278

N

National Labor Relations Act (NLRA), 50, 51, 174, 188, 250, 275, 276, 317, 340, 362

National Labor Relations Board (NLRB), 39, 50, 51, 251, 264, 274, 275, 276, 285

natural disaster exception, WARN, 257, 280

needs, hierarchy of, 31, 43, 255, 278, 300, 314, 326, 338

needs analysis, 45, 47, 105, 249, 273, 308, 333

negative reinforcement, 148, 251, 276, 307, 332

negative self-talk, 70, 351

negatively accelerated learning curve, 259, 281

negligent hiring, 303, 329

nepotism, 105, 140

NLRB vs. Weingarten, Inc., 302, 328, 364

nominal group method, 208, 292, 320

noncompete agreement, 105, 282

nondirective interview questions, 139

nondisclosure agreements, 260, 282

nonsolicitation agreements, 188

nursing mothers, accommodating, 247, 272

O

O*Netn (Occupational Information Network), 35–36

Occupational Safety and Health Act (OSH Act), 363, 368

Occupational Safety and Health Administration (OSHA), 40, 45–46, 48, 303, 329

Occupational Safety and Health (OSH) programs, state-run, 246, 272

OD (organizational development), 106, 185, 307, 332

Office of Federal Contract Compliance (OFCCP), 311, 335

official exam results, getting, 71

Ohmae, Kenichi, 28

Older Workers Benefit Protection Act (OWBPA), 161, 364, 368

Oldham, Greg R., 44

ombudsman, 305, 330

Omnibus Budget Reconciliation Act (OBRA), 338, 365

onboarding, 105, 141, 199–200, 268

Oncale vs. Sundowner Offshore Services, 250, 275, 366

one-on-ones, 106, 231

online application process, 11–12

online business sites, 28–29

online media recruiting, 243, 269

online practice exams, 3, 25

online research, 24

on-the-job training, 106, 150, 244, 270, 324, 335

open-door policy, 317, 340

operant conditioning, 44, 148, 251, 255, 276, 278, 307, 332

operating expense, pay and benefits as percentage of, 308, 332

operational functions of business, 122–124

organizational climate, 168–169, 225–226, 227, 303, 317, 328, 340

organizational commitment, 229

organizational crises, 305, 330–331

organizational culture, 90, 167–168, 225–226, 227–228, 306, 314, 331–332, 338

organizational development (OD), 106, 185, 307, 332

organizational research, 228

orientation, 141, 199

OSH (Occupational Safety and Health) programs, state-run, 246, 272

OSH Act (Occupational Safety and Health Act), 363, 368

OSHA (Occupational Safety and Health Administration), 40, 45–46, 48, 303, 329

outlines, using to study, 30, 355

outplacement, 106, 310, 334

outsourcing
    BPO services, 312, 336
    compensation and benefits, 264, 285
    defined, 106
    recruiting function, 295, 322
    usefulness of, 244, 256, 270, 279
    workforce planning, 195

overhead, 106, 157–158

overthinking, avoiding, 348

overtime, 106, 160, 164, 218–219

OWBPA (Older Workers Benefit Protection Act), 161, 364, 368

ownership culture, 216

P

parent-country nationals, 106, 296, 323

Pareto chart, 106, 260, 276

partial public workers, 305, 330

"pass it ugly" term, 21

passing scores, 71, 106

Patient Protection and Affordable Care Act (PPACA), 162, 272, 273, 367

pay adjustments, 159

pay compression, 159, 263, 284, 300, 315, 326, 338

pay discrimination, 300, 326

pay disparity, 220

pay for performance, 106, 107, 247, 273, 301, 315, 327, 338

pay openness, 301, 327

pay systems, structuring, 156–159

pay transparency, 220, 301, 327

Paycheck Protection Program (PPP), 180

payroll, processing, 159

payroll vendor selection, 249, 273

Pearson VUE, 12, 66, 67, 350

pedagogy, 208

peer review panel, 316, 339

Penn Central, 202

PEO (professional employer organization), 258, 280, 311, 335, 336

peppermint gum, 354

performance, 147, 148, 217

performance appraisals, 107, 171

performance compensation philosophy, 156–157

performance feedback, 170–171, 230–232, 313, 337

performance improvement plan (PIP), 266, 286

performance management, 107, 169–171, 231, 260, 266, 282, 286

performance management system, 107, 299, 325

performance reviews, 107, 209, 298, 299, 324–325, 326

performance-based pay, 106, 107, 247, 273, 301, 315, 327, 338

perquisites (perks), 107, 300, 326

personal values, defining, 233

personnel files, 256, 279

PEST/PESTLE tool, 77–78, 107, 121–122, 182, 241, 268

phone conversations, listening to employee, 316, 339

PHR exam. *See* exam preparation; practice exams; Professional in Human Resources exam; questions, exam; *specific functional areas*

physical risks, 45

physiological needs, 314, 338

piece rate, 107, 248, 273, 285

pilot programs, 260, 282

PIP (performance improvement plan), 266, 286

planning horizon, 293, 320–321

plateaued careers, 107, 312, 336

playing field, business, 121–122

plumber's test, 219, 326

point method of job evaluation, 157, 316, 339

policies, 107, 127, 172–174, 184, 266, 286, 328

political environment, 77, 121

political forecasting, 191

polycentric staffing, 107, 323

polygraph tests, 257, 279

Portal-to-Portal Act, 158, 160, 247, 251, 262, 272, 275, 283, 362

Porter, Michael, 28, 179, 182, 227, 295, 322

positive correlation, 252, 276

positive reinforcement, 148, 276, 332

positive thinking, on test day, 68–69

positively accelerated learning curve, 259, 281

post-hire activities, 240, 267

power, role in motivation, 232

PPACA (Patient Protection and Affordable Care Act), 162, 272, 273, 367

PPP (Paycheck Protection Program), 180

practice exams

  best answers, finding, 61

  changing answers in, 63

  overview, 3, 11

  PHR, 239–266

  as preparation tactic, 14

  resources for, 26

  role in exam preparation, 23–25

  SPHR, 289, 290–318

  spotting correct answer, 58

Prahalad, C.K., 28

predictive validity, 107, 139

pre-employment drug screens, 243, 269

pre-employment tests, 138–139, 240, 243, 267, 270, 296, 311, 323, 334

preliminary results report, 71

preparation for exam. *See also* questions, exam; *specific exam subjects*

  applying core knowledge, 40–41

  asking employer to pay for certification, 33

  exam weights by functional area, 21–23

  Glossary of Terms overview, 85–86

  goal-setting, 31

  internet resources, 34–40

  leading up to test day, 65–67

  motivation, 43–44

  outlines, making when studying, 30

  overview, 1–4, 21

  practicing, 23–25

  preparation tactics, 14–15

unfair labor practices related to, 249, 274

social responsibility, 111, 292, 320

Social Security, 161, 362

social stage, hierarchy of needs, 255, 278

socialization, 200, 241, 268

Society for Human Resource Management (SHRM), 34, 75

Socratic seminars, 208, 244, 270

spaced practice, 358

span of control, 112, 241, 268, 294, 321

specialized certifications, 76–77

SPHR exam. *See* exam preparation; practice exams; questions, exam; Senior Professional in Human Resources exam; *specific functional areas*

spiral career paths, 147

S-shaped learning curve, 259, 281

staff meetings, 169

staffing, 112, 197–199

stakeholders, 112, 120–121

state-run OSH programs, 246, 272

state-specific applications, unlearning, 347

statistical analysis, 304, 329

statutory rights, 53

"Stay, Groom, Go" method, 209

stereotypes, 70, 112, 260, 282

stock options, 112, 216, 301, 327

strategic business units (SBU), 308, 333

strategic partnership, 112, 180

strategic planning

  and compensation strategies, 215–216

  defined, 112, 180, 325

  objectives, interpreting, 181

  overview, 179–180

  stages of planning, 181–183, 294, 321

  when entering new competitive market, 306, 331

strategy, defined, 112, 179

strategy evaluation, 183

strategy formulation, 182–183

strategy implementation, 183

strength summary, 210

strikes, 50, 51, 251, 275

student debt, cost of, 207

study groups, 14, 30–33

study plan, 4, 14, 25–27, 354

studying for exam, 24, 29–30, 85–86, 153, 353–359. *See also* exam preparation

subject areas, 15–17

succession planning

  data management, 149

  defined, 113, 325

  impact of lack of, 307, 332

Learning and Development activities, 207

  in PHR practice exam, 252, 276

  workforce planning, 196–197

suggestion systems, 173–174

supervisors, 52–53, 54, 113, 139–140, 312, 336

supplemental exam materials, 28–29

supplier power, 295, 322

Supreme Court, diversity in, 41

SWOT analysis, 113, 182

synchronous learning, 113, 298, 325

synchronous training, 145, 151

synthesis, questions focused on, 13

systems thinking, 253, 277

T

tactile (kinesthetic) learners, 86, 146, 354

Taft-Hartley Act. *See* Labor-Management Relations Act

talent. *See also* employees

  ability to compete for, 158

  assessing, 209–210

Talent Management subscription service, 37

Talent Planning and Acquisition (functional area 02). *See also specific related topics*

  credible internet resources, 35–36

  exam objectives, 133–134, 193–194

  important areas of, 134–135

  overview, 16, 17, 133, 193

tangible employment action, 250, 274

tangible rewards, 148

task significance, 299, 325

Taylor, Frederick, 228, 232

teach-to-learn technique, 357

team incentives, 216

technical training, 145

technological forecasting, 192

technology, 77, 78, 121, 187–192

tentative nonconfirmation (TNC) email, 296, 323

termination, 172, 201–203, 265, 285

terrorism threats, 48

test day, 14–15, 65–71

testing environment, 67

testing facilities, 66, 68

360-degree reviews, 171, 313, 336

three-stage model of change, 185–186

time off requests, 173

tipped employees, 254, 277

TIPS doctrine, 302, 328

Title VII of the Civil Rights Act, 135, 138, 256, 273, 279, 363, 368

About the Author

Sandra M. Reed is a leading expert in the certification of HR professionals. She is the author of the 2nd edition of The Official Guide to the Human Resource Body of Knowledge, and the 5th edition of the *PHR and SPHR Professional in Human Resources Certification Complete Study Guide: 2018 Exams.* Reed is also the author of case studies and learning modules for the Society of Human Resource Management, teaching and writing content for undergraduate studies at both public and private universities.

Reed is a sought-after, engaging facilitator and trainer of human resources and management principles, with a strong focus on leadership development and exam preparation. She is a Master Practitioner of the MBTI personality assessment, and a certified trainer in leadership. She holds her Master of Arts in Organizational Leadership and Bachelor of Arts in Industrial-Organizational Psychology. Ms. Reed is currently the owner of epocHResource Group (www.epochresources.com), a management and consulting company based in California.

Dedication

This book is dedicated to my children, Calvin and Clara, who inspire me to be the most authentic version of myself I can be. And to Chris, my champion, whose own hard work and dedication gives me the freedom to explore. I am thankful.

Author's Acknowledgments

Writing a book feels like a highly personal experience, when in reality it requires a community of experts. In fact, the overriding theme of this text is that you need multiple resources to prepare for these exams; nowhere does that principle apply better than when publishing a book.

Many thanks to Tim Gallan, a calm and focused presence in the face of impeding deadlines, and Lindsay Lefevere, for trusting my talent and process. I know there are several key players that work behind the scenes at John Wiley & Sons, and I am thankful for their collective efforts.

Finally, thanks so much to the best clients in the world for giving me a hall pass for an intense few months without giving me permission to disappear entirely. The candidness, transparency, and boots-on-the-ground feedback became critical resources to call upon for real-world examples of HR in the trenches.

Publisher's Acknowledgments

Executive Editor: Lindsay Lefevere

Project Editor: Tim Gallan

Copy Editor: Christine Pingleton

Technical Editor: Ed Hernandez, PhD

Production Editor: Tamilmani Varadharaj

Cover Image: © SrdjanPav/Getty Images